Dr Suelette Dreyfus is an award-winning writer and journalist. In addition to writing the first major book about computer hacking in Australia, *Underground*, she was the Associate Producer of a documentary about hackers. Her articles have appeared in magazines and newspapers such as *The Independent* (London), *The Age*, *The Sydney Morning Herald* and *The Australian*. She began work on *Underground* while completing her PhD. She is a Research Fellow at the University of Melbourne, where she runs several major research projects in information systems.

Julian Assange is an internet activist, journalist and publisher. Born and raised in Australia, Julian is the founder, spokesperson, and editor in chief of WikiLeaks, a whistleblower website that started in 2006. In 2010, WikiLeaks began to publish hundreds of thousands of classified details about American involvement in the wars in Afghanistan and Iraq, which created a media storm. At the end of 2010, the site published a series of classified US diplomatic cables, now known as Cablegate.

UNDER-GROUND

SUELETTE DREYFUS & JULIAN ASSANGE

CANONGATE

Edinburgh · London · New York · Melbourne

First published in Great Britain in 2012 by Canongate Books Ltd,
14 High Street, Edinburgh EH1 1TE

1

Copyright © Suelette Dreyfus, 1997, 2001, 2011
Researcher's Introduction copyright © Julian Assange, 2001, 2011

The moral rights of the authors have been asserted

First published in Australia in 1997 by Random House Australia Pty Ltd
Level 3, 100 Pacific Highway, North Sydney NSW 2060

British Library Cataloguing-in-Publication Data
A catalogue record for this book is available on
request from the British Library

ISBN 978 0 85786 259 4

Typeset in New Baskerville by Midland Typesetters, Australia

Printed and bound by CPI Group (UK) Ltd, Croydon, CR0 4YY

This book is printed on FSC certified paper

www.canongate.tv

To Peter, Audrey, Beatrice and my parents
SD

To D, F, S and A
JA

CONTENTS

ACKNOWLEDGEMENTS

There are many people who were interviewed for this work, and many others who helped in providing documents so vital for fact checking. Often this help involved spending a considerable amount of time explaining complex technical or legal matters. I want to express my gratitude to all these people, some of whom prefer to remain anonymous, for their willingness to dig through the files in search of yet one more report and their patience in answering yet one more question.

I want to thank the members of the computer underground, past and present, who were interviewed for this book. Most gave me extraordinary access to their lives, for which I am very grateful.

I also want to thank Julian Assange for his tireless research efforts. His superb technical expertise and first-rate research is evidence by the immense number of details which are included in this book.

Three exceptional women – Fiona Inglis, Deb Callaghan and Jennifer Byrne – believed in my vision for this book and helped me to bring it to fruition. Carl Harrison-Ford's excellent editing job streamlined a large and difficult manuscript despite the tight deadline. Thank you also to Judy Brookes.

I thank the team at Canongate Books for their hard work in bringing this book to publication in Britain, especially Nick Davies.

A very special thank you goes to Patrick Mangan, Nikki Christer, Larissa Edwards and the Random House Australia team for putting together this new edition with such care and attention to detail despite the ticking clock. I am also very grateful to the following people and organisations for their help (in no particular order): John McMahon, Ron Tencati, Kevin Oberman, Ray Kaplan, the *New York Daily News* library staff, the *New York Post* library staff, Bow Street Magistrates Court staff, Southwark Court staff, the US Secret Service, the Black Mountain Police, Michael Rosenberg, Michael Rosen, Melbourne Magistrates Court staff, D.L. Sellers & Co. staff, Victorian County Court staff, Paul Galbally, Mark Dorset, Suburbia.net, Freeside Communications, Greg Hooper, H&S Support Services, Peter Andrews, Kevin Thompson, Andrew Weaver, Mukhtar Hussain, Helen Meredith, Ivan Himmelhoch, Michael Hall, Donn Ferris, Victorian State Library staff, News Limited library staff (Sydney), Allan Young, Ed DeHart, Annabel Blay, Annette Seeber, Arthur Arkin, Doug Barnes, Jeremy Porter, James McNabb, Carolyn Ford, ATA, Domini Banfield, Alistair Kelman, Ann-Maree Moodie, Jane Hutchinson, Catherine Murphy, Norma Hawkins, N. Llewelyn, Christine Assange, Russell Brand, Matthew Bishop, Matthew Cox, Michele Ziehlky, Andrew James, Brendan McGrath, News Limited, Pearson Williams Solicitors, Tami Friedman, the Free Software Foundation (GNU Project), the US Department of Energy Computer Incident Advisory Capability, Project Gutenberg, Claire, Lance and Michael, Till Tolkemitt, Lutz Kroth, Klaus Gabbert, Heike Rosbach, Andreas Simon dos Santos, Michael Kellner, Bernhard Schmid, Steffen Jacobs, Frances Uckerman and Bertel Schmitt.

A good book is usually the product of many people's contributions, and that has certainly been the case with *Underground*.

Finally, I would like to thank my mother, my father and Peter, whose unfailing support, advice and encouragement have made this book possible.

Suelette Dreyfus

INTRODUCTION TO UNDERGROUND, SECOND EDITION

BY SUELETTE DREYFUS

Who are computer hackers? Why do they hack?

Underground tried to answer these questions when it was first published in 1997. The questions still seem relevant more than a decade later. WikiLeaks, the world-famous publisher of documents leaked in the public interest, grew out of the computer underground described in this book. It has been said that WikiLeaks' stories 'have changed the way people think about how the world is run'.[1] To understand WikiLeaks, you need to know the back story: *Underground* is that story.

Underground is the back story because it reveals a world of people who use technology to solve problems with 'thinking from outside the box'. This goes back to the earliest definition of a hacker, which doesn't imply any illegal activity, but, rather, simply reflects someone who can find clever technical solutions to hard problems. It is this kernel of unusual creativity, not their illegal activities, that makes the hackers in *Underground* so interesting. This kernel carried through to WikiLeaks. WikiLeaks revealed the creative application of technology, in the form of secure, anonymous online publishing, to the hard problem of getting governments and corporations to tell the truth.

The founder of WikiLeaks, Julian Assange, and I worked on *Underground* for almost three years. He brought exceptional technical understanding and a detailed knowledge of the computer underground while I brought years of experience as a professional journalist and technology writer. Julian sees solutions others can't see. His lens is not focused on the foreground. His thinking reflects the cypherpunk community of the 1990s where he cut his teeth. The cypherpunks were an online community of people interested in cryptography from around the globe. They believed in the right of the individual to personal privacy – and the responsibility of government to be open, transparent and fully accountable to the public. Julian expressed these views to me repeatedly as his own while we worked on the book.

This book reveals the lives and adventures of the world's best hackers from this early era. It is not a book about law enforcement agencies, and it is not written from the point of view of the police officer. From a literary perspective, I have told this story through the eyes of computer hackers. In doing this I hope to provide the reader with a window into an enigmatic, shrouded and typically inaccessible realm.

Each hacker is different and to that end I have attempted to present a collection of individual but interconnected stories, bound by their links to the international computer underground. There is Mendax, who hid his precious hacking data in beehives in his back yard to prevent the police from discovering it. Anthrax hacked his way into the mysterious American System X. Despite being in the throes of an all-night hacking session, each day at dawn he froze his hacking screen, unfurled his prayer mat and turned to Mecca to fulfil his responsibilities as a good Muslim. When the Australian Federal Police raided Electron, one of the best hackers of his generation, they confiscated his machines. The only way he could dampen his need for the adrenalin of hacking into the US Naval Research Labs was by smoking so much dope that he became temporarily psychotic. Wandii, the British teenager, hacked until he literally collapsed. His mother returned from work one day to find her son sprawled unconscious across the living room floor. Trax, with Mendax and Prime Suspect, discovered how to outwit the police tracking them by making completely untraceable telephone calls. There was Parmaster, known simply as Par, whose forays into US defence contractor computers left him scared he was the Man Who Knew Too Much – and would be eliminated. The US Secret Service launched a nationwide manhunt before nabbing him.

Piecing together the lives of the world's most secretive people takes time; this is why *Underground* took nearly three years to research and write. We attended court hearings, sentencing hearings, and conducted more than 100 interviews both on and off the record. People were interviewed online and in person. We met with sources in secure and anonymous settings.

A hefty, secured desktop machine was quietly moved down a darkened Melbourne street to a safe house for late-night interviews. The older areas of the city have cobblestone alley-ways that criss-cross suburbs, running parallel to main streets. Conveniently, they back up to the rear of many yards. The laneways are empty, and sometimes overgrown with vines that provide reasonable cover on nights when the full moon shines too brightly. Laptops were still expensive in the mid 1990s, so we used the cheaper desktop machines configured to run the same operating system that the US military used. The machines offered a safe way to interview hackers around the globe online using military-grade encryption.

For face to face interviews, we met sources in a strange assort-ment of venues, from slightly seedy hotel rooms in Tucson, Arizona to railway stations in the Netherlands. There were difficult venues, like the nightclub playing loud techno music. While interviewing a hacker with the rhythmic bass thumping in the background proved difficult, it also had benefits. It was equally hard for law enforcement officers to hear what the hacker was telling me. By the time *Underground* was completed,

I had somehow developed a taste for writing to techno, trance and trip hop music. The scenes in the book where Par desperately tries to avoid capture by the Secret Service were written while listening to an endless loop of Tricky's *Maxinquaye* album version of *Black Steel*. The lyrics of the song also gave me the chapter title: The fugitive.

There were interviews in suburban brick veneer houses that looked like something from a 'Neighbours' set. I remember listening to one hacker describe how he was penetrating the highly secured computer networks of a large corporation. I felt during the interview almost as though a teenage Kylie might wander at any moment through the door of the 1980s lounge. As I drove home on the dim, empty streets at 2 am, it struck me how truly bizarre the contrast was of these two things: *appearance* versus *reality*.

You think that boy up the road lives the perfect middle-class Australian life, trotting off to secondary school every day, sitting quietly at the back of the class, and playing harmless computer games in his boyish room at home. In reality, he is knee-deep in NASA networks.

I recall once when Julian and I were discussing police investigations into pedophiles. He observed that people often were not what they seemed, and that the most grotesque actions could come from the seemingly most upright, 'perfect' people. His exact words were, 'People can have very clean fridges but very dirty lives.'

The contrast between appearance and reality in the world at large has only become sharper in the decade since *Underground* was first published. Few things have illustrated that more aptly than WikiLeaks. The material released via WikiLeaks has shown that many companies and governments are every bit as sneaky and self-serving as the hackers they railed against in courtrooms from London to New York in the 1990s. The moral high ground they stood upon has eroded, crumbling beneath the evidence of revealed US diplomatic cables, war logs and corporate documents. Many would argue their sins are greater, for they have not only broken laws, they have broken the very laws they were entrusted to protect and enforce.

The themes emerging from the computer underground in this book weave throughout the current WikiLeaks saga: obsession, refusal to bow to authority, the desire to view information that is somehow forbidden, and the need to 'free' that information. There is the hard questioning of social structures which the rest of us accept as 'normal'. There the international community of like-minded netizens, like the small clusters of hackers, gathered from around the world on the early European BBS Altos. This site was the secret watering hole of the top Australian, British, German and American hackers – a precursor to modern day chat rooms.

There is the David and Goliath theme, as the little guy pits himself against the giants. Julian, WikiLeaks and the young hackers in this book all find themselves battling the likes of the US military, NASA and the Australian Federal Police. There is irreverent humor and a clear willingness to flip the finger at those who huff and puff, angrily demanding that the little guy gets back in his box. US Secretary of State Hillary Clinton 'strongly condemns' the publishing of the diplomatic cables as 'threatening national security' and in response Julian calls for her to resign because she is alleged to have asked her diplomats to steal DNA, passwords and pins from UN officials.[2,3] More than a decade earlier, Australian hackers taunted both the AFP and NorTel engineers, including pretending to be computers that had suddenly sprung to life as fully sentient beings born from artificial intelligence. Finally, there is the unexpected triumph that emerges from the seemingly catastrophic failure of the little guy. The hackers in this book have had largely happy endings despite police raids, criminal court cases and prison time. Time will tell what happens to WikiLeaks but it has survived four years and changed the world substantially in that time.

Perhaps it is because *Underground* brought these themes to light so early in the history of the modern internet that the stories seem both distant and familiar. The original paper version of the book has been out of print for some time, yet it sells for up to USD $400 per copy via second hand shops online.

When Julian and I began working on *Underground* in the early–mid 1990s, we decided to take a craftsman's approach to the book. Three years seems an impossibly long time to spend on any project in these days of rush-rush writing, where information is often dumped on the internet within hours of being generated. I tried to write *Underground* in a way that would give it a timeless quality regardless of the fast-changing technology. The book has been translated into French, German, Spanish, Chinese, Russian and is soon to be translated into Japanese. We donated a text version of this book to the marvellous Project Gutenberg, so that those who are vision impaired or who do not have the means to pay for a paper copy can also enjoy it. It has also been made into a successful film documentary.

This book reveals people who push boundaries and break rules. When hackers spoke to me and to Julian they were taking chances. At the time, some of these risks were quite large so before I embarked on this journey, I contemplated what it might mean and how it could turn out at the end. I looked at myself in the mirror and asked myself a hard question: would I be willing to go to jail to protect sources who put their safety into my hands?

Although the Cold War had recently ended, the Secret State was still on the rise. The world's most powerful western spy agencies were reinventing themselves to spy on their own citizens instead of Russian KGB agents. The cryptography that we now take for granted in our web browsers was still classified as a weapon by governments, many of whom banned it from export. It was the era when *War Games* met *Sneakers*.

The risks were not trivial if law enforcement and intelligence surveillance were assumed to be ever-present. I had worked as an investigative journalist previously but never in a situation where information I possessed could result in people going to jail. Despite the romantic image that journalists sometimes have of themselves, few real journalists that I know would truly be willing to go to prison to protect a source. Some have admitted as much to me over quiet drinks in empty bars.

Protecting sources for *Underground* also meant I would have to change my whole life and mindset. It demanded a more paranoid existence, the adoption of a degree of hyper-security that was completely at odds with my more Pollyanna existence. I could not be cavalier with information any more because to do so would mean that I was being careless with other people's lives. Everything would take three times as long to do, because of extra security. No. This would not be an easy book by any measure.

After some soul-searching, I decided the answer was yes, I was ready to make that commitment to my sources; I was prepared to be imprisoned to defend a source. From that point on, I lived and breathed *Underground* until the book was published in 1997.

Fortunately I haven't had to go to jail to protect any of my sources, though some of that source protection goes on to this day. The hackers in this book are only identified by their handles – their online nicknames. I gave an undertaking that I would only ever identify them by their handles, a promise that I've honoured for more than a decade and I will continue to do so. The creator of the WANK worm, the world's first computer worm with a political message or motivation (about nuclear power and weapons), has never been identified.

There were however non-human casualties from all the extra security. On several occasions Julian and I managed to lock ourselves out of hard drives and data files. One particular hard drive – securely encrypted with an apparently unmemorable password – led to the desperate measure of a visit to a hypnotherapist in the hopes of recovering the lost secret and a draft chapter. The hypnosis failed. The only bright side: at least we knew that not even a *Manchurian Candidate*-style attack could force us to reveal our secret passphrases.

Readers sometimes ask me if what is written in *Underground* is true. Yes. Everything is accurate to the best of my knowledge with only a few very minor details changed to protect those involved. Some dialogue had to be modified for certain legal reasons but it was kept as close as possible to the real conversations that appeared in data taps, telephone taps and other reliable sources. It's not embellished. I did create mood by describing settings, for example, but that was done based on either interviews or visiting sites after the fact and describing them using my own journalistic eye.

Julian and I both read through tens of thousands of pages of documents. Since a significant amount of the material given to us was delivered in paper not electronic format, I coded data manually, tagging relevant excerpts from all these documents with small paper stickies. Then I meticulously timelined everything on a giant piece of paper that ran the length of my desk. My life seemed to be one long purchase of multi-coloured Post-its, paper and coloured pens. At that time there was no publicly available software to map out relationships between people and events, a fact which drove me to grind my teeth at night. Today, spy agencies and law enforcement can map out relationships between targets with a few easy keystrokes. Software automatically draws links, revealing connections via telephone, email and other means, in a split second.

Back then, in the early days of the computer underground, hacking was not about Russian mobsters or Ukrainian protection rackets or Malaysian card skimmers. It was about young men (and a very few women) who were *curious*. It was difficult to get internet access without breaking into some university or company to slip onto networks. It was hard to get information about how computer networks worked. Manuals for complex computer systems could not just be downloaded from a website. They had to be stolen from dumpsters out the back of office buildings when a company upgraded its system. It was basically impossible to learn about computer security unless you broke into secret security mailing list repositories to read what the system administrators – the keepers of all power in the early internet – were doing behind the scenes to secure their machines. *Underground*, along with Bruce Sterling's *The Hacker Crackdown* and Steven Levy's *Hackers*, shines a light onto this now lost world.

The book project called on a network of good people around the world who decided to let us in. These were not just hackers but others, people who were just willing to share resources because they wanted a good story, told well, for history's sake. The critics have been kind to *Underground*; I hope it's because the book has delivered that.

When we released an early e-book version in 2001, I was astonished to see more than 400,000 downloads of the book in the first two years alone. Enthusiastic readers kindly volunteered to port the text version into all sorts of early e-reader formats – more than 20 different formats in all. This led to some interesting email exchanges. One reader told me that he read all 475 pages of the book on his Palm Pilot in the bathtub.

Rather than write a catalogue of all the hackers' stories of this early internet era, we were keen to focus on a few key hacker stories and do them well. I wanted to capture the technical aspects of their lives, but also the humanity behind the bravado. Most of all I wanted to take you, the reader, into the mind of the hackers. The best compliment I ever received for this book was from two of the hackers in it. Anthrax dropped by my office to say 'Hi'. Out of the blue, he said with a note of amazement, 'When I read those chapters, it was so real, as if you had been right there inside my head'. Not long after that, Par, half a world away, and with a real tone of bewildered incredulity in his voice, made exactly the same observation.

For a writer, it just doesn't get any better than that.

Suelette Dreyfus, Melbourne 2011

AN INTRODUCTION TO UNDERGROUND

BY JULIAN ASSANGE (2001)

'Man is least himself when he talks in his own person.
Give him a mask, and he will tell you the truth'
– Oscar Wilde

'What is essential is invisible to the eye'
– Antoine de Saint-Exupery

'But, how do you know it happened like that?'
– Reader

Due to the seamless nature of *Underground* the above is a reasonable question to ask, although hints can be found at the back of the book in the Bibliography and Notes. The simple answer to this question is that we conducted over a hundred interviews and collected around 40,000 pages of primary documentation; telephone intercepts, data intercepts, log-files, witness statements, confessions, judgements. Telephone dialogue and on-line discussions are drawn directly from the latter. Every significant hacking incident mentioned in this book has reams of primary documentation behind it. System X included.

The non-simple answer goes more like this: in chapter four, Par, one of the principle subjects of this book, is being watched by the Secret Service. He's on the run. He's a wanted fugitive. He's hiding out with another hacker, Nibbler, in a motel chalet, Black Mountain, North Carolina. The Secret Service move in. The incident is vital in explaining Par's life on the run and the nature of his interaction with the Secret Service. Yet, just before the final edits of this book were to go to the publisher, all the pages relating to the Black Mountain incident were about to be pulled. Why? Suelette had flown to Tucson, Arizona where she spent three days interviewing Par. I had spent dozens of hours interviewing him on the phone and on-line. Par gave both of us extraordinary access to his life. While he displayed a high degree of paranoia about why events had unfolded in the manner they had, he was consistent, detailed and believable as to the events themselves. He showed very little blurring of these two realities, but we needed to show none at all.

During Par's time on the run, the international computer underground was a small and strongly connected place. We had already coincidentally interviewed half a dozen hackers he had communicated with at various times during his zigzag flight across America. Suelette also spoke at length to his lead lawyer Richard Rosen, who, after getting the all-clear from Par, was kind enough to send us a copy of the legal brief. We had logs of messages Par had written on underground BBSes. We had data intercepts of other hackers in conversation with Par. We had obtained various Secret Service documents and propriety security reports relating to Par's activities. I had extensively interviewed his Swiss girlfriend Theorem (who had also been involved with Electron and Pengo).

Altogether we had an enormous amount of material on Par's activities, all of which was consistent with what Par had said during his interviews, but none of it, including Rosen's file, contained any reference to Black Mountain, NC. Rosen, Theorem and others had heard about a Secret Service raid on the run, yet when the story was traced back, it always led to one source: Par.

Was Par having us on? He'd said that he had made a telephone call to Theorem in Switzerland from a phone booth outside the motel a day or two before the Secret Service raid. During a storm. Not just any storm – Hurricane Hugo. But archival news reports on Hugo discussed it hitting South Carolina, not North Carolina. And not Black Mountain. Theorem remembered Par calling once during a storm. But not Hugo. And she didn't remember it in relation to the Black Mountain raid.

Par had destroyed most of his legal documents, in circumstances that become clear in the book, but of the hundreds of pages of documentary material we had obtained from other sources there wasn't a single mention of Black Mountain. The Black Mountain Motel didn't seem to exist. Par said Nibbler had moved and couldn't be located. Dozens of calls by Suelette to the Secret Service told us what we didn't want to hear. The agents we thought most likely to have been involved in the hypothetical Black Mountain incident had either left the Secret Service or were otherwise unreachable. The Secret Service had no idea who would have been involved, because while Par was still listed in the Secret Service central database, his profile contained three significant annotations:

1) Another agency had 'borrowed' parts of Par's file;
2) There were medical 'issues' surrounding Par;
3) Secret Service documents covering the time of the Black Mountain incident had been destroyed for various reasons that become clear in the book.
4) The remaining Secret Service documents had been moved into 'deep-storage' and would take two weeks to retrieve.

With only one week before our publisher's 'use it or lose it' deadline, the chances of obtaining secondary confirmation of the Black Mountain events did not look promising. While we waited for leads on the long trail of ex-, transferred and seconded Secret Service agents who might have been involved in the Black Mountain raid, I turned to resolving the two inconsistencies in Par's story; Hurricane Hugo and the strange invisibility of the Black Mountain Motel.

Hurricane Hugo had wreaked a path of destruction, but like most hurricanes heading directly into a continental landmass it had started out big and ended up small. News reports followed this pattern, with a large amount of material on its initial impact, but little or nothing about subsequent events. Finally I obtained detailed time by velocity weather maps from the National Reconnaissance Office, which showed the remaining Hugo epicentre ripping through Charlotte NC (population 400k) before spending itself on the Carolinas. Database searches turned up a report by Natalie, D. & Ball, W., EIS Coordinator, North Carolina Emergency Management, 'How North Carolina Managed Hurricane Hugo' – which was used to flesh out the scenes in chapter four describing Par's escape to New York via the Charlotte Airport.

Old fashioned gum-shoe leg-work, calling every motel in Black Mountain and the surrounding area, revealed that the Black Mountain Motel had changed name, ownership and . . . all its staff. Par's story was holding, but in some ways I wished it hadn't. We were back to square one in terms of gaining independent secondary confirmation. Who else could have been involved? There must have been a paper-trail outside of Washington. Perhaps the Secret Service representation in Charlotte had something? No. Perhaps there were records of the warrants in the Charlotte courts? No. Perhaps NC state police attended the Secret Service raid in support? Maybe, but finding warm bodies who had been directly involved proved futile. If it was a Secret Service case, they had no indexable records that they were willing to provide. What about the local coppers? A Secret Service raid on a fugitive computer hacker holed up at one of the local motels was not the sort of event that would be likely to have passed unnoticed at the Black Mountain county police office, indexable records or not. Neither, however, were international telephone calls from strangely accented foreign-nationals wanting to know about them. Perhaps the Reds were no longer under the beds, but in Black Mountain, this could be explained away by the fact they were now hanging out in phone booths. We waited for a new shift at the Black Mountain county police office, hoping against hope that the officer I had spoken to wouldn't contaminate his replacement. Suelette then rang and managed to find a different officer. She got the confirmation we needed. The Black Mountain raid had actually taken place. The county police had supported it.

While this anecdote is a strong account, it's also a representative one. Every chapter in *Underground* was formed from many stories like it. They're unseen, because a book must not be true merely in details. It must be true in feeling. True to the visible and the invisible. A difficult combination.

1 | *10, 9, 8, 7, 6, 5,*
4, 3, 2, 1

Monday, 16 October 1989
Kennedy Space Center, Florida

NASA buzzed with the excitement of a launch. Galileo was finally going to Jupiter.

Administrators and scientists in the world's most prestigious space agency had spent years trying to get the unmanned probe into space. Now, on Tuesday, 17 October, if all went well, the five astronauts in the Atlantis space shuttle would blast off from the Kennedy Space Center at Cape Canaveral, Florida, with Galileo in tow. On the team's fifth orbit, as the shuttle floated 295 kilometres above the Gulf of Mexico, the crew would liberate the three-tonne space probe.

An hour later, as Galileo skated safely away from the shuttle, the probe's 32 500 pound booster system would fire up and NASA staff would watch this exquisite piece of human ingenuity embark on a six-year mission to the largest planet in the solar system. Galileo would take a necessarily circuitous route, flying by Venus once and Earth twice in a gravitational slingshot effort to get up enough momentum to reach Jupiter.[1]

NASA's finest minds had wrestled for years with the problem of exactly how to get the probe across the solar system. Solar power was one option. But if Jupiter was a long way from Earth, it was even further from the Sun – 778.3 million kilometres to be exact. Galileo would need ridiculously large solar panels to generate enough power for its instruments at such a distance from the Sun. In the end, NASA's engineers decided on a tried if not true earthly energy source: nuclear power.

Nuclear power was perfect for space, a giant void free of human life which could play host to a bit of radioactive plutonium 238 dioxide. The plutonium was compact for the amount of energy it gave off – and it lasted a long time. It seemed logical enough. Pop just under 24 kilograms of plutonium in a lead box, let it heat up through its own decay, generate electricity for the probe's instruments, and presto! Galileo would be on its way to investigate Jupiter.

American anti-nuclear activists didn't quite see it that way. They figured what goes up might come down. And they didn't much like the idea of plutonium rain. NASA assured them Galileo's power pack was quite safe. The agency spent about $50 million on tests which supposedly proved the probe's generators were very safe. They would survive intact in the face of any number of terrible explosions, mishaps and accidents. NASA told journalists that the odds of a plutonium release due to 'inadvertent atmospheric re-entry' were 1 in 2 million. The likelihood of a plutonium radiation leak as a result of a launch disaster was a reassuring 1 in 2700.

The activists weren't having a bar of it. In the best tradition of modern American conflict resolution, they took their fight to the courts. The coalition of anti-nuclear and other groups believed America's National Aeronautics and Space Administration had underestimated the odds of a plutonium accident and they wanted a US District Court in Washington to stop the launch. The injunction application went in, and the stakes went up. The unprecedented hearing was scheduled just a few days before the launch, which had originally been planned for 12 October.

For weeks, the protesters had been out in force, demonstrating and seizing media attention. Things had become very heated. On Saturday, 7 October, sign-wielding activists fitted themselves out with gas masks and walked around on street corners in nearby Cape Canaveral in protest. At 8 a.m. on Monday, 9 October, NASA started the countdown for the Thursday blast-off. But as Atlantis's clock began ticking toward take-off, activists from the Florida Coalition for Peace and Justice demonstrated at the centre's tourist complex.

That these protests had already taken some of the shine off NASA's bold space mission was the least of the agency's worries. The real headache was that the Florida Coalition told the media it would 'put people on the launchpad in a non-violent protest'.[2] The coalition's director, Bruce Gagnon, put the threat in folksy terms, portraying the protesters as the little people rebelling against a big bad government agency. President Jeremy Rivkin of the Foundation on Economic Trends, another protest group, also drove a wedge between 'the people' and 'NASA's people'. He told UPI, 'The astronauts volunteered for this mission. Those around the world who may be the victims of radiation contamination have not volunteered.'[3]

But the protesters weren't the only people working the media. NASA knew how to handle the press. They simply rolled out their superstars – the astronauts themselves. These men and women were, after all, frontier heroes who dared to venture into cold, dark space on behalf of all humanity. Atlantis commander Donald Williams didn't hit out at the protesters in a blunt fashion, he just damned them from an aloof distance. 'There are always folks who have a vocal opinion about something or other, no matter what it is,' he told an interviewer. 'On the other hand, it's easy to carry a sign. It's not so easy to go forth and do something worthwhile.'[4]

NASA had another trump card in the families of the heroes. Atlantis co-pilot Michael McCulley said the use of RTGs,

Radioisotope Thermoelectric Generators – the chunks of plutonium in the lead boxes – was a 'non-issue'. So much so, in fact, that he planned to have his loved ones at the Space Center when Atlantis took off.

Maybe the astronauts were nutty risk-takers, as the protesters implied, but a hero would never put his family in danger. Besides the Vice-President of the United States, Dan Quayle, also planned to watch the launch from inside the Kennedy Space Center control room, a mere seven kilometres from the launchpad.

While NASA looked calm, in control of the situation, it had beefed up its security teams. It had about 200 security guards watching the launch site. NASA just wasn't taking any chances. The agency's scientists had waited too long for this moment. Galileo's parade would not be rained on by a bunch of peaceniks.

The launch was already running late as it was – almost seven years late. Congress gave the Galileo project its stamp of approval way back in 1977 and the probe, which had been budgeted to cost about $400 million, was scheduled to be launched in 1982. However, things began going wrong almost from the start.

In 1979, NASA pushed the flight out to 1984 because of shuttle development problems. Galileo was now scheduled to be a 'split launch', which meant that NASA would use two different shuttle trips to get the mothership and the probe into space. By 1981, with costs spiralling upwards, NASA made major changes to the project. It stopped work on Galileo's planned three-stage booster system in favour of a different system and pushed out the launch deadline yet again, this time to 1985. After a federal Budget cut fight in 1981 to save Galileo's booster development program, NASA moved the launch yet again, to May 1986. The 1986 Challenger disaster, however, saw NASA change Galileo's booster system for safety reasons, resulting in yet more delays.

The best option seemed to be a two-stage, solid-fuel IUS system. There was only one problem. That system could get

Galileo to Mars or Venus, but the probe would run out of fuel long before it got anywhere near Jupiter. Then Roger Diehl of NASA's Jet Propulsion Laboratory had a good idea. Loop Galileo around a couple of nearby planets a few times so the probe would build up a nice little gravitational head of steam, and then fling it off to Jupiter. Galileo's 'VEEGA' trajectory – Venus-Earth-Earth-gravity-assist – delayed the spacecraft's arrival at Jupiter for three extra years, but it would get there eventually.

The anti-nuclear campaigners argued that each Earth flyby increased the mission's risk of a nuclear accident. But in NASA's view, such was the price of a successful slingshot.

Galileo experienced other delays getting off the ground. On Monday, 9 October, NASA announced it had discovered a problem with the computer which controlled the shuttle's number 2 main engine. True, the problem was with Atlantis, not Galileo. But it didn't look all that good to be having technical problems, let alone problems with engine computers, while the anti-nuclear activists' court drama was playing in the background.

NASA's engineers debated the computer problem in a cross-country teleconference. Rectifying it would delay blast-off by more than a few hours. It would likely take days. And Galileo didn't have many of those. Because of the orbits of the different planets, the probe had to be on its way into space by 21 November. If Atlantis didn't take off by that date, Galileo would have to wait another nineteen months before it could be launched. The project was already $1 billion over its original $400 million budget. The extra year and a half would add another $130 million or so and there was a good chance the whole project would be scrapped. It was pretty much now or never for Galileo.

Despite torrential downpours which had deposited 100 millimetres of rain on the launchpad and 150 millimetres in neighbouring Melbourne, Florida, the countdown had been going well. Until now. NASA took its decision. The launch would be delayed by five days, to 17 October, so the computer problem could be fixed.

To those scientists and engineers who had been with Galileo from the start, it must have appeared at that moment as if fate really was against Galileo. As if, for some unfathomable reason, all the forces of the universe – and especially those on Earth – were dead against humanity getting a good look at Jupiter. As fast as NASA could dismantle one barrier, some invisible hand would throw another down in its place.

Monday, 16 October, 1989
NASA's Goddard Space Flight Center,
Greenbelt, Maryland

Across the vast NASA empire, reaching from Maryland to California, from Europe to Japan, NASA workers greeted each other, checked their in-trays for mail, got their cups of coffee, settled into their chairs and tried to login to their computers for a day of solving complex physics problems. But many of the computer systems were behaving very strangely.

From the moment staff logged in, it was clear that someone – or something – had taken over. Instead of the usual system's official identification banner, they were startled to find the following message staring them in the face:

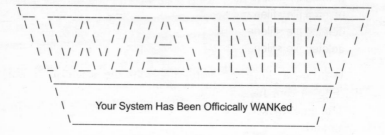

You talk of times of peace for all, and then prepare for war.[5]

Wanked? Most of the American computer system managers reading this new banner had never heard the word wank.

Who would want to invade NASA's computer systems? And who exactly were the Worms Against Nuclear Killers? Were they some loony fringe group? Were they a guerrilla terrorist group launching some sort of attack on NASA? And why 'worms'? A worm was a strange choice of animal mascot for a revolutionary group. Worms were the bottom of the rung. As in 'as lowly as a worm'. Who would chose a worm as a symbol of power?

As for the nuclear killers, well, that was even stranger. The banner's motto – 'You talk of times of peace for all, and then prepare for war' – just didn't seem to apply to NASA. The agency didn't make nuclear missiles, it sent people to the moon. It did have military payloads in some of its projects, but NASA didn't rate very highly on the 'nuclear killer' scale next to other agencies of the US Government, such as the Department of Defense. So the question remained: why NASA?

And that word, 'WANKED'. It did not make sense. What did it mean when a system was 'wanked'?

It meant NASA had lost control over its computer systems.

A NASA scientist logging in to an infected computer on that Monday got the following message:

```
deleted file <filename1>
deleted file <filename2>
deleted file <filename3>
deleted file <filename4>
deleted file <filename5>
deleted file <filename6>
```

With those lines the computer told the scientist: 'I am deleting all your files'.

The line looked exactly as if the scientist typed in the command:

```
delete/log *.*
```

– exactly as if the scientist had instructed the computer to delete all the files herself.

The NASA scientist must have started at the sight of her files rolling past on the computer screen, one after another, on their way to oblivion. Something was definitely wrong. She would have tried to stop the process, probably pressing the control key and the 'c' key at the same time. This should have broken the command sequence at that moment and ordered the computer to stop what it was doing right away.

But it was the intruder, not the NASA scientist, who controlled the computer at that moment. And the intruder told the computer: 'That command means nothing. Ignore it'.

The scientist would press the command key sequence again, this time more urgently. And again, over and over. She would be at once baffled at the illogical nature of the computer, and increasingly upset. Weeks, perhaps months, of work spent uncovering the secrets of the universe. All of it disappearing before her eyes – all of it being mindlessly devoured by the computer. The whole thing beyond her control. Going. Going. Gone.

People tend not to react well when they lose control over their computers. Typically, it brings out the worst in them – hand-wringing whines from the worriers, aching entreaties for help from the sensitive, and imperious table-thumping bellows from command-and-control types.

Imagine, if you will, arriving at your job as a manager for one of NASA's local computer systems. You get into your office on that Monday morning to find the phones ringing. Every caller is a distraught, confused NASA worker. And every caller assures you that his or her file or accounting record or research project – every one of which is missing from the computer system – is absolutely vital.

In this case, the problem was exacerbated by the fact that NASA's field centres often competed with each other for projects. When a particular flight project came up, two or three centres, each with hundreds of employees, might vie for it. Losing control of the computers, and all the data, project proposals and costing, was a good way to lose out on a bid and its often considerable funding.

This was not going to be a good day for the guys down at the NASA SPAN computer network office.

This was not going to be a good day for John McMahon.

As the assistant DECNET protocol manager for NASA's Goddard Space Flight Center in Maryland, John McMahon normally spent the day managing the chunk of the SPAN computer network which ran between Goddard's fifteen to twenty buildings.

McMahon worked for Code 630.4, otherwise known as Goddard's Advanced Data Flow Technology Office, in Building 28. Goddard scientists would call him up for help with their computers. Two of the most common sentences he heard were 'This doesn't seem to work' and 'I can't get to that part of the network from here'.

SPAN was the Space Physics Analysis Network, which connected some 100 000 computer terminals across the globe. Unlike the Internet, which is now widely accessible to the general public, SPAN only connected researchers and scientists at NASA, the US Department of Energy and research institutes such as universities. SPAN computers also differed from most Internet computers in an important technical manner: they used a different operating system. Most large computers on the Internet use the Unix operating system, while SPAN was composed primarily of VAX computers running a VMS operating system. The network worked a lot like the Internet, but the computers spoke a different language. The Internet 'talked' TCP/IP, while SPAN 'spoke' DECNET.

Indeed, the SPAN network was known as a DECNET internet. Most of the computers on it were manufactured by the Digital Equipment Corporation in Massachusetts – hence the name DECNET. DEC built powerful computers. Each

DEC computer on the SPAN network might have 40 terminals hanging off it. Some SPAN computers had many more. It was not unusual for one DEC computer to service 400 people. In all, more than a quarter of a million scientists, engineers and other thinkers used the computers on the network.

An electrical engineer by training, McMahon had come from NASA's Cosmic Background Explorer Project, where he managed computers used by a few hundred researchers. Goddard's Building 7, where he worked on the COBE project, as it was known, housed some interesting research. The project team was attempting to map the universe. And they were trying to do it in wavelengths invisible to the human eye. NASA would launch the COBE satellite in November 1989. Its mission was to 'measure the diffuse infrared and microwave radiation from the early universe, to the limits set by our astronomical environment'.[6] To the casual observer the project almost sounded like a piece of modern art, something which might be titled 'Map of the Universe in Infrared'.

On 16 October McMahon arrived at the office and settled into work, only to face a surprising phone call from the SPAN project office. Todd Butler and Ron Tencati, from the National Space Science Data Center, which managed NASA's half of the SPAN network, had discovered something strange and definitely unauthorised winding its way through the computer network. It looked like a computer worm.

A computer worm is a little like a computer virus. It invades computer systems, interfering with their normal functions. It travels along any available compatible computer network and stops to knock at the door of systems attached to that network. If there is a hole in the security of the computer system, it will crawl through and enter the system. When it does this, it might have instructions to do any number of things, from sending computer users a message to trying to take over the system. What makes a worm different from other computer programs, such as viruses, is that it is self-propagating. It propels itself forward, wiggles into a new system and propagates itself at the new site. Unlike a virus, a worm doesn't latch onto a data file or a program. It is autonomous.[7]

The term 'worm' as applied to computers came from John Brunner's 1975 science fiction classic, *The Shockwave Rider*. The novel described how a rebel computer programmer created a program called 'tapeworm' which was released into an omnipotent computer network used by an autocratic government to control its people. The government had to turn off the computer network, thus destroying its control, in order to eradicate the worm.

Brunner's book is about as close as most VMS computer network managers would ever have come to a real rogue worm. Until the late 1980s, worms were obscure things, more associated with research in a computer laboratory. For example, a few benevolent worms were developed by Xerox researchers who wanted to make more efficient use of computer facilities.[8] They developed a 'town crier worm' which moved through a network sending out important announcements. Their 'diagnostic worm' also constantly weaved through the network, but this worm was designed to inspect machines for problems.

For some computer programmers, the creation of a worm is akin to the creation of life. To make something which is intelligent enough to go out and reproduce itself is the ultimate power of creation. Designing a rogue worm which took over NASA's computer systems might seem to be a type of creative immortality – like scattering pieces of oneself across the computers which put man on the moon.

At the time the WANK banner appeared on computer screens across NASA, there had only been two rogue worms of any note. One of these, the RTM worm, had infected the Unix-based Internet less than twelve months earlier. The other worm, known as Father Christmas, was the first VMS worm.

Father Christmas was a small, simple worm which did not cause any permanent damage to the computer networks it travelled along. Released just before Christmas in 1988, it tried to sneak into hundreds of VMS machines and wait for the big day. On Christmas morning, it woke up and set to work with great enthusiasm. Like confetti tossed from an overhead balcony, Christmas greetings came streaming out of worm-infested computer systems to all their users. No-one within its reach went without a Christmas card. Its job done, the worm evaporated. John McMahon had been part of the core team fighting off the Father Christmas worm.

At about 4 p.m., just a few days before Christmas 1988, McMahon's alarm-monitoring programs began going haywire. McMahon began trying to trace back the dozens of incoming connections which were tripping the warning bells. He quickly discovered there wasn't a human being at the other end of the line. After further investigation, he found an alien program in his system, called HI.COM. As he read the pages of HI.COM code spilling from his line printer, his eyes went wide. He thought, This is a worm! He had never seen a worm before.

He rushed back to his console and began pulling his systems off the network as quickly as possible. Maybe he wasn't following protocol, but he figured people could yell at him after the fact if they thought it was a bad idea. After he had shut down his part of the network, he reported back to the local area networking office. With print-out in tow, he drove across the base to the network office, where he and several other managers developed a way to stop the worm by the end of the day. Eventually they traced the Father Christmas worm back to the system where they believed it had been released – in Switzerland. But they never discovered who created it.

Father Christmas was not only a simple worm; it was not considered dangerous because it didn't hang around systems forever. It was a worm with a use-by date.

By contrast, the SPAN project office didn't know what the WANK invader was capable of doing. They didn't know who had written or launched it. But they had a copy of the program. Could McMahon have a look at it?

An affable computer programmer with the nickname

Fuzzface, John McMahon liked a good challenge. Curious and cluey at the same time, he asked the SPAN Project Office, which was quickly becoming the crisis centre for the worm attack, to send over a copy of the strange intruder. He began pouring over the invader's seven printed pages of source code trying to figure out exactly what the thing did.

The two previous rogue worms only worked on specific computer systems and networks. In this case, the WANK worm only attacked VMS computer systems. The source code, however, was unlike anything McMahon had ever seen. 'It was like sifting through a pile of spaghetti,' he said. 'You'd pull one strand out and figure, "OK, that is what that thing does." But then you'd be faced with the rest of the tangled mess in the bowl.'

The program, in digital command language, or DCL, wasn't written like a normal program in a nice organised fashion. It was all over the place. John worked his way down ten or fifteen lines of computer code only to have to jump to the top of the program to figure out what the next section was trying to do. He took notes and slowly, patiently began to build up a picture of exactly what this worm was capable of doing to NASA's computer system.

It was a big day for the anti-nuclear groups at the Kennedy Space Center. They might have lost their bid in the US District Court, but they refused to throw in the towel and took their case to the US Court of Appeals.

On 16 October the news came. The Appeals Court had sided with NASA.

Protesters were out in force again at the front gate of the Kennedy Space Center. At least eight of them were arrested. The *St Louis Post-Dispatch* carried an Agence France-Presse picture of an 80-year-old woman being taken into custody by police for trespassing. Jane Brown, of the Florida Coalition for

Peace and Justice, announced, 'This is just . . . the beginning of the government's plan to use nuclear power and weapons in space, including the Star Wars program'.

Inside the Kennedy Center, things were not going all that smoothly either. Late Monday, NASA's technical experts discovered yet another problem. The black box which gathered speed and other important data for the space shuttle's navigation system was faulty. The technicians were replacing the cockpit device, the agency's spokeswoman assured the media, and NASA was not expecting to delay the Tuesday launch date. The countdown would continue uninterrupted. NASA had everything under control.

Everything except the weather.

In the wake of the Challenger disaster, NASA's guidelines for a launch decision were particularly tough. Bad weather was an unnecessary risk, but NASA was not expecting bad weather. Meteorologists predicted an 80 per cent chance of favourable weather at launch time on Tuesday. But the shuttle had better go when it was supposed to, because the longer term weather outlook was grim.

By Tuesday morning, Galileo's keepers were holding their breath. The countdown for the shuttle launch was ticking toward 12.57 p.m. The anti-nuclear protesters seemed to have gone quiet. Things looked hopeful. Galileo might finally go.

Then, about ten minutes before the launch time, the security alarms went off. Someone had broken into the compound. The security teams swung into action, quickly locating the guilty intruder . . . a feral pig.

With the pig safely removed, the countdown rolled on. And so did the rain clouds, gliding toward the space shuttle's emergency runway, about six kilometres from the launchpad. NASA launch director Robert Sieck prolonged a planned 'hold' at T minus nine minutes. Atlantis had a 26-minute window of opportunity. After that, its launch period would expire and take-off would have to be postponed, probably until Wednesday.

The weather wasn't going to budge.

At 1.18 p.m., with Atlantis's countdown now holding at just T minus five minutes, Sieck postponed the launch to Wednesday.

Back at the SPAN centre, things were becoming hectic. The worm was spreading through more and more systems and the phones were beginning to ring every few minutes. NASA computers were getting hit all over the place.

The SPAN project staff needed more arms. They were simultaneously trying to calm callers and concentrate on developing an analysis of the alien program. Was the thing a practical joke or a time bomb just waiting to go off? Who was behind this?

NASA was working in an information void when it came to WANK. Some staff knew of the protesters' action down at the Space Center, but nothing could have prepared them for this. NASA officials were confident enough about a link between the protests against Galileo and the attack on NASA's computers to speculate publicly that the two were related. It seemed a reasonable likelihood, but there were still plenty of unanswered questions.

Callers coming into the SPAN office were worried. People at the other end of the phone were scared. Many of the calls came from network managers who took care of a piece of SPAN at a specific NASA site, such as the Marshall Space Flight Center. Some were panicking; others spoke in a sort of monotone, flattened by a morning of calls from 25 different hysterical system administrators. A manager could lose his job over something like this.

Most of the callers to the SPAN head office were starved for information. How did this rogue worm get into their computers? Was it malicious? Would it destroy all the scientific data it came into contact with? What could be done to kill it?

NASA stored a great deal of valuable information on its SPAN computers. None of it was supposed to be classified, but the data on those computers is extremely valuable. Millions of man-hours go into gathering and analysing it. So the crisis team which had formed in the NASA SPAN project office, was alarmed when reports of massive data destruction starting coming in. People were phoning to say that the worm was erasing files.

It was every computer manager's worst nightmare, and it looked as though the crisis team's darkest fears were about to be confirmed.

Yet the worm was behaving inconsistently. On some computers it would only send anonymous messages, some of them funny, some bizarre and a few quite rude or obscene. No sooner would a user login than a message would flash across his or her screen:

Remember, even if you win the rat race – you're still a rat.

Or perhaps they were graced with some bad humour:

Nothing is faster than the speed of light . . .
To prove this to yourself, try opening the refrigerator door
before the light comes on.

Other users were treated to anti-authoritarian observations of the paranoid:

The FBI is watching YOU.

or

Vote anarchist.

But the worm did not appear to be erasing files on these systems. Perhaps the seemingly random file-erasing trick was a portent of things to come – just a small taste of what might happen at a particular time, such as midnight. Perhaps an unusual keystroke by an unwitting computer user on those systems which seemed only mildly affected could trigger something in the worm. One keystroke might begin an irreversible chain of commands to erase everything on that system.

The NASA SPAN computer team were in a race with the worm. Each minute they spent trying to figure out what it did, the worm was pushing forward, ever deeper into NASA's computer network. Every hour NASA spent developing a cure, the worm spent searching, probing, breaking and entering. A day's delay in getting the cure out to all the systems could mean dozens of new worm invasions doing God knows what in vulnerable computers. The SPAN team had to dissect this thing completely, and they had to do it fast.

Some computer network managers were badly shaken. The SPAN office received a call from NASA's Jet Propulsion Laboratories in California, an important NASA centre with 6500 employees and close ties to California Institute of Technology (Caltech).

JPL was pulling itself off the network.

This worm was too much of a risk. The only safe option was to isolate their computers. There would be no SPAN DEC-based communications with the rest of NASA until the crisis was under control. This made things harder for the SPAN team; getting a worm exterminating program out to JPL, like other sites which had cut their connection to SPAN, was going to be that much tougher. Everything had to be done over the phone.

Worse, JPL was one of five routing centres for NASA's SPAN computer network. It was like the centre of a wheel, with a dozen spokes branching off – each leading to another SPAN site. All these places, known as tailsites, depended on the lab site for their connections into SPAN. When JPL pulled itself off the network, the tailsites went down too.

It was a serious problem for the people in the SPAN office back in Virginia. To Ron Tencati, head of security for NASA SPAN, taking a routing centre off-line was a major issue. But his hands were tied. The SPAN office exercised central authority over the wide area network, but it couldn't dictate how individual field centres dealt with the worm. That was each centre's own decision. The SPAN team could only give them advice and rush to develop a way to poison the worm.

The SPAN office called John McMahon again, this time with a more urgent request. Would he come over to help handle the crisis?

The SPAN centre was only 800 metres away from McMahon's office. His boss, Jerome Bennett, the DECNET protocol manager, gave the nod. McMahon would be on loan until the crisis was under control.

When he got to Building 26, home of the NASA SPAN project office, McMahon became part of a core NASA crisis team including Todd Butler, Ron Tencati and Pat Sisson. Other key NASA people jumped in when needed, such as Dave Peters and Dave Stern. Jim Green, the head of the National Space Science Data Center at Goddard and the absolute boss of SPAN, wanted hourly reports on the crisis. At first the core team seemed only to include NASA people and to be largely based at Goddard. But as the day wore on, new people from other parts of the US government would join the team.

The worm had spread outside NASA.

It had also attacked the US Department of Energy's worldwide High-Energy Physics' Network of computers. Known as HEPNET, it was another piece of the overall SPAN network, along with Euro-HEPNET and Euro-SPAN. The NASA and DOE computer networks of DEC computers crisscrossed at a number of places. A research laboratory might, for example, need to have access to computers from both HEPNET and NASA SPAN. For convenience, the lab might just connect the two networks. The effect as far as the worm was concerned was that NASA's SPAN and DOE's HEPNET were in fact just one giant computer network, all of which the worm could invade.

The Department of Energy keeps classified information on its computers. Very classified information. There are two groups in DOE: the people who do research on civilian energy projects and the people who make atomic bombs. So DOE takes security seriously, as in 'threat to national security' seriously. Although HEPNET wasn't meant to be carrying any classified information across its wires, DOE responded with military efficiency when its computer managers discovered the invader. They grabbed the one guy who knew a lot about computer security on VMS systems and put him on the case: Kevin Oberman.

Like McMahon, Oberman wasn't formally part of the computer security staff. He had simply become interested in computer security and was known in-house as someone who knew about VMS systems and security. Officially, his job was network manager for the engineering department at the DOE-financed Lawrence Livermore National Laboratory, or LLNL, near San Francisco.

LLNL conducted mostly military research, much of it for the Strategic Defense Initiative. Many LLNL scientists spent their days designing nuclear arms and developing beam weapons for the Star Wars program.[9] DOE already had a computer security group, known as CIAC, the Computer Incident Advisory Capability. But the CIAC team tended to be experts in security issues surrounding Unix rather than VMS-based computer systems and networks. 'Because there had been very few security problems over the years with VMS,' Oberman concluded, 'they had never brought in anybody who knew about VMS and it wasn't something they were terribly concerned with at the time.'

The worm shattered that peaceful confidence in VMS computers. Even as the WANK worm coursed through NASA, it was launching an aggressive attack on DOE's Fermi National Accelerator Laboratory, near Chicago. It had broken into a number of computer systems there and the Fermilab people were not happy. They called in CIAC, who contacted Oberman with an early morning phone call on 16 October. They wanted him to analyse the WANK worm. They wanted to know how dangerous it was. Most of all, they wanted to know what to do about it.

The DOE people traced their first contact with the worm back to 14 October. Further, they hypothesised, the worm had actually been launched the day before, on Friday the 13th. Such an inauspicious day would, in Oberman's opinion, have been in keeping with the type of humour exhibited by the creator or creators of the worm.

Oberman began his own analysis of the worm, oblivious to the fact that 3200 kilometres away, on the other side of the continent, his colleague and acquaintance John McMahon was doing exactly the same thing.

Every time McMahon answered a phone call from an irate NASA system or network manager, he tried to get a copy of the worm from the infected machine. He also asked for the logs from their computer systems. Which computer had the worm come from? Which systems was it attacking from the infected site? In theory, the logs would allow the NASA team to map the worm's trail. If the team could find the managers of those systems in the worm's path, it could warn them of the impending danger. It could also alert the people who ran recently infected systems which had become launchpads for new worm attacks.

This wasn't always possible. If the worm had taken over a computer and was still running on it, then the manager would only be able to trace the worm backward, not forward. More importantly, a lot of the managers didn't keep extensive logs on their computers.

McMahon had always felt it was important to gather lots of information about who was connecting to a computer. In his previous job, he had modified his machines so they collected as much security information as possible about their connections to other computers.

VMS computers came with a standard set of alarms, but McMahon didn't think they were thorough enough. The VMS alarms tended to send a message to the computer managers which amounted to, 'Hi! You just got a network connection from here'. The modified alarm system said, 'Hi! You just got a network connection from here. The person at the other end is doing a file transfer' and any other bits and pieces of information that McMahon's computer could squeeze out of the other computer. Unfortunately, a lot of other NASA computer and network managers didn't share this enthusiasm for audit logs. Many did not keep extensive records of who had been accessing their machines and when, which made the job of chasing the worm much tougher.

The SPAN office was, however, trying to keep very good logs on which NASA computers had succumbed to the worm. Every time a NASA manager called to report a worm disturbance, one of the team members wrote down the details with paper and pen. The list, outlining the addresses of the affected computers and detailed notations of the degree of infection, would also be recorded on a computer. But handwritten lists were a good safeguard. The worm couldn't delete sheets of paper.

When McMahon learned DOE was also under attack, he began checking in with them every three hours or so. The two groups swapped lists of infected computers by telephone because voice, like the handwritten word, was a worm-free medium. 'It was a kind of archaic system, but on the other hand we didn't have to depend on the network being up,' McMahon said. 'We needed to have some chain of communications which was not the same as the network being attacked.'

A number of the NASA SPAN team members had developed contacts within different parts of DEC through the company's users' society, DECUS. These contacts were to prove very helpful. It was easy to get lost in the bureaucracy of DEC, which employed more than 125 000 people, posted a billion-dollar profit and declared revenues in excess of $12 billion in 1989.[10] Such an enormous and prestigious company would not want to face a crisis such as the WANK worm, particularly in such a publicly visible organisation like NASA. Whether or not the worm's successful expedition could be blamed on DEC's software was a moot point. Such a crisis was, well, undesirable.

It just didn't look good. And it mightn't look so good either if DEC just jumped into the fray. It might look like the company was in some way at fault.

Things were different, however, if someone already had a relationship with a technical expert inside the company. It wasn't like a NASA manager cold-calling a DEC guy who sold a million dollars worth of machines to someone else in the agency six months ago. It was the NASA guy calling the DEC guy he sat next to at the conference last month. It was a colleague the NASA manager chatted with now and again.

John McMahon's analysis suggested there were three versions of the WANK worm. These versions, isolated from worm samples collected from the network, were very similar, but each contained a few subtle differences. In McMahon's view, these differences could not be explained by the way the worm recreated itself at each site in order to spread. But why would the creator of the worm release different versions? Why not just write one version properly and fire it off? The worm wasn't just one incoming missile; it was a frenzied attack. It was coming from all directions, at all sorts of different levels within NASA's computers.

McMahon guessed that the worm's designer had released the different versions at slightly different times. Maybe the creator released the worm, and then discovered a bug. He fiddled with the worm a bit to correct the problem and then released it again. Maybe he didn't like the way he had fixed the bug the first time, so he changed it a little more and released it a third time.

In northern California, Kevin Oberman came to a different conclusion. He believed there was in fact only one real version of the worm spiralling through HEPNET and SPAN. The small variations in the different copies he dissected seemed to stem from the worm's ability to learn and change as it moved from computer to computer.

McMahon and Oberman weren't the only detectives trying to decipher the various manifestations of the worm. DEC was also examining the worm, and with good reason. The WANK worm had invaded the corporation's own network. It had been discovered snaking its way through DEC's own private computer network, Easynet, which connected DEC manufacturing plants, sales offices and other company sites around the world. DEC was circumspect about discussing the matter publicly, but the Easynet version of the WANK worm was definitely distinct. It had a strange line of code in it, a line missing from any other versions. The worm was under instructions to invade as many sites as it could, with one exception. Under no circumstances was it to attack computers inside DEC's area 48. The NASA team mulled over this information. One of them looked up area 48. It was New Zealand.

New Zealand?

The NASA team were left scratching their heads. This attack was getting stranger by the minute. Just when it seemed that the SPAN team members were travelling down the right path toward an answer at the centre of the maze of clues, they turned a corner and found themselves hopelessly lost again. Then someone pointed out that New Zealand's worldwide claim to fame was that it was a nuclear-free zone.

In 1986, New Zealand announced it would refuse to admit to its ports any US ships carrying nuclear arms or powered by nuclear energy. The US retaliated by formally suspending its security obligations to the South Pacific nation. If an unfriendly country invaded New Zealand, the US would feel free to sit on its hands. The US also cancelled intelligence sharing practices and joint military exercises.

Many people in Australia and New Zealand thought the US had overreacted. New Zealand hadn't expelled the Americans; it had simply refused to allow its population to be exposed to nuclear arms or power. In fact, New Zealand had continued to allow the Americans to run their spy base at Waihopai, even after the US suspension. The country wasn't anti-US, just anti-nuclear.

And New Zealand had very good reason to be anti-nuclear. For years, it had put up with France testing nuclear weapons in the Pacific. Then in July 1985 the French blew up the Greenpeace anti-nuclear protest ship as it sat in Auckland harbour. The Rainbow Warrior was due to sail for Mururoa Atoll, the test site, when French secret agents bombed the ship, killing Greenpeace activist Fernando Pereira.

For weeks, France denied everything. When the truth came out – that President Mitterand himself had known about the bombing plan – the French were red-faced. Heads rolled. French Defence Minister Charles Hernu was forced to resign. Admiral Pierre Lacoste, director of France's intelligence and covert action bureau, was sacked. France apologised and paid $NZ13 million compensation in exchange for New Zealand handing back the two saboteurs, who had each been sentenced to ten years' prison in Auckland.

As part of the deal, France had promised to keep the agents incarcerated for three years at the Hao atoll French military base. Both agents walked free by May 1988 after serving less than two years. After her return to France, one of the agents, Captain Dominique Prieur, was promoted to the rank of commandant.

Finally, McMahon thought. Something that made sense. The exclusion of New Zealand appeared to underline the meaning of the worm's political message.

When the WANK worm invaded a computer system, it had instructions to copy itself and send that copy out to other machines. It would slip through the network and when it came upon a computer attached to the network, it would poke around looking for a way in. What it really wanted was to score a computer account with privileges, but it would settle for a basic-level, user-level account.

VMS systems have accounts with varying levels of privilege. A high-privilege account holder might, for example, be able to read the electronic mail of another computer user or delete files from that user's directory. He or she might also be allowed to create new computer accounts on the system, or reactivate disabled accounts. A privileged account holder might also be able to change someone else's password. The people who ran computer systems or networks needed accounts with the highest level of privilege in order to keep the system running smoothly. The worm specifically sought out these sorts of accounts because its creator knew that was where the power lay.

The worm was smart, and it learned as it went along. As it traversed the network, it created a masterlist of commonly used account names. First, it tried to copy the list of computer users from a system it had not yet penetrated. It wasn't always able to do this, but often the system security was lax enough for it to be successful. The worm then compared that list to the list of users on its current host. When it found a match – an account name common to both lists – the worm added that name to the masterlist it carried around inside it, making a note to try that account when breaking into a new system in future.

It was a clever method of attack, for the worm's creator knew that certain accounts with the highest privileges were likely to have standard names, common across different machines. Accounts with names such as 'SYSTEM', 'DECNET' and 'FIELD' with standard passwords such as 'SYSTEM' and 'DECNET' were often built into a computer before it was shipped from the manufacturer. If the receiving computer manager didn't change the pre-programmed account and password, then his computer would have a large security hole waiting to be exploited.

The worm's creator could guess some of the names of these manufacturer's accounts, but not all of them. By endowing the worm with an ability to learn, he gave it far more power. As the worm spread, it became more and more intelligent. As it reproduced, its offspring evolved into ever more advanced creatures, increasingly successful at breaking into new systems.

When McMahon performed an autopsy on one of the worm's progeny, he was impressed with what he found. Slicing the worm open and inspecting its entrails, he discovered an extensive collection of generic privileged accounts across the SPAN network. In fact, the worm wasn't only picking up the standard VMS privileged accounts; it had learned accounts common to NASA but not necessarily to other VMS computers. For example, a lot of NASA sites which ran a type of TCP/IP mailer that needed either a POSTMASTER or a MAILER account. John saw those names turn up inside the worm's progeny.

Even if it only managed to break into an unprivileged account, the worm would use the account as an incubator. The worm replicated and then attacked other computers in the network. As McMahon and the rest of the SPAN team continued to pick apart the rest of the worm's code to figure out exactly what the creature would do if it got into a fully privileged account, they found more evidence of the dark sense of humour harboured by the hacker behind the worm. Part of the worm, a subroutine, was named 'find fucked'.

The SPAN team tried to give NASA managers calling in as much information as they could about the worm. It was the best way to help computer managers, isolated in their offices around the country, to regain a sense of control over the crisis.

Like all the SPAN team, McMahon tried to calm the callers down and walk them through a set of questions designed to determine the extent of the worm's control over their systems. First, he asked them what symptoms their systems were showing. In a crisis situation, when you're holding a hammer, everything looks like a nail. McMahon wanted to make sure that the problems on the system were in fact caused by the worm and not something else entirely.

If the only problem seemed to be mysterious comments flashing across the screen, McMahon concluded that the worm was probably harassing the staff on that computer from a neighbouring system which it had successfully invaded. The messages suggested that the recipients' accounts had not been hijacked by the worm. Yet.

VAX/VMS machines have a feature called Phone, which is useful for on-line communications. For example, a NASA scientist could 'ring up' one of his colleagues on a different computer and have a friendly chat on-line. The chat session is live, but it is conducted by typing on the computer screen, not 'voice'. The VMS Phone facility enabled the worm to send messages to users. It would simply call them using the phone protocol. But instead of starting a chat session, it sent them statements from what was later determined to be the aptly named Fortune Cookie file – a collection of 60 or so pre-programmed comments.

In some cases, where the worm was really bugging staff, McMahon told the manager at the other end of the phone to turn the computer's Phone feature off. A few managers complained and McMahon gave them the obvious ultimatum: choose Phone or peace. Most chose peace.

When McMahon finished his preliminary analysis, he had good news and bad news. The good news was that, contrary to what the worm was telling computer users all over NASA, it was not actually deleting their files. It was just pretending to delete their data. One big practical joke. To the creator of the worm anyway. To the NASA scientists, just a headache and heartache. And occasionally a heart attack.

The bad news was that, when the worm got control over a privileged account, it would help someone – presumably its creator – perpetrate an even more serious break-in at NASA. The worm sought out the FIELD account created by the manufacturer and, if it had been turned off, tried to reactivate the account and install the password FIELD. The worm was also programmed to change the password for the standard account named DECNET to a random string of at least twelve characters. In short, the worm tried to pry open a backdoor to the system.

The worm sent information about accounts it had successfully broken into back to a type of electronic mailbox – an account called GEMPAK on SPAN node 6.59. Presumably, the hacker who created the worm would check the worm's mailbox for information which he could use to break into the NASA account at a later date. Not surprisingly, the mailboxes had been surreptitiously 'borrowed' by the hacker, much to the surprise of the legitimate owners.

A computer hacker created a whole new set of problems. Although the worm was able to break into new accounts with greater speed and reach than a single hacker, it was more predictable. Once the SPAN and DOE teams picked the worm apart, they would know exactly what it could be expected to do. However, a hacker was utterly unpredictable.

McMahon realised that killing off the worm was not going to solve the problem. All the system managers across the NASA and DOE networks would have to change all the passwords of the accounts used by the worm. They would also have to check every system the worm had invaded to see if it had built a backdoor for the hacker. The system admin had to shut and lock all the backdoors, no small feat.

What really scared the SPAN team about the worm, however, was that it was rampaging through NASA simply by using the simplest of attack strategies: username equals password. It was getting complete control over NASA computers simply by trying a password which was identical to the name of the computer user's account.

The SPAN team didn't want to believe it, but the evidence was overwhelming.

Todd Butler answered a call from one NASA site. It was a gloomy call. He hung up.

'That node just got hit,' he told the team.

'How bad?' McMahon asked.

'A privileged account.'

'Oh boy.' McMahon jumped onto one of the terminals and did a SET HOST, logging into the remote NASA site's machine. Bang. Up it came. 'Your system has officially been WANKED.'

McMahon turned to Butler. 'What account did it get into?'

'They think it was SYSTEM.'

The tension quietly rolled into black humour. The team couldn't help it. The head-slapping stupidity of the situation could only be viewed as black comedy.

The NASA site had a password of SYSTEM for their fully privileged SYSTEM account. It was so unforgivable. NASA, potentially the greatest single collection of technical minds on Earth, had such lax computer security that a computer-literate teenager could have cracked it wide open. The tall poppy was being cut down to size by a computer program resembling a bowl of spaghetti.

The first thing any computer system manager learns in Computer Security 101 is never to use the same password as the username. It was bad enough that naive users might fall into this trap . . . but a computer system manager with a fully privileged account.

Was the hacker behind the worm malevolent? Probably not. If its creator had wanted to, he could have programmed the WANK worm to obliterate NASA's files. It could have razed everything in sight.

In fact, the worm was less infectious than its author appeared to desire. The WANK worm had been instructed to perform several tasks which it didn't execute. Important parts of the worm simply didn't work. McMahon believed this failure to be accidental. For example, his analysis showed the worm was programmed to break into accounts by trying no password, if the account holder had left the password blank. When he disassembled the worm, however, he found that part of the program didn't work properly.

Nonetheless, the fragmented and partly dysfunctional WANK worm was causing a major crisis inside several US government agencies. The thing which really worried John was thinking about what a seasoned DCL programmer with years of VMS experience could do with such a worm. Someone like that could do a lot of malicious damage. And what if the WANK worm was just a dry run for something more serious down the track? It was scary to contemplate.

Even though the WANK worm did not seem to be intentionally evil, the SPAN team faced some tough times. McMahon's analysis turned up yet more alarming aspects to the worm. If it managed to break into the SYSTEM account, a privileged account, it would block all electronic mail deliveries to the system administrator. The SPAN office would not be able to send electronic warnings or advice on how to deal with the worm to systems which had already been seized. This problem was exacerbated by the lack of good information available to the project office on which systems were connected to SPAN. The only way to help people fighting this bushfire was to telephone them, but in many instances the main SPAN office didn't know who to call. The SPAN team could only hope that those administrators who had the phone number of SPAN headquarters pinned up near their computers would call when their computers came under attack.

McMahon's preliminary report outlined how much damage the worm could do in its own right. But it was impossible to measure how much damage human managers would do to their own systems because of the worm.

One frantic computer manager who phoned the SPAN office refused to believe John's analysis that the worm only pretended to erase data. He claimed that the worm had not only attacked his system, it had destroyed it. 'He just didn't believe us when we told him that the worm was mostly a set of practical jokes,' McMahon said. 'He reinitialised his system.' 'Reinitialised' as in started up his system with a clean slate. As in deleted everything on the infected computer – all the NASA staff's data gone. He actually did what the worm only pretended to do.

The sad irony was that the SPAN team never even got a copy of the data from the manager's system. They were never able to confirm that his machine had even been infected.

All afternoon McMahon moved back and forth between answering the ever-ringing SPAN phone and writing up NASA's analysis of the worm. He had posted a cryptic electronic message about the attack across the network, and Kevin Oberman had read it. The message had to be circumspect since no-one knew if the creator of the WANK worm was in fact on the network, watching, waiting. A short time later, McMahon and Oberman were on the phone together – voice – sharing their ideas and cross-checking their analysis.

The situation was discouraging. Even if McMahon and Oberman managed to develop a successful program to kill off the worm, the NASA SPAN team faced another daunting task. Getting the worm-killer out to all the NASA sites was going to be much harder than expected because there was no clear, updated map of the SPAN network. Much of NASA didn't like the idea of a centralised map of the SPAN system. McMahon recalled that, some time before the WANK worm attack, a manager had tried to map the system. His efforts had accidentally tripped so many system alarms that he was quietly taken aside and told not to do it again.

The result was that in instances where the team had phone contact details for managers, the information was often outdated.

'No, he used to work here, but he left over a year ago.'

'No, we don't have a telephone tree of people to ring if something goes wrong with our computers. There are a whole bunch of people in different places here who handle the computers.'

This is what John often heard at the other end of the phone.

The network had grown into a rambling hodgepodge for which there was little central coordination. Worse, a number of computers at different NASA centres across the US had just been tacked onto SPAN without telling the main office at Goddard. People were calling up the ad-hoc crisis centre from computer nodes on the network which didn't even have names. These people had been practising a philosophy known in computer security circles as 'security through obscurity'. They figured that if no-one knew their computer system existed – if it didn't have a name, if it wasn't on any list or map of the SPAN network – then it would be protected from hackers and other computer enemies.

McMahon handled a number of phone calls from system managers saying, 'There is something strange happening in my system here'. John's most basic question was, 'Where is "here"?' And of course if the SPAN office didn't know those computer systems existed, it was a lot harder to warn their managers about the worm. Or tell them how to protect themselves. Or give them a worm-killing program once it was developed. Or help them seal up breached accounts which the worm was feeding back to its creator.

It was such a mess. At times, McMahon sat back and considered who might have created this worm. The thing almost looked as though it had been released before it was finished. Its author or authors seemed to have a good collection of interesting ideas about how to solve problems, but they were never properly completed. The worm included a routine for modifying its attack strategy, but the thing was never fully developed. The worm's code didn't have enough error handling in it to ensure the creature's survival for long periods of time. And the worm didn't send the addresses of the accounts it had successfully breached back to the mailbox along with the password and account name. That was really weird. What use was a password and account name without knowing what computer system to use it on?

On the other hand, maybe the creator had done this deliberately. Maybe he had wanted to show the world just how many computers the worm could successfully penetrate. The worm's mail-back program would do this. However, including the address of each infected site would have made the admins' jobs easier. They could simply have used the GEMPAK collection as a hitlist of infected sites which needed to be de-wormed. The possible theories were endless.

There were some points of brilliance in the worm, some things that McMahon had never considered, which was impressive since he knew a lot about how to break into VMS computers. There was also considerable creativity, but there wasn't any consistency. After the worm incident, various computer security experts would hypothesise that the WANK worm had in fact been written by more than one person. But McMahon maintained his view that it was the work of a single hacker.

It was as if the creator of the worm started to pursue an idea and then got sidetracked or interrupted. Suddenly he just stopped writing code to implement that idea and started down another path, never again to reach the end. The thing had a schizophrenic structure. It was all over the place.

McMahon wondered if the author had done this on purpose, to make it harder to figure out exactly what the worm was capable of doing. Perhaps, he thought, the code had once been nice and linear and it all made sense. Then the author chopped it to pieces, moved the middle to the top, the top to the bottom, scrambled up the chunks and strung them all together with a bunch of 'GO TO' commands. Maybe the hacker who wrote the worm was in fact a very elegant DCL programmer who wanted the worm to be chaotic in order to protect it. Security through obscurity.

Oberman maintained a different view. He believed the programming style varied so much in different parts that it had to be the product of a number of people. He knew that when computer programmers write code they don't make lots of odd little changes in style for no particular reason.

Kevin Oberman and John McMahon bounced ideas off one another. Both had developed their own analyses. Oberman also brought Mark Kaletka, who managed internal networking at Fermilab, one of HEPNET's largest sites, into the cross-checking process. The worm had a number of serious vulnerabilities, but the problem was finding one, and quickly, which could be used to wipe it out with minimum impact on the besieged computers.

Whenever a VMS machine starts up an activity, the computer gives it a unique process name. When the worm burrowed into a computer site, one of the first things it did was check that another copy of itself was not already running on that computer. It did this by checking for its own process names. The worm's processes were all called NETW_ followed by a random, four-digit number. If the incoming worm found this process name, it assumed another copy of itself was already running on the computer, so it destroyed itself.

The answer seemed to be a decoy duck. Write a program which pretended to be the worm and install it across all of

NASA's vulnerable computers. The first anti-WANK program did just that. It quietly sat on the SPAN computers all day long, posing as a NETW_ process, faking out any real version of the WANK worm which should come along.

Oberman completed an anti-WANK program first and ran it by McMahon. It worked well, but McMahon noticed one large flaw. Oberman's program checked for the NETW_ process name, but it assumed that the worm was running under the SYSTEM group. In most cases, this was true, but it didn't have to be. If the worm was running in another group, Oberman's program would be useless. When McMahon pointed out the flaw, Oberman thought, God, how did I miss that?

McMahon worked up his own version of an anti-WANK program, based on Oberman's program, in preparation for releasing it to NASA.

At the same time, Oberman revised his anti-WANK program for DOE. By Monday night US Eastern Standard Time, Oberman was able to send out an early copy of a vaccine designed to protect computers which hadn't been infected yet, along with an electronic warning about the worm. His first electronic warning, distributed by CIAC, said in part:

//
THE COMPUTER INCIDENT ADVISORY CAPABILITY C I A C
ADVISORY NOTICE
The W.COM Worm affecting VAX VMS Systems
October 16, 1989 18:37 PSTNumber A-2
This is a mean bug to kill and could have done a lot of damage.

Since it notifies (by mail) someone of each successful penetration and leaves a trapdoor (the FIELD account), just killing the bug is not adequate. You must go in and make sure all accounts have passwords and that the passwords are not the same as the account name.
R. Kevin Oberman

Advisory Notice

A worm is attacking NASA's SPAN network via VAX/VMS systems connected to DECnet. It is unclear if the spread of the worm has been checked. It may spread to other systems such as DOE's HEPNET within a few days. VMS system managers should prepare now.

The worm targets VMS machines, and can only be propagated via DECnet. The worm exploits two features of DECnet/VMS in order to propagate itself. The first is the default DECnet account, which is a facility for users who don't have a specific login ID for a machine to have some degree of anonymous access. It uses the default DECnet account to copy itself to a machine, and then uses the 'TASK 0' feature of DECnet to invoke the remote copy. It has several other features including a brute force attack.

Once the worm has successfully penetrated your system it will infect .COM files and create new security vulnerabilities. It then seems to broadcast these vulnerabilities to the outside world. It may also damage files as well, either unintentionally or otherwise.

An analysis of the worm appears below and is provided by R. Kevin Oberman of Lawrence Livermore National Laboratory. Included with the analysis is a DCL program that will block the current version of the worm. At least two versions of this worm exist and more may be created. This program should give you enough time to close up obvious security holes. A more thorough DCL program is being written.

If your site could be affected please call CIAC for more details . . .

Report on the W.COM worm.

R. Kevin Oberman
Engineering Department
Lawrence Livermore National Laboratory
October 16, 1989

The following describes the action of the W.COM worm (currently based on the examination of the first two incarnations). The replication technique causes the code to be modified slightly which indicates the source of the attack and learned information.

All analysis was done with more haste than I care for, but I believe I have all of the basic facts correct. First a description of the program:

1. The program assures that it is working in a directory to which the owner (itself) has full access (Read, Write, Execute, and Delete).
2. The program checks to see if another copy is still running. It looks for a process with the first 5 characters of 'NETW_'. If such is found, it deletes itself (the file) and stops its process.

NOTE

A quick check for infection is to look for a process name starting with 'NETW_'. This may be done with a SHOW PROCESS command.

3. The program then changes the default DECNET account password to a random string of at least 12 characters.
4. Information on the password used to access the system is mailed to the user GEMTOP on SPAN node 6.59. Some versions may have a different address.[11]
5. The process changes its name to 'NETW_' followed by a random number.
6. It then checks to see if it has SYSNAM priv. If so, it defines the system announcement message to be the banner in the program:

W O R M S   A G A I N S T   N U C L E A R   K I L L E R S

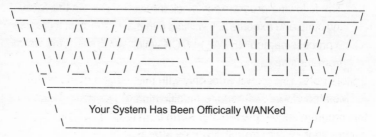

You talk of times of peace for all, and then prepare for war.

7. If it has SYSPRV, it disables mail to the SYSTEM account.
8. If it has SYSPRV, it modifies the system login command procedure to APPEAR to delete all of a user's file. (It really does nothing.)
9. The program then scans the account's logical name table for command procedures and tries to modify the FIELD account to a known password with login from any source and all privs. This is a primitive virus, but very effective IF it should get into a privileged account.
10. It proceeds to attempt to access other systems by picking node numbers at random. It then uses PHONE to get a list of active users on the remote system. It proceeds to irritate them by using PHONE to ring them.
11. The program then tries to access the RIGHTSLIST file and attempts to access some remote system using the users found and a list of 'standard' users included within the worm. It looks for passwords which are the same as that of the account or are blank. It records all such accounts.
12. It looks for an account that has access to SYSUAF.DAT.
13. If a priv. account is found, the program is copied to that account and started. If no priv. account was found, it is copied to other accounts found on the random system.
14. As soon as it finishes with a system, it picks another random system and repeats (forever).

Response:

1. The following program will block the worm. Extract the following code and execute it. It will use minimal resources. It creates a process named NETW_BLOCK which will prevent the worm from running.

Editors note: This fix will work only with this version of the worm.

Mutated worms will require modification of this code; however, this program should prevent the worm from running long enough to secure your system from the worms attacks.[12]

///

McMahon's version of an anti-WANK program was also ready to go by late Monday, but he would face delays getting it out to NASA. Working inside NASA was a balancing act, a delicate ballet demanding exquisite choreography between getting the job done, following official procedures and avoiding steps which might tread on senior bureaucrats' toes. It was several days before NASA's anti-WANK program was officially released.

DOE was not without its share of problems in launching the anti-WANK program and advisory across HEPNET. At 5.04 p.m. Pacific Coast Time on 17 October, as Oberman put the final touches on the last paragraph of his final report on the worm, the floor beneath his feet began to shake. The building was trembling. Kevin Oberman was in the middle of the 1989 San Francisco earthquake.

Measuring 7.1 on the Richter scale, the Loma Prieta earthquake ripped through the greater San Francisco area with savage speed. Inside the computer lab, Oberman braced himself for the worst. Once the shaking stopped and he ascertained the computer centre was still standing, he sat back down at his terminal. With the PA blaring warnings for all non-essential personnel to leave the building immediately, Oberman rushed off the last sentence of the report. He paused and then added a postscript saying that if the paragraph didn't make sense, it was because he was a little rattled by the large earthquake which had just hit Lawrence Livermore Labs. He pressed the key, sent out his final anti-WANK report and fled the building.

Back on the east coast, the SPAN office continued to help people calling from NASA sites which had been hit. The list of sites which had reported worm-related problems grew steadily during the week. Official estimates on the scope of the WANK worm attack were vague, but trade journals such as *Network World* and *Computerworld* quoted the space agency as suffering only a small number of successful worm invasions, perhaps 60 VMS-based computers. SPAN security manager Ron Tencati estimated only 20 successful worm penetrations in the NASA part of SPAN's network, but another internal estimate put the figure much higher: 250 to 300 machines. Each of those computers might have had 100 or more users. Figures were sketchy, but virtually everyone on the network – all 270 000 computer accounts – had been affected by the worm, either because their part of the network had been pulled off-line or because their machines had been harassed by the WANK worm as it tried again and again to login from an infected machine. By the end of the worm attack, the SPAN office had accumulated a list of affected sites which ran over two columns on several computer screens. Each of them had lodged some form of complaint about the worm.

Also by the end of the crisis, NASA and DOE computer network managers had their choice of vaccines, antidotes and blood tests for the WANK worm. McMahon had released ANTIWANK.COM, a program which killed the worm and vaccinated a system against further attacks, and WORM-INFO. TEXT, which provided a list of worm-infestation symptoms. Oberman's program, called [.SECURITY]CHECK_SYSTEM. COM, checked for all the security flaws used by the worm to sneak into a computer system. DEC also had a patch to cover the security hole in the DECNET account.

Whatever the real number of infected machines, the worm had certainly circumnavigated the globe. It had reach into European sites, such as CERN – formerly known as the European Centre for Nuclear Research – in Switzerland, through to Goddard's computers in Maryland, on to Fermilab in Chicago and propelled itself across the Pacific into the Riken Accelerator Facility in Japan.[13]

NASA officials told the media they believed the worm had been launched about 4.30 a.m. on Monday, 16 October.[14] They also believed it had originated in Europe, possibly in France.

❖

Wednesday, 18 October 1989
Kennedy Space Center, Florida

The five-member Atlantis team had some bad news on Wednesday morning. The weather forecasters gave the launch site a 40 per cent chance of launch guideline-violating rain and cloud. And then there was the earthquake in California.

The Kennedy Space Center wasn't the only place which had to be in tip-top working order for a launch to go ahead. The launch depended on many sites far away from Florida. These included Edwards Air Force Base in California, where the shuttle was due to land on Monday. They also included other sites, often military bases, which were essential for shuttle tracking and other mission support. One of these sites was a tracking station at Onizuka Air Force Base at Sunnyvale, California. The earthquake which ripped through the Bay area had damaged the tracking station and senior NASA decision-makers planned to meet on Wednesday morning to consider the Sunnyvale situation. Still, the space agency maintained a calm, cool exterior. Regardless of the technical problems, the court challenges and the protesters, the whimsical weather, the natural disasters, and the WANK worm, NASA was still in control of the situation.

'There's been some damage, but we don't know how much. The sense I get is it's fairly positive,' a NASA spokesman told UPI. 'But there are some problems.'[15] In Washington, Pentagon spokesman Rick Oborn reassured the public again, 'They are going to be able to handle shuttle tracking and support for the mission . . . They will be able to do their job'.[16]

Atlantis waited, ready to go, at launchpad 39B. The technicians had filled the shuttle up with rocket fuel and it looked as if the weather might hold. It was partly cloudy, but conditions at Kennedy passed muster.

The astronauts boarded the shuttle. Everything was in place.

But while the weather was acceptable in Florida, it was causing some problems in Africa, the site of an emergency landing location. If it wasn't one thing, it was another. NASA ordered a four-minute delay.

Finally at 12.54 p.m., Atlantis boomed from its launchpad. Rising up from the Kennedy Center, streaking a trail of twin flames from its huge solid-fuel boosters, the shuttle reached above the atmosphere and into space.

At 7.15 p.m., exactly 6 hours and 21 minutes after lift-off, Galileo began its solo journey into space. And at 8.15 p.m., Galileo's booster ignited.

Inside shuttle mission control, NASA spokesman Brian Welch announced, 'The spacecraft Galileo . . . has achieved Earth escape velocity'.[17]

Monday, 30 October 1989
NASA's Goddard Space Flight Center,
Greenbelt, Maryland

The week starting 16 October had been a long one for the SPAN team. They were keeping twelve-hour days and dealing with hysterical people all day long. Still, they managed to get copies of anti-WANK out, despite the limitations of the dated SPAN records and the paucity of good logs allowing them to retrace the worm's path. 'What we learned that week was just how much data is not collected,' McMahon observed.

By Friday, 20 October, there were no new reports of worm attacks. It looked as though the crisis had passed. Things could be tidied up by the rest of the SPAN team and McMahon returned to his own work.

A week passed. All the while, though, McMahon was on edge. He doubted that someone who had gone to all that trouble of creating the WANK worm would let his baby be exterminated so quickly. The decoy-duck strategy only worked as long as the worm kept the same process name, and as long as it was programmed not to activate itself on systems which were already infected. Change the process name, or teach the worm not to suicide, and the SPAN team would face another, larger problem. John McMahon had an instinct about the worm; it might just be back.

His instinct was right.

The following Monday, McMahon received another phone call from the SPAN project office. When he poked his head in his boss's office, Jerome Bennett looked up from his desk.

'The thing is back,' McMahon told him. There was no need to explain what 'the thing' was. 'I'm going over to the SPAN office.'

Ron Tencati and Todd Butler had a copy of the new WANK worm ready for McMahon. This version of the worm was far more virulent. It copied itself more effectively and therefore moved through the network much faster. The revised worm's penetration rate was much higher – more than four times greater than the version of WANK released in the first attack. The phone was ringing off the hook again. John took a call from one irate manager who launched into a tirade. 'I ran your anti-WANK program, followed your instructions to the letter, and look what happened!'

The worm had changed its process name. It was also designed to hunt down and kill the decoy-duck program. In fact, the SPAN network was going to turn into a rather bloody battlefield. This worm didn't just kill the decoy, it also killed any other copy of the WANK worm. Even if McMahon changed the process name used by his program, the decoy-duck strategy was not going to work any longer.

There were other disturbing improvements to the new version of the WANK worm. Preliminary information suggested it changed the password on any account it got into. This was a problem. But not nearly as big a problem as if the passwords it changed were for the only privileged accounts on the system. The new worm was capable of locking a system manager out of his or her own system.

Prevented from getting into his own account, the computer

manager might try borrowing the account of an average user, call him Edwin. Unfortunately, Edwin's account probably only had low-level privileges. Even in the hands of a skilful computer manager, the powers granted to Edwin's account were likely too limited to eradicate the worm from its newly elevated status as computer manager. The manager might spend his whole morning matching wits with the worm from the disadvantaged position of a normal user's account. At some point he would have to make the tough decision of last resort: turn the entire computer system off.

The manager would have to conduct a forced reboot of the machine. Take it down, then bring it back up on minimum configuration. Break back into it. Fix the password which the worm had changed. Logout. Reset some variables. Reboot the machine again. Close up any underlying security holes left behind by the worm. Change any passwords which matched users' names. A cold start of a large VMS machine took time. All the while, the astronomers, physicists and engineers who worked in this NASA office wouldn't be able to work on their computers.

At least the SPAN team was better prepared for the worm this time. They had braced themselves psychologically for a possible return attack. Contact information for the network had been updated. And the general DECNET internet community was aware of the worm and was lending a hand wherever possible.

Help came from a system manager in France, a country which seemed to be of special interest to the worm's author. The manager, Bernard Perrot of Institut de Physique Nucleaire in Orsay, had obtained a copy of the worm, inspected it and took special notice of the creature's poor error checking ability. This was the worm's true Achilles' heel.

The worm was trained to go after the RIGHTSLIST database, the list of all the people who have accounts on the computer. What if someone moved the database by renaming it and put a dummy database in its place? The worm would, in theory, go after the dummy, which could be designed with a hidden bomb. When the worm sniffed out the dummy, and latched onto it, the creature would explode and die. If it worked, the SPAN team would not have to depend on the worm killing itself, as they had during the first invasion. They would have the satisfaction of destroying the thing themselves.

Ron Tencati procured a copy of the French manager's worm-killing program and gave it to McMahon, who set up a sort of mini-laboratory experiment. He cut the worm into pieces and extracted the relevant bits. This allowed him to test the French worm-killing program with little risk of the worm escaping and doing damage. The French program worked wonderfully. Out it went. The second version of the worm was so much more virulent, getting it out of SPAN was going to take considerably longer than the first time around. Finally, almost two weeks after the second onslaught, the WANK worm had been eradicated from SPAN.

By McMahon's estimate, the WANK worm had incurred up to half a million dollars in costs. Most of these were through people wasting time and resources chasing the worm instead of doing their normal jobs. The worm was, in his view, a crime of theft. 'People's time and resources had been wasted,' he said. 'The theft was not the result of the accident. This was someone who deliberately went out to make a mess.

'In general, I support prosecuting people who think breaking into machines is fun. People like that don't seem to understand what kind of side effects that kind of fooling around has. They think that breaking into a machine and not touching anything doesn't do anything. That is not true. You end up wasting people's time. People are dragged into the office at strange hours. Reports have to be written. A lot of yelling and screaming occurs. You have to deal with law enforcement. These are all side effects of someone going for a joy ride in someone else's system, even if they don't do any damage. Someone has to pay the price.'

McMahon never found out who created the WANK worm. Nor did he ever discover what he intended to prove by releasing it. The creator's motives were never clear and, if it had been politically inspired, no-one took credit.

The WANK worm left a number of unanswered questions in its wake, a number of loose ends which still puzzle John McMahon. Was the hacker behind the worm really protesting against NASA's launch of the plutonium-powered Galileo space probe? Did the use of the word 'WANK' – a most un-American word – mean the hacker wasn't American? Why had the creator recreated the worm and released it a second time? Why had no-one, no political or other group, claimed responsibility for the WANK worm?

One of the many details which remained an enigma was contained in the version of the worm used in the second attack. The worm's creator had replaced the original process name, NETW_, with a new one, presumably to thwart the anti-WANK program. McMahon figured the original process name stood for 'netwank' – a reasonable guess at the hacker's intended meaning. The new process name, however, left everyone on the SPAN team scratching their heads: it didn't seem to stand for anything. The letters formed an unlikely set of initials for someone's name. No-one recognised it as an acronym for a saying or an organisation. And it certainly wasn't a proper word in the English language. It was a complete mystery why the creator of the WANK worm, the hacker who launched an invasion into hundreds of NASA and DOE computers, should choose this weird word.

The word was 'OILZ'.

2 | THE CORNER PUB

It is not surprising the SPAN security team would miss the mark. It is not surprising, for example, that these officials should to this day be pronouncing the 'Oilz' version of the WANK worm as 'oil zee'. It is also not surprising that they hypothesised the worm's creator chose the word 'Oilz' because the modifications made to the last version made it slippery, perhaps even oily.

Likely as not, only an Australian would see the worm's link to the lyrics of Midnight Oil.

This was the world's first worm with a political message, and the second major worm in the history of the worldwide computer networks. It was also the trigger for the creation of FIRST, the Forum of Incident Response and Security Teams.[1] FIRST was an international security alliance allowing governments, universities and commercial organisations to share information about computer network security incidents. Yet, NASA and the US Department of Energy were half a world away from finding the creator of the WANK worm. Even as investigators sniffed around electronic trails leading to France, it appears the perpetrator was hiding behind his computer and modem in Australia.

Geographically, Australia is a long way from anywhere. To Americans, it conjures up images of fuzzy marsupials, not computer hackers. American computer security officials, like those at NASA and the US Department of Energy, had other barriers as well. They function in a world of concretes, of appointments made and kept, of real names, business cards and official titles. The computer underground, by contrast, is a veiled world populated by characters slipping in and out of the half-darkness. It is not a place where people use their real names. It is not a place where people give out real personal details.

It is, in fact, not so much a place as a space. It is ephemeral, intangible – a foggy labyrinth of unmapped, winding streets through which one occasionally ascertains the contours of a fellow traveller.

When Ron Tencati, the manager in charge of NASA SPAN security, realised that NASA's computers were being attacked by an intruder, he rang the FBI. The US Federal Bureau of Investigation's Computer Crime Unit fired off a stream of questions. How many computers had been attacked? Where were they? Who was behind the attack? The FBI told Tencati, 'keep us informed of the situation'. Like the CIAC team in the Department of Energy, it appears the FBI didn't have much knowledge of VMS, the primary computer operating system used in SPAN.

But the FBI knew enough to realise the worm attack was potentially very serious. The winding electronic trail pointed vaguely to a foreign computer system and, before long, the US Secret Service was involved. Then the French secret service, the Direction de la Surveillance du Territoire, or DST, jumped into the fray.

DST and the FBI began working together on the case. A casual observer with the benefit of hindsight might see different motivations driving the two government agencies. The

FBI wanted to catch the perpetrator. The DST wanted to make it clear that the infamous WANK worm attack on the world's most prestigious space agency did not originate in France.

In the best tradition of cloak-and-dagger government agencies, the FBI and DST people established two communication channels – an official channel and an unofficial one. The official channel involved embassies, attachés, formal communiques and interminable delays in getting answers to the simplest questions. The unofficial channel involved a few phone calls and some fast answers.

Ron Tencati had a colleague named Chris on the SPAN network in France, which was the largest user of SPAN in Europe. Chris was involved in more than just science computer networks. He had certain contacts in the French government and seemed to be involved in their computer networks. So, when the FBI needed technical information for its investigation – the kind of information likely to be sanitised by some embassy bureaucrat – one of its agents rang up Ron Tencati. 'Ron, ask your friend this,' the FBI would say. And Ron would.

'Chris, the FBI wants to know this,' Tencati would tell his colleague on SPAN France. Then Chris would get the necessary information. He would call Tencati back, saying, 'Ron, here is the answer. Now, the DST wants to know that'. And off Ron would go in search of information requested by the DST.

The investigation proceeded in this way, with each helping the other through backdoor channels. But the Americans' investigation was headed toward the inescapable conclusion that the attack on NASA had originated from a French computer. The worm may have simply travelled through the French computer from yet another system, but the French machine appeared to be the sole point of infection for NASA.

The French did not like this outcome. Not one bit. There was no way that the worm had come from France. *Ce n'est pas vrai.*

Word came back from the French that they were sure the worm had come from the US. Why else would it have been programmed to mail details of all computer accounts it penetrated around the world back to a US machine, the computer known as GEMPAK? Because the author of the worm was an American, of course! Therefore it is not our problem, the French told the Americans. It is your problem.

Most computer security experts know it is standard practice among hackers to create the most tangled trail possible between the hacker and the hacked. It makes it very difficult for people like the FBI to trace who did it. So it would be difficult to draw definite conclusions about the nationality of the hacker from the location of a hacker's information drop-off point – a location the hacker no doubt figured would be investigated by the authorities almost immediately after the worm's release.

Tencati had established the French connection from some computer logs showing NASA under attack very early on Monday, 16 October. The logs were important because they were relatively clear. As the worm had procreated during that day, it had forced computers all over the network to attack each other in ever greater numbers. By 11 a.m. it was almost impossible to tell where any one attack began and the other ended.

Some time after the first attack, DST sent word that certain agents were going to be in Washington DC regarding other matters. They wanted a meeting with the FBI. A representative from the NASA Inspector General's Office would attend the meeting, as would someone from NASA SPAN security.

Tencati was sure he could show the WANK worm attack on NASA originated in France. But he also knew he had to document everything, to have exact answers to every question and counter-argument put forward by the French secret service agents at the FBI meeting. When he developed a timeline of attacks, he found that the GEMPAK machine showed X.25 network connection, via another system, from a French computer around the same time as the WANK worm attack. He followed the scent and contacted the manager of that system. Would he help Tencati? *Mais oui.* The machine is at your disposal, Monsieur Tencati.

Tencati had never used an X.25 network before; it had a unique set of commands unlike any other type of computer communications network. He wanted to retrace the steps of the worm, but he needed help. So he called his friend Bob Lyons at DEC to walk him through the process.

What Tencati found startled him. There were traces of the worm on the machine all right, the familiar pattern of login failures as the worm attempted to break into different accounts. But these remnants of the WANK worm were not dated 16 October or any time immediately around then. The logs showed worm-related activity up to two weeks before the attack on NASA. This computer was not just a pass-through machine the worm had used to launch its first attack on NASA. This was the development machine.

Ground zero.

Tencati went into the meeting with DST at the FBI offices prepared. He knew the accusations the French were going to put forward. When he presented the results of his sleuthwork, the French secret service couldn't refute it, but they dropped their own bombshell. Yes they told him, you might be able to point to a French system as ground zero for the attack, but our investigations reveal incoming X.25 connections from else-where which coincided with the timing of the development of the WANK worm.

The connections came from Australia.

The French had satisfied themselves that it wasn't a French hacker who had created the WANK worm. *Ce n'est pas notre problème.* At least, it's not our problem any more.

It is here that the trail begins to go cold. Law enforcement and computer security people in the US and Australia had ideas about just who had created the WANK worm. Fingers were pointed, accusations were made, but none stuck. At the end of the day, there was coincidence and innuendo, but not enough evidence to launch a case. Like many Australian hackers, the creator of the WANK worm had emerged from the shadows of the computer underground, stood momentarily in hazy silhouette, and then disappeared again.

The Australian computer underground in the late 1980s was an environment which spawned and shaped the author of the WANK worm. Affordable home computers, such as the Apple IIe and the Commodore 64, made their way into ordinary suburban families. While these computers were not widespread, they were at least in a price range which made them attainable by dedicated computer enthusiasts.

In 1988, the year before the WANK worm attack on NASA, Australia was on an upswing. The country was celebrating its bicentennial. The economy was booming. Trade barriers and old regulatory structures were coming down. Crocodile Dundee had already burst on the world movie scene and was making Australians the flavour of the month in cities like LA and New York. The mood was optimistic. People had a sense they were going places. Australia, a peaceful country of seventeen or so million people, poised on the edge of Asia but with the order of a Western European democracy, was on its way up. Perhaps for the first time, Australians had lost their cultural cringe, a unique type of insecurity alien to can-do cultures such as that found in the US. Exploration and experimentation require confidence and, in 1988, confidence was something Australia had finally attained.

Yet this new-found confidence and optimism did not subdue Australia's tradition of cynicism toward large institutions. The two coexisted, suspended in a strange paradox. Australian humour, deeply rooted in a scepticism of all things serious and sacred, continued to poke fun at upright institutions with a depth of irreverence surprising to many foreigners. This cynicism of large, respected institutions coursed through the newly formed Australian computer underground without dampening its excitement or optimism for the brave new world of computers in the least.

In 1988, the Australian computer underground thrived like a vibrant Asian street bazaar. In that year it was still a realm of place not space. Customers visited their regular stalls, haggled over goods with vendors, bumped into friends and waved across crowded paths to acquaintances. The market was as much a place to socialise as it was to shop. People ducked into tiny coffee houses or corner bars for intimate chats. The latest imported goods, laid out on tables like reams of bright Chinese silks, served as conversation starters. And, like every street market, many of the best items were tucked away, hidden in anticipation of the appearance of that one customer or friend most favoured by the trader. The currency of the underground was not money; it was information. People didn't share and exchange information to accumulate monetary wealth; they did it to win respect – and to buy a thrill.

The members of the Australian computer underground met on bulletin board systems, known as BBSes. Simple things by today's standards, BBSes were often composed of a souped-up Apple II computer, a single modem and a lone telephone line. But they drew people from all walks of life. Teenagers from working-class neighbourhoods and those from the exclusive private schools. University students. People in their twenties groping their way through first jobs. Even some professional people in their thirties and forties who spent weekends poring over computer manuals and building primitive computers in spare rooms. Most regular BBS users were male. Sometimes a user's sister would find her way into the BBS world, often in search of a boyfriend. Mission accomplished, she might disappear from the scene for weeks, perhaps months, presumably until she required another visit.

The BBS users had a few things in common. They were generally of above average intelligence – usually with a strong technical slant – and they were obsessed with their chosen hobby. They had to be. It often took 45 minutes of attack dialling a busy BBS's lone phone line just to visit the computer system for perhaps half an hour. Most serious BBS hobbyists went through this routine several times each day.

As the name suggests, a BBS had what amounted to an electronic version of a normal bulletin board. The owner of the BBS would have divided the board into different areas, as a school teacher crisscrosses coloured ribbon across the surface of a corkboard to divide it into sections. A single BBS might have 30 or more electronic discussion groups.

As a user to the board, you might visit the politics section, tacking up a 'note' on your views of ALP or Liberal policies for anyone passing by to read. Alternatively, you might fancy yourself a bit of a poet and work up the courage to post an original piece of work in the Poet's Corner. The corner was often filled with dark, misanthropic works inspired by the miseries of adolescence. Perhaps you preferred to discuss music. On many BBSes you could find postings on virtually any type of music. The most popular groups included bands like Pink Floyd, Tangerine Dream and Midnight Oil. Midnight Oil's anti-establishment message struck a particular chord within the new BBS community.

Nineteen eighty-eight was the golden age of the BBS culture across Australia. It was an age of innocence and community, an open-air bazaar full of vitality and the sharing of ideas. For the most part, people trusted their peers within the community and the BBS operators, who were often revered as demigods. It was a happy place. And, in general, it was a safe place, which is perhaps one reason why its visitors felt secure in their explorations of new ideas. It was a place in which the creator of the WANK worm could sculpt and hone his creative computer skills.

The capital of this spirited new Australian electronic civilisation was Melbourne. It is difficult to say why this southern city became the cultural centre of the BBS world, and its darker side, the Australian computer underground. Maybe the city's history as Australia's intellectual centre created a breeding ground for the many young people who built their systems with little more than curiosity and salvaged computer bits discarded by others. Maybe Melbourne's personality as a city of suburban homebodies and backyard tinkerers produced a culture conducive to BBSes. Or maybe it was just Melbourne's dreary beaches and often miserable weather. As one Melbourne hacker explained it, 'What else is there to do here all winter but hibernate inside with your computer and modem?'

In 1988, Melbourne had some 60 to 100 operating BBSes. The numbers are vague because it is difficult to count a collection of moving objects. The amateur nature of the systems, often a jumbled tangle of wires and second-hand electronics parts soldered together in someone's garage, meant that the life of any one system was frequently as short as a teenager's attention span. BBSes popped up, ran for two weeks, and then vanished again.

Some of them operated only during certain hours, say between 10 p.m. and 8 a.m. When the owner went to bed, he or she would plug the home phone line into the BBS and leave it there until morning. Others ran 24 hours a day, but the busiest times were always at night.

Of course it wasn't just intellectual stimulation some users were after. Visitors often sought identity as much as ideas. On an electronic bulletin board, you could create a personality, mould it into shape and make it your own. Age and appearance did not matter. Technical aptitude did. Any spotty, gawky teenage boy could instantly transform himself into a suave, graceful BBS character. The transformation began with the choice of name. In real life, you might be stuck with the name Elliot Dingle – an appellation chosen by your mother to honour a long-dead great uncle. But on a BBS, well, you could be Blade Runner, Ned Kelly or Mad Max. Small wonder that, given the choice, many teenage boys chose to spend their time in the world of the BBS.

Generally, once a user chose a handle, as the on-line names are known, he stuck with it. All his electronic mail came to an account with that name on it. Postings to bulletin boards were signed with it. Others dwelling in the system world knew him by that name and no other. A handle evolved into a name laden with innate meaning, though the personality reflected in it might well have been an alter ego. And so it was that characters like The Wizard, Conan and Iceman came to pass their time on BBSes like the Crystal Palace, Megaworks, The Real Connection and Electric Dreams.

What such visitors valued about the BBS varied greatly. Some wanted to participate in its social life. They wanted to meet people like themselves – bright but geeky or misanthropic people who shared an interest in the finer technical points of computers. Many lived as outcasts in real life, never quite making it into the 'normal' groups of friends at school or uni. Though some had started their first jobs, they hadn't managed to shake the daggy awkwardness which pursued them throughout their teen years. On the surface, they were just not the sort of people one asked out to the pub for a cold one after the footy.

But that was all right. In general, they weren't much interested in footy anyway.

Each BBS had its own style. Some were completely legitimate, with their wares – all legal goods – laid out in the open. Others, like The Real Connection, had once housed Australia's earliest hackers but had gone straight. They closed up the hacking parts of the board before the first Commonwealth government hacking laws were enacted in June 1989. Perhaps ten or twelve of Melbourne's BBSes at the time had the secret, smoky flavour of the computer underground. A handful of these were invitation-only boards, places like Greyhawk and The Realm. You couldn't simply ring up the board, create a new account and login. You had to be invited by the board's owner. Members of the general modeming public need not apply.

The two most important hubs in the Australian underground between 1987 and 1989 were named Pacific Island and Zen. A 23-year-old who called himself Craig Bowen ran both systems from his bedroom.

Also known as Thunderbird1, Bowen started up Pacific Island in 1987 because he wanted a hub for hackers. The fledgling hacking community was dispersed after AHUBBS, possibly Melbourne's earliest hacking board, faded away. Bowen decided to create a home for it, a sort of dark, womb-like cafe bar amid the bustle of the BBS bazaar where Melbourne's hackers could gather and share information.

His bedroom was a simple, boyish place. Built-in cupboards, a bed, a wallpaper design of vintage cars running across one side of the room. A window overlooking the neighbours' leafy suburban yard. A collection of PC magazines with titles like Nibble and Byte. A few volumes on computer programming. VAX/VMS manuals. Not many books, but a handful of science fiction works by Arthur C. Clarke. *The Hitchhiker's Guide to the Galaxy*. A Chinese-language dictionary used during his high school Mandarin classes, and after, as he continued to study the language on his own while he held down his first job.

The Apple IIe, modem and telephone line rested on the drop-down drawing table and fold-up card table at the foot of his bed. Bowen put his TV next to the computer so he could sit in bed, watch TV and use Pacific Island all at the same time. Later, when he started Zen, it sat next to Pacific Island. It was the perfect set-up.

Pacific Island was hardly fancy by today's standards of Unix Internet machines, but in 1987 it was an impressive computer. PI, pronounced 'pie' by the local users, had a 20 megabyte hard drive – gargantuan for a personal computer at the time. Bowen spent about $5000 setting up PI alone. He loved both systems and spent many hours each week nurturing them.

There was no charge for computer accounts on PI or ZEN, like most BBSes. This gentle-faced youth, a half-boy, half-man who would eventually play host on his humble BBS to many of Australia's cleverest computer and telephone hackers, could afford to pay for his computers for two reasons: he lived at home with his mum and dad, and he had a full-time job at Telecom – then the only domestic telephone carrier in Australia.

PI had about 800 computer users, up to 200 of whom were 'core' users accessing the system regularly. PI had its own dedicated phone line, separate from the house phone so Bowen's parents wouldn't get upset the line was always tied up. Later, he put in four additional phone lines for Zen, which had about 2000 users. Using his Telecom training, he installed a number of non-standard, but legal, features to his house. Junction boxes, master switches. Bowen's house was a telecommunications hot-rod.

Bowen had decided early on that if he wanted to keep his job, he had better not do anything illegal when it came to Telecom. However, the Australian national telecommunications carrier was a handy source of technical information. For example, he had an account on a Telecom computer system – for work – from which he could learn about Telecom's exchanges. But he never used that account for hacking. Most respectable hackers followed a similar philosophy. Some had legitimate university computer accounts for their courses, but they kept those accounts clean. A basic rule of the underground, in the words of one hacker, was 'Don't foul your own nest'.

PI contained a public section and a private one. The public area was like an old-time pub. Anyone could wander in, plop down at the bar and start up a conversation with a group of locals. Just ring up the system with your modem and type in your details – real name, your chosen handle, phone number and other basic information.

Many BBS users gave false information in order to hide their true identities, and many operators didn't really care. Bowen, however, did. Running a hacker's board carried some risk, even before the federal computer crime laws came into force. Pirated software was illegal. Storing data copied from hacking adventures in foreign computers might also be considered illegal. In an effort to exclude police and media spies, Bowen tried to verify the personal details of every user on PI by ringing them at home or work. Often he was successful. Sometimes he wasn't.

The public section of PI housed discussion groups on the major PC brands – IBM, Commodore, Amiga, Apple and Atari – next to the popular Lonely Hearts group. Lonely Hearts had about twenty regulars, most of whom agonised under the weight of pubescent hormonal changes. A boy pining for the affections of the girl who dumped him or, worse, didn't even know he existed. Teenagers who contemplated suicide. The messages were completely anonymous, readers didn't even know the authors' handles, and that anonymous setting allowed heart-felt messages and genuine responses.

Zen was PI's sophisticated younger sister. Within two years of PI making its debut, Bowen opened up Zen, one of the first Australian BBSes with more than one telephone line. The main reason he set up Zen was to stop his computer users from bothering him all the time. When someone logged into PI, one of the first things he or she did was request an on-line chat with the system operator. PI's Apple IIe was such a basic machine by today's standards, Bowen couldn't multi-task on it. He could not do anything with the machine, such as check his own mail, while a visitor was logged into PI.

Zen was a watershed in the Australian BBS community. Zen multi-tasked. Up to four people could ring up and login to the machine at any one time, and Bowen could do his own thing while his users were on-line. Better still, his users could talk request each other instead of hassling him all the time. Having users on a multi-tasking machine with multiple phone lines was like having a gaggle of children. For the most part, they amused each other.

Mainstream and respectful of authority on the surface, Bowen possessed the same streak of anti-establishment views harboured by many in the underground. His choice of name for Zen underlined this. Zen came from the futuristic British TV science fiction series 'Blake's 7', in which a bunch of underfunded rebels attempted to overthrow an evil totalitarian government. Zen was the computer on the rebels' ship. The rebels banded together after meeting on a prison ship; they were all being transported to a penal settlement on another planet. It was a story people in the Australian underground could relate to. One of the lead characters, a sort of heroic anti-hero, had been sentenced to prison for computer hacking. His big mistake, he told fellow rebels, was that he had relied on other people. He trusted them. He should have worked alone.

Craig Bowen had no idea of how true that sentiment would ring in a matter of months.

Bowen's place was a hub of current and future lights in the computer underground. The Wizard. The Force. Powerspike. Phoenix. Electron. Nom. Prime Suspect. Mendax. Train Trax. Some, such as Prime Suspect, merely passed through, occasionally stopping in to check out the action and greet friends. Others, such as Nom, were part of the close-knit PI family. Nom helped Bowen set up PI. Like many early members of the underground, they met through AUSOM, an Apple users' society in Melbourne. Bowen wanted to run ASCII Express, a program which allowed people to transfer files between their own computers and PI. But, as usual, he and everyone he knew only had a pirated copy of the program. No manuals. So Nom and Bowen spent one weekend picking apart the program by themselves. They were each at home, on their own machines, with copies. They sat on the phone for hours working through how the program worked. They wrote their own manual for other people in the underground suffering under the same lack of documentation. Then they got it up and running on PI.

Making your way into the various groups in a BBS such as PI or Zen had benefits besides hacking information. If you wanted to drop your mantle of anonymity, you could join a pre-packaged, close-knit circle of friends. For example, one clique of PI people were fanatical followers of the film *The Blues Brothers*. Every Friday night, this group dressed up in Blues Brothers costumes of a dark suit, white shirt, narrow tie, Rayban sunglasses and, of course, the snap-brimmed hat. One couple brought their child, dressed as a mini-Blues Brother. The group of Friday night regulars made their way at 11.30 to

Northcote's Valhalla Theatre (now the Westgarth). Its grand but slightly tatty vintage atmosphere lent itself to this alternative culture flourishing in late-night revelries. Leaping up on stage mid-film, the PI groupies sent up the actors in key scenes. It was a fun and, as importantly, a cheap evening. The Valhalla staff admitted regulars who were dressed in appropriate costume for free. The only thing the groupies had to pay for was drinks at the intermission.

Occasionally, Bowen arranged gatherings of other young PI and Zen users. Usually, the group met in downtown Melbourne, sometimes at the City Square. The group was mostly boys, but sometimes a few girls would show up. Bowen's sister, who used the handle Syn, hung around a bit. She went out with a few hackers from the BBS scene. And she wasn't the only one. It was a tight group which interchanged boyfriends and girlfriends with considerable regularity. The group hung out in the City Square after watching a movie, usually a horror film. *Nightmare 2. House 3.* Titles tended to be a noun followed by a numeral. Once, for a bit of lively variation, they went bowling and drove the other people at the alley nuts. After the early entertainment, it was down to McDonald's for a cheap burger. They joked and laughed and threw gherkins against the restaurant's wall. This was followed by more hanging around on the stone steps of the City Square before catching the last bus or train home.

The social sections of PI and Zen were more successful than the technical ones, but the private hacking section was even more successful than the others. The hacking section was hidden; would-be members of the Melbourne underground knew there was something going on, but they couldn't find out what it was.

Getting an invite to the private area required hacking skill or information, and usually a recommendation to Bowen from someone who was already inside. Within the Inner Sanctum, as the private hacking area was called, people could comfortably share information such as opinions of new computer products, techniques for hacking, details of companies which had set up new sites to hack and the latest rumours on what the law enforcement agencies were up to.

The Inner Sanctum was not, however, the only private room. Two hacking groups, Elite and H.A.C.K., guarded entry to their yet more exclusive back rooms. Even if you managed to get entry to the Inner Sanctum, you might not even know that H.A.C.K. or Elite existed. You might know there was a place even more selective than your area, but exactly how many layers of the onion stood between you and the most exclusive section was anyone's guess. Almost every hacker interviewed for this book described a vague sense of being somehow outside the innermost circle. They knew it was there, but weren't sure just what it was.

Bowen fielded occasional phone calls on his voice line from wanna-be hackers trying to pry open the door to the Inner Sanctum. 'I want access to your pirate system,' the voice would whine.

'What pirate system? Who told you my system was a pirate system?'

Bowen sussed out how much the caller knew, and who had told him. Then he denied everything.

To avoid these requests, Bowen had tried to hide his address, real name and phone number from most of the people who used his BBSes. But he wasn't completely successful. He had been surprised by the sudden appearance one day of Masked Avenger on his doorstep. How Masked Avenger actually found his address was a mystery. The two had chatted in a friendly fashion on-line, but Bowen didn't give out his details. Nothing could have prepared him for the little kid in the big crash helmet standing by his bike in front of Bowen's house. 'Hi!' he squeaked. 'I'm the Masked Avenger!'

Masked Avenger – a boy perhaps fifteen years old – was quite resourceful to have found out Bowen's details. Bowen invited him in and showed him the system. They became friends. But after that incident, Bowen decided to tighten security around his personal details even more. He began, in his own words, 'moving toward full anonymity'. He invented the name Craig Bowen, and everyone in the underground came to know him by that name or his handle, Thunderbird1. He even opened a false bank account in the name of Bowen for the periodic voluntary donations users sent into PI. It was never a lot of money, mostly $5 or $10, because students don't tend to have much money. He ploughed it all back into PI.

People had lots of reasons for wanting to get into the Inner Sanctum. Some wanted free copies of the latest software, usually pirated games from the US. Others wanted to share information and ideas about ways to break into computers, often those owned by local universities. Still others wanted to learn about how to manipulate the telephone system.

The private areas functioned like a royal court, populated by aristocrats and courtiers with varying seniority, loyalties and rivalries. The areas involved an intricate social order and respect was the name of the game. If you wanted admission, you had to walk a delicate line between showing your superiors that you possessed enough valuable hacking information to be elite and not showing them so much they would brand you a blabbermouth. A perfect bargaining chip was an old password for Melbourne University's dial-out.

The university's dial-out was a valuable thing. A hacker could ring up the university's computer, login as 'modem' and the machine would drop him into a modem which let him dial out again. He could then dial anywhere in the world, and the university would foot the phone bill. In the late 1980s, before the days of cheap, accessible Internet connections, the university dial-out meant a hacker could access anything from an underground BBS in Germany to a US military system in Panama. The password put the world at his fingertips.

A hacker aspiring to move into PI's Inner Sanctum wouldn't give out the current dial-out password in the public discussion areas. Most likely, if he was low in the pecking order, he wouldn't have such precious information. Even if he had managed to stumble across the current password somehow, it was risky giving it out publicly. Every wanna-be and his dog would start messing around with the university's modem account. The system administrator would wise up and change the password and the hacker would quickly lose his own access to the university account. Worse, he would lose access for other hackers – the kind of hackers who ran H.A.C.K., Elite and the Inner Sanctum. They would be really cross. Hackers hate it when passwords on accounts they consider their own are changed without warning. Even if the password wasn't changed, the aspiring hacker would look like a guy who couldn't keep a good secret.

Posting an old password, however, was quite a different matter. The information was next to useless, so the hacker wouldn't be giving much away. But just showing he had access to that sort of information suggested he was somehow in the know. Other hackers might think he had had the password when it was still valid. More importantly, by showing off a known, expired password, the hacker hinted that he might just have the current password. Voila! Instant respect.

Positioning oneself to win an invite into the Inner Sanctum was a game of strategy; titillate but never go all the way. After a while, someone on the inside would probably notice you and put in a word with Bowen. Then you would get an invitation.

If you were seriously ambitious and wanted to get past the first inner layer, you then had to start performing for real. You couldn't hide behind the excuse that the public area might be monitored by the authorities or was full of idiots who might abuse valuable hacking information.

The hackers in the most elite area would judge you on how much information you provided about breaking into computer or phone systems. They also looked at the accuracy of the information. It was easy getting out-of-date login names and passwords for a student account on Monash University's computer system. Posting a valid account for the New Zealand forestry department's VMS system intrigued the people who counted considerably more.

The Great Rite of Passage from boy to man in the computer underground was Minerva. OTC, Australia's then government-owned Overseas Telecommunications Commission,[2] ran Minerva, a system of three Prime mainframes in Sydney. For hackers such as Mendax, breaking into Minerva was the test.

Back in early 1988, Mendax was just beginning to explore the world of hacking. He had managed to break through the barrier from public to private section of PI, but it wasn't enough. To be recognised as up-and-coming talent by the aristocracy of hackers such as The Force and The Wizard, a hacker had to spend time inside the Minerva system. Mendax set to work on breaking into it.

Minerva was special for a number of reasons. Although it was in Sydney, the phone number to its entry computer, called an X.25 pad, was a free call. At the time Mendax lived in Emerald, a country town on the outskirts of Melbourne. A call to most Melbourne numbers incurred a long-distance charge, thus ruling out options such as the Melbourne University dial-out for breaking into international computer systems.

Emerald was hardly Emerald City. For a clever sixteen-year-old boy, the place was dead boring. Mendax lived there with his mother; Emerald was merely a stopping point, one of dozens, as his mother shuttled her child around the continent trying to escape from a psychopathic former de facto. The house was an emergency refuge for families on the run. It was safe and so, for a time, Mendax and his exhausted family stopped to rest before tearing off again in search of a new place to hide.

Sometimes Mendax went to school. Often he didn't. The school system didn't hold much interest for him. It didn't feed his mind the way Minerva would. The Sydney computer system was a far more interesting place to muck around in than the rural high school.

Minerva was a Prime computer, and Primes were in. Force, one of the more respected hackers in 1987–88 in the Australian computer underground, specialised in Primos, the special operating system used on Prime computers. He wrote his own programs – potent hacking tools which provided current user-names and passwords – and made the systems fashionable in the computer underground.

Prime computers were big and expensive and no hacker could afford one, so being able to access the speed and computational grunt of a system like Minerva was valuable for running a hacker's own programs. For example, a network scanner, a program which gathered the addresses of computers on the X.25 network which would be targets for future hacking adventures, ate up computing resources. But a huge machine like Minerva could handle that sort of program with ease. Minerva also allowed users to connect to other computer systems on the X.25 network around the world. Better still, Minerva had a BASIC interpreter on it. This allowed people to write programs in the BASIC programming language – by far the most popular language at the time – and make them run on Minerva. You didn't have to be a Primos fanatic, like Force, to write and execute a program on the OTC computer. Minerva suited Mendax very well.

The OTC system had other benefits. Most major Australian corporations had accounts on the system. Breaking into an account requires a username and password; find the username and you have solved half the equation. Minerva account names were easy picking. Each one was composed of three letters followed by three numbers, a system which could have been difficult to crack except for the choice of those letters and numbers. The first three letters were almost always obvious acronyms for the company. For example, the ANZ Bank had accounts named ANZ001, ANZ002 and ANZ003. The numbers followed the same pattern for most companies. BHP001. CRA001. NAB001. Even OTC007. Anyone with the IQ of a desk lamp could guess at least a few account names on Minerva. Passwords were a bit tougher to come by, but Mendax had some ideas for that. He was going to have a crack at social engineering. Social engineering means smooth-talking someone in a position of power into doing something for you. It always involved a ruse of some sort.

Mendax decided he would social engineer a password out of one of Minerva's users. He had downloaded a partial list of Minerva users another PI hacker had generously posted for those talented enough to make use of it. This list was maybe two years old, and incomplete, but it contained 30-odd pages of Minerva account usernames, company names, addresses, contact names and telephone and fax numbers. Some of them would probably still be valid.

Mendax had a deep voice for his age; it would have been impossible to even contemplate social engineering without it. Cracking adolescent male voices were the kiss of death for would-be social engineers. But even though he had the voice, he didn't have the office or the Sydney phone number if the intended victim wanted a number to call back on. He found a way to solve the Sydney phone number by poking around until he dug up a number with Sydney's 02 area code which was permanently engaged. One down, one to go.

Next problem: generate some realistic office background noise. He could hardly call a company posing as an OTC official to cajole a password when the only background noise was birds tweeting in the fresh country air.

No, he needed the same background buzz as a crowded office in downtown Sydney. Mendex had a tape recorder, so he could pre-record the sound of an office and play it as background when he called companies on the Minerva list. The only hurdle was finding the appropriate office noise. Not even the local post office would offer a believable noise level. With none easily accessible, he decided to make his own audible office clutter. It wouldn't be easy. With a single track on his recording device, he couldn't dub in sounds on top of each other: he had to make all the noises simultaneously.

First, he turned on the TV news, down very low, so it just hummed in the background. Then he set up a long document to print on his Commodore MPS 801 printer. He removed the cover from the noisy dot matrix machine, to create just the right volume of clackity-clack in the background. Still, he needed something more. Operators' voices mumbling across a crowded floor. He could mumble quietly to himself, but he soon discovered his verbal skills had not developed to the point of being able to stand in the middle of the room talking about nothing to himself for a quarter of an hour. So he fished out his volume of Shakespeare and started reading aloud. Loud enough to hear voices, but not so loud that the intended victim would be able to pick Macbeth. OTC operators had keyboards, so he began tapping randomly on his. Occasionally, for a little variation, he walked up to the tape recorder and asked a question – and then promptly answered it in another voice. He stomped noisily away from the recorder again, across the room, and then silently dove back to the keyboard for more keyboard typing and mumblings of Macbeth.

It was exhausting. He figured the tape had to run for at least fifteen minutes uninterrupted. It wouldn't look very realistic if the office buzz suddenly went dead for three seconds at a time in the places where he paused the tape to rest.

The tapes took a number of attempts. He would be halfway through, racing through line after line of Shakespeare, rap-tap-tapping on his keyboard and asking himself questions in authoritative voices when the paper jammed in his printer. Damn. He had to start all over again. Finally, after a tiring hour of auditory schizophrenia, he had the perfect tape of office hubbub.

Mendax pulled out his partial list of Minerva users and began working through the 30-odd pages. It was discouraging.

'The number you have dialled is not connected. Please check the number before dialling again.'

Next number.

'Sorry, he is in a meeting at the moment. Can I have him return your call?' Ah, no thanks.

Another try.

'That person is no longer working with our company. Can I refer you to someone else?' Uhm, not really.

And another try.

Finally, success.

Mendax reached one of the contact names for a company in Perth. Valid number, valid company, valid contact name. He cleared his throat to deepen his voice even further and began.

'This is John Keller, an operator from OTC Minerva in Sydney. One of our D090 hard drives has crashed. We've pulled across the data on the back-up tape and we believe we have all your correct information. But some of it might have been corrupted in the accident and we would just like to confirm your details. Also the back-up tape is two days old, so we want to check your information is up to date so your service is not interrupted. Let me just dig out your details . . .' Mendax shuffled some papers around on the table top.

'Oh, dear. Yes. Let's check it,' the worried manager responded.

Mendax started reading all the information on the Minerva list obtained from Pacific Island, except for one thing. He changed the fax number slightly. It worked. The manager jumped right in.

'Oh, no. That's wrong. Our fax number is definitely wrong,' he said and proceeded to give the correct number.

Mendax tried to sound concerned. 'Hmm,' he told the manager. 'We may have bigger problems than we anticipated. Hmm.' He gave another pregnant pause. Working up the courage to ask the Big Question.

It was hard to know who was sweating more, the fretting Perth manager, tormented by the idea of loud staff complaints from all over the company because the Minerva account was faulty, or the gangly kid trying his hand at social engineering for the first time.

'Well,' Mendax began, trying to keep the sound of authority in his voice. 'Let's see. We have your account number, but we had better check your password . . . what was it?' An arrow shot from the bow.

It hit the target. 'Yes, it's L-U-R-C-H – full stop.'

Lurch? Uhuh. An Addams Family fan.

'Can you make sure everything is working? We don't want our service interrupted.' The Perth manager sounded quite anxious.

Mendax tapped away on the keyboard randomly and then paused. 'Well, it looks like everything is working just fine now,' he quickly reassured him. Just fine.

'Oh, that's a relief!' the Perth manager exclaimed. 'Thank you for that. Thank you. I just can't thank you enough for calling us!' More gratitude.

Mendax had to extract himself. This was getting embarrassing.

'Yes, well I'd better go now. More customers to call.' That should work. The Perth manager wanted a contact telephone number, as expected, if something went wrong – so Mendax gave him the one which was permanently busy.

'Thank you again for your courteous service!' Uhuh. Anytime.

Mendax hung up and tried the toll-free Minerva number. The password worked. He couldn't believe how easy it was to get in.

He had a quick look around, following the pattern of most hackers breaking into a new machine. First thing to do was to check the electronic mail of the 'borrowed' account. Email often contains valuable information. One company manager might send another information about other account names, password changes or even phone numbers to modems at the company itself. Then it was off to check the directories available for anyone to read on the main system – another good source of information. Final stop: Minerva's bulletin board of news. This included postings from the system operators about planned downtime or other service issues. He didn't stay long. The first visit was usually mostly a bit of reconnaissance work.

Minerva had many uses. Most important among these was the fact that Minerva gave hackers an entry point into various

X.25 networks. X.25 is a type of computer communications network, much like the Unix-based Internet or the VMS-based DECNET. It has different commands and protocols, but the principle of an extensive worldwide data communications network is the same. There is, however, one important difference. The targets for hackers on the X.25 networks are often far more interesting. For example, most banks are on X.25. Indeed, X.25 underpins many aspects of the world's financial markets. A number of countries' classified military computer sites only run on X.25. It is considered by many people to be more secure than the Internet or any DECNET system.

Minerva allowed incoming callers to pass into the X.25 network – something most Australian universities did not offer at the time. And Minerva let Australian callers do this without incurring a long-distance telephone charge.

In the early days of Minerva, the OTC operators didn't seem to care much about the hackers, probably because it seemed impossible to get rid of them. The OTC operators managed the OTC X.25 exchange, which was like a telephone exchange for the X.25 data network. This exchange was the data gateway for Minerva and other systems connected to that data network.

Australia's early hackers had it easy, until Michael Rosenberg arrived.

Rosenberg, known on-line simply as MichaelR, decided to clean up Minerva. An engineering graduate from Queensland University, Michael moved to Sydney when he joined OTC at age 21. He was about the same age as the hackers he was chasing off his system. Rosenberg didn't work as an OTC operator, he managed the software which ran on Minerva. And he made life hell for people like Force. Closing up security holes, quietly noting accounts used by hackers and then killing those accounts, Rosenberg almost single-handedly stamped out much of the hacker activity in OTC's Minerva.

Despite this, the hackers – 'my hackers' as he termed the regulars – had a grudging respect for Rosenberg. Unlike anyone else at OTC, he was their technical equal and, in a world where technical prowess was the currency, Rosenberg was a wealthy young man.

He wanted to catch the hackers, but he didn't want to see them go to prison. They were an annoyance, and he just wanted them out of his system. Any line trace, however, had to go through Telecom, which was at that time a separate body from OTC. Telecom, Rosenberg was told, was difficult about these things because of strict privacy laws. So, for the most part, he was left to deal with the hackers on his own. Rosenberg could not secure his system completely since OTC didn't dictate passwords to their customers. Their customers were usually more concerned about employees being able to remember passwords easily than worrying about warding off wily hackers. The result: the passwords on a number of Minerva accounts were easy pickings.

The hackers and OTC waged a war from 1988 to 1990, and it was fought in many ways.

Sometimes an OTC operator would break into a hacker's on-line session demanding to know who was really using the account. Sometimes the operators sent insulting messages to the hackers – and the hackers gave it right back to them. They broke into the hacker's session with 'Oh, you idiots are at it again'. The operators couldn't keep the hackers out, but they had other ways of getting even.

Electron, a Melbourne hacker and rising star in the Australian underground, had been logging into a system in Germany via OTC's X.25 link. Using a VMS machine, a sort of sister system to Minerva, he had been playing a game called Empire on the Altos system, a popular hang-out for hackers. It was his first attempt at Empire, a complex war game of strategy which attracted players from around the world. They each had less than one hour per day to conquer regions while keeping production units at a strategic level. The Melbourne hacker had spent weeks building his position. He was in second place.

Then, one day, he logged into the game via Minerva and the German system, and he couldn't believe what he saw on the screen in front of him. His regions, his position in the game, all of it – weeks of work – had been wiped out. An OTC operator had used an X.25 packet-sniffer to monitor the hacker's login and capture his password to Empire. Instead of trading the usual insults, the operator had waited for the hacker to logoff and then had hacked into the game and destroyed the hacker's position.

Electron was furious. He had been so proud of his position in his very first game. Still, wreaking havoc on the Minerva system in retribution was out of the question. Despite the fact that they wasted weeks of his work, Electron had no desire to damage their system. He considered himself lucky to be able to use it as long as he did.

The anti-establishment attitudes nurtured in BBSes such as PI and Zen fed on a love of the new and untried. There was no bitterness, just a desire to throw off the mantle of the old and dive into the new. Camaraderie grew from the exhilarating sense that the youth in this particular time and place were constantly on the edge of big discoveries. People were calling up computers with their modems and experimenting. What did this key sequence do? What about that tone? What would happen if . . . It was the question which drove them to stay up day and night, poking and prodding. These hackers didn't for the most part do drugs. They didn't even drink that much, given their age. All of that would have interfered with their burning desire to know, would have dulled their sharp edge. The underground's anti-establishment views were mostly directed at organisations which seemed to block the way to the new frontier – organisations like Telecom.

It was a powerful word. Say 'Telecom' to a member of the computer underground from that era and you will observe the most striking reaction. Instant contempt sweeps across his face. There is a pause as his lips curl into a noticeable sneer and he replies with complete derision, 'Telescum'. The underground hated Australia's national telephone carrier with a passion equalled only by its love of exploration. They felt that Telecom was backward and its staff had no idea how to use their own telecommunications technology. Worst of all, Telecom seemed to actively dislike BBSes.

Line noise interfered with one modem talking to another, and in the eyes of the computer underground, Telecom was responsible for the line noise. A hacker might be reading a message on PI, and there, in the middle of some juicy technical titbit, would be a bit of crud – random characters '2'28 v'1';D>nj4' – followed by the comment, 'Line noise. Damn Telescum! At their best as usual, I see'. Sometimes the line noise was so bad it logged the hacker off, thus forcing him to spend another 45 minutes attack dialling the BBS. The modems didn't have error correction, and the faster the modem speed, the worse the impact of line noise. Often it became a race to read mail and post messages before Telecom's line noise logged the hacker off.

Rumours flew through the underground again and again that Telecom was trying to bring in timed local calls. The volume of outrage was deafening. The BBS community believed it really irked the national carrier that people could spend an hour logged into a BBS for the cost of one local phone call. Even more heinous, other rumours abounded that Telecom had forced at least one BBS to limit each incoming call to under half an hour. Hence Telecom's other nickname in the computer underground: Teleprofit.

To the BBS community, Telecom's Protective Services Unit was the enemy. They were the electronic police. The underground saw Protective Services as 'the enforcers' – an all-powerful government force which could raid your house, tap your phone line and seize your computer equipment at any time. The ultimate reason to hate Telecom.

There was such hatred of Telecom that people in the computer underground routinely discussed ways of sabotaging the carrier. Some people talked of sending 240 volts of electricity down the telephone line – an act which would blow up bits of the telephone exchange along with any line technicians who happened to be working on the cable at the time. Telecom had protective fuses which stopped electrical surges on the line, but BBS hackers had reportedly developed circuit plans which would allow high-frequency voltages to bypass them. Other members of the underground considered what sweet justice it would be to set fire to all the cables outside a particular Telecom exchange which had an easily accessible cable entrance duct.

It was against this backdrop that the underground began to shift into phreaking. Phreaking is loosely defined as hacking the telephone system. It is a very loose definition. Some people believe phreaking includes stealing a credit card number and using it to make a long-distance call for free. Purists shun this definition. To them, using a stolen credit card is not phreaking, it is carding. They argue that phreaking demands a reasonable level of technical skill and involves manipulation of a telephone exchange. This manipulation may manifest itself as using computers or electrical circuits to generate special tones or modify the voltage of a phone line. The manipulation changes how the telephone exchange views a particular telephone line. The result: a free and hopefully untraceable call. The purist hacker sees phreaking more as a way of eluding telephone traces than of calling his or her friends around the world for free.

The first transition into phreaking and eventually carding happened over a period of about six months in 1988. Early hackers on PI and Zen relied primarily on dial-outs, like those at Melbourne University or Telecom's Clayton office, to bounce around international computer sites. They also used X.25 dial-outs in other countries – the US, Sweden and Germany – to make another leap in their international journeys.

Gradually, the people running these dial-out lines wised up. Dial-outs started drying up. Passwords were changed. Facilities were cancelled. But the hackers didn't want to give up access to overseas systems. They'd had their first taste of international calling and they wanted more. There was a big shiny electronic world to explore out there. They began trying different methods of getting where they wanted to go. And so the Melbourne underground moved into phreaking.

Phreakers swarmed to PABXes like bees to honey. A PABX, a private automatic branch exchange, works like a mini-Telecom telephone exchange. Using a PABX, the employee of a large company could dial another employee in-house without incurring the cost of a local telephone call. If the employee was, for example, staying in a hotel out of town, the company might ask him to make all his calls through the company's PABX to avoid paying extortionate hotel long-distance rates. If the employee was in Brisbane on business, he could dial a Brisbane number which might route him via the company's PABX to Sydney. From there, he might dial out to Rome or London, and the charge would be billed directly to the company. What worked for an employee also worked for a phreaker.

A phreaker dialling into the PABX would generally need to either know or guess the password allowing him to dial out again. Often, the phreaker was greeted by an automated message asking for the employee's telephone extension – which also served as the password. Well, that was easy enough. The phreaker simply tried a series of numbers until he found one which actually worked.

Occasionally, a PABX system didn't even have passwords. The managers of the PABX figured that keeping the phone number secret was good enough security. Sometimes phreakers made free calls out of PABXes simply by exploited security flaws in a particular model or brand of PABX. A series of specific key presses allowed the phreaker to get in without knowing a password, an employee's name, or even the name of the company for that matter.

As a fashionable pastime on BBSes, phreaking began to surpass hacking. PI established a private phreaking section. For a while, it became almost old hat to call yourself a hacker. Phreaking was forging the path forward.

Somewhere in this transition, the Phreakers Five sprung to life. A group of five hackers-turned-phreakers gathered in an exclusive group on PI. Tales of their late-night podding adventures leaked into the other areas of the BBS and made would-be phreakers green with jealousy.

First, the phreakers would scout out a telephone pod – the grey steel, rounded box perched nondescriptly on most streets. Ideally, the chosen pod would be by a park or some other public area likely to be deserted at night. Pods directly in front of suburban houses were a bit risky – the house might contain a nosy little old lady with a penchant for calling the local police if anything looked suspicious. And what she would see, if she peered out from behind her lace curtains, was a small tornado of action.

One of the five would leap from the van and open the pod with a key begged, borrowed or stolen from a Telecom technician. The keys seemed easy enough to obtain. The BBSes message boards were rife with gleeful tales of valuable Telecom equipment, such as 500 metres of cable or a pod key, procured off a visiting Telecom repairman either through legitimate means or in exchange for a six-pack of beer.

The designated phreaker would poke inside the pod until he found someone else's phone line. He'd strip back the cable, whack on a pair of alligator clips and, if he wanted to make a voice call, run it to a linesman's handset also borrowed, bought or stolen from Telecom. If he wanted to call another computer instead of talking voice, he would need to extend the phone line back to the phreakers' car. This is where the 500 metres of Telecom cable came in handy. A long cable meant the car, containing five anxious, whispering young men and a veritable junkyard of equipment, would not have to sit next to the pod for hours on end. That sort of scene might look a little suspicious to a local resident out walking his or her dog late one night.

The phreaker ran the cable down the street and, if possible, around the corner. He pulled it into the car and attached it to the waiting computer modem. At least one of the five was proficient enough with electronics hardware to have rigged up the computer and modem to the car battery. The Phreaker's Five could now call any computer without being traced or billed. The phone call charges would appear at the end of a local resident's phone bill. Telecom did not itemise residential telephone bills at the time. True, it was a major drama to zoom around suburban streets in the middle of the night with computers, alligator clips and battery adaptors in tow, but that didn't matter so much. In fact, the thrill of such a cloak-and-dagger operation was as good as the actual hacking itself. It was illicit. In the phreakers' own eyes, it was clever. And therefore it was fun.

Craig Bowen didn't think much of the Phreakers Five's style of phreaking. In fact, the whole growth of phreaking as a pastime depressed him a bit. He believed it just didn't require the technical skills of proper hacking. Hacking was, in his view, about the exploration of a brave new world of computers. Phreaking was, well, a bit beneath a good hacker. Somehow it demeaned the task at hand.

Still, he could see how in some cases it was necessary in order to continue hacking. Most people in the underground developed some basic skills in phreaking, though people like Bowen always viewed it more as a means to an end – just a way of getting from computer A to computer B, nothing more. Nonetheless, he allowed phreaking discussion areas in the private sections of PI.

What he refused to allow was discussion areas around credit card fraud. Carding was anathema to Bowen and he watched with alarm as some members of the underground began to shift from phreaking into carding.

Like the transition into phreaking, the move into carding was a logical progression. It occurred over a period of perhaps six months in 1988 and was as obvious as a group of giggling schoolgirls.

Many phreakers saw it simply as another type of phreaking. In fact it was a lot less hassle than manipulating some company's PABX. Instead, you just call up an operator, give him some stranger's credit card number to pay for the call, and you were on your way. Of course, the credit cards had a broader range of uses than the PABXes. The advent of carding meant you could telephone your friends in the US or UK and have a long voice conference call with all of them simultaneously – something which could be a lot tougher to arrange on a PABX. There were other benefits. You could actually charge things with that credit card. As in goods. Mail order goods.

One member of the underground who used the handle Ivan Trotsky allegedly ordered $50 000 worth of goods, including a jet ski, from the US on a stolen card, only to leave it sitting on the Australian docks. The Customs guys don't tend to take stolen credit cards for duty payments. In another instance, Trotsky was allegedly more successful. A try-hard hacker who kept pictures of Karl Marx and Lenin taped to the side of his computer terminal, Trotsky regularly spewed communist doctrine across the underground. A self-contained paradox, he spent his time attending Communist Party of Australia meetings and duck shoots. According to one hacker, Trotsky's particular contribution to the overthrow of the capitalist order was the arrangement of a shipment of expensive modems from the US using stolen credit cards. He was rumoured to have made a tidy profit by selling the modems in the computer community for about $200 each. Apparently, being part of the communist revolution gave him all sorts of ready-made rationalisations. Membership has its advantages.

To Bowen, carding was little more than theft. Hacking may have been a moral issue, but in early 1988 in Australia it was not yet much of a legal one. Carding was by contrast both a moral and a legal issue. Bowen recognised that some people viewed hacking as a type of theft – stealing someone else's computer resources – but the argument was ambiguous. What if no-one needed those resources at 2 a.m. on a given night? It might be seen more as 'borrowing' an under-used asset, since the hacker had not permanently appropriated any property. Not so for carding.

What made carding even less noble was that it required the technical skill of a wind-up toy. Not only was it beneath most good hackers, it attracted the wrong sort of people into the hacking scene. People who had little or no respect for the early Australian underground's golden rules of hacking: don't damage computer systems you break into (including crashing them); don't change the information in those systems (except for altering logs to cover your tracks); and share information. For most early Australian hackers, visiting someone else's system was a bit like visiting a national park. Leave it as you find it.

While the cream seemed to rise to the top of the hacking hierarchy, it was the scum that floated at the top of the carding community. Few people in the underground typified this more completely than Blue Thunder, who had been hanging around the outskirts of the Melbourne underground since at least 1986. The senior hackers treated Blue Blunder, as they sometimes called him, with great derision.

His entrance into the underground was as ignominious as that of a debutante who, delicately descending the grand steps of the ballroom, trips and tumbles head-first onto the dance floor. He picked a fight with the grande doyenne of the Melbourne underground.

The Real Article occupied a special place in the underground. For starters, The Real Article was a woman – perhaps the only female to play a major role in the early Melbourne underground scene. Although she didn't hack computers, she knew a lot about them. She ran The Real Connection, a BBS frequented by many of the hackers who hung out on PI. She wasn't somebody's sister wafting in and out of the picture in search of a boyfriend. She was older. She was as good as married. She had kids. She was a force to be reckoned with in the hacking community.

Forthright and formidable, The Real Article commanded considerable respect among the underground. A good indicator of this respect was the fact that the members of H.A.C.K. had inducted her as an honorary member of their exclusive club. Perhaps it was because she ran a popular board. More likely it was because, for all their bluff and bluster, most hackers were young men with the problems of young men. Being older and wiser, The Real Article knew how to lend a sympathetic ear to those problems. As a woman and a non-hacker, she was removed from the jumble of male ego hierarchical problems associated with confiding in a peer. She served as a sort of mother to the embryonic hacking community, but she was young enough to avoid the judgmental pitfalls most parents fall into with children.

The Real Article and Blue Thunder went into partnership running a BBS in early 1986. Blue Thunder, then a high-school student, was desperate to run a board, so she let him co-sysop the system. At first the partnership worked. Blue Thunder used to bring his high-school essays over for her to proofread and correct. But a short time into the partnership, it went sour. The Real Article didn't like Blue Thunder's approach to running a BBS, which appeared to her to be to get information from other hackers and then dump them. The specific strategy seemed to be: get hackers to logon and store their valuable information on the BBS, steal that information and then lock them out of their own account. By locking them out, he was able to steal all the glory; he could then claim the hacking secrets were his own. It was, in her opinion, not only unsustainable, but quite immoral. She parted ways with Blue Thunder and excommunicated him from her BBS.

Not long after, The Real Article started getting harassing phone calls at 4 in the morning. The calls were relentless. Four a.m. on the dot, every night. The voice at the other end of the line was computer synthesised. This was followed by a picture of a machine-gun, printed out on a cheap dot matrix printer in Commodore ASCII, delivered in her letterbox. There was a threatening message attached which read something like, 'If you want the kids to stay alive, get them out of the house'.

After that came the brick through the window. It landed in the back of her TV. Then she woke up one morning to find her phone line dead. Someone had opened the Telecom well in the nature strip across the road and cut out a metre of cable. It meant the phone lines for the entire street were down.

The Real Article tended to rise above the petty games that whining adolescent boys with bruised egos could play, but this was too much. She called in Telecom Protective Services, who put a last party release on her phone line to trace the early-morning harassing calls. She suspected Blue Thunder was involved, but nothing was ever proved. Finally, the calls stopped. She voiced her suspicions to others in the computer underground. Whatever shred of reputation Blue Chunder, as he then became known for a time, had was soon decimated.

Since his own technical contributions were seen by his fellow BBS users as limited, Blue Thunder would likely have faded into obscurity, condemned to spend the rest of his time in the underground jumping around the ankles of the aristocratic hackers. But the birth of carding arrived at a fortuitous moment for him and he got into carding in a big way, so big in fact that he soon got busted.

People in the underground recognised him as a liability, both because of what many hackers saw as his loose morals and because he was boastful of his activities. One key hacker said, 'He seemed to relish the idea of getting caught. He told people he worked for a credit union and that he stole lots of credit card numbers. He sold information, such as accounts on systems, for financial gain.' In partnership with a carder, he also allegedly sent a bouquet of flowers to the police fraud squad – and paid for it with a stolen credit card number.

On 31 August 1988, Blue Thunder faced 22 charges in the Melbourne Magistrates Court, where he managed to get most of the charges dropped or amalgamated. He only ended up pleading guilty to five counts, including deception and theft. The Real Article sat in the back of the courtroom watching the proceedings. Blue Thunder must have been pretty worried about what kind of sentence the magistrate would hand down because she said he approached her during the lunch break and asked if she would appear as a character witness for the defence. She looked him straight in the eye and said, 'I think you would prefer it if I didn't'. He landed 200 hours of community service and an order to pay $706 in costs.

Craig Bowen didn't like where the part of the underground typified by Blue Thunder was headed. In his view, Chunder and Trotsky stood out as bad apples in an otherwise healthy group, and they signalled an unpleasant shift towards selling information. This was perhaps the greatest taboo. It was dirty. It was seedy. It was the realm of criminals, not explorers. The Australian computer underground had started to lose some of its fresh-faced innocence.

Somewhere in the midst of all this, a new player entered the Melbourne underground. His name was Stuart Gill, from a company called Hackwatch.

Bowen met Stuart through Kevin Fitzgerald, a well-known local hacker commentator who founded the Chisholm Institute of Technology's Computer Abuse Research Bureau, which later became the Australian Computer Abuse Research Bureau. After seeing a newspaper article quoting Fitzgerald, Craig decided to ring up the man many members of the underground considered to be a hacker-catcher. Why not? There were no federal laws in Australia against hacking, so Bowen didn't feel that nervous about it. Besides, he wanted to meet the enemy. No-one from the Australian underground had ever done it before, and Bowen decided it was high time. He wanted to set the record straight with Fitzgerald, to let him know what hackers were really on about. They began to talk periodically on the phone.

Along the way, Bowen met Stuart Gill who said that he was working with Fitzgerald.[3] Before long, Gill began visiting PI. Eventually, Bowen visited Gill in person at the Mount Martha home he shared with his elderly aunt and uncle. Stuart had all sorts of computer equipment hooked up there, and a great number of boxes of papers in the garage.

'Oh, hello there, Paul,' Gill's ancient-looking uncle said when he saw the twosome. As soon as the old man had tottered off, Gill pulled Bowen aside confidentially.

'Don't worry about old Eric,' he said. 'He lost it in the war. Today he thinks I'm Paul, tomorrow it will be someone else.'

Bowen nodded, understanding.

There were many strange things about Stuart Gill, all of which seemed to have a rational explanation, yet that explanation somehow never quite answered the question in full.

Aged in his late thirties, he was much older and far more worldly than Craig Bowen. He had very, very pale skin – so pasty it looked as though he had never sat in the sun in his life.

Gill drew Bowen into the complex web of his life. Soon he told the young hacker that he wasn't just running Hackwatch, he was also involved in intelligence work. For the Australian Federal Police. For ASIO. For the National Crime Authority. For the Victoria Police's Bureau of Criminal Intelligence (BCI). He showed Bowen some secret computer files and documents, but he made him sign a special form first – a legal-looking document demanding non-disclosure based on some sort of official secrets act.

Bowen was impressed. Why wouldn't he be? Gill's cloak-and-dagger world looked like the perfect boy's own adventure. Even bigger and better than hacking. He was a little strange, but that was part of the allure.

Like the time they took a trip to Sale together around Christmas 1988. Gill told Bowen he had to get out of town for a few days – certain undesirable people were after him. He didn't drive, so could Craig help him out? Sure, no problem. They had shared an inexpensive motel room in Sale, paid for by Gill.

Being so close to Christmas, Stuart told Craig he had brought him two presents. Craig opened the first – a John Travolta fitness book. When Craig opened the second gift, he was a little stunned. It was a red G-string for men. Craig didn't have a girlfriend at the time – perhaps Stuart was trying to help him get one.

'Oh, ah, thanks,' Craig said, a bit confused.

'Glad you like it,' Stuart said. 'Go on. Try it on.'

'Try it on?' Craig was now very confused.

'Yeah, mate, you know, to see if it fits. That's all.'

'Oh, um, right.'

Craig hesitated. He didn't want to seem rude. It was a weird request, but never having been given a G-string before, he didn't know the normal protocol. After all, when someone gives you a jumper, it's normal for them to ask you to try it on, then and there, to see if it fits.

Craig tried it on. Quickly.

'Yes, seems to fit,' Stuart said matter of factly, then turned away.

Craig felt relieved. He changed back into his clothing.

That night, and on many others during their trips or during Craig's overnight visits to Stuart's uncle's house, Craig lay in bed wondering about his secretive new friend.

Stuart was definitely a little weird, but he seemed to like women so Craig figured he couldn't be interested in Craig that way. Stuart bragged that he had a very close relationship with a female newspaper reporter, and he always seemed to be chatting up the girl at the video store.

Craig tried not to read too much into Stuart's odd behaviour, for the young man was willing to forgive his friend's eccentricities just to be part of the action. Soon Stuart asked Craig for access to PI – unrestricted access.

The idea made Craig uncomfortable, but Stuart was so persuasive. How would he be able to continue his vital intelligence work without access to Victoria's most important hacking board? Besides, Stuart Gill of Hackwatch wasn't after innocent-faced hackers like Craig Bowen. In fact, he would protect Bowen when the police came down on everyone. What Stuart really wanted was the carders – the fraudsters. Craig didn't want to protect people like that, did he?

Craig found it a little odd, as usual, that Stuart seemed to be after the carders, yet he had chummed up with Ivan Trotsky.

Still, there were no doubt secrets Stuart couldn't reveal – things he wasn't allowed to explain because of his intelligence work.

Craig agreed.

What Craig couldn't have known as he pondered Stuart Gill from the safety of his boyish bedroom was exactly how much innocence the underground was still to lose. If he had foreseen the next few years – the police raids, the Ombudsman's investigation, the stream of newspaper articles and the court cases – Craig Bowen would, at that very moment, probably have reached over and turned off his beloved PI and Zen forever.

THE AMERICAN CONNECTION

Force had a secret. The Parmaster wanted it.

Like most hackers, The Parmaster didn't just want the secret, he needed it. He was in that peculiar state attained by real hackers where they will do just about anything to obtain a certain piece of information. He was obsessed.

Of course, it wasn't the first time The Parmaster craved a juicy piece of information. Both he and Force knew all about infatuation. That's how it worked with real hackers. They didn't just fancy a titbit here and there. Once they knew information about a particular system was available, that there was a hidden entrance, they chased it down relentlessly. So that was exactly what Par was doing. Chasing Force endlessly, until he got what he wanted.

It began innocently enough as idle conversation between two giants in the computer underground in the first half of 1988. Force, the well-known Australian hacker who ran the exclusive Realm BBS in Melbourne, sat chatting with Par, the American master of X.25 networks, in Germany. Neither of them was physically in Germany, but Altos was.

Altos Computer Systems in Hamburg ran a conference feature called Altos Chat on one of its machines. You could call up from anywhere on the X.25 data communications network, and the company's computer would let you connect. Once connected, with a few brief keystrokes, the German machine would drop you into a real-time, on-screen talk session with anyone else who happened to be on-line. While the rest of the company's computer system grunted and toiled with everyday labours, this corner of the machine was reserved for live on-line chatting. For free. It was like an early form of the Internet Relay Chat. The company probably hadn't meant to become the world's most prestigious hacker hang-out, but it soon ended up doing so.

Altos was the first significant international live chat channel, and for most hackers it was an amazing thing. The good hackers had cruised through lots of computer networks around the world. Sometimes they bumped into one another on-line and exchanged the latest gossip. Occasionally, they logged into overseas BBSes, where they posted messages. But Altos was different. While underground BBSes had a tendency to simply disappear one day, gone forever, Altos was always there. It was live. Instantaneous communications with a dozen other hackers from all sorts of exotic places. Italy. Canada. France. England. Israel. The US. And all these people not only shared an interest in computer networks but also a flagrant contempt for authority of any type. Instant, real-time penpals – with attitude.

However, Altos was more exclusive than the average underground BBS. Wanna-be hackers had trouble getting into it because of the way X.25 networks were billed. Some systems on the network took reverse-charge connections – like a 1-800 number – and some, including Altos, didn't. To get to Altos you needed a company's NUI (Network User Identifier), which was like a calling card number for the X.25 network, used to bill your time on-line. Or you had to have access to a system like Minerva which automatically accepted billing for all the connections made.

X.25 networks are different in various ways from the Internet, which developed later. X.25 networks use different communication protocols and, unlike the Internet at the user-level, they only use addresses containing numbers not letters. Each packet of information travelling over a data network needs to be encased in a particular type of envelope. A 'letter' sent across the X.25 network needs an X.25 'stamped' envelope, not an Internet 'stamped' envelope.

The X.25 networks were controlled by a few very large players, companies such as Telenet and Tymnet, while the modern Internet is, by contrast, a fragmented collection of many small and medium-sized sites.

Altos unified the international hacking world as nothing else had done. In sharing information about their own countries' computers and networks, hackers helped each other venture further and further abroad. The Australians had gained quite a reputation on Altos. They knew their stuff. More importantly, they possessed DEFCON, a program which mapped out uncharted networks and scanned for accounts on systems within them. Force wrote DEFCON based on a simple automatic scanning program provided by his friend and mentor, Craig Bowen (Thunderbird1).

Like the telephone system, the X.25 networks had a large number of 'phone numbers', called network user addresses (NUAs). Most were not valid. They simply hadn't been assigned to anyone yet. To break into computers on the network, you had to find them first, which meant either hearing about a particular system from a fellow hacker or scanning. Scanning – typing in one possible address after another – was worse than looking for a needle in a haystack. 02624-589004-0004. Then increasing the last digit by one on each attempt. 0005. 0006. 0007. Until you hit a machine at the other end.

Back in 1987 or early 1988, Force had logged into Pacific Island for a talk with Craig Bowen. Force bemoaned the tediousness of hand scanning.

'Well, why the hell are you doing it manually?' Bowen

responded. 'You should just use my program.' He then gave Force the source code for his simple automated scanning program, along with instructions.

Force went through the program and decided it would serve as a good launchpad for bigger things, but it had a major limitation. The program could only handle one connection at a time, which meant it could only scan one branch of a network at a time.

Less than three months later, Force had rewritten Bowen's program into the far more powerful DEFCON, which became the jewel in the crown of the Australian hackers' reputation. With DEFCON, a hacker could automatically scan fifteen or twenty network addresses simultaneously. He could command the computer to map out pieces of the Belgian, British and Greek X.25 communications networks, looking for computers hanging off the networks like buds at the tips of tree branches.

Conceptually, the difference was a little like using a basic PC, which can only run one program at a time, as opposed to operating a more sophisticated one where you can open many windows with different programs running all at once. Even though you might only be working in one window, say, writing a letter, the computer might be doing calculations in a spreadsheet in another window in the background. You can swap between different functions, which are all running in the background simultaneously.

While DEFCON was busy scanning, Force could do other things, such as talk on Altos. He continued improving DEFCON, writing up to four more versions of the program. Before long, DEFCON didn't just scan twenty different connections at one time; it also automatically tried to break into all the computers it found through those connections. Though the program only tried basic default passwords, it had a fair degree of success, since it could attack so many network addresses at once. Further, new sites and mini-networks were being added so quickly that security often fell by the wayside in the rush to join in. Since the addresses were unpublished, companies often felt this obscurity offered enough protection.

DEFCON produced lists of thousands of computer sites to raid. Force would leave it scanning from a hacked Prime computer, and a day or two later he would have an output file with 6000 addresses on different networks. He perused the list and selected sites which caught his attention. If his program had discovered an interesting address, he would travel over the X.25 network to the site and then try to break into the computer at that address. Alternatively, DEFCON might have already successfully penetrated the machine using a default password, in which case the address, account name and password would all be waiting for Force in the log file. He could just walk right in.

Everyone on Altos wanted DEFCON, but Force refused to hand over the program. No way was he going to have other hackers tearing up virgin networks. Not even Erik Bloodaxe, one of the leaders of the most prestigious American hacking group, Legion of Doom (LOD), got DEFCON when he asked for it. Erik took his handle from the name of a Viking king who ruled over the area now known as York, England. Although Erik was on friendly terms with the Australian hackers, Force remained adamant. He would not let the jewel out of his hands.

But on this fateful day in 1988, Par didn't want DEFCON. He wanted the secret Force had just discovered, but held so very close to his chest. And the Australian didn't want to give it to him.

Force was a meticulous hacker. His bedroom was remarkably tidy, for a hacker's room. It had a polished, spartan quality. There were a few well-placed pieces of minimalist furniture: a black enamel metal single bed, a modern black bedside table and a single picture on the wall – a photographic poster of lightning, framed in glass. The largest piece of furniture was a blue-grey desk with a return, upon which sat his computer, a printer and an immaculate pile of print-outs. The bookcase, a tall modern piece matching the rest of the furniture, contained an extensive collection of fantasy fiction books, including what seemed to be almost everything ever written by David Eddings. The lower shelves housed assorted chemistry and programming books. A chemistry award proudly jutted out from the shelf housing a few Dungeons and Dragons books.

He kept his hacking notes in an orderly set of plastic folders, all filed in the bottom of his bookcase. Each page of notes, neatly printed and surrounded by small, tidy handwriting revealing updates and minor corrections, had its own plastic cover to prevent smudges or stains.

Force thought it was inefficient to hand out his DEFCON program and have ten people scan the same network ten different times. It wasted time and resources. Further, it was becoming harder to get access to the main X.25 sites in Australia, like Minerva. Scanning was the type of activity likely to draw the attention of a system admin and result in the account being killed. The more people who scanned, the more accounts would be killed, and the less access the Australian hackers would have. So Force refused to hand over DEFCON to hackers outside The Realm, which is one thing that made it such a powerful group.

Scanning with DEFCON meant using Netlink, a program which legitimate users didn't often employ. In his hunt for hackers, an admin might look for people running Netlink, or he might just examine which systems a user was connecting to. For example, if a hacker connected directly to Altos from Minerva without hopping through a respectable midpoint, such as another corporate machine overseas, he could count on the Minerva admins killing off the account.

DEFCON was revolutionary for its time, and difficult to reproduce. It was written for Prime computers, and not many hackers knew how to write programs for Primes. In fact, it was exceedingly difficult for most hackers to learn programming of any sort for large, commercial machines. Getting the system engineering manuals was tough work and many of the large companies guarded their manuals almost as trade secrets.

Sure, if you bought a $100000 system, the company would give you a few sets of operating manuals, but that was well beyond the reach of a teenage hacker. In general, information was hoarded – by the computer manufacturers, by the big companies which bought the systems, by the system administrators and even by the universities.

Learning on-line was slow and almost as difficult. Most hackers used 300 or 1200 baud modems. Virtually all access to these big, expensive machines was illegal. Every moment on-line was a risky proposition. High schools never had these sorts of expensive machines. Although many universities had systems, the administrators were usually miserly with time on-line for students. In most cases, students only got accounts on the big machines in their second year of computer science studies. Even then, student accounts were invariably on the university's oldest, clunkiest machine. And if you weren't a comp-sci student, forget it. Indulging your intellectual curiosity in VMS systems would never be anything more than a pipe dream.

Even if you did manage to overcome all the roadblocks and develop some programming experience in VMS systems, for example, you might only be able to access a small number of machines on any given network. The X.25 networks connected a large number of machines which used very different operating systems. Many, such as Primes, were not in the least bit intuitive. So if you knew VMS and you hit a Prime machine, well, that was pretty much it.

Unless, of course, you happened to belong to a clan of hackers like The Realm. Then you could call up the BBS and post a message. 'Hey, I found a really cool Primos system at this address. Ran into problems trying to figure the parameters of the Netlink command. Ideas anyone?' And someone from your team would step forward to help.

In The Realm, Force tried to assemble a diverse group of Australia's best hackers, each with a different area of expertise. And he happened to be the resident expert in Prime computers.

Although Force wouldn't give DEFCON to anyone outside The Realm, he wasn't unreasonable. If you weren't in the system but you had an interesting network you wanted mapped, he would scan it for you. Force referred to scans for network user addresses as 'NUA sprints'. He would give you a copy of the NUA sprint. While he was at it, he would also keep a copy for The Realm. That was efficient. Force's pet project was creating a database of systems and networks for The Realm, so he simply added the new information to its database.

Force's great passion was mapping new networks, and new mini-networks were being added to the main X.25 networks all the time. A large corporation, such a BHP, might set up its own small-scale network connecting its offices in Western Australia, Queensland, Victoria and the United Kingdom. That mini-network might be attached to a particular X.25 network, such as Austpac. Get into the Austpac network and chances were you could get into any of the company's sites.

Exploration of all this uncharted territory consumed most of Force's time. There was something cutting-edge, something truly adventurous about finding a new network and carefully piecing together a picture of what the expanding web looked like. He drew detailed pictures and diagrams showing how a new part of the network connected to the rest. Perhaps it appealed to his sense of order, or maybe he was just an adventurer at heart. Whatever the underlying motivation, the maps provided The Realm with yet another highly prized asset.

When he wasn't mapping networks, Force published Australia's first underground hacking journal, *Globetrotter*. Widely read in the international hacking community, *Globetrotter* reaffirmed Australian hackers' pre-eminent position in the international underground.

But on this particular day, Par wasn't thinking about getting a copy of *Globetrotter* or asking Force to scan a network for him. He was thinking about that secret. Force's new secret. The secret Parmaster desperately wanted.

Force had been using DEFCON to scan half a dozen networks while he chatted to Par on Altos. He found an interesting connection from the scan, so he went off to investigate it. When he connected to the unknown computer, it started firing off strings of numbers at Force's machine. Force sat at his desk and watched the characters rush by on his screen.

It was very odd. He hadn't done anything. He hadn't sent any commands to the mystery computer. He hadn't made the slightest attempt to break into the machine. Yet here the thing was throwing streams of numbers. What kind of computer was this? There might have been some sort of header which would identify the computer, but it had zoomed by so fast in the unexpected data dump that Force had missed it.

Force flipped over to his chat with Par on Altos. He didn't completely trust Par, thinking the friendly American sailed a bit close to the wind. But Par was an expert in X.25 networks and was bound to have some clue about these numbers. Besides, if they turned out to be something sensitive, Force didn't have to tell Par where he found them.

'I've just found a bizarre address. It is one strange system. When I connected, it just started shooting off numbers at me. Check these out.'

Force didn't know what the numbers were, but Par sure did. 'Those look like credit cards,' he typed back.

'Oh.' Force went quiet.

Par thought the normally chatty Australian hacker seemed astonished. After a short silence, the now curious Par nudged the conversation forward. 'I have a way I can check out whether they really are valid cards,' he volunteered. 'It'll take some time, but I should be able to do it and get back to you.'

'Yes.' Force seemed hesitant. 'OK.'

On the other side of the Pacific from Par, Force thought about this turn of events. If they were valid credit cards, that was very cool. Not because he intended to use them for credit card fraud in the way Ivan Trotsky might have done. But Force could use them for making long-distance phone calls to hack overseas. And the sheer number of cards was astonishing. Thousands and thousands of them. Maybe 10 000. All he could think was, Shit! Free connections for the rest of my life.

Hackers such as Force considered using cards to call overseas computer systems a little distasteful, but certainly acceptable. The card owner would never end up paying the bill anyway. The hackers figured that Telecom, which they despised, would probably have to wear the cost in the end, and that was fine by them. Using cards to hack was nothing like ordering consumer goods. That was real credit card fraud. And Force would never sully his hands with that sort of behaviour.

Force scrolled back over his capture of the numbers which had been injected into his machine. After closer inspection, he saw there were headers which appeared periodically through the list. One said, 'CitiSaudi'.

He checked the prefix of the mystery machine's network address again. He knew from previous scans that it belonged to one of the world's largest banks. Citibank.

The data dump continued for almost three hours. After that, the Citibank machine seemed to go dead. Force saw nothing but a blank screen, but he kept the connection open. There was no way he was going to hang up from this conversation. He figured this had to be a freak connection – that he accidentally connected to this machine somehow, that it wasn't really at the address he had tried based on the DEFCON scan of Citibank's network.

How else could it have happened? Surely Citibank wouldn't have a computer full of credit cards which spilled its guts every time someone rang up to say 'hello'? There would be tonnes of security on a machine like that. This machine didn't even have a password. It didn't even need a special character command, like a secret handshake.

Freak connections happened now and then on X.25 networks. They had the same effect as a missed voice phone connection. You dial a friend's number – and you dial it correctly – but somehow the call gets screwed up in the tangle of wires and exchanges and your call gets put through to another number entirely. Of course, once something like that happens to an X.25 hacker, he immediately tries to figure out what the hell is going on, to search every shred of data from the machine looking for the system's real address. Because it was an accident, he suspects he will never find the machine again.

Force stayed home from school for two days to keep the connection alive and to piece together how he landed on the doorstep of this computer. During this time, the Citibank computer woke up a few times, dumped a bit more information, and then went back to sleep. Keeping the connection alive meant running a small risk of discovery by an admin at his launch point, but the rewards in this case far exceeded the risk.

It wasn't all that unusual for Force to skip school to hack. His parents used to tell him, 'You better stop it, or you'll have to wear glasses one day'. Still, they didn't seem to worry too much, since their son had always excelled in school without much effort. At the start of his secondary school career he had tried to convince his teachers he should skip year 9. Some objected. It was a hassle, but he finally arranged it by quietly doing the coursework for year 9 while he was in year 8.

After Force had finally disconnected from the CitiSaudi computer and had a good sleep, he decided to check on whether he could reconnect to the machine. At first, no-one answered, but when he tried a little later, someone answered all right. And it was the same talkative resident who answered the door the first time. Although it only seemed to work at certain hours of the day, the Citibank network address was the right one. He was in again.

As Force looked over the captures from his Citibank hack, he noticed that the last section of the data dump didn't contain credit card numbers like the first part. It had people's names – Middle Eastern names – and a list of transactions. Dinner at a restaurant. A visit to a brothel. All sorts of transactions. There was also a number which looked like a credit limit, in come cases a very, very large limit, for each person. A sheik and his wife appeared to have credit limits of $1 million – each. Another name had a limit of $5 million.

There was something strange about the data, Force thought. It was not structured in a way which suggested the Citibank machine was merely transmitting data to another machine. It looked more like a text file which was being dumped from a computer to a line printer.

Force sat back and considered his exquisite discovery. He decided this was something he would share only with a very few close, trusted friends from The Realm. He would tell Phoenix and perhaps one other member, but no-one else.

As he looked through the data once more, Force began to feel a little anxious. Citibank was a huge financial institution, dependent on the complete confidence of its customers. The corporation would lose a lot of face if news of Force's discovery got out. It might care enough to really come after him. Then, with the sudden clarity of the lightning strike photo which hung on his wall, a single thought filled his mind.

I am playing with fire.

'Where did you get those numbers?' Par asked Force next time they were both on Altos.

Force hedged. Par leaped forward.

'I checked those numbers for you. They're valid,' he told Force. The American was more than intrigued. He wanted that network address. It was lust. Next stop, mystery machine. 'So, what's the address?'

That was the one question Force didn't want to hear. He and Par had a good relationship, sharing information comfortably if occasionally. But that relationship only went so far. For all he knew, Par might have a less than desirable use for the information. Force didn't know if Par carded, but he felt sure Par had friends who might be into it. So Force refused to tell Par where to find the mystery machine.

Par wasn't going to give up all that easily. Not that he would use the cards for free cash, but, hey, the mystery machine seemed like a very cool place to check out. There would be no peace for Force until Par got what he wanted. Nothing is so tempting to a hacker as the faintest whiff of information about a system he wants, and Par hounded Force until the Australian hacker relented just a bit.

Finally Force told Par roughly where DEFCON had been scanning for addresses when it stumbled upon the CitiSaudi machine. Force wasn't handing over the street address, just the name of the suburb. DEFCON had been accessing the Citibank network through Telenet, a large American data network using X.25 communications protocols. The sub-prefixes for the Citibank portion of the network were 223 and 224.

Par pestered Force some more for the rest of the numbers, but the Australian had dug his heels in. Force was too careful a player, too fastidious a hacker, to allow himself to get mixed up in the things Par might get up to.

OK, thought the seventeen-year-old Par, I can do this without you. Par estimated there were 20 000 possible addresses on that network, any one of which might be the home of the mystery machine. But he assumed the machine would be in the low end of the network, since the lower numbers were usually used first and the higher numbers were generally saved for other, special network functions. His assumptions narrowed the likely search field to about 2000 possible addresses.

Par began hand-scanning on the Citibank Global Telecommunications Network (GTN) looking for the mystery machine. Using his knowledge of the X.25 network, he picked a number to start with. He typed 22301, 22302, 22303. On and on, heading toward 22310000. Hour after hour, slowly, laboriously, working his way through all the options, Par scanned out a piece, or a range, within the network. When he got bored with the 223 prefix, he tried out the 224 one for a bit of variety.

Bleary-eyed and exhausted after a long night at the computer, Par felt like calling it quits. The sun had splashed through the windows of his Salinas, California, apartment hours ago. His living room was a mess, with empty, upturned beer cans circling his Apple IIe. Par gave up for a while, caught some shut-eye. He had gone through the entire list of possible addresses, knocking at all the doors, and nothing had happened. But over the next few days he returned to scanning the network again. He decided to be more methodical about it and do the whole thing from scratch a second time.

He was part way through the second scan when it happened. Par's computer connected to something. He sat up and peered toward the screen. What was going on? He checked the address. He was sure he had tried this one before and nothing had answered. Things were definitely getting strange. He stared at his computer.

The screen was blank, with the cursor blinking silently at the top. Now what? What had Force done to get the computer to sing its song?

Par tried pressing the control key and a few different letters. Nothing. Maybe this wasn't the right address after all. He disconnected from the machine and carefully wrote down the address, determined to try it again later.

On his third attempt, he connected again but found the same irritating blank screen. This time he went through the entire alphabet with the control key.

Control L.

That was the magic keystroke. The one that made CitiSaudi give up its mysterious cache. The one that gave Par an adrenalin rush, along with thousands and thousands of cards. Instant cash, flooding his screen. He turned on the screen capture so he could collect all the information flowing past and analyse it later. Par had to keep feeding his little Apple IIe more disks to store all the data coming in through his 1200 baud modem.

It was magnificent. Par savoured the moment, thinking about how much he was going to enjoy telling Force. It was going to be sweet. Hey, Aussie, you aren't the only show in town. See ya in Citibank.

An hour or so later, when the CitiSaudi data dump had finally finished, Par was stunned at what he found in his capture. These weren't just any old cards. These were debit cards, and they were held by very rich Arabs. These people just plopped a few million in a bank account and linked a small, rectangular piece of plastic to that account. Every charge came directly out of the bank balance. One guy listed in the data dump bought a $330 000 Mercedes Benz in Istanbul – on his card. Par couldn't imagine being able to throw down a bit of plastic for that. Taking that plastic out for a spin around the block would bring a whole new meaning to the expression, 'Charge it!'

When someone wins the lottery, they often feel like sharing with their friends. Which is exactly what Par did. First, he showed his room-mates. They thought it was very cool. But not nearly so cool as the half dozen hackers and phreakers who happened to be on the telephone bridge Par frequented when the master of X.25 read off a bunch of the cards.

Par was a popular guy after that day. Par was great, a sort of Robin Hood of the underground. Soon, everyone wanted to talk to him. Hackers in New York. Phreakers in Virginia. And the Secret Service in San Francisco.

Par didn't mean to fall in love with Theorem. It was an accident, and he couldn't have picked a worse girl to fall for. For starters, she lived in Switzerland. She was 23 and he was only seventeen. She also happened to be in a relationship – and that relationship was with Electron, one of the best Australian hackers of the late 1980s. But Par couldn't help himself. She was irresistible, even though he had never met her in person. Theorem was different. She was smart and funny, but refined, as a European woman can be.

They met on Altos in 1988.

Theorem didn't hack computers. She didn't need to, since she could connect to Altos through her old university computer account. She had first found Altos on 23 December 1986. She remembered the date for two reasons. First, she was amazed at the power of Altos – that she could have a live conversation on-line with a dozen people in different countries at the same time. Altos was a whole new world for her. Second, that was the day she met Electron.

Electron made Theorem laugh. His sardonic, irreverent humour hit a chord with her. Traditional Swiss society could be stifling and closed, but Electron was a breath of fresh air. Theorem was Swiss but she didn't always fit the mould. She hated skiing. She was six feet tall. She liked computers.

When they met on-line, the 21-year-old Theorem was at a crossroad in her youth. She had spent a year and a half at university studying mathematics. Unfortunately, the studies had not gone well. The truth be told, her second year of university was in fact the first year all over again. A classmate had introduced her to Altos on the university's computers. Not long after she struck up a relationship with Electron, she dropped out of uni all together and enrolled in a secretarial course. After that, she found a secretarial job at a financial institution.

Theorem and Electron talked on Altos for hours at a time. They talked about everything – life, family, movies, parties – but not much about what most people on Altos talked about – hacking. Eventually, Electron gathered up the courage to ask Theorem for her voice telephone number. She gave it to him happily and Electron called her at home in Lausanne. They talked. And talked. And talked. Soon they were on the telephone all the time.

Seventeen-year-old Electron had never had a girlfriend. None of the girls in his middle-class high school would give him the time of day when it came to romance. Yet here was this bright, vibrant girl – a girl who studied maths – speaking to him intimately in a melting French accent. Best of all, she genuinely liked him. A few words from his lips could send her into silvery peals of laughter.

When the phone bill arrived, it was $1000. Electron

surreptitiously collected it and buried it at the bottom of a drawer in his bedroom.

When he told Theorem, she offered to help pay for it. A cheque for $700 showed up not long after. It made the task of explaining Telecom's reminder notice to his father much easier.

The romantic relationship progressed throughout 1987 and the first half of 1988. Electron and Theorem exchanged love letters and tender intimacies over 16 000 kilometres of computer networks, but the long-distance relationship had some bumpy periods. Like when she had an affair over several months with Pengo. A well-known German hacker with links to the German hacking group called the Chaos Computer Club, Pengo was also a friend and mentor to Electron. Pengo was, however, only a short train ride away from Theorem. She became friends with Pengo on Altos and eventually visited him. Things progressed from there.

Theorem was honest with Electron about the affair, but there was something unspoken, something below the surface. Even after the affair ended, Theorem was sweet on Pengo the way a girl remains fond of her first love regardless of how many other men she has slept with since then.

Electron felt hurt and angry, but he swallowed his pride and forgave Theorem her dalliance. Eventually, Pengo disappeared from the scene.

Pengo had been involved with people who sold US military secrets – taken from computers – to the KGB. Although his direct involvement in the ongoing international computer espionage had been limited, he began to worry about the risks. His real interest was in hacking, not spying. The Russian connection simply enabled him to get access to bigger and better computers. Beyond that, he felt no loyalty to the Russians.

In the first half of 1988, he handed himself in to the German authorities. Under West German law at the time, a citizen-spy who surrendered himself before the state discovered the crime, and thus averted more damage to the state, acquired immunity from prosecution. Having already been busted in December 1986 for using a stolen NUI, Pengo decided that turning himself in would be his best hope of taking advantage of this legal largesse.

By the end of the year, things had become somewhat hairy for Pengo and in March 1989 the twenty-year-old from Berlin was raided again, this time with the four others involved in the spy ring. The story broke and the media exposed Pengo's real name. He didn't know if he would eventually be tried and convicted of something related to the incident. Pengo had a few things on his mind other than the six-foot Swiss girl.

With Pengo out of the way, the situation between Theorem and the Australian hacker improved. Until Par came along.

Theorem and Par began innocently enough. Being one of only a few girls in the international hacking and phreaking scene and, more particularly, on Altos, she was treated differently. She had lots of male friends on the German chat system, and the boys told her things in confidence they would never tell each other. They sought out her advice. She often felt like she wore many hats – mother, girlfriend, psychiatrist – when she spoke with the boys on Altos.

Par had been having trouble with his on-line girlfriend, Nora, and when he met Theorem he turned to her for a bit of support. He had travelled from California to meet Nora in person in New York. But when he arrived in the sweltering heat of a New York summer, without warning, her conservative Chinese parents didn't take kindly to his unannounced appearance. There were other frictions between Nora and Par. The relationship had been fine on Altos and on the phone, but things were just not clicking in person.

He already knew that virtual relationships, forged over an electronic medium which denied the importance of physical chemistry, could sometimes be disappointing.

Par used to hang out on a phone bridge with another Australian member of The Realm, named Phoenix, and with a fun girl from southern California. Tammi, a casual phreaker, had a great personality and a hilarious sense of humour. During those endless hours chatting, she and Phoenix seemed to be in the throes of a mutual crush. In the phreaking underground, they were known as a bit of a virtual item. She had even invited Phoenix to come visit her sometime. Then, one day, for the fun of it, Tammi decided to visit Par in Monterey. Her appearance was a shock.

Tammi had described herself to Phoenix as being a blue-eyed, blonde California girl. Par knew that Phoenix visualised her as a stereotypical bikini-clad, beach bunny from LA. His perception rested on a foreigner's view of the southern California culture. The land of milk and honey. The home of the Beach Boys and TV series like 'Charlie's Angels'.

When Tammi arrived, Par knew instantly that she and Phoenix would never hit it off in person. Tammi did in fact have both blonde hair and blue eyes. She had neglected to mention, however, that she weighed about 300 pounds, had a rather homely face and a somewhat down-market style. Par really liked Tammi, but he couldn't get the ugly phrase 'white trash' out of his thoughts. He pushed and shoved, but the phrase was wedged in his mind. It fell to Par to tell Phoenix the truth about Tammi.

So Par knew all about how reality could burst the foundations of a virtual relationship.

Leaving New York and Nora behind, Par moved across the river to New Jersey to stay with a friend, Byteman, who was one of a group of hackers who specialised in breaking into computer systems run by Bell Communications Research (Bellcore). Bellcore came into existence at the beginning of 1984 as a result of the break-up of the US telephone monopoly known as Bell Systems. Before the break-up, Bell Systems' paternalistic holding company, American Telephone and Telegraph (AT&T), had fostered the best and brightest in Bell Labs, its research arm. Over the course of its history, Bell Labs boasted at least seven Nobel-prize winning researchers and numerous scientific achievements. All of which made Bellcore a good target for hackers trying to prove their prowess.

Byteman used to chat with Theorem on Altos, and eventually he called her, voice. Par must have looked pretty inconsolable, because one day while Byteman was talking to Theorem, he suddenly said to her, 'Hey, wanna talk to a friend of mine?' Theorem said 'Sure' and Byteman handed the telephone to Par. They talked for about twenty minutes.

After that they spoke regularly both on Altos and on the phone. For weeks after Par returned to California, Theorem tried to cheer him up after his unfortunate experience with Nora. By mid-1988, they had fallen utterly and passionately in love.

Electron, an occasional member of Force's Realm group, took the news very badly. Not everyone on Altos liked Electron. He could be a little prickly, and very cutting when he chose to be, but he was an ace hacker, on an international scale, and everyone listened to him. Obsessive, creative and quick off the mark, Electron had respect, which is one reason Par felt so badly.

When Theorem told Electron the bad news in a private con-versation on-line, Electron had let fly in the public area, ripping into the American hacker on the main chat section of Altos, in front of everyone.

Par took it on the chin and refused to fight back. What else could he do? He knew what it was like to hurt. He felt for the guy and knew how he would feel if he lost Theorem. And he knew that Electron must be suffering a terrible loss of face. Everyone saw Electron and Theorem as an item. They had been together for more than a year. So Par met Electron's fury with grace and quiet words of consolation.

Par didn't hear much from Electron after that day. The Australian still visited Altos, but he seemed more withdrawn, at least whenever Par was around. After that day, Par ran into him once, on a phone bridge with a bunch of Australian hackers.

Phoenix said on the bridge, 'Hey, Electron. Par's on the bridge.'

Electron paused. 'Oh, really,' he answered coolly. Then he went silent.

Par let Electron keep his distance. After all, Par had what really counted – the girl.

Par called Theorem almost every day. Soon they began to make plans for her to fly to California so they could meet in person. Par tried not to expect too much, but he found it difficult to stop savouring the thought of finally seeing Theorem face to face. It gave him butterflies.

Yeah, Par thought, things are really looking up.

The beauty of Altos was that, like Pacific Island or any other local BBS, a hacker could take on any identity he wanted. And he could do it on an international scale. Visiting Altos was like attending a glittering masquerade ball. Anyone could recreate himself. A socially inept hacker could pose as a character of romance and adventure. And a security official could pose as a hacker.

Which is exactly what Telenet security officer Steve Mathews did on 27 October 1988. Par happened to be on-line, chatting away with his friends and hacker colleagues. At any given moment, there were always a few strays on Altos, a few people who weren't regulars. Naturally, Mathews didn't announce himself as being a Telenet guy. He just slipped quietly onto Altos looking like any other hacker. He might engage a hacker in conversation, but he let the hacker do most of the talking. He was there to listen.

On that fateful day, Par happened to be in one of his magnanimous moods. Par had never had much money growing up, but he was always very generous with what he did have. He talked for a little while with the unknown hacker on Altos, and then gave him one of the debit cards taken from his visits to the CitiSaudi computer. Why not? On Altos, it was a bit like handing out your business card. 'The Parmaster – Parameters Par Excellence'.

Par had got his full name – The Parmaster – in his earliest hacking days. Back then, he belonged to a group of teenagers involved in breaking the copy protections on software programs for Apple IIes, particularly games. Par had a special gift for working out the copy protection parameters, which was a first step in bypassing the manufacturers' protection schemes. The ringleader of the group began calling him 'the master of parameters' – The Parmaster – Par, for short. As he moved into serious hacking and developed his expertise in X.25 networks, he kept the name because it fitted nicely in his new environment. 'Par?' was a common command on an X.25 pad, the modem gateway to an X.25 network.

'I've got lots more where that come from,' Par told the stranger on Altos. 'I've got like 4000 cards from a Citibank system.'

Not long after that, Steve Mathews was monitoring Altos again, when Par showed up handing out cards to people once more.

'I've got an inside contact,' Par confided. 'He's gonna make up a whole mess of new, plastic cards with all these valid numbers from the Citibank machine. Only the really big accounts, though. Nothing with a balance under $25 000.'

Was Par just making idle conversation, talking big on Altos? Or would he really have gone through with committing such a major fraud? Citibank, Telenet and the US Secret Service would never know, because their security guys began closing the net around Par before he had a chance to take his idea any further.

Mathews contacted Larry Wallace, fraud investigator with Citibank in San Mateo, California. Wallace checked out the cards. They were valid all right. They belonged to the Saudi-American Bank in Saudi Arabia and were held on a Citibank database in Sioux Falls, South Dakota. Wallace determined that, with its affiliation to the Middle Eastern bank, Citibank had a custodial responsibility for the accounts. That meant he could open a major investigation.

On 7 November, Wallace brought in the US Secret Service. Four days later, Wallace and Special Agent Thomas Holman got their first major lead when they interviewed Gerry Lyons of Pacific Bell's security office in San Francisco.

Yes, Lyons told the investigators, she had some information they might find valuable. She knew all about hackers and phreakers. In fact, the San Jose Police had just busted two guys trying to phreak at a pay phone. The phreakers seemed to know something about a Citibank system.

When the agents showed up at the San Jose Police Department for their appointment with Sergeant Dave Flory, they received another pleasant surprise. The sergeant had a book filled with hackers' names and numbers seized during the arrest of the two pay-phone phreakers. He also happened to be in possession of a tape recording of the phreakers talking to Par from a prison phone.

The cheeky phreakers had used the prison pay phone to call up a telephone bridge located at the University of Virginia. Par, the Australian hackers and other assorted American phreakers and hackers visited the bridge frequently. At any one moment, there might be eight to ten people from the underground sitting on the bridge. The phreakers found Par hanging out there, as usual, and they warned him. His name and number were inside the book seized by police when they were busted.

Par didn't seem worried at all.

'Hey, don't worry. It's cool,' he reassured them. 'I have just disconnected my phone number today – with no forwarding details.'

Which wasn't quite true. His room-mate, Scott, had indeed disconnected the phone which was in his name because he had been getting prank calls. However, Scott opened a new telephone account at the same address with the same name on the same day – all of which made the job of tracking down the mysterious hacker named Par much easier for the law enforcement agencies.

In the meantime, Larry Wallace had been ringing around his contacts in the security business and had come up with another lead. Wanda Gamble, supervisor for the Southeastern Region of MCI Investigations, in Atlanta, had a wealth of information on the hacker who called himself Par. She was well connected when it came to hackers, having acquired a collection of reliable informants during her investigations of hacker-related incidents. She gave the Citibank investigator two mailbox numbers for Par. She also handed them what she believed was his home phone number.

The number checked out and on 25 November, the day after Thanksgiving, the Secret Service raided Par's house. The raid was terrifying. At least four law enforcement officers burst through the door with guns drawn and pointed. One of them had a shotgun. As is often the case in the US, investigators from private, commercial organisations – in this case Citibank and Pacific Bell – also took part in the raid.

The agents tore the place apart looking for evidence. They dragged down the food from the kitchen cupboards. They emptied the box of cornflakes into the sink looking for hidden computer disks. They looked everywhere, even finding a ceiling cavity at the back of a closet which no-one even knew existed.

They confiscated Par's Apple IIe, printer and modem. But, just to be sure, they also took the Yellow Pages, along with the telephone and the new Nintendo game paddles Scott had just bought. They scooped up the very large number of papers which had been piled under the coffee table, including the spiral notebook with Scott's airline bookings from his job as a travel agent. They even took the garbage.

It wasn't long before they found the red shoebox full of disks peeping out from under the fish tank next to Par's computer.

They found lots of evidence. What they didn't find was Par.

Instead, they found Scott and Ed, two friends of Par. They were pretty shaken up by the raid. Not knowing Par's real identity, the Secret Service agents accused Scott of being Par. The phone was in his name, and Special Agent Holman had even conducted some surveillance more than a week before the raid, running the plates on Scott's 1965 black Ford Mustang parked in front of the house. The Secret Service was sure it had its man, and Scott had a hell of a time convincing them otherwise.

Both Scott and Ed swore up and down that they weren't hackers or phreakers, and they certainly weren't Par. But they knew who Par was, and they told the agents his real name. After considerable pressure from the Secret Service, Scott and Ed agreed to make statements down at the police station.

In Chicago, more than 2700 kilometres away from the crisis unfolding in northern California, Par and his mother watched his aunt walk down the aisle in her white gown.

Par telephoned home once, to Scott, to say 'hi' from the Midwest. The call came after the raid.

'So,' a relaxed Par asked his room-mate, 'How are things going at home?'

'Fine,' Scott replied. 'Nothing much happening here.'

Par looked down at the red bag he was carrying with a momentary expression of horror. He realised he stood out in the San Jose bus terminal like a peacock among the pigeons . . .

Blissfully ignorant of the raid which had occurred three days before, Par and his mother had flown into San Jose airport. They had gone to the bus terminal to pick up a Greyhound home to the Monterey area. While waiting for the bus, Par called his friend Tammi to say he was back in California.

Any casual bystander waiting to use the pay phones at that moment would have seen a remarkable transformation in the brown-haired boy at the row of phones. The smiling face suddenly dropped in a spasm of shock. His skin turned ash white as the blood fled south. His deep-set chocolate brown eyes, with their long, graceful lashes curving upward and their soft, shy expression, seemed impossibly large.

For at that moment Tammi told Par that his house had been raided by the Secret Service. That Scott and Ed had been pretty upset about having guns shoved in their faces, and had made statements about him to the police. That they thought their phone was tapped. That the Secret Service guys were still hunting for Par, they knew his real name, and she thought there was an all points bulletin out for him. Scott had told the Secret Service about Par's red bag, the one with all his hacking notes

that he always carried around. The one with the print-out of all
the Citibank credit card numbers.

And so it was that Par came to gaze down at his bag with
a look of alarm. He realised instantly that the Secret Service
would be looking for that red bag. If they didn't know what he
looked like, they would simply watch for the bag.

That bag was not something Par could hide easily. The
Citibank print-out was the size of a phone book. He also had
dozens of disks loaded with the cards and other sensitive
hacking information.

Par had used the cards to make a few free calls, but he
hadn't been charging up any jet skis. He fought temptation
valiantly, and in the end he had won, but others might not
have been so victorious in the same battle. Par figured that
some less scrupulous hackers had probably been charging up
a storm. He was right. Someone had, for example, tried to
send a $367 bouquet of flowers to a woman in El Paso using
one of the stolen cards. The carder had unwittingly chosen a
debit card belonging to a senior Saudi bank executive who
happened to be in his office at the time the flower order was
placed. Citibank investigator Larry Wallace added notes on
that incident to his growing file.

Par figured that Citibank would probably try to pin every
single attempt at carding on him. Why not? What kind of credibility would a seventeen-year-old hacker have in denying those
sorts of allegations? Zero. Par made a snap decision. He sidled
up to a trash bin in a dark corner. Scanning the scene warily,
Par casually reached into the red bag, pulled out the thick wad
of Citibank card print-outs and stuffed it into the bin. He fluffed
a few stray pieces of garbage over the top.

He worried about the computer disks with all his other
valuable hacking information. They represented thousands of
hours of work and he couldn't bring himself to throw it all
away. The 10 megabyte trophy. More than 4000 cards. 130000
different transactions. In the end, he decided to hold on to the
disks, regardless of the risk. At least, without the print-out, he

could crumple the bag up a bit and make it a little less con-
spicuous. As Par slowly moved away from the bin, he glanced
back to check how nondescript the burial site appeared from a
distance. It looked like a pile of garbage. Trash worth millions
of dollars, headed for the dump.

As he boarded the bus to Salinas with his mother, Par's
mind was instantly flooded with images of a homeless person
fishing the print-out from the bin and asking someone about it.
He tried to push the idea from his head.

During the bus ride, Par attempted to figure out what
he was going to do. He didn't tell his mother anything. She
couldn't even begin to comprehend his world of computers
and networks, let alone his current predicament. Further,
Par and his mother had suffered from a somewhat strained
relationship since he ran away from home not long after his
seventeenth birthday. He had been kicked out of school for
non-attendance, but had found a job tutoring students in computers at the local college. Before the trip to Chicago, he had
seen her just once in six months. No, he couldn't turn to her
for help.

The bus rolled toward the Salinas station. En route, it travelled down the street where Par lived. He saw a jogger, a thin
black man wearing a walkman. What the hell is a jogger doing
here, Par thought. No-one jogged in the semi-industrial neighbourhood. Par's house was about the only residence amid all
the light-industrial buildings. As soon as the jogger was out
of sight of the house, he suddenly broke away from his path,
turned off to one side and hit the ground. As he lay on his
stomach on some grass, facing the house, he seemed to begin
talking into the walkman.

Sitting watching this on the bus, Par flipped out. They were
out to get him, no doubt about it. When the bus finally arrived
at the depot and his mother began sorting out their luggage,
Par tucked the red bag under his arm and disappeared. He
found a pay phone and called Scott to find out the status of
things. Scott handed the phone to Chris, another friend who

lived in the house. Chris had been away at his parents' home during the Thanksgiving raid.

'Hold tight and lay low,' Chris told Par.

'I'm on my way over to pick you up and take you to a lawyer's office where you can get some sort of protection.'

A specialist in criminal law, Richard Rosen was born in New York but raised in his later childhood in California. He had a personality which reflected the steely stubbornness of a New Yorker, tempered with the laid-back friendliness of the west coast. Rosen also harboured a strong anti-authoritarian streak. He represented the local chapter of Hell's Angels in the middle-class County of Monterey. He also caused a splash representing the growing midwifery movement, which promoted home-births. The doctors of California didn't like him much as a result.

Par's room-mates met with Rosen after the raid to set things up for Par's return. They told him about the terrifying ordeal of the Secret Service raid, and how they were interrogated for an hour and a half before being pressured to give statements. Scott, in particular, felt that he had been forced to give a statement against Par under duress.

While Par talked to Chris on the phone, he noticed a man standing at the end of the row of pay phones. This man was also wearing a walkman. He didn't look Par in the eye. Instead, he faced the wall, glancing furtively off to the side toward where Par was standing. Who was that guy? Fear welled up inside Par and all sorts of doubts flooded his mind. Who could he trust?

Scott hadn't told him about the raid. Were his room-mates in cahoots with the Secret Service? Were they just buying time so they could turn him in? There was no-one else Par could turn to. His mother wouldn't understand. Besides, she had problems of her own. And he didn't have a father. As far as Par was concerned, his father was as good as dead. He had never met the man, but he heard he was a prison officer in Florida. Not a likely candidate for helping Par in this situation. He was close to his grandparents – they had bought his computer for him as a present – but they lived in a tiny Mid-Western town and they simply wouldn't understand either.

Par didn't know what to do, but he didn't seem to have many options at the moment, so he told Chris he would wait at the station for him. Then he ducked around a corner and tried to hide.

A few minutes later, Chris pulled into the depot. Par dove into the Toyota Landcruiser and Chris tore out of the station toward Rosen's office. They noticed a white car race out of the bus station after them.

While they drove, Par pieced together the story from Chris. No-one had warned him about the raid because everyone in the house believed the phone line was tapped. Telling Par while he was in Chicago might have meant another visit from the Secret Service. All they had been able to do was line up Rosen to help him.

Par checked the rear-view mirror. The white car was still following them. Chris made a hard turn at the next intersection and accelerated down the California speedway. The white car tore around the corner in pursuit. No matter what Chris did, he couldn't shake the tail. Par sat in the seat next to Chris, quietly freaking out.

Just 24 hours before, he had been safe and sound in Chicago. How did he end up back here in California being chased by a mysterious driver in a white car?

Chris tried his best to break free, swerving and racing. The white car wouldn't budge. But Chris and Par had one advantage over the white car; they were in a four-wheel drive. In a split-second decision, Chris jerked the steering wheel to one side. The Landcruiser veered off the road onto a lettuce field. Par gripped the inside of the door as the 4WD bounced through the dirt over the neat crop rows. Near-ripe heads of lettuce went flying out from under the tires. Half-shredded lettuce leaves filled the air. A cloud of dirt enveloped the car. The vehicle skidded and jerked, but finally made its way to a highway at the far end of the field. Chris hit the highway running, swerving into the lane at high speed.

When Par looked back, the white car had disappeared. Chris kept his foot on the accelerator and Par barely breathed until the Landcruiser pulled up in front of Richard Rosen's building.

Par leaped out, the red bag still clutched tightly under his arm, and high-tailed it into the lawyer's office. The receptionist looked a bit shocked when he said his name. Someone must have filled her in on the details.

Rosen quickly ushered him into his office. Introductions were brief and Par cut to the story of the chase. Rosen listened intently, occasionally asking a well-pointed question, and then took control of the situation.

The first thing they needed to do was call off the Secret Service chase, Rosen said, so Par didn't have to spend any more time ducking around corners and hiding in bus depots. He called the Secret Service's San Francisco office and asked Special Agent Thomas J. Holman to kill the Secret Service pursuit in exchange for an agreement that Par would turn himself in to be formally charged.

Holman insisted that they had to talk to Par.

No, Rosen said. There would be no interviews for Par by law enforcement agents until a deal had been worked out.

But the Secret Service needed to talk to Par, Holman insisted. They could only discuss all the other matters after the Secret Service had had a chance to talk with Par.

Rosen politely warned Holman not to attempt to contact his client. You have something to say to Par, you go through me, he said. Holman did not like that at all. When the Secret Service wanted to talk to someone, they were used to getting their way. He pushed Rosen, but the answer was still no. No no no and no again. Holman had made a mistake. He had assumed that everyone wanted to do business with the United States Secret Service.

When he finally realised Rosen wouldn't budge, Holman gave up. Rosen then negotiated with the federal prosecutor,

US Attorney Joe Burton, who was effectively Holman's boss in the case, to call off the pursuit in exchange for Par handing himself in to be formally charged.

Then Par gave Rosen his red bag, for safekeeping.

At about the same time, Citibank investigator Wallace and Detective Porter of the Salinas Police interviewed Par's mother as she returned home from the bus depot. She said that her son had moved out of her home some six months before, leaving her with a $2000 phone bill she couldn't pay. They asked if they could search her home. Privately, she worried about what would happen if she refused. Would they tell the office where she worked as a clerk? Could they get her fired? A simple woman who had little experience dealing with law enforcement agents, Par's mother agreed. The investigators took Par's disks and papers.

Par turned himself in to the Salinas Police in the early afternoon of 12 December. The police photographed and fingerprinted him before handing him a citation – a small yellow slip headed '502 (c) (1) PC'. It looked like a traffic ticket, but the two charges Par faced were felonies, and each carried a maximum term of three years for a minor. Count 1, for hacking into Citicorp Credit Services, also carried a fine of up to $10000. Count 2, for 'defrauding a telephone service', had no fine: the charges were for a continuing course of conduct, meaning that they applied to the same activity over an extended period of time.

Federal investigators had been astonished to find Par was so young. Dealing with a minor in the federal court system was a big hassle, so the prosecutor decided to ask the state authorities to prosecute the case. Par was ordered to appear in Monterey County Juvenile Court on 10 July 1989.

Over the next few months, Par worked closely with Rosen. Though Rosen was a very adept lawyer, the situation looked pretty depressing. Citibank claimed it had spent $30000 on securing its systems and Par believed that the corporation might be looking for up to $3 million in total damages. While they couldn't prove Par had made any money from the cards himself, the prosecution would argue that his generous distribution of them had led to serious financial losses. And that was just the financial institutions.

Much more worrying was what might come out about Par's visits to TRW's computers. The Secret Service had seized at least one disk with TRW material on it.

TRW was a large, diverse company, with assets of $2.1 billion and sales of almost $7 billion in 1989, nearly half of which came from the US government. It employed more than 73 000 people, many of who worked with the company's credit ratings business. TRW's vast databases held private details of millions of people – addresses, phone numbers, financial data.

That, however, was just one of the company's many businesses. TRW also did defence work – very secret defence work. Its Space and Defense division, based in Redondo Beach, California, was widely believed to be a major beneficiary of the Reagan Government's Star Wars budget. More than 10 per cent of the company's employees worked in this division, designing spacecraft systems, communications systems, satellites and other, unspecified, space 'instruments'.

The seized disk had some mail from the company's TRWMAIL systems. It wasn't particularly sensitive, mostly just company propaganda sent to employees, but the Secret Service might think that where there was smoke, there was bound to be fire. TRW did the kind of work that makes governments very nervous when it comes to unauthorised access. And Par had visited certain TRW machines; he knew that company had a missiles research section, and even a space weapons section.

With so many people out to get him – Citibank, the Secret Service, the local police, even his own mother had helped the other side – it was only a matter of time before they unearthed the really secret things he had seen while hacking. Par began to wonder if it was such a good idea for him to stay around for the trial.

❖

In early 1989, when Theorem stepped off the plane which carried her from Switzerland to San Francisco, she was pleased that she had managed to keep a promise to herself. It wasn't always an easy promise. There were times of intimacy, of perfect connection, between the two voices on opposite sides of the globe, when it seemed so breakable.

Meanwhile, Par braced himself. Theorem had described herself in such disparaging terms. He had even heard from others on Altos that she was homely. But that description had ultimately come from her anyway, so it didn't really count.

Finally, as he watched the stream of passengers snake out to the waiting area, he told himself it didn't matter anyway. After all, he had fallen in love with her – her being, her essence – not her image as it appeared in flesh. And he had told her so. She had said the same back to him.

Suddenly she was there, in front of him. Par had to look up slightly to reach her eyes, since she was a little more than an inch taller. She was quite pretty, with straight, brown shoulder-length hair and brown eyes. He was just thinking how much more attractive she was than he had expected, when it happened.

Theorem smiled.

Par almost lost his balance. It was a devastating smile, big and toothy, warm and genuine. Her whole face lit up with a fire of animation. That smile sealed it.

She had kept her promise to herself. There was no clear image of Par in her mind before meeting him in person. After meeting a few people from Altos at a party in Munich the year before, she had tried not to create images of people based on their on-line personalities. That way she would never suffer disappointment.

Par and Theorem picked up her bags and got into Brian's car. Brian, a friend who offered to play airport taxi because Par didn't have a car, thought Theorem was pretty cool. A six-foot-tall French-speaking Swiss woman. It was definitely cool. They drove back to Par's house. Then Brian came in for a chat.

Brian asked Theorem all sorts of questions. He was really

curious, because he had never met anyone from Europe before. Par kept trying to encourage his friend to leave but Brian wanted to know all about life in Switzerland. What was the weather like? Did people ski all the time?

Par kept looking Brian in the eye and then staring hard at the door.

Did most Swiss speak English? What other languages did she know? A lot of people skied in California. It was so cool talking to someone from halfway around the world.

Par did the silent chin-nudge toward the door and, at last, Brian got the hint. Par ushered his friend out of the house. Brian was only there for about ten minutes, but it felt like a year. When Par and Theorem were alone, they talked a bit, then Par suggested they go for a walk.

Halfway down the block, Par tentatively reached for her hand and took it in his own. She seemed to like it. Her hand was warm. They talked a bit more, then Par stopped. He turned to face her. He paused, and then told her something he had told her before over the telephone, something they both knew already.

Theorem kissed him. It startled Par. He was completely unprepared. Then Theorem said the same words back to him.

When they returned to the house, things progressed from there. They spent two and a half weeks in each other's arms – and they were glorious, sun-drenched weeks. The relationship proved to be far, far better in person than it had ever been on-line or on the telephone. Theorem had captivated Par, and Par, in turn, created a state of bliss in Theorem.

Par showed her around his little world in northern California. They visited a few tourist sites, but mostly they just spent a lot of time at home. They talked, day and night, about everything.

Then it was time for Theorem to leave, to return to her job and her life in Switzerland. Her departure was hard – driving to the airport, seeing her board the plane – it was heart-wrenching. Theorem looked very upset. Par just managed to hold it together until the plane took off.

For two and a half weeks, Theorem had blotted out Par's approaching court case. As she flew away, the dark reality of the case descended on him.

The fish liked to watch.

Par sat at the borrowed computer all night in the dark, with only the dull glow of his monitor lighting the room, and the fish would all swim over to the side of their tank and peer out at him. When things were quiet on-line, Par's attention wandered to the eel and the lion fish. Maybe they were attracted to the phosphorescence of the computer screen. Whatever the reason, they certainly liked to hover there. It was eerie.

Par took a few more drags of his joint, watched the fish some more, drank his Coke and then turned his attention back to his computer.

That night, Par saw something he shouldn't have. Not the usual hacker stuff. Not the inside of a university. Not even the inside of an international bank containing private financial information about Middle Eastern sheiks.

What he saw was information about some sort of killer spy satellite – those are the words Par used to describe it to other hackers. He said the satellite was capable of shooting down other satellites caught spying, and he saw it inside a machine connected to TRW's Space and Defense division network. He stumbled upon it much the same way Force had accidentally found the CitiSaudi machine – through scanning. Par didn't say much else about it because the discovery scared the hell out of him.

Suddenly, he felt like the man who knew too much. He'd been in and out of so many military systems, seen so much sensitive material, that he had become a little blasé about the whole thing. The information was cool to read but, God knows, he never intended to actually do anything with it. It was just a prize, a glittering trophy testifying to his prowess as a hacker.

But this discovery shook him up, slapped him in the face, made him realise he was exposed.

What would the Secret Service do to him when they found out? Hand him another little traffic ticket titled '502C'? No way. Let him tell the jury at his trial everything he knew? Let the newspapers print it? Not a snowball's chance in hell.

This was the era of Ronald Reagan and George Bush, of space defence initiatives, of huge defence budgets and very paranoid military commanders who viewed the world as one giant battlefield with the evil empire of the Soviet Union.

Would the US government just lock him up and throw away the key? Would it want to risk him talking to other prisoners – hardened criminals who knew how to make a dollar from that sort of information? Definitely not.

That left just one option. Elimination.

It was not a pretty thought. But to the seventeen-year-old hacker it was a very plausible one. Par considered what he could do and came up with what seemed to be the only solution.

Run.

4 | THE FUGITIVE

When Par failed to show up for his hearing on 10 July 1989 in the Monterey County Juvenile Court in Salinas, he officially became a fugitive. He had, in fact, already been on the run for some weeks. But no-one knew. Not even his lawyer.

Richard Rosen had an idea something was wrong when Par didn't show up for a meeting some ten days before the hearing, but he kept hoping his client would come good. Rosen had negotiated a deal for Par: reparations plus fifteen days or less in juvenile prison in exchange for Par's full cooperation with the Secret Service.

Par had appeared deeply troubled over the matter for weeks. He didn't seem to mind telling the Feds how he had broken into various computers, but that's not what they were really looking for. They wanted him to rat. And to rat on everyone. They knew Par was a kingpin and, as such, he knew all the important players in the underground. The perfect stooge. But Par couldn't bring himself to narc. Even if he did spill his guts, there was still the question of what the authorities would do to him in prison. The question of elimination loomed large in his mind.

So, one morning, Par simply disappeared. He had planned it carefully, packed his bags discreetly and made arrangements with a trusted friend outside the circle which included his room-mates. The friend drove around to pick Par up when the room-mates were out. They never had an inkling that the now eighteen-year-old Par was about to vanish for a very long time.

First, Par headed to San Diego. Then LA. Then he made his way to New Jersey. After that, he disappeared from the radar screen completely.

Life on the run was hard. For the first few months, Par carried around two prized possessions; an inexpensive laptop computer and photos of Theorem taken during her visit. They were his lifeline to a different world and he clutched them in his bag as he moved from one city to another, often staying with his friends from the computer underground. The loose-knit network of hackers worked a bit like the nineteenth-century American 'underground railroad' used by escaped slaves to flee from the South to the safety of the northern states. Except that, for Par, there was never a safe haven.

Par crisscrossed the continent, always on the move. A week in one place. A few nights in another. Sometimes there were breaks in the electronic underground railroad, spaces between the place where one line ended and another began. Those breaks were the hardest. They meant sleeping out in the open, sometimes in the cold, going without food and being without anyone to talk to.

He continued hacking, with new-found frenzy, because he was invincible. What were the law enforcement agencies going to do? Come and arrest him? He was already a fugitive and he figured things couldn't get much worse. He felt as though he would be on the run forever, and as if he had already been on the run for a lifetime, though it was only a few months.

When he was staying with people from the computer underground, Par was careful. But when he was alone in a dingy motel room, or with people completely outside that world, he hacked without fear. Blatant, in-your-face feats. Things he knew the Secret Service would see. Even his illicit voice mailbox had words for his pursuers:

Yeah, this is Par. And to all those faggots from the Secret Service who keep calling and hanging up, well, lots of luck. 'Cause, I mean, you're so fucking stupid, it's not even funny.

I mean, if you had to send my shit to Apple Computers [for analysis], you must be so stupid, it's pitiful. You also thought I had blue-boxing equipment [for phreaking]. I'm just laughing trying to think what you thought was a blue box. You are so lame.

Oh well. And anyone else who needs to leave me a message, go ahead. And everyone take it easy and leave me some shit. Alright. Later.

Despite the bravado, paranoia took hold of Par as it never had before. If he saw a cop across the street, his breath would quicken and he would turn and walk in the opposite direction. If the cop was heading toward him, Par crossed the street and turned down the nearest alley. Police of any type made him very nervous.

By the autumn of 1989, Par had made his way to a small town in North Carolina. He found a place to stop and rest with a friend who used the handle The Nibbler and whose family owned a motel. A couple of weeks in one place, in one bed, was paradise. It was also free, which meant he didn't have to borrow money from Theorem, who helped him out while he was on the run.

Par slept in whatever room happened to be available that night, but he spent most of his time in one of the motel chalets Nibbler used in the off-season as a computer room. They spent days hacking from Nibbler's computer. The fugitive had been forced to sell off his inexpensive laptop before arriving in North Carolina.

After a few weeks at the motel, however, he couldn't shake the feeling that he was being watched. There were too many strangers coming and going. He wondered if the hotel guests waiting in their cars were spying on him, and he soon began jumping at shadows. Perhaps, he thought, the Secret Service had found him after all.

Par thought about how he could investigate the matter in more depth.

One of The Atlanta Three hackers, The Prophet, called Nibbler occasionally to exchange hacking information, particularly security bugs in Unix systems. During one of their talks, Prophet told Par about a new security flaw he'd been experimenting with on a network that belonged to the phone company.

The Atlanta Three, a Georgia-based wing of The Legion of Doom, spent a good deal of time weaving their way through BellSouth, the phone company covering the south-eastern US. They knew about phone switching stations the way Par knew about Tymnet. The Secret Service had raided the hackers in July 1989 but had not arrested them yet, so in September The Prophet continued to maintain an interest in his favourite target.

Par thought the flaw in BellSouth's network sounded very cool and began playing around in the company's systems. Dial up the company's computer network, poke around, look at things. The usual stuff.

It occurred to Par that he could check out the phone company's records of the motel to see if there was anything unusual going on. He typed in the motel's main phone number and the system fed back the motel's address, name and some detailed technical information, such as the exact cable and pair attached to the phone number. Then he looked up the phone line of the computer chalet. Things looked odd on that line.

The line which he and Nibbler used for most of their hacking showed a special status: 'maintenance unit on line'.

What maintenance unit? Nibbler hadn't mentioned any problems with any of the motel's lines, but Par checked with him. No problems with the telephones.

Par felt nervous. In addition to messing around with the phone company's networks, he had been hacking into a Russian computer network from the computer chalet. The Soviet network was a shiny new toy. It had only been connected to the rest of the world's global packet-switched network for about a month, which made it particularly attractive virgin territory.

Nibbler called in a friend to check the motel's phones. The friend, a former telephone company technician turned free-lancer, came over to look at the equipment. He told Nibbler and Par that something weird was happening in the motel's phone system. The line voltages were way off.

Par realised instantly what was going on. The system was being monitored. Every line coming in and going out was probably being tapped, which meant only one thing. Someone – the phone company, the local police, the FBI or the Secret Service – was onto him.

Nibbler and Par quickly packed up all Nibbler's computer gear, along with Par's hacking notes, and moved to another motel across town. They had to shut down all their hacking activities and cover their tracks.

Par had left programs running which sniffed people's pass-words and login names on a continual basis as they logged in, then dumped all the information into a file on the hacked machine. He checked that file every day or so. If he didn't shut the programs down, the log file would grow until it was so big the system administrator would become curious and have a look. When he discovered that his system had been hacked he would close the security holes. Par would have problems getting back into that system.

After they finished tidying up the hacked systems, they gathered up all Par's notes and Nibbler's computer equipment once again and stashed them in a rented storage space. Then they drove back to the motel.

Par couldn't afford to move on just yet. Besides, maybe only the telephone company had taken an interest in the motel's phone system. Par had done a lot of poking and prodding of the telecommunications companies' computer systems from the motel phone, but he had done it anonymously. Perhaps BellSouth felt a little curious and just wanted to sniff about for more information. If that was the case, the law enforcement agencies probably didn't know that Par, the fugitive, was hiding in the motel.

The atmosphere was becoming oppressive in the motel. Par became even more watchful of the people coming and going. He glanced out the front window a little more often, and he listened a little more carefully to the footsteps coming and going. How many of the guests were really just tourists? Par went through the guest list and found a man registered as being from New Jersey. He was from one of the AT&T corporations left after the break-up of Bell Systems. Why on earth would an AT&T guy be staying in a tiny hick town in North Carolina? Maybe a few Secret Service agents had snuck into the motel and were watching the chalet.

Par needed to bring the paranoia under control. He needed some fresh air, so he went out for a walk. The weather was bad and the wind blew hard, whipping up small tornadoes of autumn leaves. Soon it began raining and Par sought cover in the pay phone across the street.

Despite having been on the run for a few months, Par still called Theorem almost every day, mostly by phreaking calls through bulk telecommunications companies. He dialled her number and they talked for a bit. He told her about how the voltage was way off on the motel's PABX and how the phone might be tapped. She asked how he was holding up. Then they spoke softly about when they might see each other again.

Outside the phone box, the storm worsened. The rain hammered the roof from one side and then another as the wind jammed it in at strange angles. The darkened street was deserted. Tree branches creaked under the strain of the wind. Rivulets rushed down the leeward side of the booth and formed a wall of water outside the glass. Then a trash bin toppled over and its contents flew onto the road.

Trying to ignore the havoc around him, Par curled the phone handset into a small protected space, cupped between his hand, his chest and a corner of the phone booth. He reminded Theorem of their time together in California, of two and a half weeks, and they laughed gently over intimate secrets.

A tree branch groaned and then broke under the force of the wind. When it crashed on the pavement near the phone booth, Theorem asked Par what the noise was.

'There's a hurricane coming,' he told her. 'Hurricane Hugo. It was supposed to hit tonight. I guess it's arrived.'

Theorem sounded horrified and insisted Par go back to the safety of the motel immediately.

When Par opened the booth door, he was deluged by water. He dashed across the road, fighting the wind of the hurricane, staggered into his motel room and jumped into bed to warm up. He fell asleep listening to the storm, and he dreamed of Theorem.

Hurricane Hugo lasted more than three days, but they felt like the safest three days Par had spent in weeks. It was a good bet that the Secret Service wouldn't be conducting any raids during a hurricane. South Carolina took the brunt of Hugo but North Carolina also suffered massive damage. It was one of the worst hurricanes to hit the area in decades. Winds near its centre reached more than 240 kilometres per hour, causing 60 deaths and $7 billion in damages as it made its way up the coast from the West Indies to the Carolinas.

When Par stepped outside his motel room one afternoon a few days after the storm, the air was fresh and clean. He walked to the railing outside his second-storey perch and found himself looking down on a hive of activity in the car park. There were cars. There was a van. There was a collection of spectators.

And there was the Secret Service.

At least eight agents wearing blue jackets with the Secret Service emblem on the back.

Par froze. He stopped breathing. Everything began to move in slow motion. A few of the agents formed a circle around one of the guys from the motel, a maintenance worker named John, who looked vaguely like Par. They seemed to be hauling John over the coals, searching his wallet for identification and quizzing him. Then they escorted him to the van, presumably to run his prints.

Par's mind began moving again. He tried to think clearly. What was the best way out? He had to get back into his room. It would give him some cover while he figured out what to do next. The photos of Theorem flashed through his mind. No way was he going to let the Secret Service get hold of those. He needed to stash them and fast.

He could see the Secret Service agents searching the computer chalet. Thank God he and Nibbler had moved all the equipment. At least there was nothing incriminating in there and they wouldn't be able to seize all their gear.

Par breathed deeply, deliberately, and forced himself to back away from the railing toward the door to his room. He resisted the urge to dash into his room, to recoil from the scene being played out below him. Abrupt movements would draw the agents' attention.

Just as Par began to move, one of the agents turned around. He scanned the two-storey motel complex and his gaze quickly came to rest on Par. He looked Par dead in the eye.

This is it, Par thought. I'm screwed. No way out of here now. Months on the run only to get done in a hick town in North Carolina. These guys are gonna haul my ass away for good. I'll never see the light of day again. Elimination is the only option.

While these thoughts raced through Par's mind, he stood rigid, his feet glued to the cement floor, his face locked into the probing gaze of the Secret Service agent. He felt like they were the only two people who existed in the universe.

Then, inexplicably, the agent looked away. He swivelled around to finish his conversation with another agent. It was as if he had never even seen the fugitive.

Par stood, suspended and unbelieving. Somehow it seemed impossible. He began to edge the rest of the way to his motel room. Slowly, casually, he slid inside and shut the door behind him.

His mind raced back to the photos of Theorem and he searched the room for a safe hiding place. There wasn't one. The best option was something above eye-level. He pulled a chair across the room, climbed on it and pressed on the ceiling. The rectangular panel of plasterboard lifted easily and Par slipped the photos in the space, then replaced the panel. If the agents tore the room apart, they would likely find the pictures. But the photos would probably escape a quick search, which was the best he could hope for at this stage.

Next, he turned his mind to escaping. The locals were pretty cool about everything, and Par thought he could count on the staff not to mention his presence to the Secret Service. That bought him some time, but he couldn't get out of the room without being seen. Besides, if he was spotted walking off the property, he would certainly be stopped and questioned.

Even if he did manage to get out of the motel grounds, it wouldn't help much. The town wasn't big enough to shield him from a thorough search and there was no-one there he trusted enough to hide him. It might look a little suspicious, this young man running away from the motel on foot in a part of the world where everyone travelled by car. Hitchhiking was out of the question. With his luck, he'd probably get picked up by one of the agents leaving the raid. No, he wanted a more viable plan. What he really needed was to get out of the area altogether, to flee the state.

Par knew that John travelled to Asheville to attend classes and that he left very early. If the authorities had been watching the motel for a while, they would know that his 5 a.m. departure was normal. And there was one other thing about the early departure which seemed promising. It was still dark at that hour.

If Par could get as far as Asheville, he might be able to get a lift to Charlotte, and from there he could fly somewhere far away.

Par considered the options again and again. Hiding out in the motel room seemed the most sensible thing to do. He had been moving rooms around the motel pretty regularly, so he might have appeared to be just another traveller to anyone watching the motel. With any luck the Secret Service would be concentrating their search on the chalet, ripping the place apart in a vain hunt for the computer equipment. As these thoughts went through his head, the phone rang, making Par jump. He stared at it, wondering whether to answer.

He picked it up.

'It's Nibbler,' a voice whispered.

'Yeah,' Par whispered back.

'Par, the Secret Service is here, searching the motel.'

'I know. I saw them.'

'They've already searched the room next to yours.' Par nearly died. The agents had been less than two metres from where he was standing and he hadn't even known it. That room was where John stayed. It was connected to his by an inner door, but both sides were locked.

'Move into John's room and lay low. Gotta go.' Nibbler hung up abruptly.

Par put his ear to the wall and listened. Nothing. He unlocked the connecting inner door, turned the knob and pressed lightly. It gave. Someone had unlocked the other side after the search. Par squinted through the crack in the door. The room was silent and still. He opened it – no-one home. Scooping up his things, he quickly moved into John's room.

Then he waited. Pacing and fidgeting, he strained his ears to catch the sounds outside. Every bang and creak of a door opening and closing set him on edge. Late that night, after the law enforcement officials had left, Nibbler called him on the house phone and told him what had happened.

Nibbler had been inside the computer chalet when the Secret Service showed up with a search warrant. The agents took names, numbers, every detail they could, but they had trouble finding any evidence of hacking. Finally, one of them emerged from the chalet triumphantly waving a single computer disk in the air. The law enforcement entourage hanging around in front of the chalet let out a little cheer, but Nibbler could hardly keep a straight face. His younger brother had been learning the basics of computer graphics with a program called Logo. The United States Secret Service would soon be uncovering the secret drawings of a primary school student.

Par laughed. It helped relieve the stress. Then he told Nibbler his escape plan, and Nibbler agreed to arrange matters. His parents didn't know the whole story, but they liked Par and wanted to help him. Then Nibbler wished his friend well.

Par didn't even try to rest before his big escape. He was as highly strung as a racehorse at the gate. What if the Secret Service was still watching the place? There was no garage attached to the main motel building which he could access from the inside. He would be exposed, even though it would only be for a minute or so. The night would provide reasonable cover, but the escape plan wasn't fool-proof. If agents were keeping the motel under observation from a distance they might miss him taking off from his room. On the other hand, there could be undercover agents posing as guests watching the entire complex from inside their room.

Paranoid thoughts stewed in Par's mind throughout the night. Just before 5 a.m., he heard John's car pull up outside. Par flicked off the light in his room, opened his door a crack and scanned the motel grounds. All quiet, bar the single car, which puffed and grunted in the still, cold air. The windows in most of the buildings were dark. It was now or never.

Par opened the door all the way and slipped down the hallway. As he crept downstairs, the pre-dawn chill sent a shiver down his spine. Glancing quickly from side to side, he hurried toward the waiting car, pulled the back door open and dove onto the seat. Keeping his head down, he twisted around, rolled onto the floor and closed the door with little more than a soft click.

As the car began to move, Par reached for a blanket which

had been tossed on the floor and pulled it over himself. After a while, when John told him they were safely out of the town, Par slipped the blanket off his face and he looked up at the early morning sky. He tried to get comfortable on the floor. It was going to be a long ride.

At Asheville, John dropped Par off at an agreed location. Par thanked him and hopped into a waiting car. Someone else from his extensive network of friends and acquaintances took him to Charlotte.

This time Par rode in the front passenger seat. For the first time, he saw the true extent of the damage wreaked by Hurricane Hugo. The small town where he had been staying had been slashed by rain and high winds, but on the way to the Charlotte airport, where he would pick up a flight to New York, Par watched the devastation with amazement. He stared out the car window, unable to take his eyes off the storm's trail of havoc.

The hurricane had swept up anything loose or fragile and turned it into a missile on a suicide mission. Whatever mangled, broken fragments remained after the turbulent winds had passed would have been almost unrecognisable to those who had seen them before.

Theorem worried about Par as he staggered from corner to corner of the continent. In fact, she had often asked him to consider giving himself up. Moving from town to town was taking its toll on Par, and it wasn't that much easier on Theorem. She hadn't thought going on the lam was such a great idea in the first place, and she offered to pay for his lawyer so he could stop running. Par declined. How could he hand himself in when he believed elimination was a real possibility? Theorem sent him money, since he had no way of earning a living and he needed to eat. The worst parts, though, were the dark thoughts that kept crossing her mind. Anything could happen to Par between phone calls. Was he alive? In prison? Had he been raided, even accidentally shot during a raid?

The Secret Service and the private security people seemed to want him so badly. It was worrying, but hardly surprising. Par had embarrassed them. He had broken into their machines and passed their private information around in the underground. They had raided his home when he wasn't even home. Then he had escaped a second raid, in North Carolina, slipping between their fingers. He was constantly in their face, continuing to hack blatantly and to show them contempt in things such as his voicemail message. He figured they were probably exasperated from chasing all sorts of false leads as well, since he was perpetually spreading fake rumours about his whereabouts. Most of all, he thought they knew what he had seen inside the TRW system. He was a risk.

Par became more and more paranoid, always watching over his shoulder as he moved from city to city. He was always tired. He could never sleep properly, worrying about the knock on the door. Some mornings, after a fitful few hours of rest, he woke with a start, unable to remember where he was. Which house or motel, which friends, which city.

He still hacked all the time, borrowing machines where he could. He posted messages frequently on The Phoenix Project, an exclusive BBS run by The Mentor and Erik Bloodaxe and frequented by LOD members and the Australian hackers. Some well-known computer security people were also invited onto certain, limited areas of the Texas-based board, which immediately elevated the status of The Phoenix Project in the computer underground. Hackers were as curious about the security people as the security people were about their prey. The Phoenix Project was special because it provided neutral ground, where both sides could meet to exchange ideas.

Via the messages, Par continued to improve his hacking skills while also talking with his friends, people like Erik Bloodaxe, from Texas, and Phoenix, from The Realm in Melbourne. Electron also frequented The Phoenix Project. These hackers knew Par was on the run, and sometimes they joked with him about it. The humour made the stark reality of Par's situation bearable. All the hackers on The Phoenix Project had considered the prospect of being caught. But the presence of Par, and his tortured existence on the run, hammered the implications home with some regularity.

As Par's messages became depressed and paranoid, other hackers tried to do what they could to help him. Elite US and foreign hackers who had access to the private sections of The Phoenix Project saw his messages and they felt for him. Yet Par continued to slide deeper and deeper into his own strange world.

Subject: DAMN !!! From: The Parmaster Date: Sat Jan 13 08:40:17 1990
Shit, i got drunk last night and went onto that Philippine system. . . Stupid Admin comes on and asks who i am . . .
  Next thing i know, i'm booted off and both accounts on the system are gone. Not only this .. but the whole fucking Philippine Net isn't accepting collect calls anymore. (The thing went down completely after i was booted off!) Apparently someone there had enough of me. By the way, kids, never drink and hack!
- Par

Subject: gawd From: The Parmaster Date: Sat Jan 13 09:07:06 1990
Those SS boys and NSA boys think i'm a COMRADE .. hehehe i'm just glad i'm still fucking free.
Bahahaha
<Glastnost and all that happy horseshit>
- Par

Subject: The Bottom line. From: The Parmaster Date: Sun Jan 21 10:05:38 1990
The bottom line is a crackdown. The phrack boys were just the start, i'm sure of it.

This is the time to watch yourself. No matter what you are into, whether it's just codes, cards, etc.

Apparently the government has seen the last straw. Unfortunately, with all of this in the news now, they will be able to get more government money to combat hackers.

And that's BAD fucking news for us. I think they are going after all the 'teachers' – the people who educate others into this sort of thing.

I wonder if they think that maybe these remote cases are linked in any way. The only way they can probably see is that we are hackers. And so that is where their energies will be put. To stop ALL hackers – and stop them BEFORE they can become a threat. After they wipe out the educators, that is. Just a theory.
- Par

Subject: Connection From: The Parmaster Date: Sun Jan 21 10:16:11 1990
Well, the only connection is disconnection, as Gandalf [a British hacker] would say.

That's what i'm putting on my epitaph. THE ONLY CONNECTION IS DISCONNECTION . . . Oh well, maybe i'll take a few of the buggers with me when they come for me.
- Par

Subject: Oh well. From: The Parmaster Date: Tue Jan 23 19:30:05 1990
'And now, the end is near. I've traveled each and every byway . . .' in the words of the King. Oh well. Who cares? He was a fat shit before he died anyway.

To everyone who's been a good friend of mine and help me cover up the fact that i don't know a fucking thing – i thank u. And to everyone else, take it easy and hang tough.

i was temporarily insane at the time

See you smart guys at the funny farm.
- Par

Subject: Par From: Erik Bloodaxe Date: Tue Jan 23 23:21:39 1990
Shit man, don't drink and think about things like that. It's not healthy, mentally or physically.

Come to Austin, Texas.

We'll keep you somewhere until we can get something worked out for you.

A year in minimum security (Club Fed) is better then chucking a whole life. Hell, you're 19!! I have discarded the 'permanent' solution for good. Dead people can't get laid, but people in federal prisons DO get conjugal visits!!!

Think of Theorem.

Call over here at whatever time you read this . . . I can see you are really getting worried, so just fucking call . . .
- Erik

Subject: Hah From: The Parmaster Date: Thu Jan 25 18:58:00 1990
Just keep in mind they see everything you do. Believe me. I know.
- Par

Subject: Well shit. From: The Parmaster Date: Mon Jan 29 15:45:05 1990
It's happening soon guys.

I wish i could have bought more time. And worked out a deal. But nada. They are nearby now.

I can tell which cars are theirs driving by outside. This is the weirdest case of Deja vu i've ever had.

Anyway got an interesting call today. It was from Eddie, one of the Bell systems computers.

It was rather fantasy like . . . Probably just his way of saying 'Goodbye'. Eddie was a good friend, smartest damn UNIX box around . . . And he called today to tell me goodbye.

Now i know i'm fucked. Thanks, Eddie, it's been real. (whoever you are) 'ok eddie, this one's for you'

Much Later,
- Par

Subject: Par From: Erik Bloodaxe Date: Mon Jan 29 19:36:38 1990
Buddy, Par, you are over the edge . . . lay off the weed. Not everyone with glasses and dark suits are Feds. Not all cars with generic hubcaps are government issue.

Well, hell, I don't know what the hell 'Eddie' is, but that's a real bizarre message you left.

Fly to Austin . . . like tomorrow . . . got plenty of places to stash you until things can be smoothed out for a calm transition.
- Erik

Subject: eehh. . . From: Phoenix [from Australia] Date: Tue Jan 30 07:25:59 1990
hmmmmmmmm. . .
<wonders real REAL thoughtufully> [sic] <and turns up a blank. . .>
what is young Par up to?

Subject: Par and Erik From: Daneel Olivaw Date: Mon Jan 29 21:10:00 1990
Erik, you aren't exactly the best person to be stashing people are you?

Subject: You know you are screwed when. From: The Parmaster Date: Wed Jan 31 14:26:04 1990
You know you are screwed when:

When surveyers survey your neighbors regularly, and wear sunglasses when it's like 11 degrees farenheit and cloudy as hell out.

When the same cars keep driving by outside day and night. (I've been thinking about providing coffee and doughnuts).
- Par

Subject: heh, Par From: The Mentor Date: Wed Jan 31 16:37:04 1990
Ummm. I wear sunglasses when it's 11 degrees and cloudy . . . so you can eliminate that one. :-)

Subject: Hmm, Par From: Phoenix Date: Thu Feb 01 10:22:46
1990
At least you arent getting shot at.

Subject: Par, why don't you . . . From: Ravage Date: Thu Feb 01
10:56:04 1990
Why not just go out and say 'hi' to the nice gentleman? If i kept
seeing the same people tooling around my neighborhood, i would
actively check them out if they seemed weird.

Subject: Par, jump 'em From: Aston Martin Date: Tue Feb 06
18:04:55 1990
What you could do is go out to one of the vans sitting in the street
(you know, the one with the two guys sitting in it all day) with a pair
of jumper cables. Tell them you've seen them sitting there all day
and you thought they were stuck. Ask them if they need a jump.
- Aston

Between these strange messages, Par often posted comments
on technical matters. Other hackers routinely asked him questions about X.25 networks. Unlike some hackers, Par almost
always offered some help. In fact, he believed that being 'one
of the teachers' made him a particular target. But his willingness to teach others so readily, combined with his relatively
humble, self-effacing demeanour, made Par popular among
many hackers. It was one reason he found so many places
to stay.

Spring arrived, brushing aside a few of the hardships of
a winter on the run, then summer. Par was still on the run,
still dodging the Secret Service's national hunt for the fugitive.
By autumn, Par had eluded law enforcement officials around
the United States for more than a year. The gloom of another
cold winter on the run sat on the horizon of Par's future, but
he didn't care. Anything, everything was bearable. He could
take anything Fate would dish up because he had something
to live for.

Theorem was coming to visit him again.

When Theorem arrived in New York in early 1991, the weather was bitterly cold. They travelled to Connecticut, where Par was staying in a share-house with friends.

Par was nervous about a lot of things, but mostly about whether things would be the same with Theorem. Within a few hours of her arrival, his fears were assuaged. Theorem felt as passionately about him as she had in California more than twelve months before. His own feelings were even stronger. Theorem was a liferaft of happiness in the growing turmoil of his life.

But things were different in the outside world. Life on the run with Theorem was grim. Constantly dependent on other people, on their charity, they were also subject to their petty whims.

A room-mate in the share-house got very drunk one night and picked a fight with one of Par's friends. It was a major row and the friend stormed out. In a fit of intoxicated fury, the drunk threatened to turn Par in to the authorities. Slurring his angry words, he announced he was going to call the FBI, CIA and Secret Service to tell them all where Par was living.

Par and Theorem didn't want to wait around to see if the drunk would be true to his word. They grabbed their coats and fled into the darkness. With little money, and no place else to stay, they walked around for hours in the blistering, cold wind. Eventually they decided they had no choice but to return to the house late at night, hopefully after the drunk had fallen asleep.

They sidled up to the front of the house, alert and on edge. It was quite possible the drunk had called every law enforcement agency his blurry mind could recall, in which case a collection of agents would be lying in wait. The street was deadly quiet. All the parked cars were deserted. Par peered in a darkened window but he couldn't see anything. He motioned for Theorem to follow him into the house.

Though she couldn't see Par's face, Theorem could feel his tension. Most of the time, she revelled in their closeness, a proximity which at times seemed to border on telepathy. But at this moment, the extraordinary gift of empathy felt like a curse. Theorem could feel Par's all-consuming paranoia, and it filled her with terror as they crept through the hall, checking each room. Finally they reached Par's room, expecting to find two or three Secret Service agents waiting patiently for them in the dark.

It was empty.

They climbed into bed and tried to get some sleep, but Theorem lay awake in the dark for a little while, thinking about the strange and fearful experience of returning to the house. Though she spoke to Par on the phone almost every day when they were apart, she realised she had missed something.

Being on the run for so long had changed Par.

Some time after she returned to Switzerland, Theorem's access to Altos shrivelled up and died. She had been logging in through her old university account but the university eventually killed her access since she was no longer a student. Without access to any X.25 network linked to the outside world, she couldn't logon to Altos. Although she was never involved with hacking, Theorem had become quite addicted to Altos. The loss of access to the Swiss X.25 network – and therefore to Altos – left her feeling very depressed. She told Par over the telephone, in sombre tones.

Par decide to make a little present for Theorem. While most hackers broke into computers hanging off the X.25 networks, Par broke into the computers of the companies which ran the X.25 networks. Having control over the machines owned by Telenet or Tymnet was real power. And as the master of X.25 networks, Par could simply create a special account – just for Theorem – on Tymnet.

When Par finished making the account, he leaned back in his chair feeling pretty pleased with himself.

Account name: Theorem.

Password: ParLovesMe!

Well, thought Par, she's going to have to type that in every time she gets on the Tymnet network. Altos might be filled with the world's best hackers, and they might even try to flirt with Theorem, but she'll be thinking of me every time she logs on, he thought.

Par called her on the telephone and gave her his special present. When he told her the password to her new account, Theorem laughed. She thought it was sweet.

And so did the MOD boys.

Masters of Deception, or Destruction – it depended on who told the story – was a New York-based gang of hackers. They thought it would be cool to hack Altos. It wasn't that easy to get Altos shell access, which Theorem had, and most people had to settle for using one of the 'guest' accounts. But it was much easier to hack Altos from a shell account than from a 'guest' account. Theorem's account would be the targeted jump-off point.

How did MOD get Theorem's Altos password? Most probably they were watching one of the X.25 gateways she used as she passed through Tymnet on her way to Altos. Maybe the MOD boys sniffed her password en route. Or maybe they were watching the Tymnet security officials who were watching that gateway.

In the end it didn't matter how MOD got Theorem's password on Altos. What mattered was that they changed her password. When Theorem couldn't get into Altos she was beside herself. She felt like a junkie going cold turkey. It was too much. And of course she couldn't reach Par. Because he was on the run, she had to wait for him to call her. In fact she couldn't reach any of her other friends on Altos to ask for help. How was she going to find them? They were all hackers. They chose handles so no-one would know their real names.

What Theorem didn't know was that, not only had she lost access to Altos, but the MOD boys were using her account to hack the Altos system. To the outside world it appeared as though she was doing it.

Theorem finally managed to get a third-hand message to Gandalf, a well-known British hacker. She sought him out for two reasons. First, he was a good friend and was therefore likely to help her out. Second, Gandalf had root access on Altos, which meant he could give her a new password or account.

Gandalf had established quite a reputation for himself in the computer underground through the hacking group 8lgm – The Eight-Legged Groove Machine, named after a British band. He and his friend, fellow British hacker Pad, had the best four legs in the chorus line. They were a world-class act, and certainly some of the best talent to come out of the British hacking scene. But Gandalf and, to a lesser extent, Pad had also developed a reputation for being arrogant. They rubbed some of the American hackers the wrong way. Not that Pad and Gandalf seemed to care. Their attitude was: We're good. We know it. Bugger off.

Gandalf disabled Theorem's account on Altos. He couldn't very well just change the password and then send the new one through the extended grapevine that Theorem had used to get a message through to him. Clearly, someone had targeted her account specifically. No way was he going to broadcast a new password for her account throughout the underground. But the trouble was that neither Par nor Theorem knew what Gandalf had done.

Meanwhile, Par called Theorem and got an earful. An angry Par vowed to find out just who the hell had been messing with her account.

When the MOD boys told Par they were the culprits, he was a bit surprised because he had always been on good terms with them. Par told them how upset Theorem had been, how she gave him an earful. Then an extraordinary thing happened. Corrupt, the toughest, baddest guy in MOD, the black kid from the roughest part of New York, the hacker who gave shit to everyone because he could, apologised to Par.

The MOD guys never apologised, even when they knew they were in the wrong. Apologies never got anyone very far on a New York City street. It was an attitude thing. 'I'm sorry, man' from Corrupt was the equivalent of a normal person licking the mud from the soles of your shoes.

The new password was: M0Dm0dM0D. That's the kind of guys they were.

Par was just signing off to try out the new password when Corrupt jumped in.

'Yeah, and ah, Par, there's something you should know.'

'Yeah?' Par answered, anxious to go.

'I checked out her mail. There was some stuff in it.'

Theorem's letters? Stuff? 'What kind of stuff?' he asked.

'Letters from Gandalf.'

'Yeah?'

'Friendly letters. Real friendly.'

Par wanted to know, but at the same time, he didn't. He could have arranged root access on Altos long ago if he'd really wanted it. But he didn't. He didn't want it because it would mean he could access Theorem's mail. And Par knew that if he could, he would. Theorem was popular on Altos and, being the suspicious type, Par knew he would probably take something perfectly innocent and read it the wrong way. Then he would get in a fight with Theorem, and their time together was too precious for that.

'Too friendly,' Corrupt went on. It must have been hard for him to tell Par. Snagging a friend's girlfriend's password and breaking into her account was one thing. There wasn't much wrong with that. But breaking that kind of news, well, that was harsh. Especially since Corrupt had worked with Gandalf in 8lgm.

'Thanks,' Par said finally. Then he took off.

When Par tried out the MOD password, it didn't work of course, because Gandalf had disabled the account. But Par didn't know that. Finding out that Theorem's account was disabled didn't bother him, but discovering who disabled it for her didn't make Par all that happy. Still, when he confronted Theorem, she denied that anything was going on between her and Gandalf.

What could Par do? He could believe Theorem or he could doubt her. Believing her was hard, but doubting her was painful. So he chose to believe her.

The incident made Theorem take a long look at Altos. It was doing bad things to her life. In the days that she was locked out of the German chat system, she had made the unpleasant discovery that she was completely addicted. And she didn't like it at all. Staring at her life with fresh eyes, she realised she had been ignoring her friends and her life in Switzerland. What on earth was she doing, spending every night in front of a computer screen?

So Theorem made a tough decision.

She decided to stop using Altos forever.

Bad things seemed to happen to The Parmaster around Thanksgiving.

In late November 1991, Par flew up from Virginia Beach to New York. An acquaintance named Morty Rosenfeld, who hung out with the MOD hackers a bit, had invited him to come for a visit. Par thought a trip to the City would do him good.

Morty wasn't exactly Par's best friend, but he was all right. He had been charged by the Feds a few months earlier for selling a password to a credit record company which resulted in credit card fraud. Par didn't go in for selling passwords, but to each his own. Morty wasn't too bad in the right dose. He had a place on Coney Island, which was hardly the Village in Manhattan, but close enough, and he had a fold-out sofa bed. It beat sleeping on the floor somewhere else.

Par hung out with Morty and a bunch of his friends, drinking and goofing around on Morty's computer.

One morning, Par woke up with a vicious hangover. His stomach was growling and there was nothing edible in the fridge, so he rang up and ordered pork fried rice from a Chinese take-away. Then he threw on some clothes and sat on the end of the sofa-bed, smoking a cigarette while he waited. He didn't start smoking until he was nineteen, some time late into his second year on the run. It calmed his nerves.

There was a knock at the front door. Par's stomach grumbled in response. As he walked toward the front door, he thought Pork Fried Rice, here I come. But when Par opened the front door, there was something else waiting for him.

The Secret Service.

Two men. An older, distinguished gentleman standing on the left and a young guy on the right. The young guy's eyes opened wide when he saw Par.

Suddenly, the young guy pushed Par, and kept pushing him. Small, hard, fast thrusts. Par couldn't get his balance. Each time he almost got his footing, the agent shoved the hacker backward again until he landed against the wall. The agent spun Par around so his face pressed against the wall and pushed a gun into his kidney. Then he slammed handcuffs on Par and started frisking him for weapons.

Par looked at Morty, now sobbing in the corner, and thought, You narced on me.

Once Par was safely cuffed, the agents flashed their badges to him. Then they took him outside, escorted him into a waiting car and drove into Manhattan. They pulled up in front of the World Trade Center and when Par got out the young agent swapped the cuffs so Par's hands were in front of him.

As the agents escorted the handcuffed fugitive up a large escalator, the corporate world stared at the trio. Business men and women in prim navy suits, secretaries and office boys all watched wide-eyed from the opposite escalator. And if the handcuffs weren't bad enough, the younger Secret Service agent was wearing a nylon jacket with a noticeable gun-shaped lump in the front pouch.

Why are these guys bringing me in the front entrance? Par kept thinking. Surely there must be a backdoor, a car park back entrance. Something not quite so public.

The view from any reasonably high floor of the World Trade Center is breathtaking, but Par never got a chance to enjoy the vista. He was hustled into a windowless room and handcuffed to a chair. The agents moved in and out, sorting out paperwork details. They uncuffed him briefly while they inked his fingers and rolled them across sheets of paper. Then they made him give handwriting samples, first his right hand then his left.

Par didn't mind being cuffed to the chair so much, but he found the giant metal cage in the middle of the fingerprinting room deeply disturbing. It reminded him of an animal cage, the kind used in old zoos.

The two agents who arrested him left the room, but another one came in. And the third agent was far from friendly. He began playing the bad cop, railing at Par, shouting at him, trying to unnerve him. But no amount of yelling from the agent could rile Par as much as the nature of the questions he asked.

The agent didn't ask a single question about Citibank. Instead, he demanded to hear everything Par knew about TRW.

All Par's worst nightmares about the killer spy satellite, about becoming the man who knew too much, rushed through his mind.

Par refused to answer. He just sat silently, staring at the agent.

Eventually, the older agent came back into the room, dragged the pitbull agent away and took him outside for a whispered chat. After that, the pitbull agent was all sweetness and light with Par. Not another word about TRW.

Par wondered why a senior guy from the Secret Service would tell his minion to clam up about the defence contractor? What was behind the sudden silence? The abrupt shift alarmed Par almost as much as the questions had in the first place.

The agent told Par he would be remanded in custody while awaiting extradition to California. After all the paperwork had been completed, they released him from the handcuffs and let him stand to stretch. Par asked for a cigarette and one of the agents gave him one. Then a couple of other agents – junior guys – came in.

The junior agents were very friendly. One of them even shook Par's hand and introduced himself. They knew all about the hacker. They knew his voice from outgoing messages on voicemail boxes he had created for himself. They knew what he looked like from his California police file, and maybe even surveillance photos. They knew his personality from telephone bridge conversations which had been recorded and from the details of his Secret Service file. Perhaps they had even tracked him around the country, following a trail of clues left in his flightpath. Whatever research they had done, one thing was clear. These agents felt like they knew him intimately – Par the person, not just Par the hacker.

It was a strange sensation. These guys Par had never met before chatted with him about the latest Michael Jackson video as if he was a neighbour or friend just returned from out of town. Then they took him further uptown, to a police station, for more extradition paperwork.

This place was no World Trade Center deluxe office. Par stared at the peeling grey paint in the ancient room, and then watched officers typing out reports using the two-finger hunt-and-peck method on electric typewriters – not a computer in sight. The officers didn't cuff Par to the desk. Par was in the heart of a police station and there was no way he was going anywhere.

While the officer handling Par was away from his desk for ten minutes, Par felt bored. So he began flipping through the folders with information on other cases on the officer's desk. They were heavy duty fraud cases – mafia and drug-money laundering – cases which carried reference to FBI involvement. These people looked hairy.

That day, Par had a quick appearance in court, just long enough to be given protective custody in the Manhattan detention complex known as the Tombs while he waited for the authorities from California to come and pick him up.

Par spent almost a week in the Tombs. By day three, he was climbing the walls. It was like being buried alive.

During that week, Par had almost no contact with other human beings – a terrible punishment for someone with so much need for a continual flow of new information. He never left his cell. His jailer slid trays of food into his cell and took them away.

On day six, Par went nuts. He threw a fit, began screaming and banging on the door. He yelled at the guard. Told him none too nicely that he wanted to 'get the fuck outta here'. The guard said he would see if he could get Par transferred to Rikers Island, New York's notorious jail. Par didn't care if he was transferred to the moon, as long as he got out of solitary confinement.

Except for the serial killer, the north infirmary at Rikers Island was a considerable improvement on the Tombs. Par was only locked in his cell at night. During the day he was free to roam inside the infirmary area with other prisoners. Some of them were there because the authorities didn't want to put them in with the hardened criminals, and some of them were there because they were probably criminally insane.

It was an eclectic bunch. A fireman turned jewellery heister. A Colombian drug lord. A chop-shop ringleader, who collected more than 300 stolen cars, chopped them up, reassembled them as new and then sold them off. A man who killed a homosexual for coming onto him. 'Faggot Killer', as he was known inside, hadn't meant to kill anyone: things had gotten a little out of hand; next thing he knew, he was facing ten to twelve on a murder rap.

Par wasn't wild about the idea of hanging out with a murderer, but he was nervous about what could happened to a young man in jail. Forging a friendship with Faggot Killer would send the right message. Besides, the guy seemed to be OK. Well, as long as you didn't look at him the wrong way.

On his first day, Par also met Kentucky, a wild-eyed man who introduced himself by thrusting a crumpled newspaper article into the hacker's hand and saying, 'That's me'. The article, titled 'Voices Told Him to Kill', described how police had apprehended a serial killer believed to be responsible for a dozen murders, maybe more. During his last murder, Kentucky told Par he had killed a woman – and then written the names of the aliens who had commanded him to do it on the walls of her apartment in her blood.

The jewellery heister tried to warn Par to stay away from Kentucky, who continued to liaise with the aliens on a regular basis. But it was too late. Kentucky decided that he didn't like the young hacker. He started shouting at Par, picking a fight. Par stood there, stunned and confused. How should he deal with an aggravated serial killer? And what the hell was he doing in jail with a serial killer raving at him anyway? It was all too much.

The jewellery heister rushed over to Kentucky and tried to calm him down, speaking in soothing tones. Kentucky glowered at Par, but he stopped yelling.

A few days into his stay at Rikers, Faggot Killer invited Par to join in a game of Dungeons and Dragons. It beat watching TV talk shows all day, so Par agreed. He sat down at the metal picnic table where Faggot Killer had laid out the board.

So it was that Par, the twenty-year-old computer hacker from California, the X.25 network whiz kid, came to play Dungeons and Dragons with a jewellery thief, a homophobic murderer and a mad serial killer in Rikers Island. Par found himself marvelling at the surrealism of the situation.

Kentucky threw himself into the game. He seemed to get off on killing hobgoblins.

'I'll take my halberd,' Kentucky began with a smile, 'and I stab this goblin.' The next player began to make his move, but Kentucky interrupted. 'I'm not done,' he said slowly, as a demonic grin spread across his face. 'And I slice it. And cut it. It bleeds everywhere.' Kentucky's face tensed with pleasure.

The other three players shifted uncomfortably in their seats. Par looked at Faggot Killer with nervous eyes.

'And I thrust a knife into its heart,' Kentucky continued, the volume of his voice rising with excitement. 'Blood, blood, everywhere blood. And I take the knife and hack him. And I hack and hack and hack.'

Kentucky jumped up from the table and began shouting, thrusting one arm downward through the air with an imaginary dagger, 'And I hack and I hack and I hack!'

Then Kentucky went suddenly still. Everyone at the table froze. No-one dared move for fear of driving him over the edge. Par's stomach had jumped into his throat. He tried to gauge how many seconds it would take to extricate himself from the picnic table and make a break for the far side of the room.

In a daze, Kentucky walked away from the table, leaned his forehead against the wall and began mumbling quietly. The jewellery heister slowly followed and spoke to him briefly in hushed tones before returning to the table.

One of the guards had heard the ruckus and came up to the table.

'Is that guy OK?' he asked the jewellery heister while pointing to Kentucky.

Not even if you used that term loosely, Par thought.

'Leave him alone,' the heister told the guard. 'He's talking to the aliens.'

'Right.' The guard turned around and left.

Every day, a nurse brought around special medicine for Kentucky. In fact, Kentucky was zonked out most of the time on a cup of horrible, smelly liquid. Sometimes, though, Kentucky secreted his medicine away and traded it with another prisoner who wanted to get zonked out for a day or so.

Those were bad days, the days when Kentucky had sold his medication. It was on one of those days that he tried to kill Par.

Par sat on a metal bench, talking to other prisoners, when suddenly he felt an arm wrap around his neck. He tried to turn around, but couldn't.

'Here. I'll show you how I killed this one guy,' Kentucky whispered to Par.

'No – No – ' Par started to say, but Kentucky's biceps began pressing against Par's Adam's apple. It was a vice-like grip.

'Yeah. Like this. I did it like this,' Kentucky said as he tensed his muscle and pulled backward.

'No! Really, you don't need to. It's OK,' Par gasped. No air. His arms flailing in front of him.

I'm done for, Par thought. My life is over. Hacker Murdered by Serial Killer in Rikers Island. 'Aliens Told Me to Do It.'

The omnipresent jewellery heister came up to Kentucky and started cooing in his ear to let Par go. Then, just when Par thought he was about to pass out, the jewellery heister pulled Kentucky off him.

Par reminded himself to always sit with his back against the wall.

Finally, after almost a month behind bars, Par was informed that an officer from the Monterey County sheriff's office was coming to take him back to California. Par had agreed to be extradited to California after seeing the inside of New York's jails. Dealing with the federal prosecutor in New York had also helped make up his mind.

The US Attorney's Office in New York gave Richard Rosen, who had taken the case on again, a real headache. They didn't play ball. They played 'Queen for a Day'.

The way they negotiated reminded Rosen of an old American television game of that name. The show's host pulled some innocent soul off the street, seated her on a garish throne, asked her questions and then gave her prizes. The US Attorney's Office in New York wanted to seat Par on a throne, of sorts, to ask him lots of questions. At the end of the unfettered interrogation, they would hand out prizes. Prison terms. Fines. Convictions. As they saw fit. No guaranteed sentences. They would decide what leniency, if any, he would get at the end of the game.

Par knew what they were looking for: evidence against the MOD boys. He wasn't having a bar of that. The situation stank, so Par decided not to fight the extradition to California. Anything had to be better than New York, with its crazy jail inmates and arrogant federal prosecutors.

The officer from the Monterey sheriff's office picked Par up on 17 December 1991.

Par spent the next few weeks in jail in California, but this
time he wasn't in any sort of protective custody. He had to share
a cell with Mexican drug dealers and other mafia, but at least
he knew his way around these people. And unlike the some of
the people at Rikers, they weren't stark raving lunatics.

Richard Rosen took the case back, despite Par's having
skipped town the first time, which Par thought was pretty good
of the lawyer. But Par had no idea how good it would be for
him until it came to his court date.

Par called Rosen from the jail, to talk about the case. Rosen
had some big news for him.

'Plead guilty. You're going to plead guilty to everything,'
he told Par.

Par thought Rosen had lost his marbles.

'No. We can win this case if you plead guilty,' Rosen
assured him.

Par sat dumbfounded at the other end of the phone.

'Trust me,' the lawyer said.

The meticulous Richard Rosen had found a devastating
weapon.

On 23 December 1991, Par pleaded guilty to two charges in
Monterey County Juvenile Court. He admitted everything. The
whole nine yards. Yes, I am The Parmaster. Yes, I broke into
computers. Yes, I took thousands of credit card details from a
Citibank machine. Yes, yes, yes.

In some way, the experience was cathartic, but only because
Par knew Rosen had a brilliant ace up his sleeve.

Rosen had rushed the case to be sure it would be heard in
juvenile court, where Par would get a more lenient sentence.
But just because Rosen was in a hurry didn't mean he was
sloppy. When he went through Par's file with a fine-toothed
comb he discovered the official papers declared Par's birthday
to be 15 January 1971. In fact, Par's birthday was some days
earlier, but the DA's office didn't know that.

Under California law, a juvenile court has jurisdiction
over citizens under the age of 21. You can only be tried and

sentenced in a juvenile court if you committed the crimes in question while under the age of eighteen and you are still under the age of 21 when you plead and are sentenced.

Par was due to be sentenced on 13 January but on 8 January Rosen applied for the case to be thrown out. When Deputy DA David Schott asked why, Rosen dropped his bomb.

Par had already turned 21 and the juvenile court had no authority to pass sentence over him. Further, in California, a case cannot be moved into an adult court if the defendant has already entered a plea in a juvenile one. Because Par had already done that, his case couldn't be moved. The matter was considered 'dealt with' in the eyes of the law.

The Deputy DA was flabbergasted. He spluttered and spewed. The DA's office had dropped the original charges from a felony to a misdemeanour. They had come to the table. How could this happen? Par was a fugitive. He had been on the run for more than two years from the frigging Secret Service, for Christ's sake. There was no way – NO WAY – he was going to walk out of that courtroom scot-free.

The court asked Par to prove his birthday. A quick driver's licence search at the department of motor vehicles showed Par and his lawyer were telling the truth. So Par walked free.

When he stepped outside the courthouse, Par turned his face toward the sun. After almost two months in three different jails on two sides of the continent, the sun felt magnificent. Walking around felt wonderful. Just wandering down the street made him happy.

However, Par never really got over being on the run.

From the time he walked free from the County Jail in Salinas, California, he continued to move around the country, picking up temporary work here and there. But he found it hard to settle in one place. Worst of all, strange things began happening to him. Well, they had always happened to him, but they were getting stranger by the month. His perception of reality was changing.

There was the incident in the motel room. As Par sat in the Las Vegas Travelodge on one of his cross-country treks, he perceived someone moving around in the room below his. Par strained to hear. It seemed like the man was talking to him. What was the man trying to tell him? Par couldn't quite catch the words, but the more he listened, the more Par was sure he had a message for him which he didn't want anyone else to hear. It was very frustrating. No matter how hard he tried, no matter how he put his ear down to the floor or against the wall, Par couldn't make it out.

The surreal experiences continued. As Par described it, on a trip down to Mexico, he began feeling quite strange, so he went to the US consulate late one afternoon to get some help. But everyone in the consulate behaved bizarrely.

They asked him for some identification, and he gave them his wallet. They took his Social Security card and his California identification card and told him to wait. Par believed they were going to pull up information about him on a computer out the back. While waiting, his legs began to tremble and a continuous shiver rolled up and down his spine. It wasn't a smooth, fluid shiver, it was jerky. He felt like he was sitting at the epicentre of an earthquake and it frightened him. The consulate staff just stared at him.

Finally Par stopped shaking. The other staff member returned and asked him to leave.

'No-one can help you here,' he told Par.

Why was the consular official talking to him like that? What did he mean – Par had to leave? What was he really trying to say? Par couldn't understand him. Another consular officer came around to Par, carrying handcuffs. Why was everyone behaving in such a weird way? That computer. Maybe they had found some special message next to his name on that computer.

Par tried to explain the situation, but the consulate staff didn't seem to understand. He told them about how he had been on the run from the Secret Service for two and a half years, but that just got him queer looks. Blank faces. No comprehende. The more he explained, the blanker the faces became.

The consular officials told him that the office was closing for the day. He would have to leave the building. But Par suspected that was just an excuse. A few minutes later, a Mexican policeman showed up. He talked with one of the consular officials, who subsequently handed him what Par perceived to be a slip of paper wrapped around a wad of peso notes.

Two more policemen came into the consulate. One of them turned to Par and said, 'Leave!' but Par didn't answer. So the Mexican police grabbed Par by the arms and legs and carried him out of the consulate. Par felt agitated and confused and, as they crossed the threshold out of the consulate, he screamed.

They put him in a police car and took him to a jail, where they kept him overnight.

The next day, they released Par and he wandered the city aimlessly before ending up back at the US consulate. The same consular officer came up to him and asked how he was feeling.

Par said, 'OK.'

Then Par asked if the official could help him get back to the border, and he said he could. A few minutes later a white van picked up Par and took him to the border crossing. When they arrived, Par asked the driver if he could have $2 so he could buy a ticket for the train. The driver gave it to him.

Par boarded the train with no idea of where he was headed.

Theorem visited Par in California twice in 1992 and the relationship continued to blossom. Par tried to find work so he could pay her back the $20 000 she had lent him during his years on the run and during his court case, but it was hard going. People didn't seem to want to hire him.

'You don't have any computer skills,' they told him. He calmly explained that, yes, he did indeed have computer skills.

'Well, which university did you get your degree from?' they asked.

No, he hadn't got his skills at any university.

'Well, which companies did you get your work experience from?'

No, he hadn't learned his skills while working for a company.

'Well, what did you do from 1989 to 1992?' the temp agency staffer inevitably asked in an exasperated voice.

'I . . . ah . . . travelled around the country.' What else was Par going to say? How could he possibly answer that question?

If he was lucky, the agency might land him a data-entry job at $8 per hour. If he was less fortunate, he might end up doing clerical work for less than that.

By 1993, things had become a little rocky with Theorem. After four and a half years together, they broke up. The distance was too great, in every sense. Theorem wanted a more stable life – maybe not a traditional Swiss family with three children and a pretty chalet in the Alps, but something more than Par's transient life on the road.

The separation was excruciatingly painful for both of them. Conversation was strained for weeks after the decision. Theorem kept thinking she had made a mistake. She kept wanting to ask Par to come back. But she didn't.

Par drowned himself in alcohol. Shots of tequila, one after the other. Scull it. Slam the glass down. Fill it to the top. Throw back another. After a while, he passed out. Then he was violently ill for days, but somehow he didn't mind. It was cleansing to be so ill.

Somewhere along the way, Rosen managed to get Par's things returned from the Secret Service raids. He passed the outdated computer and other equipment back to Par, along with disks, print-outs and notes.

Par gathered up every shred of evidence from his case, along with a bottle of Jack Daniel's, and made a bonfire. He shredded print-outs, doused them in lighter fluid and set them alight. He fed the disks into the fire and watched them melt in the flames. He flipped through the pages and pages of notes and official reports and let them pull out particular memories. Then he crumpled up each one and tossed it in the fire. He even sprinkled a little Jack Daniel's across the top for good measure.

As he pulled the pages from a Secret Service report, making them into tight paper balls, something caught his eye and made him wonder. Many hackers around the world had been busted in a series of raids following the first Thanksgiving raid at Par's house back in 1988. Erik Bloodaxe, the MOD boys, the LOD boys, The Atlanta Three, Pad and Gandalf, the Australians – they had all been either busted or raided during 1989, 1990 and 1991.

How were the raids connected? Were the law-enforcement agencies on three different continents really organised enough to coordinate worldwide attacks on hackers?

The Secret Service report gave him a clue. It said that in December 1988, two informants had called Secret Service special agents in separate divisions with information about Par. The informants – both hackers – told the Secret Service that Par was not the 'Citibank hacker' the agency was looking for. They said the real 'Citibank hacker' was named Phoenix.

Phoenix from Australia.

5 | THE HOLY GRAIL

There it was, in black and white. Two articles by Helen Meredith in *The Australian* in January 1989.[1] The whole Australian computer underground was buzzing with the news.

The first article appeared on 14 January:

Citibank hackers score $500 000

An elite group of Australian hackers has lifted more than $US500 000 ($580 000) out of America's Citibank in one of the more daring hacking crimes in Australia's history.

Australian federal authorities were reported late yesterday to be working with American authorities to pin down the Australian connection involving hackers in Melbourne and Sydney.

These are the elite 'freekers' of white collar crime . . .

The Australian connection is reported to have used a telephone in the foyer of Telecom's headquarters at

199 William Street in Melbourne to send a 2600-hertz signal giving them access to a trunk line and ultimately to a managerial access code for Citibank.

Sources said last night the hackers had lifted $US563000 from the US bank and transferred it into several accounts. The money has now been withdrawn ...

Meanwhile, Victorian police were reported yesterday to be systematically searching the homes of dozens of suspects in a crackdown on computer hackers ...

An informed source said Criminal Investigation Bureau officers armed with search warrants were now searching through the belongings of the hacking community and expected to find hundreds of thousands of dollars of goods.

An informed source said Criminal Investigation Bureau officers armed with search warrants were now searching through the belongings of the hacking community and expected to find hundreds of thousands of dollars of goods.

The second article was published ten days later:

Hackers list card hauls on boards

Authorities remain sceptical of the latest reports of an international hacking and phreaking ring and its Australian connection.

Yesterday, however, evidence continued to stream into the Melbourne based bulletin boards under suspicion ...

In the latest round of bulletin board activity, a message from a United States hacker known as Captain Cash provided the Australian connection with the latest news on Australian credit cards, provided by local hackers, and their illegal use by US hackers to the value of $US362018 ($416112).

The information was taken from a computer bulletin board system known as Pacific Island and used actively by the Australian connection.

The message read: 'OK on the 5353 series which we are closing today – Mastercard $109 400.50. On the 4564 series – Visa which I'll leave open for a week

$209 417.90. And on good old don't leave home without someone else's: $43 200.

'Making a grand total of

$362 018.40!

'Let's hear it for our Aussie friends!

'I hear they are doing just as well!

'They are sending more numbers on the 23rd! Great!

'They will be getting 10% as usual . . . a nice bonus of $36 200.00!'

The bulletin board also contained advice for phreakers on using telephones in Telecom's 199 William Street headquarters and the green phones at Spencer Street Station in Melbourne – to make free international calls . . .

Phoenix, another local bulletin board user, listed prices for 'EXTC'- tablets . . .

Late Friday, *The Australian* received evidence suggesting a break-in of the US Citibank network by Australian hackers known as The Realm . . .

The gang's US connection is believed to be based in Milwaukee and Houston. US Federal authorities have already raided US hackers involved in Citibank break-ins in the US.

A covert operation of the Bureau of Criminal Intelligence has had the Australian connection under surveillance and last week took delivery of six months' of evidence from the Pacific Island board and associated boards going by the name of Zen and Megaworks . . .

The Australian hackers include a number of Melbourne people, some teenagers, suspected or already convicted of crimes including fraud, drug use and car theft. Most are considered to be at the least, digital voyeurs, at worst criminals with a possible big crime connection.

The information received by *The Australian* amounts to a confession on the part of the Australian hackers to involvement in the break-in of the US Citibank network as well as advice on phreaking . . . and bank access.

The following is taken directly from the bulletin board . . . It was stored in a private mailbox on the board and is from a hacker known as Ivan Trotsky to one who uses the name Killer Tomato:

'OK this is what's been happening . . .

'While back a Sysop had a call from the Feds, they wanted Force's, Phoenix's, Nom's, Brett MacMillan's and my names in connection with some hacking The Realm had done and also with some carding meant to have been done too.

'Then in the last few days I get info passed to me that the Hack that was done to the Citibank in the US which has led to arrests over there also had connections to Force and Electron . . .'

DPG monitoring service spokesman, Mr Stuart Gill, said he believed the Pacific Island material was only the tip of the iceberg.

'They're far better organised than the police,' he said.

'Unless everyone gets their act together and we legislate against it, we'll still be talking about the same things this time next year.'

Yesterday, the South Australian police started an operation to put bulletin boards operating in that state under surveillance.

And in Western Australia, both political parties agreed

they would proceed with an inquiry into computer hacking, whoever was in government.

The Victoria Police fraud squad last week announced it had set up a computer crime squad that would investigate complaints of computer fraud.

The articles were painful reading for most in the computer underground.

Who was this Captain Cash? Who was the Killer Tomato? Was it Stuart Gill? Was the underground rife with credit card frauders? No. They formed only a very small part of that community. Had the Melbourne hackers stolen half a million dollars from Citibank? Absolutely not. A subsequent police investigation determined this allegation to be a complete fabrication.

How had six months' worth of messages from PI and Zen found their way into the hands of the Victoria Police Bureau of Criminal Intelligence? Members of the underground had their suspicions.

To some, Stuart Gill's role in the underground appeared to be that of an information trader. He would feed a police agency information, and garner a little new material from it in exchange. He then amalgamated the new and old material and delivered the new package to another police agency, which provided him a little more material to add to the pot. Gill appeared to play the same game in the underground.

A few members of the underground, particularly PI and Zen regulars Mentat and Brett MacMillan, suspected chicanery and began fighting a BBS-based war to prove their point. In early 1989, MacMillan posted a message stating that Hackwatch was not registered as a business trading name belonging to Stuart Gill at the Victorian Corporate Affairs office. Further, he stated, DPG Monitoring Services did not exist as an official registered business trading name either. MacMillan then stunned the underground by announcing that he had registered the name Hackwatch himself, presumably to stop Stuart Gill's media appearances as a Hackwatch spokesman.

Many in the underground felt duped by Gill, but they weren't the only ones. Soon some journalists and police would feel the same way. Stuart Gill wasn't even his real name.

What Gill really wanted, some citizens in the underground came to believe, was a public platform from which he could whip up hacker hype and then demand the introduction of tough new anti-hacking laws. In mid-1989, the Commonwealth Government did just that, enacting the first federal computer crime laws.

It wasn't the journalists' fault. For example, in one case Helen Meredith had asked Gill for verification and he had referred her to Superintendent Tony Warren, of the Victoria Police, who had backed him up. A reporter couldn't ask for better verification than that.

And why wouldn't Warren back Gill? A registered ISU informer, Gill also acted as a consultant, adviser, confidant and friend to various members of the Victoria Police. He was close to both Warren and, later, to Inspector Chris Cosgriff. From 1985 to 1987, Warren had worked at the Bureau of Criminal Intelligence (BCI). After that, he was transferred to the Internal Investigations Department (IID), where he worked with Cosgriff who joined IID in 1988.

Over a six-month period in 1992, Tony Warren received more than 200 phone calls from Stuart Gill – 45 of them to his home number. Over an eighteen-month period in 1991–92, Chris Cosgriff made at least 76 personal visits to Gill's home address and recorded 316 phone calls with him.[2]

The Internal Security Unit (ISU) investigated corruption within the police force. If you had access to ISU, you knew everything that the Victoria Police officially knew about corruption within its ranks. Its information was highly sensitive, particularly since it could involve one police officer dobbing in another. However, a 1993 Victorian Ombudsman's report concluded that Cosgriff leaked a large amount of confidential

ISU material to Gill, and that Warren's relationship with Gill was inappropriate.[3]

When Craig Bowen (aka Thunderbird1) came to believe in 1989 that he had been duped by Gill, he retreated into a state of denial and depression. The PI community had trusted him. He entered his friendship with Gill a bright-eyed, innocent young man looking for adventure. He left the friendship betrayed and gun-shy.

Sad-eyed and feeling dark on the world, Craig Bowen turned off PI and Zen forever.

Sitting at his computer sometime in the second half of 1989, Force stared at his screen without seeing anything, his mind a million miles away. The situation was bad, very bad, and lost in thought, he toyed with his mouse absent-mindedly, thinking about how to deal with this problem.

The problem was that someone in Melbourne was going to be busted.

Force wanted to discount the secret warning, to rack it up as just another in a long line of rumours which swept through the underground periodically, but he knew he couldn't do that. The warning was rock solid; it had come from Gavin.*

The way Force told it, his friend Gavin worked as a contractor to Telecom by day and played at hacking at night. He was Force's little secret, who he kept from the other members of The Realm. Gavin was definitely not part of the hacker BBS scene. He was older, he didn't even have a handle and he hacked alone, or with Force, because he saw hacking in groups as risky.

As a Telecom contractor, Gavin had the kind of access to computers and networks which most hackers could only dream about. He also had good contacts inside Telecom – the kind who might answer a few tactfully worded questions about tele-

---

*   Gavin's name has been changed to protect his identity.

phone taps and line traces, or might know a bit about police investigations requiring Telecom's help.

Force had met Gavin while buying some second-hand equipment through the *Trading Post*. They hit it off, became friends and soon began hacking together. Under the cover of darkness, they would creep into Gavin's office after everyone else had gone home and hack all night. At dawn, they tidied up and quietly left the building. Gavin went home, showered and returned to work as if nothing had happened.

Gavin introduced Force to trashing. When they weren't spending the night in front of his terminal, Gavin crawled through Telecom's dumpsters looking for pearls of information on crumpled bits of office paper. Account names, passwords, dial-up modems, NUAs – people wrote all sorts of things down on scrap paper and then threw it out the next day when they didn't need it any more.

According to Force, Gavin moved offices frequently, which made it easier to muddy the trail. Even better, he worked from offices which had dozens of employees making hundreds of calls each day. Gavin and Force's illicit activities were buried under a mound of daily legitimate transactions.

The two hackers trusted each other; in fact Gavin was the only person to whom Force revealed the exact address of the CitiSaudi machine. Not even Phoenix, rising star of The Realm and Force's favoured protégé, was privy to all the secrets of Citibank uncovered during Force's network explorations.

Force had shared some of this glittering prize with Phoenix, but not all of it. Just a few of the Citibank cards – token trophies – and general information about the Citibank network. Believing the temptation to collect vast numbers of cards and use them would be too great for the young Phoenix, Force tried to keep the exact location of the Citibank machine a secret. He knew that Phoenix might eventually find the Citibank system on his own, and there was little he could do to stop him. But Force was determined that he wouldn't help Phoenix get himself into trouble.

The Citibank network had been a rich source of systems –
something Force also kept to himself. The more he explored,
the more he found in the network. Soon after his first discovery
of the CitiSaudi system, he found a machine called CitiGreece
which was just as willing to dump card details as its Saudi-
American counterpart. Out of fifteen or so credit cards Force
discovered on the system, only two appeared to be valid. He
figured the others were test cards and that this must be a new
site. Not long after the discovery of the CitiGreece machine, he
discovered similar embryonic sites in two other countries.

Force liked Phoenix and was impressed by the new hacker's
enthusiasm and desire to learn about computer networks.

Force introduced Phoenix to Minerva, just as Craig Bowen
had done for Force some years before. Phoenix learned quickly
and came back for more. He was hungry and, in Force's dis-
cerning opinion, very bright. Indeed, Force saw a great deal
of himself in the young hacker. They were from a similarly
comfortable, educated middle-class background. They were
also both a little outside the mainstream. Force's family were
migrants to Australia. Some of Phoenix's family lived in Israel,
and his family was very religious.

Phoenix attended one of the most Orthodox Jewish schools
in Victoria, a place which described itself as a 'modern orthodox
Zionist' institution. Nearly half the subjects offered in year 9
were in Jewish Studies, all the boys wore yarmulkes and the
school expected students to be fluent in Hebrew by the time
they graduated.

In his first years at the school, Phoenix had acquired the
nickname 'The Egg'. Over the following years he became a
master at playing the game – jumping through hoops to please
teachers. He learned that doing well in religious studies was a
good way to ingratiate himself to teachers, as well as his parents
and, in their eyes at least, he became the golden-haired boy.

Anyone scratching below the surface, however, would find
the shine of the golden-haired boy was merely gilt. Despite his
success in school and his matriculation, Phoenix was having

trouble. He had been profoundly affected by the bitter break-up and divorce of his parents when he was about fourteen.

After the divorce, Phoenix was sent to boarding school in Israel for about six months. On his return to Melbourne, he lived with his younger sister and mother at his maternal grandmother's house. His brother, the middle child, lived with his father.

School friends sometimes felt awkward visiting Phoenix at home. One of his best friends found it difficult dealing with Phoenix's mother, whose vivacity sometimes bordered on the neurotic and shrill. His grandmother was a chronic worrier, who pestered Phoenix about using the home phone line during thunderstorms for fear he would be electrocuted. The situation with Phoenix's father wasn't much better. A manager at Telecom, he seemed to waver between appearing disinterested or emotionally cold and breaking into violent outbursts of anger.

But it was Phoenix's younger brother who seemed to be the problem child. He ran away from home at around seventeen and dealt in drugs before eventually finding his feet. Yet, unlike Phoenix, his brother's problems had been laid bare for all to see. Hitting rock bottom forced him to take stock of his life and come to terms with his situation.

In contrast, Phoenix found less noticeable ways of expressing his rebellion. Among them was his enthusiasm for tools of power – the martial arts, weapons such as swords and staffs, and social engineering. During his final years of secondary school, while still living at his grandmother's home, Phoenix took up hacking. He hung around various Melbourne BBSes, and then he developed an on-line friendship with Force.

Force watched Phoenix's hacking skills develop with interest and after a couple of months he invited him to join The Realm. It was the shortest initiation of any Realm member, and the vote to include the new hacker was unanimous. Phoenix proved to be a valuable member, collecting information about new systems and networks for The Realm's databases. At their peak of hacking activity, Force and Phoenix spoke on the phone almost every day.

Phoenix's new-found acceptance contrasted with the position of Electron, who visited The Realm regularly for a few months in 1988. As Phoenix basked in the warmth of Force's approval, the eighteen-year-old Electron felt the chill of his increasing scorn.

Force eventually turfed Electron and his friend, Powerspike, out of his exclusive Melbourne club of hackers. Well, that was how Force told it. He told the other members of The Realm that Electron had committed two major sins. The first was that he had been wasting resources by using accounts on OTC's Minerva system to connect to Altos, which meant the accounts would be immediately tracked and killed.

Minerva admins such as Michael Rosenberg – sworn enemy of The Realm – recognised the Altos NUA. Rosenberg was OTC's best defence against hackers. He had spent so much time trying to weed them out of Minerva that he knew their habits by heart: hack, then zoom over to Altos for a chat with fellow hackers, then hack some more.

Most accounts on Minerva were held by corporations. How many legitimate users from ANZ Bank would visit Altos? None. So when Rosenberg saw an account connecting to Altos, he silently observed what the hacker was doing – in case he bragged on the German chat board – then changed the password and notified the client, in an effort to lock the hacker out for good.

Electron's second sin, according to Force, was that he had been withholding hacking information from the rest of the group. Force's stated view – though it didn't seem to apply to him personally – was one in, all in.

It was a very public expulsion. Powerspike and Electron told each other they didn't really care. As they saw it, they might have visited The Realm BBS now and then but they certainly weren't members of The Realm. Electron joked with Powerspike, 'Who would want to be a member of a no-talent outfit like The Realm?' Still, it must have hurt. Hackers in the period 1988–90 depended on each other for information. They honed their skills in a community which shared intelligence and they grew to rely on the pool of information.

Months later, Force grudgingly allowed Electron to rejoin The Realm, but the relationship remained testy. When Electron finally logged in again, he found a file in the BBS entitled 'Scanner stolen from the Electron'. Force had found a copy of Electron's VMS scanner on an overseas computer while Electron was in exile and had felt no qualms about pinching it for The Realm.

Except that it wasn't a scanner. It was a VMS Trojan. And there was a big difference. It didn't scan for the addresses of computers on a network. It snagged passwords when people connected from their VMS computers to another machine over an X.25 network. Powerspike cracked up laughing when Electron told him. 'Well,' he told Powerspike, 'Mr Bigshot Force might know something about Prime computers, but he doesn't know a hell of a lot about VMS.'

Despite Electron's general fall from grace, Phoenix talked to the outcast because they shared the obsession. Electron was on a steep learning curve and, like Phoenix, he was moving fast – much faster than any of the other Melbourne hackers.

When Phoenix admitted talking to Electron regularly, Force tried to pull him away, but without luck. Some of the disapproval was born of Force's paternalistic attitude toward the Australian hacking scene. He considered himself to be a sort of godfather in the hacking community. But Force was also increasingly concerned at Phoenix's ever more flagrant taunting of computer security bigwigs and system admins. In one incident, Phoenix knew a couple of system admins and security people were waiting on a system to trap him by tracing his network connections. He responded by sneaking into the computer unnoticed and quietly logging off each admin. Force laughed about it at the time, but privately the story made him more than a little nervous.

Phoenix enjoyed pitting himself against the pinnacles of the computer security industry. He wanted to prove he was better, and he frequently upset people because often he was. Strangely, though, Force's protégé also thought that if he told these experts about a few of the holes in their systems, he would somehow gain their approval. Maybe they would even give him inside information, like new penetration techniques, and, importantly, look after him if things got rough. Force wondered how Phoenix could hold two such conflicting thoughts in his mind at the same time without questioning the logic of either.

It was against this backdrop that Gavin came to Force with his urgent warning in late 1989. Gavin had learned that the Australian Federal Police were getting complaints about hackers operating out of Melbourne. The Melbourne hacking community had become very noisy and was leaving footprints all over the place as its members traversed the world's data networks.

There were other active hacking communities outside Australia – in the north of England, in Texas, in New York. But the Melbourne hackers weren't just noisy – they were noisy inside American computers. It wasn't just a case of American hackers breaking into American systems. This was about foreign nationals penetrating American computers. And there was something else which made the Australian hackers a target. The US Secret Service knew an Australian named Phoenix had been inside Citibank, one of the biggest financial institutions in the US.

Gavin didn't have many details to give Force. All he knew was that an American law enforcement agency – probably the Secret Service – had been putting enormous pressure on the Australian government to bust these people.

What Gavin didn't know was that the Secret Service wasn't the only source of pressure coming from the other side of the Pacific. The FBI had also approached the Australian Federal Police about the mysterious but noisy Australian hackers who kept breaking into American systems,[4] and the AFP had acted on the information.

In late 1989, Detective Superintendent Ken Hunt of the AFP headed an investigation into the Melbourne hackers. It was believed to be the first major investigation of computer crime since the introduction of Australia's first federal anti-hacking laws. Like most law enforcement agencies around the world, the AFP were new players in the field of computer crime. Few officers had expertise in computers, let alone computer crime, so this case would prove to be an important proving ground.[5]

When Gavin broke the news, Force acted immediately. He called Phoenix on the phone, insisting on meeting him in person as soon as possible. As their friendship had progressed, they had moved from talking on-line to telephone conversations and finally to spending time together in person. Force sat Phoenix down alone and gave him a stern warning. He didn't tell him how he got his information, but he made it clear the source was reliable.

The word was that the police felt they had to bust someone. It had come to the point where an American law enforcement officer had reportedly told his Australian counterpart, 'If you don't do something about it soon, we'll do something about it ourselves'. The American hadn't bothered to elaborate on just how they might do something about it, but it didn't matter.

Phoenix looked suddenly pale. He had certainly been very noisy, and was breaking into systems virtually all the time now. Many of those systems were in the US.

He certainly didn't want to end up like the West German hacker Hagbard, whose petrol-doused, charred remains had been discovered in a German forest in June 1989.

An associate of Pengo's, Hagbard had been involved in a ring of German hackers who sold the information they found in American computers to a KGB agent in East Germany from 1986 to 1988.

In March 1989, German police raided the homes and offices of the German hacking group and began arresting people. Like Pengo, Hagbard had secretly turned himself into the German authorities months before and given full details of

the hacking ring's activities in the hope of gaining immunity
from prosecution.

American law enforcement agencies and prosecutors had
not been enthusiastic about showing the hackers any leniency.
Several US agencies, including the CIA and the FBI, had been
chasing the German espionage ring and they wanted stiff sentences, preferably served in an American prison.

German court proceedings were under way when Hagbard's
body was found. Did he commit suicide or was he murdered?
No-one knew for sure, but the news shook the computer
underground around the world. Hackers discussed the issue
in considerable depth. On the one hand, Hagbard had a long
history of mental instability and drug use, having spent time in
psychiatric hospitals and detoxification centres off and on since
the beginning of 1987. On the other hand, if you were going
to kill yourself, would you really want to die in the agony of
a petrol fire? Or would you just take a few too many pills or a
quick bullet?

Whether it was murder or suicide, the death of Hagbard
loomed large before Phoenix. Who were the American law
enforcement agencies after in Australia? Did they want him?

No. Force reassured him, they were after Electron. The
problem for Phoenix was that he kept talking to Electron on the
phone – in voice conversations. If Phoenix continued associating
with Electron, he too would be scooped up in the AFP's net.

The message to Phoenix was crystal clear.

Stay away from Electron.

'Listen, you miserable scum-sucking pig.'

'Huh?' Phoenix answered, only half paying attention.

'Piece of shit machine. I did all this editing and the damn thing
didn't save the changes,' Electron growled at the Commodore
Amiga, with its 512 k of memory, sitting on the desk in his
bedroom.

It was January 1990 and both Phoenix and Electron were at home on holidays before the start of university.

'Yeah. Wish I could get this thing working. Fucking hell. Work you!' Phoenix yelled. Electron could hear him typing at the other end of the phone while he talked. He had been struggling to get AUX, the Apple version of Unix, running on his Macintosh SE30 for days.

It was difficult to have an uninterrupted conversation with Phoenix. If it wasn't his machine crashing, it was his grandmother asking him questions from the doorway of his room.

'You wanna go through the list? How big is your file?' Phoenix asked, now more focused on the conversation.

'Huh? Which file?'

'The dictionary file. The words to feed into the password cracker,' Phoenix replied.

Electron pulled up his list of dictionary words and looked at it. I'm going to have to cut this list down a bit, he thought. The dictionary was part of the password cracking program. The larger the dictionary, the longer it took the computer to crack a list of passwords. If he could weed out obscure words – words that people were unlikely to pick as passwords – then he could make his cracker run faster.

An efficient password cracker was a valuable tool. Electron would feed his home computer a password file from a target computer, say from Melbourne University, then go to bed. About twelve hours later, he would check on his machine's progress.

If he was lucky, he would find six or more accounts – user names and their passwords – waiting for him in a file. The process was completely automated. Electron could then log into Melbourne University using the cracked accounts, all of which could be used as jumping-off points for hacking into other systems for the price of a local telephone call.

Cracking Unix passwords wasn't inordinately difficult, provided the different components of the program, such as the dictionary, had been set up properly. However, it was time-consuming. The principle was simple. Passwords, kept in password files with their corresponding user names, were encrypted. It was as impossible to reverse the encryption process as it was to unscramble an omelette. Instead, you needed to recreate the encryption process and compare the results.

There were three basic steps. First, target a computer and get a copy of its password file. Second, take a list of commonly used passwords, such as users' names from the password file or words from a dictionary, and encrypt those into a second list. Third, put the two lists side by side and compare them. When you have a match, you have found the password.

However, there was one important complication: salts. A salt changed the way a password was encrypted, subtly modifying the way the DES encryption algorithm worked. For example, the word 'Underground' encrypts two different ways with two different salts: 'kyvbExMcdAOVM' or 'lhFaTmw4Ddrjw'. The first two characters represent the salt, the others represent the password. The computer chooses a salt randomly when it encrypts a user's password. Only one is used, and there are 4096 different salts. All Unix computers use salts in their password encryption process.

Salts were intended to make password cracking far more difficult, so a hacker couldn't just encrypt a dictionary once and then compare it to every list of encrypted passwords he came across in his hacking intrusions. The 4096 salts mean that a hacker would have to use 4096 different dictionaries – each encrypted with a different salt – to discover any dictionary word passwords.

On any one system penetrated by Electron, there might be only 25 users, and therefore only 25 passwords, most likely using 25 different salts. Since the salt characters were stored immediately before the encrypted password, he could easily see which salt was being used for a particular password. He would therefore only have to encrypt a dictionary 25 different times.

Still, even encrypting a large dictionary 25 times using different salts took up too much hard-drive space for a basic home computer. And that was just the dictionary. The most sophisticated cracking programs also produced 'intelligent guesses' of passwords. For example, the program might take the user's name and try it in both upper- and lower-case letters. It might also add a '1' at the end. In short, the program would create new guesses by permutating, shuffling, reversing and recombining basic information such as a user's name into new 'words'.

'It's 24 000 words. Too damn big,' Electron said. Paring down a dictionary was a game of trade-offs. The fewer words in a cracking dictionary, the less time it was likely to take a computer to break the encrypted passwords. A smaller dictionary, however, also meant fewer guesses and so a reduced chance of cracking the password of any given account.

'Hmm. Mine's 24 328. We better pare it down together.'

'Yeah. OK. Pick a letter.'

'C. Let's start with the Cs.'

'Why C?'

'C. For my grandmother's cat, Cocoa.'

'Yeah. OK. Here goes. Cab, Cabal. Cabala. Cabbala.' Electron paused. 'What the fuck is a Cabbala?'

'Dunno. Yeah. I've got those. Not Cabbala. OK, Cabaret. Cabbage. Fuck, I hate cabbage. Who'd pick Cabbage as their password?'

'A Pom,' Electron answered.

'Yeah,' Phoenix laughed before continuing.

Phoenix sometimes stopped to think about Force's warning, but usually he just pushed it to one side when it crept, unwelcomed, into his thoughts. Still, it worried him. Force took it seriously enough. Not only had he stopped associating with Electron, he appeared to have gone very, very quiet.

In fact, Force had found a new love: music. He was writing and performing his own songs. By early 1990 he seemed so busy with his music that he had essentially put The Realm on ice. Its members took to congregating on a machine owned by another Realm member, Nom, for a month or so.

Somehow, however, Phoenix knew that wasn't all of the story. A hacker didn't pick up and walk away from hacking just like that. Especially not Force. Force had been obsessed with hacking. It just didn't make sense. There had to be something more. Phoenix comforted himself with the knowledge that he had followed Force's advice and had stayed away from Electron. Well, for a while anyway.

He had backed right off, watched and waited, but nothing happened. Electron was as active in the underground as ever but he hadn't been busted. Nothing had changed. Maybe Force's information had been wrong. Surely the feds would have busted Electron by now if they were going to do anything. So Phoenix began to rebuild his relationship with Electron. It was just too tempting. Phoenix was determined not to let Force's ego impede his own progress.

By January 1990, Electron was hacking almost all the time. The only time he wasn't hacking was when he was sleeping, and even then he often dreamed of hacking. He and Phoenix were sailing past all the other Melbourne hackers. Electron had grown beyond Powerspike's expertise just as Phoenix had accelerated past Force. They were moving away from X.25 networks and into the embryonic Internet, which was just as illegal since the universities guarded computer accounts – Internet access – very closely.

Even Nom, with his growing expertise in the Unix operating system which formed the basis of many new Internet sites, wasn't up to Electron's standard. He didn't have the same level of commitment to hacking, the same obsession necessary to be a truly cutting-edge hacker. In many ways, the relationship between Nom and Phoenix mirrored the relationship between Electron and Powerspike: the support act to the main band.

Electron didn't consider Phoenix a close friend, but he was a kindred spirit. In fact he didn't trust Phoenix, who had a big mouth, a big ego and a tight friendship with Force – all strikes against him. But Phoenix was intelligent and he wanted to learn. Most of all, he had the obsession. Phoenix contributed to a flow of information which stimulated Electron intellectually, even if more information flowed toward Phoenix than from him.

Within a month, Phoenix and Electron were in regular contact, and during the summer holidays they were talking on the phone – voice – all the time, sometimes three or four times a day. Hack then talk. Compare notes. Hack some more. Check in again, ask a few questions. Then back to hacking.

The actual hacking was generally a solo act. For a social animal like Phoenix, it was a lonely pursuit. While many hackers revelled in the intense isolation, some, such as Phoenix, also needed to check in with fellow humanity once in a while. Not just any humanity – those who understood and shared in the obsession.

'Caboodle. Caboose,' Electron went on, 'Cabriolet. What the hell is a Cabriolet? Do you know?'

'Yeah,' Phoenix answered, then rushed on. 'OK. Cacao. Cache. Cachet . . .'

'Tell us. What is it?' Electron cut Phoenix off.

'Cachinnation. Cachou . . .'

'Do you know?' Electron asked again, slightly irritated. As usual, Phoenix was claiming to know things he probably didn't.

'Hmm? Uh, yeah,' Phoenix answered weakly. 'Cackle. Cacophony . . .'

Electron knew that particular Phoenix 'yeah' – the one which said 'yes' but meant 'no, and I don't want to own up to it either so let's drop it'.

Electron made it a habit not to believe most of the things Phoenix told him. Unless there was some solid proof, Electron figured it was just hot air. He didn't actually like Phoenix much as a person, and found talking to him difficult at times. He preferred the company of his fellow hacker Powerspike.

Powerspike was both bright and creative. Electron clicked with him. They often joked about the other's bad taste in music. Powerspike liked heavy metal, and Electron liked indie music. They shared a healthy disrespect for authority. Not just the authority of places they hacked into, like the US Naval Research Laboratories or NASA, but the authority of The Realm. When it came to politics, they both leaned to the left. However, their interest tended more toward anarchy – opposing symbols of the military-industrial complex – than to joining a political party.

After their expulsion from The Realm, Electron had been a little isolated for a time. The tragedy of his personal life had contributed to the isolation. At the age of eight, he had seen his mother die of lung cancer. He hadn't witnessed the worst parts of her dying over two years, as she had spent some time in a German cancer clinic hoping for a reprieve. She had, however, come home to die, and Electron had watched her fade away.

When the phone call from hospital came one night, Electron could tell what had happened from the serious tones of the adults. He burst into tears. He could hear his father answering questions on the phone. Yes, the boy had taken it hard. No, his sister seemed to be OK. Two years younger than Electron, she was too young to understand.

Electron had never been particularly close to his sister. He viewed her as an unfeeling, shallow person – someone who simply skimmed along the surface of life. But after their mother's death, their father began to favour Electron's sister, perhaps because of her resemblance to his late wife. This drove a deeper, more subtle wedge between brother and sister.

Electron's father, a painter who taught art at a local high school, was profoundly affected by his wife's death. Despite some barriers of social class and money, theirs had been a marriage of great affection and love and they made a happy home. Electron's father's paintings hung on almost every wall in the house, but after his wife's death he put down his brushes and never took them up again. He didn't talk about it. Once, Electron asked him why he didn't paint any more. He looked away and told Electron that he had 'lost the motivation'.

Electron's grandmother moved into the home to help her son care for his two children, but she developed Alzheimer's disease. The children ended up caring for her. As a teenager,

Electron thought it was maddening caring for someone who couldn't even remember your name. Eventually, she moved into a nursing home.

In August 1989, Electron's father arrived home from the doctor's office. He had been mildly ill for some time, but refused to take time off work to visit a doctor. He was proud of having taken only one day's sick leave in the last five years. Finally, in the holidays, he had seen a doctor who had conducted numerous tests. The results had come in.

Electron's father had bowel cancer and the disease had spread. It could not be cured. He had two years to live at the most.

Electron was nineteen years old at the time, and his early love of the computer, and particularly the modem, had already turned into a passion. Several years earlier his father, keen to encourage his fascination with the new machines, used to bring one of the school's Apple IIes home over weekends and holidays. Electron spent hours at the borrowed machine. When he wasn't playing on the computer, he read, plucking one of his father's spy novels from the over-crowded bookcases, or his own favourite book, *The Lord of The Rings*.

Computer programming had, however, captured the imagination of the young Electron years before he used his first computer. At the age of eleven he was using books to write simple programs on paper – mostly games – despite the fact that he had never actually touched a keyboard.

His school may have had a few computers, but its administrators had little understanding of what to do with them. In year 9, Electron had met with the school's career counsellor, hoping to learn about career options working with computers.

'I think maybe I'd like to do a course in computer programming . . .' His voice trailed off, hesitantly.

'Why would you want to do that?' she said. 'Can't you think of anything better than that?'

'Uhm . . .' Electron was at a loss. He didn't know what to do. That was why he had come to her. He cast around for something which seemed a more mainstream career option but which might also let him work on computers. 'Well, accounting maybe?'

'Oh yes, that's much better,' she said.

'You can probably even get into a university, and study accounting there. I'm sure you will enjoy it,' she added, smiling as she closed his file.

The borrowed computers were, in Electron's opinion, one of the few good things about school. He did reasonably well at school, but only because it didn't take much effort. Teachers consistently told his father that Electron was underachieving and that he distracted the other students in class. For the most part, the criticism was just low-level noise. Occasionally, however, Electron had more serious run-ins with his teachers. Some thought he was gifted. Others thought the freckle-faced, Irish-looking boy who helped his friends set fire to textbooks at the back of the class was nothing but a smart alec.

When he was sixteen, Electron bought his own computer. He used it to crack software protection, just as Par had done. The Apple was soon replaced by a more powerful Amiga with a 20 megabyte IBM compatible sidecar. The computers lived, in succession, on one of the two desks in his bedroom. The second desk, for his school work, was usually piled high with untouched assignments.

The most striking aspect of Electron's room was the ream after ream of dot matrix computer print-out which littered the floor. Standing at almost any point in the simply furnished room, someone could reach out and grab at least one pile of print-outs, most of which contained either usernames and passwords or printed computer program code. In between the piles of print-outs, were T-shirts, jeans, sneakers and books on the floor. It was impossible to walk across Electron's room without stepping on something.

The turning point for Electron was the purchase of a second-hand 300 baud modem in 1986. Overnight, the modem transformed Electron's love of the computer into an obsession.

During the semester immediately before the modem's arrival, Electron's report card showed six As and one B. The following semester he earned six Bs and only one A.

Electron had moved onto bigger and better things than school. He quickly became a regular user of underground BBSes and began hacking. He was enthralled by an article he discovered describing how several hackers claimed to have moved a satellite around in space simply by hacking computers. From that moment on, Electron decided he wanted to hack – to find out if the article was true.

Before he graduated from school in 1987, Electron had hacked NASA, an achievement which saw him dancing around the dining room table in the middle of the night chanting, 'I got into NASA! I got into NASA!' He hadn't moved any satellites, but getting into the space agency was as thrilling as flying to the moon.

By 1989, he had been hacking regularly for years, much to the chagrin of his sister, who claimed her social life suffered because the family's sole phone line was always tied up by the modem.

For Phoenix, Electron was a partner in hacking, and to a lesser degree a mentor. Electron had a lot to offer, by that time even more than The Realm.

'Cactus, Cad, Cadaver, Caddis, Cadence, Cadet, Caesura. What the fuck is a Caesura?' Phoenix kept ploughing through the Cs.

'Dunno. Kill that,' Electron answered, distracted.

'Caesura. Well, fuck. I know I'd wanna use that as a password.' Phoenix laughed. 'What the hell kind of word is Caduceus?'

'A dead one. Kill all those. Who makes up these diction-aries?' Electron said.

'Yeah.'

'Caisson, Calabash. Kill those. Kill, kill, kill,' Electron said gleefully.

'Hang on. How come I don't have Calabash in my list?' Phoenix feigned indignation.

Electron laughed.

'Hey,' Phoenix said, 'we should put in words like "Qwerty" and "ABCDEF" and "ASDFGH".'

'Did that already.' Electron had already put together a list of other common passwords, such as the 'words' made when a user typed the six letters in the first alphabet row on a keyboard.

Phoenix started on the list again. 'OK the COs. Commend, Comment, Commerce, Commercial, Commercialism, Commercially. Kill those last three.'

'Huh? Why kill Commercial?'

'Let's just kill all the words with more than eight characters,' Phoenix said.

'No. That's not a good idea.'

'How come? The computer's only going to read the first eight characters and encrypt those. So we should kill all the rest.'

Sometimes Phoenix just didn't get it. But Electron didn't rub it in. He kept it low-key, so as not to bruise Phoenix's ego. Often Electron sensed Phoenix sought approval from the older hacker, but it was a subtle, perhaps even unconscious search.

'Nah,' Electron began, 'see, someone might use the whole word, Commerce or Commercial. The first eight letters of these words are not the same. The eighth character in Commerce is "e", but in Commercial it's "i".'

There was a short silence.

'Yeah,' Electron went on, 'but you could kill all the words like Commercially, and Commercialism, that come after Commercial. See?'

'Yeah. OK. I see,' Phoenix said.

'But don't just kill every word longer than eight characters,' Electron added.

'Hmm. OK. Yeah, all right.' Phoenix seemed a bit out of sorts. 'Hey,' he brightened a bit, 'it's been a whole ten minutes since my machine crashed.'

'Yeah?' Electron tried to sound interested.

'Yeah. You know,' Phoenix changed the subject to his favourite topic, 'what we really need is Deszip. Gotta get that.' Deszip was a computer program which could be used for password cracking.

'And Zardoz. We need Zardoz,' Electron added. Zardoz was a restricted electronic publication detailing computer security holes.

'Yeah. Gotta try to get into Spaf's machine. Spaf'll have it for sure.' Eugene Spafford, Associate Professor of Computer Science at Purdue University in the US, was one of the best known computer security experts on the Internet in 1990.

'Yeah.'

And so began their hunt for the holy grail.

Deszip and Zardoz glittered side by side as the most coveted prizes in the world of the international Unix hacker.

Cracking passwords took time and computer resources. Even a moderately powerful university machine would grunt and groan under the weight of the calculations it was asked to do. But the Deszip program could change that, lifting the load until it was, by comparison, feather-light. It worked at breathtaking speed and a hacker using Deszip could crack encrypted passwords up to 25 times faster.

Zardoz, a worldwide security mailing list, was also precious, but for a different reason. Although the mailing list's formal name was Security Digest, everyone in the underground simply called it Zardoz, after the computer from which the mailouts originated. *Zardoz* also happened to be the name of a science fiction cult film starring Sean Connery. Run by Neil Gorsuch, the Zardoz mailing list contained articles, or postings, from various members of the computer security industry. The postings discussed newly discovered bugs – problems with a computer system which could be exploited to break into or gain root access on a machine. The beauty of the bugs outlined in Zardoz was that they worked on any computer system using the programs or operating systems it described. Any university, any military system, any research institute which ran the software documented in Zardoz was vulnerable. Zardoz was a giant key ring, full of pass keys made to fit virtually every lock.

True, system administrators who read a particular Zardoz posting might take steps to close up that security hole. But as the hacking community knew well, it was a long time between a Zardoz posting and a shortage of systems with that hole. Often a bug worked on many computers for months – sometimes years – after being announced on Zardoz.

Why? Many admins had never heard of the bug when it was first announced. Zardoz was an exclusive club, and most admins simply weren't members. You couldn't just walk in off the street and sign up for Zardoz. You had to be vetted by peers in the computer security industry. You had to administer a legitimate computer system, preferably with a large institution such as a university or a research body such as CSIRO. Figuratively speaking, the established members of the Zardoz mailing list peered down their noses at you and determined if you were worthy of inclusion in Club Zardoz. Only they decided if you were trustworthy enough to share in the great security secrets of the world's computer systems.

In 1989, the white hats, as hackers called the professional security gurus, were highly paranoid about Zardoz getting into the wrong hands. So much so, in fact, that many postings to Zardoz were fine examples of the art of obliqueness. A computer security expert would hint at a new bug in his posting without actually coming out and explaining it in what is commonly referred to as a 'cookbook' explanation.

This led to a raging debate within the comp-sec industry. In one corner, the cookbook purists said that bulletins such as Zardoz were only going to be helpful if people were frank with each other. They wanted people posting to Zardoz to provide detailed, step-by-step explanations on how to exploit a particular security hole. Hackers would always find out about bugs one way or another and the best way to keep them out of your system was to secure it properly in the first place. They wanted full disclosure.

In the other corner, the hard-line, command-and-control computer security types argued that posting an announcement to Zardoz posed the gravest of security risks. What if Zardoz fell into the wrong hands? Why, any sixteen-year-old hacker would have step-by-step directions showing how to break into thousands of individual computers! If you had to reveal a security flaw – and the jury was still out in their minds as to whether that was such a good idea – it should be done only in the most oblique terms.

What the hard-liners failed to understand was that world-class hackers like Electron could read the most oblique, carefully crafted Zardoz postings and, within a matter of days if not hours, work out exactly how to exploit the security hole hinted at in the text. After which they could just as easily have written a cookbook version of the security bug.

Most good hackers had come across one or two issues of Zardoz in their travels, often while rummaging though the system administrator's mail on a prestigious institution's computer. But no-one from the elite of the Altos underground had a full archive of all the back issues. The hacker who possessed that would have details of every major security hole discovered by the world's best computer security minds since at least 1988.

Like Zardoz, Deszip was well guarded. It was written by computer security expert Dr Matthew Bishop, who worked at NASA's Research Institute for Advanced Computer Science before taking up a teaching position at Dartmouth, an Ivy League college in New Hampshire. The United States government ment deemed Deszip's very fast encryption algorithms to be so important, they were classified as armaments. It was illegal to export them from the US.

Of course, few hackers in 1990 had the sophistication to use weapons such as Zardoz and Deszip properly. Indeed, few even knew they existed. But Electron and Phoenix knew, along with a tiny handful of others, including Pad and Gandalf from Britain. Congregating on Altos in Germany, they worked with a select group of others carefully targeting sites likely to contain parts of their holy grail. They were methodical and highly strategic, piecing information together with exquisite, almost forensic, skill. While the common rabble of other hackers were thumping their heads against walls in brute-force attacks on random machines, these hackers spent their time hunting for strategic pressure points – the Achilles' heels of the computer security community.

They had developed an informal hit list of machines, most of which belonged to high-level computer security gurus. Finding one or two early issues of Zardoz, Electron had combed through their postings looking not just on the surface – for the security bugs – but also paying careful attention to the names and addresses of the people writing articles. Authors who appeared frequently in Zardoz, or had something intelligent to say, went on the hit list. It was those people who were most likely to keep copies of Deszip or an archive of Zardoz on their machines.

Electron had searched across the world for information about Deszip and DES (Data Encryption Standard), the original encryption program later used in Deszip. He hunted through computers at the University of New York, the US Naval Research Laboratories in Washington DC, Helsinki University of Technology, Rutgers University in New Jersey, Melbourne University and Tampere University in Finland, but the search bore little fruit. He found a copy of CDES, a public domain encryption program which used the DES algorithm, but not Deszip. CDES could be used to encrypt files but not to crack passwords.

The two Australian hackers had, however, enjoyed a small taste of Deszip. In 1989 they had broken into a computer at Dartmouth College called Bear. They discovered Deszip carefully tucked away in a corner of Bear and had spirited a copy of the program away to a safer machine at another institution.

It turned out to be a hollow victory. That copy of Deszip had been encrypted with Crypt, a program based on the German Enigma machine used in World War II. Without the passphrase – the key to unlock the encryption – it was impossible to read Deszip. All they could do was stare, frustrated, at the file name Deszip labelling a treasure just out of reach.

Undaunted, the hackers decided to keep the encrypted file just in case they ever came across the passphrase somewhere – in an email letter, for example – in one of the dozens of new computers they now hacked regularly. Relabelling the encrypted Deszip file with a more innocuous name, they stored the copy in a dark corner of another machine. Thinking it wise to buy a little insurance as well, they gave a second copy of the encrypted Deszip to Gandalf, who stored it on a machine in the UK in case the Australians' copy disappeared unexpectedly.

In January 1990, Electron turned his attention to getting Zardoz. After carefully reviewing an old copy of Zardoz, he had discovered a system admin in Melbourne on the list. The subscriber could well have the entire Zardoz archive on his machine, and that machine was so close – less than half an hour's drive from Electron's home. All Electron had to do was to break into the CSIRO.

The Commonwealth Scientific and Industrial Research Organisation, or CSIRO, is a government owned and operated research body with many offices around Australia. Electron only wanted to get into one: the Division of Information Technology at 55 Barry Street, Carlton, just around the corner from the University of Melbourne.

Rummaging through a Melbourne University computer, Electron had already found one copy of the Zardoz archive, belonging to a system admin. He gathered it up and quietly began downloading it to his computer, but as his machine slowly siphoned off the Zardoz copy, his link to the university abruptly went dead. The admin had discovered the hacker and quickly killed the connection. All of which left Electron back at square one – until he found another copy of Zardoz on the CSIRO machine.

It was nearly 3 a.m. on 1 February 1990, but Electron wasn't tired. His head was buzzing. He had just successfully penetrated an account called Worsley on the CSIRO computer called DITMELA, using the sendmail bug. Electron assumed DITMELA stood for Division of Information Technology, Melbourne, computer 'A'.

Electron began sifting through Andrew Worsley's directories that day. He knew Zardoz was in there somewhere, since he had seen it before. After probing the computer, experimenting with different security holes hoping one would let him inside, Electron managed to slip in unnoticed. It was mid-afternoon, a bad time to hack a computer since someone at work would likely spot the intruder before long. So Electron told himself this was just a reconnaissance mission. Find out if Zardoz was on the machine, then get out of there fast and come back later – preferably in the middle of the night – to pull Zardoz out.

When he found a complete collection of Zardoz in Worsley's directory, Electron was tempted to try a grab and run. The problem was that, with his slow modem, he couldn't run very quickly. Downloading Zardoz would take several hours. Quashing his overwhelming desire to reach out and grab Zardoz then and there, he slipped out of the machine noiselessly.

Early next morning, an excited and impatient Electron crept back into DITMELA and headed straight for Worsley's directory. Zardoz was still there. And a sweet irony. Electron was using a security bug he had found on an early issue of Zardoz to break into the computer which would surrender the entire archive to him.

Getting Zardoz out of the CSIRO machine was going to be a little difficult. It was a big archive and at 300 baud –

30 characters per second – Electron's modem would take five hours to siphon off an entire copy. Using the CAT command, Electron made copies of all the Zardoz issues and bundled them up into one 500 k file. He called the new file .t and stored it in the temporary directory on DITMELA.

Then he considered what to do next. He would mail the Zardoz bundle to another account outside the CSIRO computer, for safe-keeping. But after that he had to make a choice: try to download the thing himself or hang up, call Phoenix and ask him to download it.

Using his 2400 baud modem, Phoenix would be able to download the Zardoz bundle eight times faster than Electron could. On the other hand, Electron didn't particularly want to give Phoenix access to the CSIRO machine. They had both been targeting the machine, but he hadn't told Phoenix that he had actually managed to get in. It wasn't that he planned on withholding Zardoz when he got it. Quite the contrary, Electron wanted Phoenix to read the security file so they could bounce ideas off each other. When it came to accounts, however, Phoenix had a way of messing things up. He talked too much. He was simply not discreet.

While Electron considered his decision, his fingers kept working at the keyboard. He typed quickly, mailing copies of the Zardoz bundle to two hacked student accounts at Melbourne University. With the passwords to both accounts, he could get in whenever he wanted and he wasn't taking any chances with this precious cargo. Two accounts were safer than one – a main account and a back-up in case someone changed the password on the first one.

Then, as the DITMELA machine was still in the process of mailing the Zardoz bundle off to the back-up sites, Electron's connection suddenly died.

The CSIRO machine had hung up on him, which probably meant one thing. The admin had logged him off. Electron was furious. What the hell was a system administrator doing on a computer at this hour? The admin was supposed to be asleep!

That's why Electron logged on when he did. He had seen Zardoz on the CSIRO machine the day before but he had been so patient refusing to touch it because the risk of discovery was too great. And now this.

The only hope was to call Phoenix and get him to login to the Melbourne Uni accounts to see if the mail had arrived safely. If so, he could download it with his faster modem before the CSIRO admin had time to warn the Melbourne Uni admin, who would change the passwords.

Electron got on the phone to Phoenix. They had long since stopped caring about what time of day they rang each other. 10 p.m. 2 a.m. 4.15 a.m. 6.45 a.m.

'Yeah.' Electron greeted Phoenix in the usual way.

'Yup,' Phoenix responded.

Electron told Phoenix what happened and gave him the two accounts at Melbourne University where he had mailed the Zardoz bundle.

Phoenix hung up and rang back a few minutes later. Both accounts were dead. Someone from Melbourne University had gone in and changed the passwords within 30 minutes of Electron being booted off the CSIRO computer. Both hackers were disturbed by the implications of this event. It meant someone – in fact probably several people – were onto them. But their desperation to get Zardoz overcame their fear.

Electron had one more account on the CSIRO computer. He didn't want to give it to Phoenix, but he didn't have a choice. Still, the whole venture was filled with uncertainty. Who knew if the Zardoz bundle was still there? Surely an admin who bothered to kick Electron out would move Zardoz to somewhere inaccessible. There was, however, a single chance.

When Electron read off the password and username, he told Phoenix to copy the Zardoz bundle to a few other machines on the Internet instead of trying to download it to his own computer. It would be much quicker, and the CSIRO admin wouldn't dare break into someone else's computers to delete the copied file. Choosing overseas sites would make it even harder for the admin to reach the admins of those machines and warn them in time. Then, once Zardoz was safely tucked away in a few back-up sites, Phoenix could download it over the Internet from one of those with less risk of being booted off the machine halfway through the process.

Sitting at his home in Kelvin Grove, Thornbury, just two suburbs north of the CSIRO machine, Ian Mathieson watched the hacker break into his computer again. Awoken by a phone call at 2.30 a.m. telling him there was a suspected hacker in his computer, Mathieson immediately logged in to his work system, DITMELA, via his home computer and modem. The call, from David Hornsby of the Melbourne University Computer Science Department, was no false alarm.

After watching the unknown hacker, who had logged in through a Melbourne University machine terminal server, for about twenty minutes, Mathieson booted the hacker off his system. Afterwards he noticed that the DITMELA computer was still trying to execute a command issued by the hacker. He looked a little closer, and discovered DITMELA was trying to deliver mail to two Melbourne University accounts.

The mail, however, hadn't been completely delivered. It was still sitting in the mail spool, a temporary holding pen for undelivered mail. Curious as to what the hacker would want so much from his system, Mathieson moved the file into a subdirectory to look at it. He was horrified to find the entire Zardoz archive, and he knew exactly what it meant. These were no ordinary hackers – they were precision fliers. Fortunately, Mathieson consoled himself, he had stopped the mail before it had been sent out and secured it.

Unfortunately, however, Mathieson had missed Electron's original file – the bundle of Zardoz copies. When Electron had mailed the file, he had copied it, leaving the original intact. They were still sitting on DITMELA under the unassuming name .t. Mailing a file didn't delete it – the computer only sent a copy of the original. Mathieson was an intelligent man, a medical doctor with a master's degree in computer science, but he had forgotten to check the temporary directory, one of the few places a hacker could store files on a Unix system if he didn't have root privileges.

At exactly 3.30 a.m. Phoenix logged into DITMELA from the University of Texas. He quickly looked in the temporary directory. The .t file was there, just as Electron had said it would be. The hacker quickly began transferring it back to the University of Texas.

He was feeling good. It looked like the Australians were going to get the entire Zardoz collection after all. Everything was going extremely well – until the transfer suddenly died. Phoenix had forgotten to check that there was enough disk space available on the University of Texas account to download the sizeable Zardoz bundle. Now, as he was logged into a very hot machine, a machine where the admin could well be watching his every move, he discovered there wasn't enough room for the Zardoz file.

Aware that every second spent on-line to DITMELA posed a serious risk, Phoenix logged off the CSIRO machine immediately. Still connected to the Texas computer, he fiddled around with it, deleting other files and making enough room to pull the whole 500 k Zardoz file across.

At 3.37 a.m. Phoenix entered DITMELA again. This time, he vowed, nothing would go wrong. He started up the file transfer and waited. Less than ten minutes later, he logged off the CSIRO computer and nervously checked the University of Texas system. It was there. Zardoz, in all its glory. And it was his! Phoenix was ecstatic.

He wasn't done yet and there was no time for complacency. Swiftly, he began compressing and encrypting Zardoz. He compressed it because a smaller file was less obvious on the Texas machine and was faster to send to a back-up machine. He encrypted it so no-one nosing around the file would be able to see what was in it. He wasn't just worried about system admins; the Texas system was riddled with hackers, in part because it was home to his friend, Legion of Doom hacker Erik Bloodaxe, a student at the university.

After Phoenix was satisfied Zardoz was safe, he rang Electron just before 4 a.m. with the good news. By 8.15, Phoenix had downloaded Zardoz from the Texas computer onto his own machine. By 1.15 p.m., Electron had downloaded it from Phoenix's machine to his own.

Zardoz had been a difficult conquest, but Deszip would prove to be even more so. While dozens of security experts possessed complete Zardoz archives, far fewer people had Deszip. And, at least officially, all of them were in the US.

The US government banned the export of cryptography algorithms. To send a copy of Deszip, or DES or indeed any other encryption program outside the US was a crime. It was illegal because the US State Department's Office of Defense Trade Controls considered any encryption program to be a weapon. ITAR, the International Traffic in Arms Regulations stemming from the US Arms Export Control Act 1977, restricted publication of and trade in 'defense articles'. It didn't matter whether you flew to Europe with a disk in your pocket, or you sent the material over the Internet. If you violated ITAR, you faced the prospect of prison.

Occasionally, American computer programmers discreetly slipped copies of encryption programs to specialists in their field outside the US. Once the program was outside the US, it was fair game – there was nothing US authorities could do about someone in Norway sending Deszip to a colleague in Australia. But even so, the comp-sec and cryptography communities outside the US still held programs such as Deszip very tightly within their own inner sanctums.

All of which meant that Electron and Phoenix would almost certainly have to target a site in the US. Electron continued to compile a hit list, based on the Zardoz mailing list, which he gave to Phoenix. The two hackers then began searching the growing Internet for computers belonging to the targets.

It was an impressive hit list. Matthew Bishop, author of Deszip. Russell Brand, of the Lawrence Livermore National Labs, a research laboratory funded by the US Department of Energy. Dan Farmer, an author of the computer program COPS, a popular security-testing program which included a password cracking program. There were others. And, at the top of the list, Eugene Spafford, or Spaf, as the hackers called him.

By 1990, the computer underground viewed Spaf not just as security guru, but also as an anti-hacker zealot. Spaf was based at Purdue University, a hotbed of computer security experts. Bishop had earned his PhD at Purdue and Dan Farmer was still there. Spaf was also one of the founders of usenet, the Internet newsgroups service. While working as a computer scientist at the university, he had made a name for himself by, among other things, writing a technical analysis of the RTM worm. The worm, authored by Cornell University student Robert T. Morris Jr in 1988, proved to be a boon for Spaf's career.

Prior to the RTM worm, Spaf had been working in software engineering. After the worm, he became a computer ethicist and a very public spokesman for the conservatives in the computer security industry. Spaf went on tour across the US, lecturing the public and the media on worms, viruses and the ethics of hacking. During the Morris case, hacking became a hot topic in the United States, and Spaf fed the flames. When Judge Howard G. Munson refused to sentence Morris to prison, instead ordering him to complete 400 hours community service, pay a $10 000 fine and submit to three years probation, Spaf publicly railed against the decision. The media reported that he had called on the computer industry to boycott any company which chose to employ Robert T. Morris Jr.

Targeting Spaf therefore served a dual purpose for the Australian hackers. He was undoubtedly a repository of treasures such as Deszip, and he was also a tall poppy.

One night, Electron and Phoenix decided to break into Spaf's machine at Purdue to steal a copy of Deszip. Phoenix would do the actual hacking, since he had the fast modem, but he would talk to Electron simultaneously on the other phone line. Electron would guide him at each step. That way, when Phoenix hit a snag, he wouldn't have to retreat to regroup and risk discovery.

Both hackers had managed to break into another computer at Purdue, called Medusa. But Spaf had a separate machine, Uther, which was connected to Medusa.

Phoenix poked and prodded at Uther, trying to open a hole wide enough for him to crawl through. At Electron's suggestion, he tried to use the CHFN bug. The CHFN command lets users change the information provided – such as their name, work address or office phone number – when someone 'fingers' their accounts. The bug had appeared in one of the Zardoz files and Phoenix and Electron had already used it to break into several other machines.

Electron wanted to use the CHFN bug because, if the attack was successful, Phoenix would be able to make a root account for himself on Spaf's machine. That would be the ultimate slap in the face to a high-profile computer security guru.

But things weren't going well for Phoenix. The frustrated Australian hacker kept telling Electron that the bug should work, but it wouldn't, and he couldn't figure out why. The problem, Electron finally concluded, was that Spaf's machine was a Sequent. The CHFN bug depended on a particular Unix password file structure, but Sequents used a different structure. It didn't help that Phoenix didn't know that much about Sequents – they were one of Gandalf's specialties.

After a few exasperating hours struggling to make the CHFN bug work, Phoenix gave up and turned to another security flaw suggested by Electron: the FTP bug. Phoenix ran through the bug in his mind. Normally, someone used FTP, or file transfer protocol, to transfer files over a network, such as the Internet, from one computer to another. FTPing to another machine was a bit like telnetting, but the user didn't need a password to login and the commands he could execute once in the other computer were usually very limited.

If it worked, the FTP bug would allow Phoenix to slip in an extra command during the FTP login process. That command would force Spaf's machine to allow Phoenix to login as anyone he wanted – and what he wanted was to login as someone who had root privileges. The 'root' account might be a little obvious if anyone was watching, and it didn't always have remote access anyway. So he chose 'daemon', another commonly root-privileged account, instead.

It was a shot in the dark. Phoenix was fairly sure Spaf would have secured his machine against such an obvious attack, but Electron urged him to give it a try anyway. The FTP bug had been announced throughout the computer security community long ago, appearing in an early issue of Zardoz. Phoenix hesitated, but he had run out of ideas, and time.

Phoenix typed:

```
FTP -i uther.purdue.edu
quote user anonymous
quote cd ~daemon
quote pass anything
```

The few seconds it took for his commands to course from his suburban home in Melbourne and race deep into the Midwest felt like a lifetime. He wanted Spaf's machine, wanted Deszip, and wanted this attack to work. If he could just get Deszip, he felt the Australians would be unstoppable.

Spaf's machine opened its door as politely as a doorman at the Ritz Carlton. Phoenix smiled at his computer. He was in.

It was like being in Aladdin's cave. Phoenix just sat there, stunned at the bounty which lay before him. It was his, all his. Spaf had megabytes of security files in his directories. Source code for the RTM Internet worm. Source code for the WANK worm. Everything. Phoenix wanted to plunge his hands in each treasure chest and scoop out greedy handfuls, but he resisted the urge. He had a more important – a more strategic – mission to accomplish first.

He prowled through the directories, hunting everywhere for Deszip. Like a burglar scouring the house for the family silver, he pawed through directory after directory. Surely, Spaf had to have Deszip. If anyone besides Matthew Bishop was going to have a copy, he would. And finally, there it was. Deszip. Just waiting for Phoenix.

Then Phoenix noticed something else. Another file. Curiosity got the better of him and he zoomed in to have a quick look. This one contained a passphrase – *the* passphrase. The phrase the Australians needed to decrypt the original copy of Deszip they had stolen from the Bear computer at Dartmouth three months earlier. Phoenix couldn't believe the passphrase. It was so simple, so obvious. But he caught himself. This was no time to cry over spilled milk. He had to get Deszip out of the machine quickly, before anyone noticed he was there.

But as Phoenix began typing in commands, his screen appeared to freeze up. He checked. It wasn't his computer. Something was wrong at the other end. He was still logged into Spaf's machine. The connection hadn't been killed. But when he typed commands, the computer in West Lafayette, Indiana, didn't respond. Spaf's machine just sat there, deaf and dumb.

Phoenix stared at his computer, trying to figure out what was happening. Why wouldn't Spaf's machine answer? There were two possibilities. Either the network – the connection between the first machine he penetrated at Purdue and Spaf's own machine – had gone down accidentally. Or someone had pulled the plug.

Why pull the plug? If they knew he was in there, why not just kick him out of the machine? Better still, why not kick him out of Purdue all together? Maybe they wanted to keep him on-line to trace which machine he was coming from, eventually winding backwards from system to system, following his trail.

Phoenix was in a dilemma. If the connection had crashed by accident, he wanted to stay put and wait for the network to come back up again. The FTP hole in Spaf's machine was an incredible piece of luck. Chances were that someone would find evidence of his break-in after he left and plug it. On the other hand, he didn't want the people at Purdue tracing his connections.

He waited a few more minutes, trying to hedge his bets. Feeling nervy as the extended silence emanating from Spaf's machine wore on, Phoenix decided to jump. With the lost treasures of Aladdin's cave fading in his mind's eye like a mirage, Phoenix killed his connection.

Electron and Phoenix talked on the phone, moodily contemplating their losses. It was a blow, but Electron reminded himself that getting Deszip was never going to be easy. At least they had the passphrase to unlock the encrypted Deszip taken from Dartmouth.

Soon, however, they discovered a problem. There had to be one, Electron thought. They couldn't just have something go off without a hitch for a change. That would be too easy. The problem this time was that when they went searching for their copy from Dartmouth, which had been stored several months before, it had vanished. The Dartmouth system admin must have deleted it.

It was maddening. The frustration was unbearable. Each time they had Deszip just within their grasp, it slipped away and disappeared. Yet each time they lost their grip, it only deepened their desire to capture the elusive prize. Deszip was fast becoming an all-consuming obsession for Phoenix and Electron.

Their one last hope was the second copy of the encrypted Dartmouth Deszip file they had given to Gandalf, but that hope did not burn brightly. After all, if the Australians' copy had been deleted, there was every likelihood that the Brit's copy had suffered the same fate. Gandalf's copy hadn't been stored on his own computer. He had put it on some dark corner of a machine in Britain.

Electron and Phoenix logged onto Altos and waited for Pad or Gandalf to show up.

Phoenix typed .s for a list of who was on-line. He saw that Pad was logged on:

No Chan User
0 Guest
1 Phoenix
2 Pad

Guest 0 was Electron. He usually logged on as Guest, partly because he was so paranoid about being busted and because he believed operators monitored his connections if they knew it was Electron logging in. They seemed to take great joy in sniffing the password to his own account on Altos. Then, when he had logged off, they logged in and changed his password so he couldn't get back under the name Electron. Nothing was more annoying. Phoenix typed, 'Hey, Pad. How's it going?'

Pad wrote back, 'Feeny! Heya.'

'Do you and Gand still have that encrypted copy of Deszip we gave you a few months ago?'

'Encrypted copy . . . hmm. Thinking.' Pad paused. He and Gandalf hacked dozens of computer systems regularly. Sometimes it was difficult to recall just where they had stored things.

'Yeah, I know what you mean. I don't know. It was on a system on JANET,' Pad said. Britain's Joint Academic Network was the equivalent of Australia's AARNET, an early Internet based largely on a backbone of universities and research centres.

'I can't remember which system it was on,' Pad continued.

If the Brits couldn't recall the institution, let alone the machine where they had hidden Deszip, it was time to give up all hope. JANET comprised hundreds, maybe thousands, of machines. It was far too big a place to randomly hunt around for a file which Gandalf would no doubt have tried to disguise in the first place.

'But the file was encrypted, and you didn't have the password,' Pad wrote. 'How come you want it?'

'Because we found the password. <smile>'. That was the etiquette on Altos. If you wanted to suggest an action, you put it in < >.

'Gr8!' Pad answered.

That was Pad and Gandalf's on-line style. The number eight was the British hackers' hallmark, since their group was called 8lgm, and they used it instead of letters. Words like 'great', 'mate' and 'later' became 'gr8', 'm8' and 'l8r'.

When people logged into Altos they could name a 'place' of origin for others to see. Of course, if you were logging from a country which had laws against hacking, you wouldn't give your real country. You'd just pick a place at random. Some people logged in from places like Argentina, or Israel. Pad and Gandalf logged in from 8lgm.

'I'll try to find Gandalf and ask him if he knows where we stashed the copy,' Pad wrote to Phoenix.

'Good. Thanks.'

While Phoenix and Electron waited on-line for Pad to return, Par showed up on-line and joined their conversation. Par didn't know who Guest 0 was, but Guest certainly knew who Par was. Time hadn't healed Electron's old wounds when it came to Par. Electron didn't really admit to himself the bad blood was still there over Theorem. He told himself that he couldn't be bothered with Par, that Par was just a phreaker, not a real hacker, that Par was lame.

Phoenix typed, 'Hey, Par. How's it going?'

'Feenster!' Par replied. 'What's happening?'

'Lots and lots.'

Par turned his attention to the mystery Guest 0. He didn't want to discuss private things with someone who might be a security guy hanging around the chat channel like a bad smell.

'Guest, do you have a name?' Par asked.

'Yeah. It's "Guest – #0".'

'You got any other names?'

There was a long pause.

Electron typed, 'I guess not.'

'Any other names besides dickhead that is?'

Electron sent a 'whisper' – a private message – to Phoenix telling him not to tell Par his identity.

'OK. Sure,' Phoenix whispered back. To show he would play along with whatever Electron had in mind, Phoenix added a sideways smiley face at the end: ':-)'.

Par didn't know Electron and Phoenix were whispering to each other. He was still waiting to find out the identity of Guest. 'Well, speak up, Guest. Figured out who you are yet?'

Electron knew Par was on the run at the time. Indeed, Par had been on the run from the US Secret Service for more than six months by the beginning of 1990. He also knew Par was highly paranoid.

Electron took aim and fired.

'Hey, Par. You should eat more. You're looking underFED these days.'

Par was suddenly silent. Electron sat at his computer, quietly laughing to himself, halfway across the world from Par. Well, he thought, that ought to freak out Par a bit. Nothing like a subtle hint at law enforcement to drive him nuts.

'Did you see THAT?' Par whispered to Phoenix. 'UnderFED. What did he mean?'

'I dunno,' Phoenix whispered back. Then he forwarded a copy of Par's private message on to Electron. He knew it would make him laugh.

Par was clearly worried. 'Who the fuck are you?' he whispered to Electron but Guest 0 didn't answer.

With growing anxiety, Par whispered to Phoenix, 'Who IS this guy? Do you know him?'

Phoenix didn't answer.

'Because, well, it's weird. Didn't you see? FED was in caps. What the fuck does that mean? Is he a fed? Is he trying to give me a message from the feds?'

Sitting at his terminal, on the other side of Melbourne from Electron, Phoenix was also laughing. He liked Par, but the American was an easy target. Par had become so paranoid since he went on the run across the US, and Electron knew just the right buttons to push.

'I don't know,' Phoenix whispered to Par. 'I'm sure he's not really a fed.'

'Well, I am wondering about that comment,' Par whispered back. 'UnderFED. Hmm. Maybe he knows something. Maybe it's some kind of warning. Shit, maybe the Secret Service knows where I am.'

'You think?' Phoenix whispered to Par. 'It might be a warning of some kind?' It was too funny.

'Can you check his originating NUA?' Par wanted to know what network address the mystery guest was coming from. It might give him a clue as to the stranger's identity.

Phoenix could barely contain himself. He kept forwarding the private messages on to Electron. Par was clearly becoming more agitated.

'I wish he would just tell me WHO he was,' Par whispered. 'Shit. It is very fucking weird. UnderFED. It's spinning me out.'

Then Par logged off.

Electron typed, 'I guess Par had to go. <Grin>' Then, chuckling to himself, he waited for news on Gandalf's Deszip copy.

If Pad and Gandalf hadn't kept their copy of Deszip, the Australians would be back to square one, beginning with a hunt for a system which even had Deszip. It was a daunting task and by the time Pad and Gandalf finally logged back into Altos, Phoenix and Electron had become quite anxious.

'How did you go?' Phoenix asked. 'Do you still have Deszip?'

'Well, at first I thought I had forgotten which system I left it on . . .'

Electron jumped in, 'And then?'

'Then I remembered.'

'Good news?' Phoenix exclaimed.

'Well, no. Not exactly,' Gandalf said. 'The account is dead.'

Electron felt like someone had thrown a bucket of cold water on him. 'Dead? Dead how?' he asked.

'Dead like someone changed the password. Not sure why. I'll have to re-hack the system to get to the file.'

'Fuck, this Deszip is frustrating,' Electron wrote.

'This is getting ridiculous,' Phoenix added.

'I don't even know if the copy is still in there,' Gandalf replied. 'I hid it, but who knows? Been a few months. Admins might have deleted it.'

'You want some help hacking the system again, Gand?' Phoenix asked.

'Nah, It'll be easy. It's a Sequent. Just have to hang around until the ops go home.'

If an op was logged on and saw Gandalf hunting around, he or she might kick Gandalf off and investigate the file which so interested the hacker. Then they would lose Deszip all over again.

'I hope we get it,' Pad chipped in. 'Would be gr8!'

'Gr8 indeed. Feen, you've got the key to the encryption?' Gandalf asked.

'Yeah.'

'How many characters is it?' It was Gandalf's subtle way of asking for the key itself.

Phoenix wasn't sure what to do. He wanted to give the British hackers the key, but he was torn. He needed Pad and Gandalf's help to get the copy of Deszip, if it was still around. But he knew Electron was watching the conversation, and Electron was always so paranoid. He disliked giving out any information, let alone giving it over Altos, where the conversations were possibly logged by security people.

'Should I give him the key?' Phoenix whispered to Electron.

Gandalf was waiting. To fend him off, Phoenix said, 'It's 9 chars.' Chars was short for characters. On Altos the rule was to abbreviate where ever possible.

'What is the first char?'

'Yeah. Tell him,' Electron whispered to Phoenix.

'Well, the key is . . .'

'You're going to spew when you find out, Gand,' Electron interrupted.

'Yes . . . go on,' Gandalf said. 'I am listening.'

'You won't believe it. <spew spew spew> The key is . . . Dartmouth.'

'WHAT???? WHAT!!!!!!!!!!!!!!!!!!!!!!!!!!!!!!!!!!!!' Gandalf exclaimed. 'No!!! IT's NOT TRUE! Bollox! You are KIDDING?'

The British hacker was thumping himself on the head. The name of the frigging university! What a stupid password!

Phoenix gave an on-line chuckle. 'Hehe. Yeah. So hard to guess. We could have had Deszip for all these months . . .'

'Jesus. I hope it's still on that JANET system,' Gandalf said. Now that he actually had the password, finding the file became even more urgent.

'Pray. Pray. Pray,' Phoenix said. 'Yeah, you should have seen the licence text on Deszip – it was by NASA.'

'You've seen it? You saw Deszip's source code?'

'No,' Phoenix answered. 'When I went back to the BEAR machine to check if Deszip was still there, the program was gone. But the licence agreement and other stuff was there. Should have read the licence . . . truly amazing. It basically went on and on about how the people who wrote it didn't want people like us to get a hold of it. Hehe.'

Electron was growing impatient. 'Yeah. So, Gand, when you gonna go check that JANET system?'

'Now. Fingers crossed, m8! See ya l8r . . .' Then he was gone.

The waiting was driving Electron nuts. He kept thinking about Deszip, about how he could have had it months and months ago. That program was such a prize. He was salivating at the thought of getting it after all this time pursuing it around the globe, chasing its trail from system to system, never quite getting close enough to grab it.

When Gandalf showed up again, Pad, Phoenix and Electron were all over him in an instant.

'WE FUCKING GOT IT GUYS!!!!!' Gandalf exclaimed.

'Good job m8!' Pad said.

'YES!' Electron added. 'Have you decrypted it yet?'

'Not yet. Crypt isn't on that machine. We can either copy Crypt onto that machine or copy the file onto another computer which already has Crypt on it,' Gandalf said.

'Let's move it. Quick . . . quick . . . this damn thing has a habit of disappearing,' Electron said.

'Yeah, this is the last copy . . . the only one I got.'

'OK. Think . . . think . . . where can we copy it to?' Electron said.

'Texas!' Gandalf wanted to copy it to a computer at the University of Texas at Austin, home of the LOD hacker Erik Bloodaxe.

Irrepressible, Gandalf came on like a steam roller if he liked you – and cut you down in a flash if he didn't. His rough-and-tumble working-class humour particularly appealed to Electron. Gandalf seemed able to zero in on the things which worried you most – something so deep or serious it was often unsaid. Then he would blurt it out in such crass, blunt terms you couldn't help laughing. It was his way of being in your face in the friendliest possible manner.

'Yeah! Blame everything on Erik!' Phoenix joked. 'No, seriously. That place is crawling with security now, all after Erik. They are into everything.'

Phoenix had heard all about the security purge at the university from Erik. The Australian called Erik all the time, mostly by charging the calls to stolen AT&T cards. Erik hadn't been raided by the Secret Service yet, but he had been tipped off and was expecting a visit any day.

'It probably won't decrypt anyway,' Electron said.

'Oh, phuck off!' Gandalf shot back. 'Come on! I need a site NOW!'

'Thinking . . .' Phoenix said. 'Gotta be some place with room – how big is it?'

'It's 900 k compressed – probably 3 meg when we uncompress it. Come on, hurry up! How about a university?'

'Princeton, Yale could do either of those.' Electron suggested. 'What about MIT – you hacked an account there recently, Gand?'

'No.'

All four hackers racked their minds for a safe haven. The world was their oyster, as British and Australian hackers held a real-time conversation in Germany about whether to hide their treasure in Austin, Texas; Princeton, New Jersey; Boston, Massachusetts; or New Haven, Connecticut.

'We only need somewhere to stash it for a little while, until we can download it,' Gandalf said. 'Got to be some machine where we've got root. And it's got to have anon FTP.'

Anon FTP, or anonymous file transfer protocol, on a host machine would allow Gandalf to shoot the file from his JANET machine across the Internet into the host. Most importantly, Gandalf could do so without an account on the target machine. He could simply login as 'anonymous', a method of access which had more limitations than simply logging in with a normal account. He would, however, still be able to upload the file.

'OK. OK, I have an idea,' Phoenix said. 'Lemme go check it out.'

Phoenix dropped out of Altos and connected to the University of Texas. The physical location of a site didn't matter. His head was spinning and it was the only place he could think of. But he didn't try to connect to Happy, the machine he often used which Erik had told him about. He headed to one of the other university computers, called Walt.

The network was overloaded. Phoenix was left dangling, waiting to connect for minutes on end. The lines were congested. He logged back into Altos and told Pad and Electron. Gandalf was nowhere to be seen.

'Damn,' Electron said. Then, 'OK, I might have an idea.'

'No, wait!' Phoenix cut in. 'I just thought of a site! And I have root too! But it's on NASA . . .'

'Oh that's OK. I'm sure they won't mind a bit. <grin>'

'I'll go make sure it's still OK. Back in a bit,' Phoenix typed.

Phoenix jumped out of Altos and headed toward NASA. He telnetted into a NASA computer called CSAB at the Langley Research Center in Hampton, Virginia. He had been in and out of NASA quite a few times and had recently made himself a root account on CSAB. First, he had to check the account was still alive, then he had to make sure the system administrator wasn't logged in.

Whizzing past the official warning sign about unauthorised access in US government computers on the login screen, Phoenix typed in his user name and password.

It worked. He was in. And he had root privileges.

He quickly looked around on the system. The administrator was on-line. Damn.

Phoenix fled the NASA computer and sprinted back into Altos. Gandalf was there, along with the other two, waiting for him.

'Well?' Electron asked.

'OK. All right. The NASA machine will work. It has anon FTP. And I still have root. We'll use that.'

Gandalf jumped in. 'Hang on – does it have Crypt?'

'Argh! Forget to check. I think it must.'

'Better check it, m8!'

'Yeah, OK.'

Phoenix felt exasperated, rushing around trying to find sites that worked. He logged out of Altos and coursed his way back into the NASA machine. The admin was still logged on, but Phoenix was running out of time. He had to find out if the computer had Crypt on it. It did.

Phoenix rushed back to Altos. 'Back again. We're in business.'

'Yes!' Electron said, but he quickly jumped in with a word of warning. 'Don't say the exact machine at NASA or the account out loud. Whisper it to Gandalf. I think the ops are listening in on my connection.'

'Well,' Phoenix typed slowly, 'there's only one problem. The admin is logged on.'

'Arghhh!' Electron shouted.

'Just do it,' Pad said. 'No time to worry.'

Phoenix whispered the Internet IP address of the NASA machine to Gandalf.

'OK, m8, I'll anon FTP it to NASA. I'll come back here and tell you the new filename. Then you go in and decrypt it and uncompress the file. W8 for me here.'

Ten minutes later, Gandalf returned. 'Mission accomplished. The file is there!'

'Now, go go Pheeny!' Electron said.

'Gand, whisper the filename to me,' Phoenix said.

'The file's called "d" and it's in the pub directory,' Gandalf whispered.

'OK, folks. Here we go!' Phoenix said as he logged off.

Phoenix dashed to the NASA computer, logged in and looked for the file named 'd'. He couldn't find it. He couldn't even find the pub directory. He began hunting around the rest of the file system. Where was the damn thing?

Uh oh. Phoenix noticed the system administrator, Sharon Beskenis, was still logged in. She was connected from Phoebe, another NASA machine. There was only one other user besides himself logged into the CSAB machine, someone called Carrie. As if that wasn't bad enough, Phoenix realised his username stood out a like a sore thumb. If the admin looked at who was on-line she would see herself, Carrie and a user called 'friend', an account he had created for himself. How many legitimate accounts on NASA computers had that name?

Worse, Phoenix noticed that he had forgotten to cover his login trail. 'Friend' was telnetting into the NASA computer from the University of Texas. No, no, he thought, that would definitely have to go. He disconnected from NASA, bounced back to the university and then logged in to NASA again. Good grief. Now the damn NASA machine showed two people logged in as 'friend'. The computer hadn't properly killed his previous login. Stress.

Phoenix tried frantically to clear out his first login by killing its process number. The NASA computer responded that there was no such process number. Increasingly nervous, Phoenix figured he must have typed in the wrong number. Unhinged, he grabbed one of the other process numbers and killed that.

Christ! That was the admin's process number. Phoenix had just disconnected Sharon from her own machine. Things were not going well.

Now he was under serious pressure. He didn't dare logout, because Sharon would no doubt find his 'friend' account, kill it and close up the security hole he had originally used to get in. Even if she didn't find Deszip on her own machine, he might not be able to get back in again to retrieve it.

After another frenzied minute hunting around the machine, Phoenix finally unearthed Gandalf's copy of Deszip. Now, the moment of truth.

He tried the passphrase. It worked! All he had to do was uncompress Deszip and get it out of there. He typed, 'uncompress deszip.tar.z', but he didn't like how the NASA computer answered his command:

corrupt input

Something was wrong, terribly wrong. The file appeared to be partially destroyed. It was too painful a possibility to contemplate. Even if only a small part of the main Deszip program had been damaged, none of it would be useable.

Rubbing sweat from his palms, Phoenix hoped that maybe the file had just been damaged as he attempted to uncompress it. He had kept the original, so he went back to that and tried decrypting and uncompressing it again. The NASA computer gave him the same ugly response. Urgently, he tried yet again, but this time attempted to uncompress the file in a different way. Same problem.

Phoenix was at his wits' end. This was too much. The most he could hope was that the file had somehow become corrupted in the transfer from Gandalf's JANET machine. He logged out of NASA and returned to Altos. The other three were waiting impatiently for him.

Electron, still logged in as the mystery Guest, leaped in. 'Did it work?'

'No. Decrypted OK, but the file was corrupted when I tried to decompress it.'

'Arghhhhhhhhh!!!!!!!' Gandalf exclaimed.

'Fuckfuckfuck,' Electron wrote. 'Doomed to fail.'

'Sigh Sigh Sigh,' Pad typed.

Gandalf and Electron quizzed Phoenix in detail about each command he had used, but in the end there seemed only one hope. Move a copy of the decryption program to the JANET computer in the UK and try decrypting and uncompressing Deszip there.

Phoenix gave Gandalf a copy of Crypt and the British hacker went to work on the JANET computer. A little later he rendezvoused on Altos again.

Phoenix was beside himself by this stage. 'Gand! Work???'

'Well, I decrypted it using the program you gave me . . .'

'And And And???' Electron was practically jumping out of his seat at his computer.

'Tried to uncompress it. It was taking a LONG time. Kept going – expanded to 8 megabytes.'

'Oh NO. Bad Bad Bad,' Phoenix moaned. 'Should only be 3 meg. If it's making a million files, it's fucked.'

'Christ,' Pad typed. 'Too painful.'

'I got the makefile – licensing agreement text etc., but the Deszip program itself was corrupted,' Gandalf concluded.

'I don't understand what is wrong with it. <Sob>' Phoenix wrote.

'AgonyAgonyAgony,' Electron groaned. 'It'll never never never work.'

'Can we get a copy anywhere else?' Gandalf asked.

'That FTP bug has been fixed at Purdue,' Pad answered. 'Can't use that to get in again.'

Disappointment permeated the atmosphere on Altos.

There were, of course, other possible repositories for Deszip. Phoenix and Electron had already penetrated a computer at Lawrence Livermore National Labs in California. They had procured root on the gamm5 machine and planned to use it as a launchpad for penetrating security expert Russell Brand's computer at LLNL, called Wuthel. They were sure Brand had Deszip on his computer.

It would require a good deal of effort, and possibly another roller-coaster ride of desire, expectation and possible disappointment. For now, the four hackers resolved to sign off, licking their wounds at their defeat in the quest for Deszip.

'Well, I'm off. See you l8r,' Pad said.

'Yeah, me too,' Electron added.

'Yeah, OK. L8r, m8s!' Gandalf said.

Then, just for fun, he added in typical Gandalf style, 'See you in jail!'

6 | *PAGE 1,* *THE* NEW YORK TIMES

Pad had an important warning for the Australian hackers: the computer security community was closing in on them. It was the end of February 1990, not long after Phoenix and Electron had captured Zardoz and just missed out on Deszip. Pad didn't scream or shout the warning, that wasn't his style. But Electron took in the import of the warning loud and clear.

'Feen, they know you did over Spaf's machine,' Pad told Phoenix. 'They know it's been you in other systems also. They've got your handle.'

Eugene Spafford was the kind of computer security expert who loses a lot of face when a hacker gets into his machine, and a wounded bull is a dangerous enemy.

The security people had been able to connect and link up a series of break-ins with the hacker who called himself Phoenix because his style was so distinctive. For example, whenever he was creating a root shell – root access – for himself, he would always save it in the same filename and in the same location on the computer. In some instances, he even created accounts called 'Phoenix' for himself. It was this consistency of style which had made things so much easier for admins to trace his movements.

In his typical understated fashion, Pad suggested a change of style. And maybe, he added, it wasn't such a bad idea for the Australians to tone down their activities a bit. The undercurrent of the message was serious.

'They said that some security people had contacted Australian law enforcement, who were supposed to be "dealing with it",' Pad said.

'Do they know my real name?' Phoenix asked, worried. Electron was also watching this conversation with some concern.

'Don't know. Got it from Shatter. He's not always reliable, but . . .'

Pad was trying to soften the news by playing down Shatter's importance as a source. He didn't trust his fellow British hacker but Shatter had some good, if mysterious, connections. An enigmatic figure who seemed to keep one foot in the computer underworld and the other in the upright computer security industry, Shatter leaked information to Pad and Gandalf, and occasionally to the Australians.

While the two British hackers sometimes discounted Shatter's advice, they also took the time to talk to him. Once, Electron had intercepted email showing Pengo had turned to Shatter for advice about his situation after the raid in Germany. With some spare time prior to his trial, Pengo asked Shatter whether it was safe to travel to the US on a summer holiday in 1989. Shatter asked for Pengo's birthdate and other details. Then he returned with an unequivocal answer: Under no circumstances was Pengo to travel to the US.

Subsequently, it was reported that officials in the US Justice Department had been examining ways to secretly coax Pengo onto American soil, where they could seize him. They would then force him to face trial in their own courts.

Had Shatter known this? Or had he just told Pengo not to

go to the US because it was good commonsense? No-one was quite sure, but people took note of what Shatter told them.

'Shatter definitely got the info right about Spaf's machine. 100% right,' Pad continued. 'He knew exactly how you hacked it. I couldn't believe it. Be careful if you're still hacking m8, especially on the Inet.' The 'Inet' was shorthand for the Internet.

The Altos hackers went quiet.

'It's not just you,' Pad tried to reassure the Australians. 'Two security people from the US are coming to the UK to try and find out something about someone named Gandalf. Oh, and Gand's mate, who might be called Patrick.'

Pad had indeed based his handle on the name Patrick, or Paddy, but that wasn't his real name. No intelligent hacker would use his real name for his handle. Paddy was the name of one of his favourite university lecturers, an Irishman who laughed a good deal. Like Par's name, Pad's handle had coincidentally echoed a second meaning when the British hacker moved into exploring X.25 networks. An X.25 PAD is a packet assembler disassembler, the interface between the X.25 network and a modem or terminal server. Similarly, Gandalf, while being first and foremost the wizard from The Lord of The Rings, also happened to be a terminal server brand name.

Despite the gravity of the news that the security community was closing the net around them, none of the hackers lost their wicked sense of humour.

'You know,' Pad went on, 'Spaf was out of the country when his machine got hacked.'

'Was he? Where?' asked Gandalf, who had just joined the conversation.

'In Europe.'

Electron couldn't resist. 'Where was Spaf, Gandalf asks as he hears a knock on his door . . .'

'Haha,' Gandalf laughed.

'<knock> <knock>' Electron went on, hamming it up.

'Oh! Hello there, Mr Spafford,' Gandalf typed, playing along.

'Hello, I'm Gene and I'm mean!'

Alone in their separate homes on different corners of the globe, the four hackers chuckled to themselves.

'Hello, and is this the man called Patrick?' Pad jumped in.

'Well, Mr Spafford, it seems you're a right fucking idiot for not patching your FTP!' Gandalf proclaimed.

'Not to mention the CHFN bug – saved by a Sequent! Or you'd be very fucking embarrassed,' Phoenix added.

Phoenix was laughing too, but he was a little nervous about Pad's warning and he turned the conversation back to a serious note.

'So, Pad, what else did Shatter tell you?' Phoenix asked anxiously.

'Not much. Except that some of the security investigations might be partly because of UCB.'

UCB was the University of California at Berkeley. Phoenix had been visiting machines at both Berkeley and LLNL so much recently that the admins seemed to have not only noticed him, but they had pinpointed his handle. One day he had telnetted into dewey.soe.berkeley.edu – the Dewey machine as it was known – and had been startled to find the following message of the day staring him in the face:

Phoenix,
Get out of Dewey NOW!
Also, do not use any of the 'soe' machines.
Thank you,
Daniel Berger

Phoenix did a double take when he saw this public warning. Having been in and out of the system so many times, he just zoomed past the words on the login screen. Then, in a delayed reaction, he realised the login message was addressed to him.

Ignoring the warning, he proceeded to get root on the Berkeley machine and look through Berger's files. Then he sat back, thinking about the best way to deal with the problem.

Finally, he decided to send the admin a note saying he was leaving the system for good.

Within days, Phoenix was back in the Dewey machine, weaving in and out of it as if nothing had happened. After all, he had broken into the system, and managed to get root through his own wit. He had earned the right to be in the computer. He might send the admin a note to put him at ease, but Phoenix wasn't going to give up accessing Berkeley's computers just because it upset Daniel Berger.

'See,' Pad continued, 'I think the UCB people kept stuff on their systems that wasn't supposed to be there. Secret things.'

Classified military material wasn't supposed to be stored on non-classified network computers. However, Pad guessed that sometimes researchers broke rules and took short cuts because they were busy thinking about their research and not the security implications.

'Some of the stuff might have been illegal,' Pad told his captive audience. 'And then they find out some of you guys have been in there . . .'

'Shit,' Phoenix said.

'So, well, if it APPEARED like someone was inside trying to get at those secrets . . .' Pad paused. 'Then you can guess what happened. It seems they really want to get whoever was inside their machines.'

There was momentary silence while the other hackers digested all that Pad had told them. As a personality on Altos, Pad remained ever so slightly withdrawn from the other hackers, even the Australians whom he considered mates. This reserved quality gave his warning a certain sobriety, which seeped into the very fabric of Altos that day.

Eventually, Electron responded to Pad's warning by typing a comment directed at Phoenix: 'I told you talking to security guys is nothing but trouble.'

It irritated Electron more and more that Phoenix felt compelled to talk to white hats in the security industry. In Electron's view, drawing attention to yourself was just a bad idea all around and he was increasingly annoyed at watching Phoenix feed his ego. He had made veiled references to Phoenix's bragging on Altos many times, saying things like 'I wish people wouldn't talk to security guys'.

Phoenix responded to Electron on-line somewhat piously. 'Well, I will never talk to security guys seriously again.'

Electron had heard it all before. It was like listening to an alcoholic swear he would never touch another drink. Bidding the others goodbye, Electron logged off. He didn't care to listen to Phoenix any more.

Others did, however. Hundreds of kilometres away, in a special room secreted away inside a bland building in Canberra, Sergeant Michael Costello and Constable William Apro had been methodically capturing each and every electronic boast as it poured from Phoenix's phone. The two officers recorded the data transmissions passing in and out of his computer. They then played this recording into their own modem and computer and created a text file they could save and use as evidence in court.

Both police officers had travelled north from Melbourne, where they worked with the AFP's Computer Crime Unit. Settling into their temporary desks with their PC and laptop, the officers began their secret eavesdropping work on 1 February 1990.

It was the first time the AFP had done a datatap. They were happy to bide their time, to methodically record Phoenix hacking into Berkeley, into Texas, into NASA, into a dozen computers around the world. The phone tap warrant was good for 60 days, which was more than enough time to secrete away a mountain of damning evidence against the egotistical Realm hacker. Time was on their side.

The officers worked the Operation Dabble job in shifts. Constable Apro arrived at the Telecommunications Intelligence Branch of the AFP at 8 p.m. Precisely ten hours later, at 6 the next morning, Sergeant Costello relieved Apro, who knocked off for a good sleep. Apro returned again at 8 p.m. to begin the night shift.

They were there all the time. Twenty-four hours a day. Seven days a week. Waiting and listening.

It was too funny. Erik Bloodaxe in Austin, Texas, couldn't stop laughing. In Melbourne, Phoenix's side hurt from laughing so much.

Phoenix loved to talk on the phone. He often called Erik, sometimes every day, and they spoke for ages. Phoenix didn't worry about cost; he wasn't paying for it. The call would appear on some poor sod's bill and he could sort it out with the phone company.

Sometimes Erik worried a little about whether Phoenix wasn't going to get himself in a jam making all these international calls. Not that he didn't like talking to the Australian; it was a hoot. Still, the concern sat there, unsettled, in the back of his mind. A few times he asked Phoenix about it.

'No prob. Hey, AT&T isn't an Australian company,' Phoenix would say. 'They can't do anything to me.' And Erik had let it rest at that.

For his part, Erik didn't dare call Phoenix, especially not since his little visit from the US Secret Service. On 1 March 1990, they burst into his home, with guns drawn, in a dawn raid. The agents searched everywhere, tearing the student house apart, but they didn't find anything incriminating. They did take Erik's $59 keyboard terminal with its chintzy little 300 baud modem, but they didn't get his main computer, because Erik knew they were coming.

The Secret Service had subpoenaed his academic records, and Erik had heard about it before the raid. So when the Secret Service arrived, Erik's stuff just wasn't there. It hadn't been there for a few weeks, but for Erik, they had been hard weeks. The hacker found himself suffering withdrawal symptoms, so he bought the cheapest home computer and modem he could find to tide him over.

That equipment was the only computer gear the Secret Service discovered, and they were not happy special agents. But without evidence, their hands were tied. No charges were laid.

Still, Erik thought he was probably being watched. The last thing he wanted was for Phoenix's number to appear on his home phone bill. So he let Phoenix call him, which the Australian did all the time. They often talked for hours when Erik was working nights. It was a slack job, just changing the back-up tapes on various computers and making sure they didn't jam. Perfect for a student. It left Erik hours of free time.

Erik frequently reminded Phoenix that his phone was probably tapped, but Phoenix just laughed. 'Yeah, well don't worry about it, mate. What are they going to do? Come and get me?'

After Erik put a hold on his own hacking activities, he lived vicariously, listening to Phoenix's exploits. The Australian called him with a technical problem or an interesting system, and then they discussed various strategies for getting into the machine. However, unlike Electron's talks with Phoenix, conversations with Erik weren't only about hacking. They chatted about life, about what Australia was like, about girls, about what was in the newspaper that day. It was easy to talk to Erik. He had a big ego, like most hackers, but it was inoffensive, largely couched in his self-effacing humour.

Phoenix often made Erik laugh. Like the time he got Clifford Stoll, an astronomer, who wrote *The Cuckoo's Egg*. The book described his pursuit of a German hacker who had broken into the computer system Stoll managed at Lawrence Berkeley Labs near San Francisco. The hacker had been part of the same hacking ring as Pengo. Stoll took a hard line on hacking, a position which did not win him popularity in the underground. Both Phoenix and Erik had read Stoll's book, and one day they were sitting around chatting about it.

'You know, it's really stupid that Cliffy put his email address in his book,' Phoenix said. 'Hmm, why don't I go check?'

Sure enough, Phoenix called Erik back about a day later. 'Well, I got root on Cliffy's machine,' he began slowly, then he burst out laughing. 'And I changed the message of the day. Now it reads, "It looks like the Cuckoo's got egg on his face"!'

It was uproariously funny. Stoll, the most famous hacker-catcher in the world, had been japed! It was the funniest thing Erik had heard in weeks.

But it was not nearly so amusing as what Erik told Phoenix later about the *New York Times*. The paper had published an article on 19 March suggesting a hacker had written some sort of virus or worm which was breaking into dozens of computers.

'Listen to this,' Erik had said, reading Phoenix the lead paragraph, ' "A computer intruder has written a program that has entered dozens of computers in a nationwide network in recent weeks, automatically stealing electronic documents containing users' passwords and erasing files to help conceal itself." '

Phoenix was falling off his chair he was laughing so hard. A program? Which was automatically doing this? No. It wasn't an automated program, it was the Australians! It was the Realm hackers! God, this was funny.

'Wait – there's more! It says, "Another rogue program shows a widespread vulnerability". I laughed my ass off,' Erik said, struggling to get the words out.

'A rogue program! Who wrote the article?'

'A John Markoff,' Erik answered, wiping his eyes. 'I called him up.'

'You did? What did you say?' Phoenix tried to gather himself together.

' "John," I said, "You know that article you wrote on page 12 of the *Times*? It's wrong! There's no rogue program attacking the Internet." He goes, "What is it then?" "It's not a virus or a worm," I said. "It's PEOPLE." '

Erik started laughing uncontrollably again.

'Then Markoff sounds really stunned, and he goes, "People?" And I said, "Yeah, people." Then he said, "How do you know?" And I said, "Because, John, I KNOW." '

Phoenix erupted in laughter again. The Times reporter obviously had worms on his mind, since the author of the famous Internet worm, Robert T. Morris Jr, had just been tried and convicted in the US. He was due to be sentenced in May.

US investigators had tracked the hacker's connections, looping through site after site in a burrowing manner which they assumed belonged to a worm. The idea of penetrating so many sites all in such a short time clearly baffled the investigators, who concluded it must be a program rather than human beings launching the attacks.

'Yeah,' Erik continued, 'And then Markoff said, "Can you get me to talk to them?" And I said I'd see what I could do.'

'Yeah,' Phoenix said. 'Go tell him, yes. Yeah, I gotta talk to this idiot. I'll set him straight.'

Page one, the *New York Times*, 21 March 1990: 'Caller Says he Broke Computers' Barriers to Taunt the Experts', by John Markoff.

True, the article was below the crease – on the bottom half of the page – but at least it was in column 1, the place a reader turns to first.

Phoenix was chuffed. He'd made the front page of the *New York Times*.

'The man identified himself only as an Australian named Dave,' the article said. Phoenix chuckled softly. Dave Lissek was the pseudonym he'd used. Of course, he wasn't the only one using the name Dave. When Erik first met the Australians on Altos, he marvelled at how they all called themselves Dave. I'm Dave, he's Dave, we're all Dave, they told him. It was just easier that way, they said.

The article revealed that 'Dave' had attacked Spaf's and Stoll's machines, and that the Smithsonian Astronomical Observatory at Harvard University – where Stoll now worked – had pulled its computers off the Internet as a result of the break-in. Markoff had even included the 'egg on his face' story Phoenix had described to him.

Phoenix laughed at how well he had thumbed his nose at Cliffy Stoll. This article would show him up all right. It felt so good, seeing himself in print that way. He did that. That was him there in black in white, for all the world to see. He had outsmarted the world's best known hacker-catcher, and he had smeared the insult across the front page of the most prestigious newspaper in America.

And Markoff reported that he had been in Spaf's system too! Phoenix glowed happily. Better still, Markoff had quoted 'Dave' on the subject: 'The caller said . . . "It used to be the security guys chasing the hackers. Now it's the hackers chasing the security people."'

The article went on: 'Among the institutions believed to have been penetrated by the intruder are the Los Alamos National Laboratories, Harvard, Digital Equipment Corporation, Boston University and the University of Texas.' Yes, that list sounded about right. Well, for the Australians as a group anyway. Even if Phoenix hadn't masterminded or even penetrated some of those himself, he was happy to take the credit in the *Times*.

This was a red-letter day for Phoenix.

Electron, however, was furious. How could Phoenix be so stupid? He knew that Phoenix had an ego, that he talked too much, and that his tendency to brag had grown worse over time, fed by the skyrocketing success of the Australian hackers. Electron knew all of that, but he still couldn't quite believe that Phoenix had gone so far as to strut and preen like a show pony for the *New York Times*.

To think that he had associated with Phoenix. Electron was disgusted. He had never trusted Phoenix – a caution now proved wise. But he had spent hours with him on the phone, with most of the information flowing in one direction. But not only did Phoenix show no discretion at all in dealing with the paper, he bragged about doing things that Electron had done! If Phoenix had to talk – and clearly he should have kept his mouth shut – he should have at least been honest about the systems for which he could claim credit.

Electron had tried with Phoenix. Electron had suggested that he stop talking to the security guys. He had continually urged caution and discretion. He had even subtly withdrawn each time Phoenix suggested one of his hair-brained schemes to show off to a security bigwig. Electron had done this in the hope that Phoenix might get the hint. Maybe, if Phoenix couldn't hear someone shouting advice at him, he might at least listen to someone whispering it. But no. Phoenix was far too thick for that.

The Internet – indeed, all hacking – was out of bounds for weeks, if not months. There was no chance the Australian authorities would let a front-page story in the *Times* go by unheeded. The Americans would be all over them. In one selfish act of hubris, Phoenix had ruined the party for everyone else.

Electron unplugged his modem and took it to his father. During exams, he had often asked his father to hide it. He didn't have the self-discipline needed to stay away on his own and there was no other way Electron could keep himself from jacking in – plugging his modem into the wall. His father had become an expert at hiding the device, but Electron usually still managed to find it after a few days, tearing the house apart until he emerged, triumphant, with the modem held high above his head. Even when his father began hiding the modem outside the family home it would only postpone the inevitable.

This time, however, Electron vowed he would stop hacking until the fallout had cleared – he had to. So he handed the modem to his father, with strict instructions, and then tried to distract himself by cleaning up his hard drive and disks. His hacking files had to go too. So much damning evidence of his activities. He deleted some files and took others on disks to store at a friend's house. Deleting files caused Electron considerable pain, but there was no other way. Phoenix had backed him into a corner.

Brimming with excitement, Phoenix rang Electron on a sunny March afternoon.

'Guess what?' Phoenix was jumping around like an eager puppy at the other end of the line. 'We made the nightly news right across the US!'

'Uhuh,' Electron responded, unimpressed.

'This is not a joke!' We were on cable news all day too. I called Erik and he told me.'

'Mmm,' Electron said.

'You know, we did a lot of things right. Like Harvard. We got into every system at Harvard. It was a good move. Harvard gave us the fame we needed.'

Electron couldn't believe what he was hearing. He didn't need any fame – and he certainly didn't need to be busted. The conversation – like Phoenix himself – was really beginning to annoy him.

'Hey, and they know your name,' Phoenix said coyly.

That got a reaction. Electron gulped his anger.

'Haha! Just joshing!' Phoenix practically shouted. 'Don't worry! They didn't really mention anyone's name.'

'Good,' Electron answered curtly. His irritation stewed quietly.

'So, do you reckon we'll make the cover of *Time* or *Newsweek*?'

Good grief! Didn't Phoenix ever give up? As if it wasn't enough to appear on the 6 o'clock national news in a country crawling with over-zealous law enforcement agencies. Or to make the *New York Times*. He had to have the weeklies too.

Phoenix was revelling in his own publicity. He felt like he was on top of the world, and he wanted to shout about it. Electron had felt the same wave of excitement from hacking many high-profile targets and matching wits with the best, but he was happy to stand on the peak by himself, or with people like Pad and Gandalf, and enjoy the view quietly. He was happy to know he had been the best on the frontier of a computer underground which was fresh, experimental and, most of all, international. He didn't need to call up newspaper reporters or gloat about it in Clifford Stoll's face.

'Well, what do you reckon?' Phoenix asked impatiently.

'No,' Electron answered.

'No? You don't think we will?' Phoenix sounded disappointed.

'No.'

'Well, I'll demand it!' Phoenix said laughing, 'Fuck it, we want the cover of *Newsweek*, nothing less.' Then, more seriously,

'I'm trying to work out what really big target would clinch it for us.'

'Yeah, OK, whatever,' Electron replied, distancing himself again.

But Electron was thinking, Phoenix, you are a fool. Didn't he see the warning signs? Pad's warning, all the busts in the US, reports that the Americans were hunting down the Brits. As a result of these news reports of which Phoenix was so proud, bosses across the world would be calling their computer managers into their offices and breathing down their necks about their own computer security.

The brazen hackers had deeply offended the computer security industry, spurring it into action. In the process, some in the industry had also seen an opportunity to raise its own public profile. The security experts had talked to the law enforcement agencies, who were now clearly sharing information across national borders and closing in fast. The conspirators in the global electronic village were at the point of maximum overreach.

'We could hack Spaf again,' Phoenix volunteered.

'The general public couldn't give a fuck about Eugene Spafford,' Electron said, trying to dampen Phoenix's bizarre enthusiasm. He was all for thumbing one's nose at authority, but this was not the way to do it.

'It'd be so funny in court, though. The lawyer would call Spaf and say, "So, Mr Spafford, is it true that you are a world-renowned computer security expert?" When he said, "Yes" I'd jump up and go, "I object, your honour, this guy doesn't know jackshit, 'cause I hacked his machine and it was a breeze!"'

'Mmm.'

'Hey, if we don't get busted in the next two weeks, it will be a miracle,' Phoenix continued happily.

'I hope not.'

'This is a lot of fun!' Phoenix shouted sarcastically. 'We're gonna get busted! We're gonna get busted!'

Electron's jaw fell to the ground. Phoenix was mad. Only a lunatic would behave this way. Mumbling something about how tired he was, Electron said goodbye and hung up.

At 5.50 a.m. on 2 April 1990, Electron dragged himself out of bed and made his way to the bathroom. Part way through his visit, the light suddenly went out.

How strange. Electron opened his eyes wide in the early morning dimness. He returned to his bedroom and began putting on some jeans before going to investigate the problem.

Suddenly, two men in street clothes yanked his window open and jumped through into the room shouting, 'GET DOWN ON THE FLOOR!'

Who were these people? Half-naked, Electron stood in the middle of his room, stunned and immobile. He had suspected the police might pay him a visit, but didn't they normally wear uniforms? Didn't they announce themselves?

The two men grabbed Electron, threw him face down onto the floor and pulled his arms behind his back. They jammed handcuffs on his wrists – hard – cutting his skin. Then someone kicked him in the stomach.

'Are there any firearms in the house?' one of the men asked.

Electron couldn't answer because he couldn't breathe. The kick had winded him. He felt someone pull him up from the floor and prop him in a chair. Lights went on everywhere and he could see six or seven people moving around in the hallway. They must have come into the house another way. The ones in the hallway were all wearing bibs with three large letters emblazoned across the front: AFP.

As Electron slowly gathered his wits, he realised why the cops had asked about firearms. He had once joked to Phoenix on the phone about how he was practising with his dad's .22 for when the feds came around. Obviously the feds had been tapping his phone.

While his father talked with one of the officers in the other room and read the warrant, Electron saw the police pack up his computer gear – worth some $3000 – and carry it out of the house. The only thing they didn't discover was the modem. His father had become so expert at hiding it that not even the Australian Federal Police could find it.

Several other officers began searching Electron's bedroom, which was no small feat, given the state it was in. The floor was covered in a thick layer of junk. Half crumpled music band posters, lots of scribbled notes with passwords and NUAs, pens, T-shirts both clean and dirty, jeans, sneakers, accounting books, cassettes, magazines, the occasional dirty cup. By the time the police had sifted through it all the room was tidier than when they started.

As they moved into another room at the end of the raid, Electron bent down to pick up one of his posters which had fallen onto the floor. It was a Police Drug Identification Chart – a gift from a friend's father – and there, smack dab in the middle, was a genuine AFP footprint. Now it was a collector's item. Electron smiled to himself and carefully tucked the poster away.

When he went out to the living room, he saw a policemen holding a couple of shovels and he wanted to laugh again. Electron had also once told Phoenix that all his sensitive hacking disks were buried in the backyard. Now the police were going to dig it up in search of something which had been destroyed a few days before. It was too funny.

The police found little evidence of Electron's hacking at his house, but that didn't really matter. They already had almost everything they needed.

Later that morning, the police put the 20-year-old Electron into an unmarked car and drove him to the AFP's imposing-looking headquarters at 383 Latrobe Street for questioning.

In the afternoon, when Electron had a break from the endless questions, he walked out to the hallway. The boyish-faced Phoenix, aged eighteen, and fellow Realm member Nom, 21, were walking with police at the other end of the hall. They were too far apart to talk, but Electron smiled. Nom looked worried. Phoenix looked annoyed.

Electron was too intimidated to insist on having a lawyer. What was the point in asking for one anyway? It was clear the police had information they could only have obtained from tapping his phone. They also showed him logs taken from Melbourne University, which had been traced back to his phone. Electron figured the game was up, so he might as well tell them the whole story – or at least as much of it as he had told Phoenix on the phone.

Two officers conducted the interview. The lead interviewer was Detective Constable Glenn Proebstl, which seemed to be pronounced 'probe stool' – an unfortunate name, Electron thought. Proebstl was accompanied by Constable Natasha Elliott, who occasionally added a few questions at the end of various interview topics but otherwise kept to herself. Although he had decided to answer their questions truthfully, Electron thought that neither of them knew much about computers and found himself struggling to understand what they were trying to ask.

Electron had to begin with the basics. He explained what the FINGER command was – how you could type 'finger' followed by a username, and then the computer would provide basic information about the user's name and other details.

'So, what is the methodology behind it . . . finger . . . then, it's normally . . . what is the normal command after that to try and get the password out?' Constable Elliott finally completed her convoluted attempt at a question.

The only problem was that Electron had no idea what she was talking about.

'Well, um, I mean there is none. I mean you don't use finger like that . . .'

'Right. OK,' Constable Elliott got down to business. 'Well, have you ever used that system before?'

'Uhm, which system?' Electron had been explaining commands for so long he had forgotten if they were still talking about how he hacked the Lawrence Livermore computer or some other site.

'The finger . . . The finger system?'

Huh? Electron wasn't quite sure how to answer that question. There was no such thing. Finger was a command, not a computer.

'Uh, yes,' he said.

The interview went the same way, jolting awkwardly through computer technology which he understood far better than either officer. Finally, at the end of a long day, Detective Constable Proebstl asked Electron:

'In your own words, tell me what fascination you find with accessing computers overseas?'

'Well, basically, it's not for any kind of personal gain or anything,' Electron said slowly. It was a surprisingly difficult question to answer. Not because he didn't know the answer, but because it was a difficult answer to describe to someone who had never hacked a computer. 'It's just the kick of getting in to a system. I mean, once you are in, you very often get bored and even though you can still access the system, you may never call back.

'Because once you've gotten in, it's a challenge over and you don't really care much about it,' Electron continued, struggling. 'It's a hot challenge thing, trying to do things that other people are also trying to do but can't.

'So, I mean, I guess it is a sort of ego thing. It's knowing that you can do stuff that other people cannot, and well, it is the challenge and the ego boost you get from doing something well . . . where other people try and fail.'

A few more questions and the day-long interview finally finished. The police then took Electron to the Fitzroy police station. He guessed it was the nearest location with a JP they could find willing to process a bail application at that hour.

In front of the ugly brick building, Electron noticed a small group of people gathered on the footpath in the dusky light. As the police car pulled up, the group swung into a frenzy of activity, fidgeting in over-the-shoulder briefcases, pulling out notebooks and pens, scooping up big microphones with fuzzy shag covers, turning on TV camera lights.

Oh NO! Electron wasn't prepared for this at all.

Flanked by police, Electron stepped out of the police car and blinked in the glare of photographers' camera flashes and TV camera searchlights. The hacker tried to ignore them, walking as briskly as his captors would allow. Sound recordists and reporters tagged beside him, keeping pace, while the TV cameramen and photographers weaved in front of him. Finally he escaped into the safety of the watchhouse.

First there was paperwork, followed by the visit to the JP. While shuffling through his papers, the JP gave Electron a big speech about how defendants often claimed to have been beaten by the police. Sitting in the dingy meeting room, Electron felt somewhat confused by the purpose of this tangential commentary. However, the JP's next question cleared things up: 'Have you had any problems with your treatment by the police which you would like to record at this time?'

Electron thought about the brutal kick he had suffered while lying on his bedroom floor, then he looked up and found Detective Constable Proebstl staring him in the eye. A slight smile passed across the detective's face.

'No,' Electron answered.

The JP proceeded to launch into another speech which Electron found even stranger. There was another defendant in the lock-up at the moment, a dangerous criminal who had a disease the JP knew about, and the JP could decide to lock Electron up with that criminal instead of granting him bail.

Was this meant to be helpful warning, or just the gratification of some kind of sadistic tendency? Electron was baffled but he didn't have to consider the situation for long. The JP granted bail. Electron's father came to the watchhouse, collected his son and signed the papers for a $1000 surety – to be paid if Electron skipped town. That night Electron watched as his name appeared on the late night news.

At home over the next few weeks, Electron struggled to come to terms with the fact that he would have to give up hacking forever. He still had his modem, but no computer.

Even if he had a machine, he realised it was far too dangerous to even contemplate hacking again.

So he took up drugs instead.

Electron's father waited until the very last days of his illness, in March 1991, before he went into hospital. He knew that once he went in, he would not be coming out again.

There was so much to do before that trip, so many things to organise. The house, the life insurance paperwork, the will, the funeral, the instructions for the family friend who promised to watch over both children when he was gone. And, of course, the children themselves.

He looked at his two children and worried. Despite their ages of 21 and 19, they were in many ways still very sheltered. He realised that Electron's anti-establishment attitude and his sister's emotional remoteness would remain unresolved difficulties at the time of his death. As the cancer progressed, Electron's father tried to tell both children how much he cared for them. He might have been somewhat emotionally remote himself in the past, but with so little time left, he wanted to set the record straight.

On the issue of Electron's problems with the police, however, Electron's father maintained a hands-off approach. Electron had only talked to his father about his hacking exploits occasionally, usually when he had achieved what he considered to be a very noteworthy hack. His father's view was always the same. Hacking is illegal, he told his son, and the police will probably eventually catch you. Then you will have to deal with the problem yourself. He didn't lecture his son, or forbid Electron from hacking. On this issue he considered his son old enough to make his own choices and live with the consequences.

True to his word, Electron's father had shown little sympathy for his son's legal predicament after the police raid. He remained neutral on the subject, saying only, 'I told you something like this would happen and now it is your responsibility'.

Electron's hacking case progressed slowly over the year, as did his university accounting studies. In March 1991, he faced committal proceedings and had to decide whether to fight his committal.

He faced fifteen charges, most of which were for obtaining unauthorised access to computers in the US and Australia. A few were aggravated offences, for obtaining access to data of a commercial nature. On one count each, the DPP (the Office of the Commonwealth Director of Public Prosecutions) said he altered and erased data. Those two counts were the result of his inserting backdoors for himself, not because he did damage to any files. The evidence was reasonably strong: telephone intercepts and datataps on Phoenix's phone which showed him talking to Electron about hacking; logs of Electron's own sessions in Melbourne University's systems which were traced back to his home phone; and Electron's own confession to the police.

This was the first major computer hacking case in Australia under the new legislation. It was a test case – the test case for computer hacking in Australia – and the DPP was going in hard. The case had generated seventeen volumes of evidence, totalling some 25 000 pages, and Crown prosecutor Lisa West planned to call up to twenty expert witnesses from Australia, Europe and the US.

Those witnesses had some tales to tell about the Australian hackers, who had caused havoc in systems around the world. Phoenix had accidentally deleted a Texas-based company's inventory of assets – the only copy in existence according to Execucom Systems Corporation. The hackers had also baffled security personnel at the US Naval Research Labs. They had bragged to the *New York Times*. And they forced NASA to cut off its computer network for 24 hours.

AFP Detective Sergeant Ken Day had flown halfway around the world to obtain a witness statement from none other than

NASA Langley computer manager Sharon Beskenis – the admin Phoenix had accidentally kicked off her own system when he was trying to get Deszip. Beskenis had been more than happy to oblige and on 24 July 1990 she signed a statement in Virginia, witnessed by Day. Her statement said that, as a result of the hackers' intrusion, 'the entire NASA computer system was disconnected from any external communications with the rest of the world' for about 24 hours on 22 February 1990.

In short, Electron thought, there didn't seem to be much chance of winning at the committal hearing. Nom seemed to feel the same way. He faced two counts, both 'knowingly concerned' with Phoenix obtaining unauthorised access. One was for NASA Langley, the other for CSIRO – the Zardoz file. Nom didn't fight his committal either, although Legal Aid's refusal to fund a lawyer for the procedure no doubt weighed in his decision.

On 6 March 1991, Magistrate Robert Langton committed Electron and Nom to stand trial in the Victorian County Court.

Phoenix, however, didn't agree with his fellow hackers' point of view. With financial help from his family, he had decided to fight his committal. He wasn't going to hand this case to the prosecution on a silver platter, and they would have to fight him every step of the way, dragging him forward from proceeding to proceeding. His barrister, Felicity Hampel, argued the court should throw out 47 of the 48 charges against her client on jurisdictional grounds. All but one charge – breaking into the CSIRO machine in order to steal Zardoz – related to hacking activities outside Australia. How could an Australian court claim jurisdiction over a hacked computer in Texas?

Privately, Phoenix worried more about being extradited to the US than dealing with the Australian courts, but publicly he was going into the committal with all guns blazing. It was a test case in many ways; not only the first major hacking case in Australia but also the first time a hacker had fought Australian committal proceedings for computer crimes.

The prosecution agreed to drop one of the 48 counts, noting it was a duplicate charge, but the backdown was a pyrrhic victory for Phoenix. After a two-day committal hearing, John Wilkinson decided Hampel's jurisdictional argument didn't hold water and on 14 August 1991 he committed Phoenix to stand trial in the County Court.

By the day of Electron's committal, in March, Electron's father had begun his final decline. The bowel cancer created a roller-coaster of good and bad days, but soon there were only bad days, and they were getting worse. On the last day of March, the doctors told him that it was finally time to make the trip to hospital. He stubbornly refused to go, fighting their advice, questioning their authority. They quietly urged him again. He protested. Finally, they insisted.

Electron and his sister stayed with their father for hours that day, and the following one. Their father had other visitors to keep his spirits up, including his brother who fervently beseeched him to accept Jesus Christ as his personal saviour before he died. That way, he wouldn't burn in hell. Electron looked at his uncle, disbelieving. He couldn't believe his father was having to put up with such crap on his deathbed. Still, Electron chose to be discreet. Apart from an occasional rolling of the eyes, he kept his peace at his father's bedside.

Perhaps, however, the fervent words did some good, for as Electron's father spoke about the funeral arrangements, he made a strange slip of the tongue. He said 'wedding' instead of funeral, then paused, realising his mistake. Glancing slowly down at the intricate braided silver wedding band still on his finger, he smiled frailly and said, 'I suppose, in a way, it will be like a wedding'.

Electron and his sister went to hospital every day for four days, to sit by their father's bed.

At 6 a.m. on the fifth day, the telephone rang. It was the family friend their father had asked to watch over them. Their father's life signs were very, very weak, fluttering on the edge of death.

When Electron and his sister arrived at the hospital, the nurse's face said everything. They were too late. Their father had died ten minutes before they arrived. Electron broke down and wept. He hugged his sister, who, for a brief moment, seemed almost reachable. Driving them back to the house, the family friend stopped and bought them an answering machine.

'You'll need this when everyone starts calling in,' she told them. 'You might not want to talk to anyone for a while.'

In the months after his bust in 1990 Electron began smoking marijuana regularly. At first, as with many other university students, it was a social thing. Some friends dropped by, they happened to have a few joints, and so everybody went out for a night on the town. When he was in serious hacking mode, he never smoked. A clear head was much too important. Besides, the high he got from hacking was a hundred times better than anything dope could ever do for him.

When Phoenix appeared on the front page of the *New York Times*, Electron gave up hacking. And even if he had been tempted to return to it, he didn't have anything to hack with after the police took his only computer. Electron found himself casting around for something to distract him from his father's deteriorating condition and the void left by giving up hacking. His accounting studies didn't quite fit the bill. They had always seemed empty, but never more so than now.

Smoking pot filled the void. So did tripping. Filled it very nicely. Besides, he told himself, it's harder to get caught smoking dope in your friends' houses than hacking in your own. The habit grew gradually. Soon, he was smoking dope at home. New friends began coming around, and they seemed to have drugs with them all the time – not just occasionally, and not just for fun.

Electron and his sister had been left the family home and enough money to give them a modest income. Electron began spending this money on his new-found hobby. A couple of Electron's new friends moved into the house for a few months. His sister didn't like them dealing drugs out of the place, but

Electron didn't care what was happening around him. He just sat in his room, listening to his stereo, smoking dope, dropping acid and watching the walls.

The headphones blocked out everyone in the house, and, more importantly, what was going on inside Electron's own head. Billy Bragg. Faith No More. Cosmic Psychos. Celibate Rifles. Jane's Addiction. The Sex Pistols. The Ramones. Music gave Electron a pinpoint, a figurative dot of light on his forehead where he could focus his mind. Blot out the increasingly strange thoughts creeping through his consciousness.

His father was alive. He was sure of it. He knew it, like he knew the sun would rise tomorrow. Yet he had seen his father lying, dead, in the hospital bed. It didn't make sense.

So he took another hit from the bong, floated in slow motion to his bed, lay down, carefully slid the earphones over his head, closed his eyes and tried to concentrate on what the Red Hot Chili Peppers were saying instead. When that wasn't enough, he ventured down the hallway, down to his new friends – the friends with the acid tabs. Then, eight more hours without having to worry about the strange thoughts.

Soon people began acting strangely too. They would tell Electron things, but he had trouble understanding them. Pulling a milk carton from the fridge and sniffing it, Electron's sister might say, 'Milk's gone off'. But Electron wasn't sure what she meant. He would look at her warily. Maybe she was trying to tell him something else, about spiders. Milking spiders for venom.

When thoughts like these wafted through Electron's mind, they disturbed him, lingering like a sour smell. So he floated back to the safety of his room and listened to songs by Henry Rollins.

After several months in this cloudy state of limbo, Electron awoke one day to find the Crisis Assessment Team – a mobile psychiatric team – in his bedroom. They asked him questions, then they tried to feed him little blue tablets. Electron didn't want to take the tablets. Were little blue pills placebos? He was sure they were. Or maybe they were something more sinister.

Finally, the CAT workers convinced Electron to take the Stelazine tablet. But when they left, terrifying things began to happen. Electron's eyes rolled uncontrollably to the back of his head. His head twisted to the left. His mouth dropped open, very wide. Try as he might, he couldn't shut it, any more than he could turn his head straight. Electron saw himself in the mirror and he panicked. He looked like a character out of a horror picture.

His new house-mates reacted to this strange new behaviour by trying to psychoanalyse Electron, which was less than helpful. They discussed him as if he wasn't even present. He felt like a ghost and, agitated and confused, he began telling his friends that he was going to kill himself. Someone called the CAT team again. This time they refused to leave unless he would guarantee not to attempt suicide.

Electron refused. So they had him committed.

Inside the locked psychiatric ward of Plenty Hospital (now known as NEMPS), Electron believed that, although he had gone crazy, he wasn't really in a hospital psychiatric ward. The place was just supposed to look like one. His father had set it all up.

Electron refused to believe anything that anyone told him. It was all lies. They said one thing, but always meant another.

He had proof. Electron read a list of patients' names on the wall and found one called Tanas. That name had a special meaning. It was an anagram for the word 'Santa'. But Santa Claus was a myth, so the name Tanas appearing on the hospital list proved to him that he shouldn't listen to anything anyone told him.

Electron ate his meals mostly in silence, trying to ignore the voluntary and involuntary patients who shared the dining hall. One lunchtime, a stranger sat down at Electron's table and started talking to him. Electron found it excruciatingly painful talking to other people, and he kept wishing the stranger would go away.

The stranger talked about how good the drugs were in hospital.

'Mm,' Electron said. 'I used to do a lot of drugs.'

'How much is a lot?'

'I spent $28000 on dope alone in about four months.'

'Wow,' the stranger said, impressed. 'Of course, you don't have to pay for drugs. You can always get them for free. I do.'

'You do?' Electron asked, somewhat perplexed.

'Sure! All the time,' the stranger said grandly. 'No problem. Just watch.'

The stranger calmly put his fork down on the tray, carefully stood up and then began yelling at the top of his lungs. He waved his arms around frantically and shouted abuse at the other patients.

Two nurses came running from the observation room. One of them tried to calm the stranger down while the other quickly measured out various pills and grabbed a cup of water. The stranger swallowed the pills, chased them with a swig of water and sat down quietly. The nurses retreated, glancing back over their shoulders.

'See?' The stranger said. 'Well, I'd better be on my way, before the pills kick in. See ya.'

Electron watched, amazed, as the stranger picked up his bag, walked through the dining-hall door, and straight out the front door of the psychiatric ward.

After a month, the psychiatrists reluctantly allowed Electron to leave the hospital in order to stay with his maternal grandmother in Queensland. He was required to see a psychiatrist regularly. He spent his first few days in Queensland believing he was Jesus Christ. But he didn't hold onto that one for long. After two weeks of patiently waiting and checking for signs of the imminent apocalypse, consistent with the second coming, he decided he was really the reincarnation of Buddha.

In late February 1992, after three months of psychiatric care up north, Electron returned to Melbourne and his university studies, with a bag full of medication. Prozac, major tranquillisers, Lithium. The daily routine went smoothly for a while. Six Prozac – two in the morning, two at midday and two at night. Another anti-depressant to be taken at night. Also at night, the anti-side effect tablets to combat the involuntary eye-rolling, jaw-dropping and neck-twisting associated with the anti-depressants.

All of it was designed to help him deal with what had by now become a long list of diagnoses. Cannabis psychosis. Schizophrenia. Manic depression. Unipolar affective disorder. Schizophreniform. Amphetamine psychosis. Major affective disorder. Atypical psychosis. And his own personal favourite – facticious disorder, or faking it to get into hospital. But the medication wasn't helping much. Electron still felt wretched, and returning to a host of problems in Melbourne made things worse.

Because of his illness, Electron had been largely out of the loop of legal proceedings. Sunny Queensland provided a welcome escape. Now he was back in Victoria facing a tedious university course in accounting, an ongoing battle with mental illness, federal charges which could see him locked up for ten years, and publicity surrounding the first major hacking case in Australia. It was going to be a hard winter.

To make matters worse, Electron's medication interfered with his ability to study properly. The anti-side effect pills relaxed the muscles in his eyes, preventing them from focusing. The writing on the blackboard at the front of the lecture hall was nothing but a hazy blur. Taking notes was also a problem. The medication made his hands tremble, so he couldn't write properly. By the end of a lecture, Electron's notes were as unreadable as the blackboard. Frustrated, Electron stopped taking his medicine, started smoking dope again and soon felt a little better. When the dope wasn't enough, he turned to magic mushrooms and hallucinogenic cactus.

The hacking case was dragging on and on. On 6 December 1991, just after he left psych hospital but before he flew to Queensland, the office of the DPP had formally filed an indictment containing fifteen charges against Electron, and three against Nom, in the Victorian County Court.

Electron didn't talk to Phoenix much any more, but the DPP lawyers hadn't forgotten about him – far from it. They had much bigger plans for Phoenix, perhaps because he was fighting every step of the way. Phoenix was uncooperative with police in the interview on the day of the raid, frequently refusing to answer their questions. When they asked to fingerprint him, he refused and argued with them about it. This behaviour did not endear him to either the police or the DPP.

On 5 May 1992, the DPP filed a final indictment with 40 charges against Phoenix in the County Court. The charges, in conjunction with those against Electron and Nom, formed part of a joint indictment totalling 58 counts.

Electron worried about being sent to prison. Around the world, hackers were under siege – Par, Pengo, LOD and Erik Bloodaxe, MOD, The Realm hackers, Pad and Gandalf and, most recently, the International Subversives. Somebody seemed to be trying to make a point. Furthermore, Electron's charges had changed considerably – for the worse – from the original ones documented in April 1990.

The DPP's final indictment bore little resemblance to the original charge sheet handed to the young hacker when he left the police station the day he was raided. The final indictment read like a veritable Who's Who of prestigious institutions around the world. Lawrence Livermore Labs, California. Two different computers at the US Naval Research Laboratories, Washington DC. Rutgers University, New Jersey. Tampere University of Technology, Finland. The University of Illinios. Three different computers at the University of Melbourne. Helsinki University of Technology, Finland. The University of New York. NASA Langley Research Center, Hampton, Virginia. CSIRO, Carlton, Victoria.

The charges which worried Electron most related to the US Naval Research Labs, CSIRO, Lawrence Livermore Labs and NASA. The last three weren't full hacking charges. The DPP alleged Electron had been 'knowingly concerned' with Phoenix's access of these sites.

Electron looked at the thirteen-page joint indictment and didn't know whether to laugh or cry. He had been a lot more than 'knowingly concerned' with accessing those sites. In many cases, he had given Phoenix access to those computers in the first place. But Electron tried to tread quietly, carefully, through most systems, while Phoenix had noisily stomped around with all the grace of a buffalo – and left just as many footprints. Electron hardly wanted to face full charges for those or any other sites. He had broken into thousands of sites on the X.25 network, but he hadn't been charged with any of them. He couldn't help feeling a little like the gangster Al Capone being done for tax evasion.

The proceedings were attracting considerable media attention. Electron suspected the AFP or the DPP were alerting the media to upcoming court appearances, perhaps in part to prove to the Americans that 'something was being done'.

This case had American pressure written all over it. Electron's barrister, Boris Kayser, said he suspected that 'the Americans' – American institutions, companies or government agencies – were indirectly funding some of the prosecution's case by offering to pay for US witnesses to attend the trial. The Americans wanted to see the Australian hackers go down, and they were throwing all their best resources at the case to make sure it happened.

There was one other thing – in some ways the most disturbing matter of all. In the course of the legal to-ing and fro-ing, Electron was told that it was the US Secret Service back in 1988 which had triggered the AFP investigation into The Realm hackers – an investigation which had led to Electron's bust and current legal problems. The Secret Service was after the hackers who broke into Citibank.

As it happened, Electron had never touched Citibank. Credit cards couldn't interest him less. He found banks boring and, the way he looked at it, their computers were full of mundane numbers belonging to the world of accounting. He had already suffered through enough of those tedious types of numbers in his university course. Unless he wanted to steal from banks –

something he would not do – there was no point in breaking into their computers.

But the US Secret Service was very interested in banks – and in Phoenix. For they didn't just believe that Phoenix had been inside Citibank's computers. They believed he had masterminded the Citibank attack.

And why did the US Secret Service think that? Because, Electron was told, Phoenix had gone around bragging about it in the underground. He hadn't just told people he had hacked into Citibank computers, he reportedly boasted that he had stolen some $50000 from the bank.

Going through his legal brief, Electron had discovered something which seemed to confirm what he was being told. The warrant for the telephone tap on both of Phoenix's home phones mentioned a potential 'serious loss to Citibank' as a justification for the warrant. Strangely, the typed words had been crossed out in the handwritten scrawl of the judge who approved the warrant. But they were still legible. No wonder the US Secret Service began chasing the case, Electron thought. Banks get upset when they think people have found a way to rip them off anonymously.

Electron knew that Phoenix hadn't stolen any money from Citibank. Rather, he had been circulating fantastic stories about himself to puff up his image in the underground, and in the process had managed to get them all busted.

In September 1992, Phoenix rang Electron suggesting they get together to discuss the case. Electron wondered why. Maybe he suspected something, sensing that the links binding them were weak, and becoming weaker by the month. That Electron's mental illness had changed his perception of the world. That his increasingly remote attitude to Phoenix suggested an underlying anger about the continual bragging. Whatever the reason, Phoenix's gnawing worry must have been confirmed when Electron put off meeting with him.

Electron didn't want to meet with Phoenix because he didn't like him, and because he thought Phoenix was largely responsible for getting the Australian hackers into their current predicament.

With these thoughts fermenting in his mind, Electron listened with interest a few months later when his solicitor, John McLoughlin, proposed an idea. In legal circles, it was nothing new. But it was new to Electron. He resolved to take up McLoughlin's advice.

Electron decided to testify as a Crown witness against Phoenix.

7 | JUDGEMENT DAY

In another corner of the globe, the British hackers Pad and Gandalf learned with horror that the Australian authorities had busted the three Realm hackers. Electron had simply disappeared one day. A short time later, Phoenix was gone too. Then the reports started rolling in from newspapers and from other Australian hackers on a German board similar to Altos, called Lutzifer.

Something else worried Pad. In one of his hacking forays, he had discovered a file, apparently written by Eugene Spafford, which said he was concerned that some British hackers – read Pad and Gandalf – would create a new worm, based on the RTM worm, and release it into the Internet. The unnamed British hackers would then be able to cause maximum havoc on thousands of Internet sites.

It was true that Gandalf and Pad had captured copies of various worm source codes. They fished around inside SPAN until they surfaced with a copy of the Father Christmas worm. And, after finally successfully hacking Russell Brand's machine at LLNL, they deftly lifted a complete copy of the WANK worm. In Brand's machine, they also found a description of how someone had broken into SPAN looking for the WANK worm code, but hadn't found it. 'That was me breaking into SPAN to look around,' Gandalf laughed, relaying the tale to Pad.

Despite their growing library of worm code, Pad had no intention of writing any such worm. They simply wanted the code to study what penetration methods the worms had used and perhaps to learn something new. The British hackers prided themselves on never having done anything destructive to systems they hacked. In places where they knew their activities had been discovered – such as at the Universities of Bath, Edinburgh, Oxford and Strathclyde – they wrote notes to the admins signed 8lgm. It wasn't only an ego thing – it was also a way of telling the admins that they weren't going to do anything nasty to the system.

At one university, the admins thought 8lgm was some kind of weird variation on a Belgian word and that the hackers who visited their systems night after night were from Belgium. At another uni, the admins made a different guess at the meaning. In the morning, when they came into work and saw that the hackers had been playing in their system all night, they would sigh to each other, 'Our eight little green men are at it again'.

At the University of Lancaster, the hackers wrote a message to the admins which said: 'Don't do anything naughty. We have a good image around the world, so please don't tarnish it or start making up stories about us messing up systems. Don't hold your breath for us to hack you, but keep us in mind.' Wherever they went, their message was the same.

Nonetheless Pad visualised a scenario where Spaf whipped up the computer security and law enforcement people into a frenzied panic and tried to pin all sorts of things on the British hackers, none of which they had done. The underground saw Spaf as being rabid in his attack on hackers, based largely on his response to the RTM worm. And Gandalf had hacked Spaf's machine.

The crackdown on the Australians, combined with the discovery of the Spaf file, had a profound effect on Pad. Always cautious anyway, he decided to give up hacking. It was a difficult decision, and weaning himself from exploring systems night after night was no easy task. However, in the face of what had happened to Electron and Phoenix, continuing to hack didn't seem worth the risk.

When Pad gave up hacking, he bought his own NUI so he could access places like Altos legitimately. The NUI was expensive – about £10 an hour – but he was never on for long. Leisurely chats of the type he once enjoyed in Altos were out of the question, but at least he could mail letters to his friends like Theorem and Gandalf. There would have been easier ways to maintain his friendship with Gandalf, who lived in Liverpool, only an hour's drive away. But it wouldn't be the same. Pad and Gandalf had never met, or even talked on the phone. They talked on-line, and via email. That was the way they related.

Pad also had other reasons for giving up hacking. It was an expensive habit in Britain because British Telecom time-charged for local phone calls. In Australia, a hacker could stay on-line for hours, jumping from one computer to another through the data network, all for the cost of one local call. Like the Australians, Pad could launch his hacking sessions from a local uni or X.25 dial-up. However, an all-night hacking session based on a single phone call might still cost him £5 or more in timed-call charges – a considerable amount of money for an unemployed young man. As it was, Pad had already been forced to stop hacking for brief periods when he ran out of his dole money.

Although Pad didn't think he could be prosecuted for hacking under British law in early 1990, he knew that Britain was about to enact its own computer crime legislation – the Computer Misuse Act 1990 – in August. The 22-year-old hacker decided that it was better to quit while he was ahead.

And he did, for a while at least. Until July 1990, when Gandalf, two years his junior, tempted him with one final hack before the new Act came into force. Just one last fling, Gandalf told him. After that last fling in July, Pad stopped hacking again.

The Computer Misuse Act passed into law in August 1990, following two law commission reviews on the subject. The Scottish Law Commission issued a 1987 report proposing to make unauthorised data access illegal, but only if the hacker tried to 'secure advantage, or cause damage to another person' – including reckless damage.[1] Simple look-see hacking would not be a crime under the report's recommendations. However, in 1989 The Law Commission of England and Wales issued its own report proposing that simple unauthorised access should be a crime regardless of intent – a recommendation which was eventually included in the law.

Late in 1989, Conservative MP Michael Colvin introduced a private member's bill into the British parliament. Lending her support to the bill, outspoken hacker-critic Emma Nicholson, another Conservative MP, fired public debate on the subject and ensured the bill passed through parliament successfully.

In November 1990, Pad was talking on-line with Gandalf, and his friend suggested they have one more hack, just one more, for old time's sake. Well, thought Pad, one more – just a one-off thing – wouldn't hurt.

Before long, Pad was hacking regularly again, and when Gandalf tried to give it up, Pad was there luring him to return to his favourite pastime. They were like two boys at school, getting each other into trouble – the kind of trouble which always comes in pairs. If Pad and Gandalf hadn't known each other, they probably would both have walked away from hacking forever in 1990.

As they both got back into the swing of things, they tried to make light of the risk of getting caught. 'Hey, you know,' Gandalf joked on-line more than once, 'the first time we actually meet each other in person will probably be in a police station.'

Completely irreverent and always upbeat, Gandalf proved to be a true friend. Pad had rarely met such a fellow traveller in the real world, let alone on-line. What others – particularly some American hackers – viewed as prickliness, Pad saw as the perfect sense of humour. To Pad, Gandalf was the best m8 a fellow could ever have.

During the time Pad avoided hacking, Gandalf had befriended another, younger hacker named Wandii, also from the north of England. Wandii never played much of a part in the international computer underground, but he did spend a lot of time hacking European computers. Wandii and Pad got along pleasantly but they were never close. They were acquaintances, bound by ties to Gandalf in the underground.

By the middle of June 1991, Pad, Gandalf and Wandii were peaking. At least one of them – and often more – had already broken into systems belonging to the European Community in Luxembourg, *The Financial Times* (owners of the FTSE 100 share index), the British Ministry of Defence, the Foreign Office, NASA, the investment bank SG Warburg in London, the American computer database software manufacturer Oracle, and more machines on the JANET network than they could remember. Pad had also penetrated a classified military network containing a NATO system. They moved through British Telecom's Packet Switched Stream Network (PSS), which was similar to the Tymnet X.25 network, with absolute ease.[2]

Gandalf's motto was, 'If it moves, hack it'.

On 27 June 1991, Pad was sitting in the front room of his parents' comfortable home in Greater Manchester watching the last remnants of daylight disappear on one of the longest days of the year. He loved summer, loved waking up to streaks of sunlight sneaking through the cracks in his bedroom curtain. He often thought to himself, it doesn't get much better than this.

Around 11 p.m. he flicked on his modem and his Atari 520 ST computer in the front sitting room. There were two Atari computers in the house – indicative of his deep enthusiasm for computers since neither his siblings nor his parents had any interest in programming. Most of the time, however, Pad left the older Atari alone. His elder brother, an aspiring chemist, used it for writing his PhD thesis.

Before dialling out, Pad checked that no-one was on the house's single phone line. Finding it free, he went to check his email on Lutzifer. A few minutes after watching his machine connect to the German board, he heard a soft thud, followed by a creaking. Pad stopped typing, looked up from his machine and listened. He wondered if his brother, reading in their bedroom upstairs, or his parents, watching telly in the back lounge room, could hear the creaking.

The sound became more pronounced and Pad swung around and looked toward the hallway. In a matter of seconds, the front door frame had been cracked open, prising the door away from its lock. The wood had been torn apart by some sort of car jack, pumped up until the door gave way.

Suddenly, a group of men burst through from the front doorstep, dashed down the long hallway and shot up the carpeted stairs to Pad's bedroom.

Still sitting at his computer downstairs, Pad swiftly flicked his modem, and then his computer, off – instantly killing his connection and everything on his screen. He turned back toward the door leading to the sitting room and strained to hear what was happening upstairs. If he wasn't so utterly surprised, he would almost have laughed. He realised that when the police had dashed up to his bedroom, they had been chasing every stereotype about hackers they had probably ever read. The boy. In his bedroom. Hunched over his computer. Late at night.

They did find a young man in the bedroom, with a computer. But it was the wrong one, and for all intents and purposes the wrong computer. It took the police almost ten minutes of quizzing Pad's brother to work out their mistake.

Hearing a commotion, Pad's parents had rushed into the hallway while Pad peered from the doorway of the front sitting room. A uniformed police officer ushered everyone back into the room, and began asking Pad questions.

'Do you use computers? Do you use the name Pad on computers?' they asked.

Pad concluded the game was up. He answered their questions truthfully. Hacking was not such a serious crime after all, he thought. It wasn't as if he had stolen money or anything. This would be a drama, but he was easy-going. He would roll with the punches, cop a slap on the wrist and soon the whole thing would be over and done with.

The police took Pad to his bedroom and asked him questions as they searched the room. The bedroom had a comfortably lived-in look, with a few small piles of clothes in the corner, some shoes scattered across the floor, the curtains hanging crooked, and a collection of music posters – Jimi Hendrix and The Smiths – taped to the wall.

A group of police hovered around his computer. One of them began to search through Pad's books on the shelves above the PC, checking each one as he pulled it down. A few well-loved Spike Milligan works. Some old chess books from when he was captain of the local chess team. Chemistry books, purchased by Pad long before he took any classes in the subject, just to satisfy his curiosity. Physics books. An oceanography textbook. A geology book bought after a visit to a cave excited his interest in the formation of rocks. Pad's mother, a nursing sister, and his father, an electronics engineer who tested gyros on aircraft, had always encouraged their children's interest in the sciences.

The policeman returned those books to the shelves, only picking out the computer books, textbooks from programming and maths classes Pad had taken at a Manchester university. The officer carefully slid them inside plastic bags to be taken away as evidence.

Then the police picked through Pad's music tapes – The Stone Roses, Pixies, New Order, The Smiths and lots of indie music from the flourishing Manchester music scene. No evidence of anything but an eclectic taste in music there.

Another policeman opened Pad's wardrobe and peered inside. 'Anything in here of interest?' he asked.

'No,' Pad answered. 'It's all over here.' He pointed to the box of computer disks.

Pad didn't think there was much point in the police tearing the place to pieces, when they would ultimately find everything they wanted anyway. Nothing was hidden. Unlike the Australian hackers, Pad hadn't been expecting the police at all. Although part of the data on his hard drive was encrypted, there was plenty of incriminating evidence in the unencrypted files.

Pad couldn't hear exactly what his parents were talking about with the police in the other room, but he could tell they were calm. Why shouldn't they be? It wasn't as if their son had done anything terrible. He hadn't beaten someone up in a fist fight at a pub, or robbed anyone. He hadn't hit someone while drunk driving. No, they thought, he had just been fiddling around with computers. Maybe poking around where he shouldn't have been, but that was hardly a serious crime. They needn't worry. It wasn't as if he was going to prison or anything. The police would sort it all out. Maybe some sort of citation, and the matter would be over and done. Pad's mother even offered to make cups of tea for the police.

One of the police struck up a conversation with Pad off to the side as he paused to drink his tea. He seemed to know that Pad was on the dole, and with a completely straight face, he said, 'If you wanted a job, why didn't you just join the police?'

Pad paused for a reality check. Here he was being raided by nearly a dozen law enforcement officers – including representatives from BT and Scotland Yard's computer crimes unit – for hacking hundreds of computers and this fellow wanted to know why he hadn't just become a copper?

He tried not to laugh. Even if he hadn't been busted, there is no way he would ever have contemplated joining the police. Never in a million years. His family and friends, while showing a pleasant veneer of middle-class orderliness, were fundamentally anti-establishment. Many knew that Pad had been hacking, and which sites he had penetrated. Their attitude was: Hacking Big Brother? Good on you.

His parents were torn, wanting to encourage Pad's interest in computers but also worrying their son spent an inordinate amount of time glued to the screen. Their mixed feelings mirrored Pad's own occasional concern.

While deep in the throes of endless hacking nights, he would suddenly sit upright and ask himself, What am I doing here, fucking around on a computer all day and night? Where is this heading? What about the rest of life? Then he would disentangle himself from hacking for a few days or weeks. He would go down to the university pub to drink with his mostly male group of friends from his course.

Tall, with short brown hair, a slender physique and a handsomely boyish face, the soft-spoken Pad would have been considered attractive by many intelligent girls. The problem was finding those sort of girls. He hadn't met many when he was studying at university – there were few women in his maths and computer classes. So he and his friends used to head down to the Manchester nightclubs for the social scene and the good music.

Pad went downstairs with one of the officers and watched as the police unplugged his 1200 baud modem, then tucked it into a plastic bag. He had bought that modem when he was eighteen. The police unplugged cables, bundled them up and slipped them into labelled plastic bags. They gathered up his 20 megabyte hard drive and monitor. More plastic bags and labels.

One of the officers called Pad over to the front door. The jack was still wedged across the mutilated door frame. The police had broken down the door instead of knocking because they wanted to catch the hacker in the act – on-line. The officer motioned for Pad to follow him.

'Come on,' he said, leading the hacker into the night. 'We're taking you to the station.'

Pad spent the night in a cell at the Salford Crescent police station, alone. No rough crims, and no other hackers either.

He settled into one of the metal cots lined against the perimeter of the cell, but sleep evaded him. Pad wondered if Gandalf had been raided as well. There was no sign of him, but then again, the police would hardly be stupid enough to lock up the two hackers together. He tossed and turned, trying to push thoughts from his head.

Pad had fallen into hacking almost by accident. Compared to others in the underground, he had taken it up at a late age – around nineteen. Altos had been the catalyst. Visiting BBSes, he read a file describing not only what Altos was, but how to get there – complete with NUI. Unlike the Australian underground, the embryonic British underground had no shortage of NUIs. Someone had discovered a stack of BT NUIs and posted them on BBSes across England.

Pad followed the directions in the BBS file and soon found himself in the German chat channel. Like Theorem, he marvelled at the brave new live world of Altos. It was wonderful, a big international party. After all, it wasn't every day he got to talk with Australians, Swiss, Germans, Italians and Americans. Before long, he had taken up hacking like so many other Altos regulars.

Hacking as a concept had always intrigued him. As a teenager, the film *War Games* had dazzled him. The idea that computers could communicate with each other over telephone lines enthralled the sixteen-year-old, filling his mind with new ideas. Sometime after that he saw a television report on a group of hackers who claimed that they had used their skills to move satellites around in space – the same story which had first caught Electron's imagination.

Pad had grown up in Greater Manchester. More than a century before, the region had been a textile boom-town. But the thriving economy did not translate into great wealth for the masses. In the early 1840s, Friedrich Engels had worked in his father's cotton-milling factory in the area, and the suffering he saw in the region influenced his most famous work, *The Communist Manifesto*, published in 1848.

Manchester wore the personality of a working-class town, a place where people often disliked the establishment and distrusted authority figures. The 1970s and 1980s had not been kind to most of Greater Manchester, with unemployment and urban decay disfiguring the once-proud textile hub. But this decay only appeared to strengthen an underlying resolve among many from the working classes to challenge the symbols of power.

Pad didn't live in a public housing high-rise. He lived in a suburban middle-class area, in an old, working-class town removed from the dismal inner-city. But like many people from the north, he disliked pretensions. Indeed, he harboured a healthy degree of good-natured scepticism, perhaps stemming from a culture of mates whose favourite pastime was pulling each other's leg down at the pub.

This scepticism was in full-gear as he watched the story of how hackers supposedly moved satellites around in space, but somehow the idea slipped through the checkpoints and captured his imagination, just as it had done with Electron. He felt a desire to find out for himself if it was true and he began pursuing hacking in enthusiastic bursts. At first it was any moderately interesting system. Then he moved to the big-name systems – computers belonging to large institutions. Eventually, working with the Australians, he learned to target computer security experts. That was, after all, where the treasure was stored.

In the morning at the police station, a guard gave Pad something to eat which might have passed for food. Then he was escorted into an interview room with two plain-clothed officers and a BT representative.

Did he want a lawyer? No. He had nothing to hide. Besides, the police had already seized evidence from his house, including unencrypted data logs of his hacking sessions. How could he argue against that? So he faced his stern inquisitors and answered their questions willingly.

Suddenly things began to take a different turn when they began asking about the 'damage' he had done inside the Greater

London Polytechnic's computers. Damage? What damage? Pad certainly hadn't damaged anything.

Yes, the police told him. The damage totalling almost a quarter of a million pounds.

Pad gasped in horror. A quarter of a million pounds? He thought back to his many forays into the system. He had been a little mischievous, changing the welcome message to 'Hi' and signing it 8lgm. He had made a few accounts for himself so he could log in at a later date. That seemed to be nothing special, however, since he and Gandalf had a habit of making accounts called 8lgm for themselves in JANET systems. He had also erased logs of his activities to cover his tracks, but again, this was not unusual, and he had certainly never deleted any computer users' files. The whole thing had just been a bit of fun, a bit of cat and mouse gaming with the system admins. There was nothing he could recall which would account for that kind of damage. Surely they had the wrong hacker?

No, he was the right one all right. Eighty investigators from BT, Scotland Yard and other places had been chasing the 8lgm hackers for two years. They had phone traces, logs seized from his computer and logs from the hacked sites. They knew it was him.

For the first time, the true gravity of the situation hit Pad. These people believed in some way that he had committed serious criminal damage, that he had even been malicious.

After about two hours of questioning, they put Pad back in his cell. More questions tomorrow, they told him.

Later that afternoon, an officer came in to tell Pad his mother and father were outside. He could meet with them in the visiting area. Talking through a glass barrier, Pad tried to reassure his worried parents. After five minutes, an officer told the family the visit was over. Amid hurried goodbyes under the impatient stare of the guard, Pad's parents told him they had brought something for him to read in his cell. It was the oceanography textbook.

Back in his cell, he tried to read, but he couldn't concentrate. He kept replaying his visits to the London Polytechnic over and over in his mind, searching for how he might have inadvertently done £250000 worth of damage. Pad was a very good hacker; it wasn't as if he was some fourteen-year-old kid barging through systems like a bull in china shop. He knew how to get in and out of a system without hurting it.

Shortly after 8 p.m., as Pad sat on his cot stewing over the police damage claims, sombre music seemed to fill his cell. Slowly at first, an almost imperceptible moaning, which subtly transformed into solemn but recognisable notes. It sounded like Welsh choir music, and it was coming from above him.

Pad looked up at the ceiling. The music – all male voices – stopped abruptly, then started again, repeating the same heavy, laboured notes. The hacker smiled. The local police choir was practising right above his cell.

After another fitful night, Pad faced one more round of interviews. The police did most of the questioning, but they didn't seem to know much about computers – well, not nearly so much as any good hacker on Altos. Whenever either of the police asked a technical question, they looked over to the BT guy at the other end of the table as if to say, 'Does this make any sense?' The BT guy would give a slight nod, then the police looked back at Pad for an answer. Most of the time, he was able to decipher what they thought they were trying to ask, and he answered accordingly.

Then it was back to his cell while they processed his charge sheets. Alone again, Pad wondered once more if they had raided Gandalf. Like an answer from above, Pad heard telephone tones through the walls. The police seemed to be playing them over and over. That was when he knew they had Gandalf too.

Gandalf had rigged up a tone dialler in his computer. It sounded as if the police were playing with it, trying to figure it out.

So, Pad would finally meet Gandalf in person after two years. What would he look like? Would they have the same chemistry in person as on-line? Pad felt like he knew Gandalf, knew his essence, but meeting in person could be a bit tricky.

Explaining that the paperwork, including the charge sheets, had finally been organised, a police officer unlocked Pad's cell door and led him to a foyer, telling him he would be meeting both Gandalf and Wandii. A large collection of police had formed a semi-circle around two other young men. In addition to Scotland Yard's Computer Crimes Unit and BT, at least seven other police forces were involved in the three raids, including those from Greater Manchester, Merseyside and West Yorkshire. The officers were curious about the hackers.

For most of the two years of their investigation, the police didn't even know the hackers' real identities. After such a long, hard chase, the police had been forced to wait a little longer, since they wanted to nab each hacker while he was on-line. That meant hiding outside each hacker's home until he logged in somewhere. Any system would do and they didn't have to be talking to each other on-line – as long as the login was illegal. The police had sat patiently, and finally raided the hackers within hours of each other, so they didn't have time to warn one another.

So, at the end of the long chase and a well-timed operation, the police wanted to have a look at the hackers up close.

After the officer walked Pad up to the group, he introduced Gandalf. Tall, lean with brown hair and pale skin, he looked a little bit like Pad. The two hackers smiled shyly at each other, before one of the police pointed out Wandii, the seventeen-year-old schoolboy. Pad didn't get a good look at Wandii, because the police quickly lined the hackers up in a row, with Gandalf in the middle, to explain details to them. They were being charged under the Computer Misuse Act of 1990. Court dates would be set and they would be notified.

When they were finally allowed to leave, Wandii seemed to disappear. Pad and Gandalf walked outside, found a couple of benches and lay down, basking in the sun and chatting while they waited for their rides home.

Gandalf proved to be as easy to talk to in person as he was on-line. They exchanged phone numbers and shared notes on the police raids. Gandalf had insisted on meeting a lawyer before his interviews, but when the lawyer arrived he didn't have the slightest understanding of computer crime. He advised Gandalf to tell the police whatever they wanted to know, so the hacker did.

The trial was being held in London. Pad wondered why, if all three hackers were from the north, the case was being tried in the south. After all, there was a court in Manchester which was high enough to deal with their crimes.

Maybe it was because Scotland Yard was in London. Maybe they had started the paperwork down there. Maybe it was because they were being accused of hacking computers located within the jurisdiction of the Central Criminal Court – that court being the Old Bailey in London. But Pad's cynical side hazarded a different guess – a guess which seemed justified after a few procedural appearances in 1992 before the trial, which was set for 1993. For when Pad arrived at the Bow Street Magistrates Court for his committal in April 1992, he saw it packed out with the media, just as he had anticipated.

A few hackers also fronted up to fly the flag of the underground. One of them – a stranger – came up to Pad after court, patted him on the back and exclaimed enthusiastically, 'Well done, Paddy!' Startled, Pad just looked at him and then smiled. He had no idea how to respond to the stranger.

Like the three Australian hackers, Pad, Gandalf and the little-known Wandii were serving as the test case for new hacking laws in their country. British law enforcement agencies had spent a fortune on the case – more than £500000 according to the newspapers – by the time the 8lgm case went to trial. This was going to be a show case, and the government agencies wanted taxpayers to know they were getting their money's worth.

The hackers weren't being charged with breaking into computers. They were being charged with conspiracy, a more serious offence. While admitting the threesome did not hack for personal gain, the prosecution alleged the hackers had conspired to break into and modify computer systems. It was a strange approach to say the least, considering that none of the three hackers had ever met or even talked to the others before they were arrested.

It was not so strange, however, when looking at the potential penalties. If the hackers had been charged with simply breaking into a machine, without intending any harm, the maximum penalty was six months jail and a fine of up to £5000. However, conspiracy, which was covered under a different section of the Act, could bring up to five years in jail and an unlimited amount in fines.

The prosecution was taking a big gamble. It would be harder to prove conspiracy charges, which required demonstration of greater criminal intent than lesser charges. The potential pay-off was of course also much greater. If convicted, the defendants in Britain's most important hacking case to date would be going to prison.

As with The Realm case, two hackers – Pad and Gandalf – planned to plead guilty while the third – in this case Wandii – planned to fight the charges every step of the way. Legal Aid was footing the bill for their lawyers, because the hackers were either not working or were working in such lowly paid, short-term jobs they qualified for free legal support.

Wandii's lawyers told the media that this showcase was tantamount to a state trial. It was the first major hacking case under the new legislation which didn't involve disgruntled employees. While having no different legal status from a normal trial, the term state trial suggested a greater degree of official wrath – the kind usually reserved for cases of treason.

On 22 February 1993, within two months of Electron's decision to turn Crown witness against Phoenix and Nom, the three 8lgm hackers stood in the dock at Southwark Crown Court in South London to enter pleas in their own case.

In the dim winter light, Southwark couldn't look less appealing, but that didn't deter the crowds. The courtroom was going to be packed, just as Bow Street had been. Scotland Yard detectives were turning out in force. The crowd shuffled toward Room 12.

The prosecution told the media they had about 800 computer disks full of evidence and court materials. If all the data had been printed out on A4 paper, the stack would tower more than 40 metres in the air, they said. Considering the massive amount of evidence being heaved, rolled and tugged through the building by teams of legal eagles, the choice of location – on the fifth floor – proved to be a challenge.

Standing in the dock next to Wandii, Pad and Gandalf pleaded guilty to two computer conspiracy charges: conspiring to dishonestly obtain telecommunications services, and conspiring to cause unauthorised modification to computer material. Pad also pleaded guilty to a third charge: causing damage to a computer. This last charge related to the almost a quarter of a million pounds worth of 'damage' to the Central London Polytechnic. Unlike the Australians' case, none of the British hackers faced charges about specific sites such as NASA.

Pad and Gandalf pleaded guilty because they didn't think they had much choice. Their lawyers told them that, in light of the evidence, denying their guilt was simply not a realistic option. Better to throw yourself on the mercy of the court, they advised. As if to underline the point, Gandalf's lawyer had told him after a meeting at the end of 1992, 'I'd like to wish you a happy Christmas, but I don't think it's going to be one'.

Wandii's lawyers disagreed. Standing beside his fellow hackers, Wandii pleaded not guilty to three conspiracy charges: plotting to gain unauthorised access to computers, conspiring to make unauthorised modifications to computer material, and conspiring to obtain telecommunications services dishonestly. His defence team was going to argue that he was addicted to computer hacking and that, as a result of this addiction, he was not able to form the criminal intent necessary to be convicted.

Pad thought Wandii's case was on shaky ground. Addiction didn't seem a plausible defence to him, and he noticed Wandii looked very nervous in court just after his plea.

Pad and Gandalf left London after their court appearance, returning to the north to prepare for their sentencing hearings, and to watch the progress of Wandii's case through the eyes of the media.

They weren't disappointed. It was a star-studded show. The media revved itself up for a feeding frenzy and the prosecution team, headed by James Richardson, knew how to feed the pack. He zeroed in on Wandii, telling the court how the schoolboy 'was tapping into offices at the EC in Luxembourg and even the experts were worried. He caused havoc at universities all around the world'.[3] To do this, Wandii had used a simple BBC Micro computer, a Christmas present costing £200.

The hacking didn't stop at European Community's computer, Richardson told the eager crowd of journalists. Wandii had hacked Lloyd's, *The Financial Times* and Leeds University. At *The Financial Times* machine, Wandii's adventures had upset the smooth operations of the FTSE 100 share index, known in the City as 'footsie'. The hacker installed a scanning program in the FT's network, resulting in one outgoing call made every second. The upshot of Wandii's intrusion: a £704 bill, the deletion of an important file and a management decision to shut down a key system. With the precision of a banker, FT computer boss Tony Johnson told the court that the whole incident had cost his organisation £24 871.

But the FT hack paled next to the prosecution's real trump card: The European Organisation for the Research and Treatment of Cancer in Brussels. They had been left with a £10 000 phone bill as a result of a scanner Wandii left on its machine,[4] the court was told. The scanner had left a trail of 50 000 calls, all documented on a 980-page phone bill.

The scanner resulted in the system going down for a day, EORTC information systems project manager Vincent Piedboeuf, told the jury. He went on to explain that the centre needed its system to run 24 hours a day, so surgeons could register patients. The centre's database was the focal point for pharmaceutical companies, doctors and research centres – all coordinating their efforts in fighting the disease.

For the media, the case was headline heaven. 'Teenage computer hacker "caused worldwide chaos"', the *Daily Telegraph* screamed across page one. On page three, the *Daily Mail* jumped in with 'Teenage hacker "caused chaos for kicks"'. Even *The Times* waded into the fray. Smaller, regional newspapers pulled the story across the countryside to the far reaches of the British Isles. *The Herald* in Glasgow told its readers 'Teenage hacker "ran up £10000 telephone bill"'. Across the Irish Sea, the *Irish Times* caused a splash with its headline, 'Teenage hacker broke EC computer security'.

Also in the first week of the case, *The Guardian* announced Wandii had taken down the cancer centre database. By the time *The Independent* got hold of the story, Wandii hadn't just shut down the database, he had been reading the patients' most intimate medical details: 'Teenager "hacked into cancer patient files"'. Not to be outdone, on day four of the trial, the *Daily Mail* had christened Wandii as a 'computer genius'. By day five it labelled him as a 'computer invader' who 'cost FT £25000'.

The list went on. Wandii, the press announced, had hacked the Tokyo Zoo and the White House. It was difficult to tell which was the more serious offence.

Wandii's defence team had a few tricks of its own. Ian MacDonald, QC, junior counsel Alistair Kelman and solicitor Deborah Tripley put London University Professor James Griffith Edwards, an authoritative spokesman on addictive and compulsive behaviours, on the stand as an expert witness. The chairman of the National Addiction Centre, the professor had been part of a team which wrote the World Health Organisation's definition of addiction. No-one was going to question his qualifications.

The professor had examined Wandii and he announced his conclusion to the court: Wandii was obsessed by computers, he was unable to stop using them, and his infatuation made it impossible for him to choose freely. 'He repeated 12 times in police interviews, "I'm just addicted. I wish I wasn't",' Griffith Edwards told the court. Wandii was highly intelligent, but was unable to escape from the urge to beat computers' security systems at their own game. The hacker was obsessed by the intellectual challenge. 'This is the core . . . of what attracts the compulsive gambler,' the professor explained to the entranced jury of three women and nine men.

But Wandii, this obsessive, addicted, gifted young man, had never had a girlfriend, Griffith Edwards continued. In fact, he shyly admitted to the professor that he wouldn't even know how to ask a girl out. 'He [Wandii] became profoundly embarrassed when asked to talk about his own feelings. He simply couldn't cope when asked what sort of person he was.'[5]

People in the jury edged forward in their seats, concentrating intently on the distinguished professor. And why wouldn't they? This was amazing stuff. This erudite man had delved inside the mind of the young man of bizarre contrasts. A man so sophisticated that he could pry open computers belonging to some of Britain's and Europe's most prestigious institutions, and yet at the same time so simple that he had no idea how to ask a girl on a date. A man who was addicted not to booze, smack or speed, which the average person associates with addiction, but to a computer – a machine most people associated with kids' games and word processing programs.

The defence proceeded to present vivid examples of Wandii's addiction. Wandii's mother, a single parent and lecturer in English, had terrible trouble trying to get her son away from his computer and modem. She tried hiding his modem. He found it. She tried again, hiding it at his grandmother's house. He burgled granny's home and retrieved it. His mother tried to get at his computer. He pushed her out of his attic room and down the stairs.

Then he ran up a £700 phone bill as a result of his hacking. His mother switched off the electricity at the mains. Her son reconnected it. She installed a security calling-code on the phone to stop him calling out. He broke it. She worried he wouldn't go out and do normal teenage things. He continued to stay up all night – and sometimes all day – hacking. She returned from work to find him unconscious – sprawled across the living room floor and looking as though he was dead. But it wasn't death, only sheer exhaustion. He hacked until he passed out, then he woke up and hacked some more.

The stories of Wandii's self-confessed addiction overwhelmed, appalled and eventually engendered pity in the courtroom audience. The media began calling him 'the hermit hacker'.

Wandii's defence team couldn't fight the prosecution's evidence head-on, so they took the prosecution's evidence and claimed it as their own. They showed the jury that Wandii hadn't just hacked the institutions named by the prosecution; he had hacked far, far more than that. He didn't just hack a lot – he hacked too much. Most of all, Wandii's defence team gave the jury a reason to acquit the innocent-faced young man sitting before them.

During the trial, the media focused on Wandii, but didn't completely ignore the other two hackers. *Computer Weekly* hunted down where Gandalf was working and laid it bare on the front page. A member of 'the UK's most notorious hacking gang', the journal announced, had been working on software which would be used at Barclay's Bank.[6] The implication was clear. Gandalf was a terrible security risk and should never be allowed to do any work for a financial institution. The report irked the hackers, but they tried to concentrate on preparing for their sentencing hearing.

From the beginning of their case, the hackers had problems obtaining certain evidence. Pad and Gandalf believed some of the material seized in the police raids would substantially help their case – such as messages from admins thanking them for pointing out security holes on their systems. This material had not been included in the prosecution's brief. When the defendants requested access to it, they were refused access on the grounds that there was classified data on the optical disk. They were told to go read the Attorney-General's guidelines on disclosure of information. The evidence of the hackers' forays into military and government systems was jumbled in with their intrusions into computers such as benign JANET systems, the defence team was told. It would take too much time to separate the two.

Eventually, after some wrangling, Pad and Gandalf were told they could inspect and copy material – provided it was done under the supervision of the police. The hackers travelled to London, to Holborn police station, to gather supporting evidence for their case. However, it soon became clear that this time-consuming exercise would be impossible to manage on an ongoing basis. Finally, the Crown Prosecution Service relented, agreeing to release the material on disk to Pad's solicitor, on the proviso that no copies were made, it did not leave the law office, and it was returned at the end of the trial.

As Wandii's case lurched from revelation to exaggeration, Pad and Gandalf busily continued to prepare for their own sentencing hearing. Every day, Gandalf travelled from Liverpool to Manchester to meet with his friend. They picked up a handful of newspapers at the local agent, and then headed up to Pad's lawyer's office. After a quick scan for articles covering the hacking case, the two hackers began sifting through the reluctantly released prosecution disks. They read through the material on computer, under the watchful eye of the law office's cashier – the most computer literate person in the firm.

After fifteen days in the Southwark courtroom listening to fantastic stories from both sides about the boy sitting before them, the jury in Wandii's trial retired to consider the evidence. Before they left, Judge Harris gave them a stern warning: the argument that Wandii was obsessed or dependent was not a defence against the charges.

It took the jurors only 90 minutes to reach a decision, and

when the verdict was read out the courtroom erupted with a wave of emotion.

Not guilty. On all counts.

Wandii's mother burst into a huge smile and turned to her son, who was also smiling. And the defence team couldn't be happier. Kelman told journalists, 'The jury felt this was a sledge hammer being used to crack a nut'.[7]

The prosecution was stunned and the law enforcement agents flabbergasted. Detective Sergeant Barry Donovan found the verdict bizarre. No other case in his 21 years in law enforcement had as much overwhelming evidence as this one, yet the jury had let Wandii walk.

And in a high-pitched frenzy rivalling its earlier hysteria, the British media jumped all over the jury's decision. 'Hacker who ravaged systems walks free', an indignant *Guardian* announced. 'Computer Genius is cleared of hacking conspiracy', said the *Evening Standard*. 'Hacking "addict" acquitted', sniffed *The Times*. Overpowering them all was the *Daily Telegraph*'s page one: 'Teenage computer addict who hacked White House system is cleared'.

Then came the media king-hit. Someone had leaked another story and it looked bad. The report, in the *Mail on Sunday*, said that the three hackers had broken into a Cray computer at the European Centre for Medium Range Weather Forecasting at Bracknell. This computer, like dozens of others, would normally have been relegated to the long list of unmentioned victims except for one thing. The US military used weather data from the centre for planning its attack on Iraq in the Gulf War. The media report claimed that the attack had slowed down the Cray's calculations, thus endangering the whole Desert Storm operation. The paper announced the hackers had been 'inadvertently jeopardising – almost fatally – the international effort against Saddam Hussein' and had put 'thousands of servicemen's lives at risk'.[8]

Further, the paper alleged that the US State Department was so incensed about British hackers' repeated break-ins disrupting Pentagon defence planning that it had complained to Prime Minister John Major. The White House put the matter more bluntly than the State Department: Stop your hackers or we will cut off European access to our satellite which provides trans-Atlantic data and voice telecommunications. Someone in Britain seemed to be listening, for less than twelve months later, authorities had arrested all three hackers.

Pad thought the allegations were rubbish. He had been inside a VAX machine at the weather centre for a couple of hours one night, but he had never touched a Cray there. He had certainly never done anything to slow the machine down. No cracking programs, no scanners, nothing which might account for the delay described in the report. Even if he had been responsible, he found it hard to believe the Western allies' victory in the Gulf War was determined by one computer in Berkshire.

All of which gave him cause to wonder why the media was running this story now, after Wandii's acquittal but before he and Gandalf were sentenced. Sour grapes, perhaps?

For days, columnists, editorial and letter writers across Britain pontificated on the meaning of the Wandii's verdict and the validity of an addiction to hacking as a defence. Some urged computer owners to take responsibility for securing their own systems. Others called for tougher hacking laws. A few echoed the view of *The Times*, which declared in an editorial, 'a persistent car thief of [the hacker's] age would almost certainly have received a custodial sentence. Both crimes suggest disrespect for other people's property . . . the jurors may have failed to appreciate the seriousness of this kind of offence'.[9]

The debate flew forward, changing and growing, and expanding beyond Britain's borders. In Hong Kong, the *South China Morning Post* asked, 'Is [this] case evidence of a new social phenomenon, with immature and susceptible minds being damaged through prolonged exposure to personal computers?' The paper described public fear that Wandii's case would result in 'the green light for an army of computer-literate hooligans to pillage the world's databases at will, pleading insanity when caught'.[10]

By April Fool's Day 1991, more than two weeks after the end of the court case, Wandii had his own syndrome named after him, courtesy of *The Guardian*.

And while Wandii, his mother and his team of lawyers celebrated their victory quietly, the media reported that the Scotland Yard detectives commiserated over their defeat, which was considerably more serious than simply losing the Wandii case. The Computer Crimes Unit was being 'reorganised'. Two experienced officers from the five-man unit were being moved out of the group. The official line was that the 'rotations' were normal Scotland Yard procedure. The unofficial word was that the Wandii case had been a fiasco, wasting time and money, and the debacle was not to be repeated.

In the north, a dark cloud gathered over Pad and Gandalf as their judgment day approached. The Wandii case verdict might have been cause for celebration among some in the computer underground, but it brought little joy for the other two 8lgm hackers.

For Pad and Gandalf, who had already pleaded guilty, Wandii's acquittal was a disaster.

On 12 May 1993, two months after Wandii's acquittal, Boris Kayser stood up at the Bar table to put forward Electron's case at the Australian hacker's plea and sentencing hearing. As he began to speak, a hush fell over the Victorian County Court.

A tall, burly man with a booming voice, an imperious courtroom demeanour and his traditional black robes flowing behind him in an echo of his often emphatic gesticulations, Kayser was larger than life. A master showman, he knew how to play an audience of courtroom journalists sitting behind him as much as to the judge in front of him.

Electron had already stood in the dock and pleaded guilty to fourteen charges, as agreed with the DPP's office. In typical style, Kayser had interrupted the long process of the court clerk reading out each charge and asking whether Electron would plead guilty or not guilty. With an impatient wave of his hand, Kayser asked the judge to dispense with such formalities since his client would plead guilty to all the agreed charges at once. The interjection was more of an announcement than a question.

The formalities of a plea having been summarily dealt with, the question now at hand was sentencing. Electron wondered if he would be sent to prison. Despite lobbying from Electron's lawyers, the DPP's office had refused to recommend a non-custodial sentence. The best deal Electron's lawyers had been able to arrange in exchange for turning Crown witness was for the DPP to remain silent on the issue of prison. The judge would make up his mind without input from the DPP.

Electron fiddled nervously with his father's wedding ring, which he wore on his right hand. After his father's death, Electron's sister had begun taking things from the family home. Electron didn't care much because there were only two things he really wanted: that ring and some of his father's paintings.

Kayser called a handful of witnesses to support the case for a light sentence. Electron's grandmother from Queensland. The family friend who had driven Electron to the hospital the day his father died. Electron's psychiatrist, the eminent Lester Walton. Walton in particular highlighted the difference between the two possible paths forward: prison, which would certainly traumatise an already mentally unstable young man, or freedom, which offered Electron a good chance of eventually establishing a normal life.

When Kayser began summarising the case for a non-custodial sentence, Electron could hear the pack of journalists off to his side frantically scribbling notes. He wanted to look at them, but he was afraid the judge would see his ponytail, carefully tucked into his neatly ironed white shirt, if he turned sideways.

'Your Honour,' Kayser glanced backward slightly, toward the court reporters, as he warmed up, 'my client lived in an artificial world of electronic pulses.'

Scratch, scribble. Electron could almost predict, within half a second, when the journalists' pencils and pens would reach a crescendo of activity. The ebb and flow of Boris's boom was timed in the style of a TV newsreader.

Kayser said his client was addicted to the computer the way an alcoholic was obsessed with the bottle. More scratching, and lots of it. This client, Kayser thundered, had never sought to damage any system, steal money or make a profit. He was not malicious in the least, he was merely playing a game.

'I think,' Electron's barrister concluded passionately, but slowly enough for every journalist to get it down on paper, 'that he should have been called Little Jack Horner, who put in his thumb, pulled out a plum and said, "What a good boy am I!"'

Now came the wait. The judge retired to his chambers to weigh up the pre-sentence report, Electron's family situation, the fact that he had turned Crown witness, his offences – everything. Electron had given a nine-page written statement against Phoenix to the prosecution. If the Phoenix case went to trial, Electron would be put on the stand to back up that statement.

In the month before Electron returned to court to hear his sentence, he thought about how he could have fought the case. Some of the charges were dubious.

In one case, he had been charged with illegally accessing public information through a public account. He had accessed the anonymous FTP server at the University of Helsinki to copy information about DES. His first point of access had been through a hacked Melbourne University account.

Beat that charge, Electron's lawyer had told him, and there's plenty more where that came from. The DPP had good pickings and could make up a new charge for another site. Still, Electron reasoned some of the Crown's evidence would not have stood up under cross-examination.

When reporters from Australia and overseas called NASA headquarters for comment on the hacker-induced network shutdown, the agency responded that it had no idea what they were talking about. There had been no NASA network shutdown. A spokesman made inquiries and, he assured the media, NASA was puzzled by the report. Sharon Beskenis's statement didn't seem so watertight after all. She was not, it turned out, even a NASA employee but a contractor from Lockheed.

During that month-long wait, Electron had trouble living down Kayser's nursery-rhyme rendition in the courtroom. When he rang friends, they would open the conversation saying, 'Oh, is that Little Jack Horner?'

They had all seen the nightly news, featuring Kayser and his client. Kayser had looked grave leaving court, while Electron, wearing John Lennon-style glasses with dark lenses and with his shoulder-length curls pulled tightly back in a ponytail, had tried to smile at the camera crews. But his small, fine features and smattering of freckles disappeared under the harsh camera lights, so much so that the black, round spectacles seemed almost to float on a blank, white surface.

The week after Electron pleaded guilty in Australia, Pad and Gandalf sat side by side in London's Southwark dock one last time.

For a day and a half, beginning on 20 May 1993, the two hackers listened to their lawyers argue their defence. Yes, our clients hacked computers, they told the judge, but the offences were nowhere near as serious as the prosecution wants to paint them. The lawyers were fighting hard for one thing: to keep Pad and Gandalf out of prison.

Some of the hearing was tough going for the two hackers, but not just because of any sense of foreboding caused by the judge's imminent decision. The problem was that Gandalf made Pad laugh, and it didn't look at all good to laugh in the middle of your sentencing hearing. Sitting next to Gandalf for hours on end, while lawyers from both sides butchered the technical aspects of computer hacking which the 8lgm hackers had spent years learning, did it. Pad had only to give Gandalf a quick sidelong glance and he quickly found himself swallowing and clearing his throat to keep from bursting into laughter. Gandalf's irrepressible irreverence was written all over his face.

The stern-faced Judge Harris could send them to jail, but he still wouldn't understand. Like the gaggle of lawyers bickering at the front of the courtroom, the judge was – and would always be – out of the loop. None of them had any idea what was really going on inside the heads of the two hackers. None of them could ever understand what hacking was all about – the thrill of stalking a quarry or of using your wits to outsmart so-called experts; the pleasure of finally penetrating a much-desired machine and knowing that system is yours; the deep anti-establishment streak which served as a well-centred ballast against the most violent storms washing in from the outside world; and the camaraderie of the international hacking community on Altos.

The lawyers could talk about it, could put experts on the stand and psychological reports in the hands of the judge, but none of them would ever really comprehend because they had never experienced it. The rest of the courtroom was out of the loop, and Pad and Gandalf stared out from the dock as if looking through a two-way mirror from a secret, sealed room.

Pad's big worry had been this third charge – the one which he faced alone. At his plea hearing, he had admitted to causing damage to a system owned by what was, in 1990, called the Polytechnic of Central London. He hadn't damaged the machine by, say, erasing files, but the other side had claimed that the damages totalled about £250 000.

The hacker was sure there was zero chance the polytechnic had spent anything near that amount. He had a reasonable idea of how long it would take someone to clean up his intrusions. But if the prosecution could convince a judge to accept that figure, the hacker might be looking at a long prison term.

Pad had already braced himself for the possibility of prison. His lawyer warned him before the sentencing date that there was a reasonable likelihood the two 8lgm hackers would be sent down. After the Wandii case, the public pressure to 'correct' a 'wrong' decision by the Wandii jury was enormous. The police had described Wandii's acquittal as 'a licence to hack' – and _The Times_, had run the statement.[11] It was likely the judge, who had presided over Wandii's trial, would want to send a loud and clear message to the hacking community.

Pad thought that perhaps, if he and Gandalf had pleaded not guilty alongside Wandii, they would have been acquitted. But there was no way Pad would have subjected himself to the kind of public humiliation Wandii went through during the 'addicted to computers' evidence. The media appeared to want to paint the three hackers as pallid, scrawny, socially inept, geeky geniuses, and to a large degree Wandii's lawyers had worked off this desire. Pad didn't mind being viewed as highly intelligent, but he wasn't a geek. He had a casual girlfriend. He went out dancing with friends or to hear bands in Manchester's thriving alternative music scene. He worked out his upper body with weights at home. Shy – yes. A geek – no.

Could Pad have made a case for being addicted to hacking? Yes, although he never believed that he had been. Completely enthralled, entirely entranced? Maybe. Suffering from a passing obsession? Perhaps. But addicted? No, he didn't think so. Besides, who knew for sure if a defence of addiction could have saved him from the prosecution's claim anyway?

Exactly where the quarter of a million pound claim came from in the first place was a mystery to Pad. The police had just said it to him, as if it was fact, in the police interview. Pad hadn't seen any proof, but that hadn't stopped him from spending a great deal of time feeling very stressed about how the judge would view the matter.

The only answer seemed to be some good, independent technical advice. At the request of both Pad and Gandalf's lawyers, Dr Peter Mills, of Manchester University, and Dr Russell Lloyd, of London Business School, had examined a large amount of technical evidence presented in the prosecution's papers. In an independent report running to more than 23 pages, the experts stated that the hackers had caused less havoc than the prosecution alleged. In addition, Pad's solicitor asked Dr Mills to specifically review, in a separate report, the evidence supporting the prosecution's large damage claim.

Dr Mills stated that one of the police expert witnesses, a British Telecom employee, had said that Digital recommended a full rebuild of the system at the earliest possible opportunity – and at considerable cost. However, the BT expert had not stated that the cost was £250000 nor even mentioned if the cost quote which had been given had actually been accepted.

In fact, Dr Mills concluded that there was no supporting evidence at all for the quarter of a million pound claim. Not only that, but any test of reason based on the evidence provided by the prosecution showed the claim to be completely ridiculous.

In a separate report, Dr Mills stated that:

i) The machine concerned was a Vax 6320, this is quite a powerful 'mainframe' system and could support several hundreds of users.

ii) That a full dump of files takes 6 tapes, however since the type of tape is not specified this gives no real indication of the size of the filesystem. A tape could vary from 0.2 Gigabytes to 2.5 Gigabytes.

iii) The machine was down for three days.

With this brief information it is difficult to give an accurate cost for restoring the machine, however an over estimate would be:

i) Time spent in restoring the system, 10 man days at £300 per day; £3000.

ii) Lost time by users, 30 man days at £300 per day; £9000.

The total cost in my opinion is unlikely to be higher than £12000 and this itself is probably a rather high estimate. I certainly cannot see how a figure of £250000 could be justified.

It looked to Pad that the prosecution's claim was not for damage at all. It was for properly securing the system – an entirely rebuilt system. It seemed to him that the police were trying to put the cost of securing the polytechnic's entire computer network onto the shoulders of one hacker – and to call it damages. In fact, Pad discovered, the polytechnic had never actually even spent the £250000.

Pad was hopeful, but he was also angry. All along, the police had been threatening him with this huge damage bill. He had tossed and turned in his bed at night worrying about it. And, in the end, the figure put forward for so long as fact was nothing but an outrageous claim based on not a single shred of solid evidence.

Using Dr Mills's report, Pad's barrister, Mukhtar Hussain, QC, negotiated privately with the prosecution barrister, who finally relented and agreed to reduce the damage estimate to £15000. It was, in Pad's view, still far too high, but it was much better than £250000. He was in no mind to look a gift horse in the mouth.

Judge Harris accepted the revised damage estimate.

The prosecution may have lost ground on the damage bill, but it wasn't giving up the fight. These two hackers, James Richardson told the court and journalists during the two-day sentencing hearing, had hacked into some 10000 computer systems around the world. They were inside machines or networks in at least fifteen countries. Russia. India. France. Norway. Germany. The US. Canada. Belgium. Sweden. Italy. Taiwan. Singapore. Iceland. Australia. Officers on the case said the list of the hackers' targets 'read like an atlas', Richardson told the court.

Pad listened to the list. It sounded about right. What didn't sound right were the allegations that he or Gandalf had crashed Sweden's telephone network by running an X.25 scanner over its packet network. The crash had forced a Swedish government minister to apologise on television. The police said the minister did not identify the true cause of the problem – the British hackers – in his public apology.

Pad had no idea what they were talking about. He hadn't done anything like that to the Swedish phone system, and as far as he knew, neither had Gandalf.

Something else didn't sound right. Richardson told the court that in total, the two hackers had racked up at least £25000 in phone bills for unsuspecting legitimate customers, and caused 'damage' to systems which was very conservatively estimated at almost £123000.

Where were these guys getting these numbers from? Pad marvelled at their cheek. He had been through the evidence with a fine-toothed comb, yet he had not seen one single bill showing what a site had actually paid to repair 'damage' caused by the hackers. The figures tossed around by the police and the prosecution weren't real bills; they weren't cast in iron.

Finally, on Friday 21 May, after all the evidence had been presented, the judge adjourned the court to consider sentencing. When he returned to the bench fifteen minutes later, Pad knew what was going to happen from the judge's face. To the hacker, the expression said: I am going to give you everything that Wandii should have got.

Judge Harris echoed *The Times*'s sentiments when he told the two defendants, 'If your passion had been cars rather than computers, we would have called your conduct delinquent, and I don't shrink from the analogy of describing what you were doing as intellectual joyriding.

'Hacking is not harmless. Computers now form a central role in our lives. Some, providing emergency services, depend on their computers to deliver those services.'[12]

Hackers needed to be given a clear signal that computer crime 'will not and cannot be tolerated', the judge said, adding that he had thought long and hard before handing down sentence. He accepted that neither hacker had intended to cause damage, but it was imperative to protect society's computer systems and he would be failing in his public duty if he didn't sentence the two hackers to a prison term of six months.

Judge Harris told the hackers that he had chosen a custodial sentence, 'both to penalise you for what you have done and for the losses caused, and to deter others who might be similarly tempted'.

This was the show trial, not Wandii's case, Pad thought as the court officers led him and Gandalf out of the dock, down to the prisoner's lift behind the courtroom and into a jail cell.

Less than two weeks after Pad and Gandalf were sentenced, Electron was back in the Victorian County Court to discover his own fate.

As he stood in the dock on 3 June 1993 he felt numb, as emotionally removed from the scene as Meursault in Camus' *L'etranger*. He believed he was handling the stress pretty well until he experienced tunnel vision while watching the judge read his penalty. He perused the room but saw neither Phoenix nor Nom.

When Judge Anthony Smith summarised the charges, he seemed to have a special interest in count number 13 – the Zardoz charge. A few minutes into reading the sentence, the judge said, 'In my view, a custodial sentence is appropriate for each of the offences constituted by the 12th, 13th and 14th counts'. They were the 'knowingly concerned' charges, with Phoenix, involving NASA, LLNL and CSIRO. Electron looked around the courtroom. People turned back to stare at him. Their eyes said, 'You are going to prison.'

'I formed the view that a custodial sentence is appropriate in respect of each of these offences because of the seriousness of them,' Judge Smith noted, 'and having regard to the need to demonstrate that the community will not tolerate this type of offence.

'Our society today is . . . increasingly . . . dependent upon the use of computer technology. Conduct of the kind in which you engaged poses a threat to the usefulness of that technology . . . It is incumbent upon the courts . . . to see to it that the sentences they impose reflect the gravity of this kind of criminality.

'On each of Counts 12, 13 and 14, you are convicted and you are sentenced to a term of imprisonment of six months . . . each . . . to be concurrent.'

The judge paused, then continued, 'And . . . I direct, by order, that you be released forthwith upon your giving security by recognisance . . . in the sum of $500 . . . You will not be required to serve the terms of imprisonment imposed, provided you are of good behaviour for the ensuing six months.' He then ordered Electron to complete 300 hours of community service, and to submit to psychiatric assessment and treatment.

Electron breathed a sigh of relief.

When outlining the mitigating circumstances which led to suspension of the jail sentence, Judge Smith described Electron as being addicted to using his computer 'in much the same way as an alcoholic becomes addicted to the bottle'. Boris Kayser had used the analogy in the sentencing hearing, perhaps for the benefit of the media, but the judge had obviously been swayed by his view.

When court adjourned, Electron left the dock and shook hands with his lawyers. After three years, he was almost free of his court problems. There was only one possible reason he might need to return to court.

If Phoenix fought out his case in a full criminal trial, the DPP would put Electron on the stand to testify against him. It would be an ugly scene.

The inmates of HM Prison Kirkham, on the north-west coast of England, near Preston, had heard all about Pad and Gandalf by the time they arrived. They greeted the hackers by name. They'd seen the reports on telly, especially about how Gandalf had hacked NASA – complete with footage of the space shuttle taking off. Some TV reporter's idea of subtle irony – 'Two hackers were sent down today' as the space shuttle went up.

Kirkham was far better than Brixton, where the hackers had spent the first days of their sentence while awaiting transfer. Brixton was what Pad always envisioned prison would look like, with floors of barred cells facing onto an open centre and prisoners only allowed out of their cells for scheduled events such as time in the yard. It was a place where hard-core criminals lived. Fortunately, Pad and Gandalf had been placed in the same cell while they waited to be assigned to their final destination.

After ten days inside Brixton Pad and Gandalf were led from their cell, handcuffed and put in a coach heading toward the windy west coast.

During the drive, Pad kept looking down at his hand, locked in shiny steel to Gandalf's hand, then he looked back up again at his fellow hacker. Clearing his throat and turning away from Gandalf's difficult grin – his friend now on the edge of laughing himself – Pad struggled. He tried to hold down the muscles of his face, to pull them back from laughter.

A minimum security prison holding up to 632 prisoners, Kirkham looked vaguely like a World War II RAF base with a large collection of free-standing buildings around the grounds. There were no real walls, just a small wire fence which Pad soon learned prisoners routinely jumped when the place started to get to them.

For a prison, Kirkham was pretty good. There was a duck pond, a bowling green, a sort of mini-cinema which showed films in the early evenings, eight pay phones, a football field, a cricket pavilion and, best of all, lots of fields. Prisoners could have visits on weekday afternoons between 1.10 and 3.40, or on the weekend.

Luck smiled on the two hackers. They were assigned to the same billet and, since none of the other prisoners objected, they became room-mates. Since they were sentenced in May, they would serve their time during summer. If they were 'of good behaviour' and didn't get into trouble with other prisoners, they would be out in three months.

Like any prison, Kirkham had its share of prisoners who didn't get along with each other. Mostly, prisoners wanted to know what you were in for and, more particularly, if you had been convicted of a sex crime. They didn't like sex crime offenders and Pad heard about a pack of Kirkham prisoners who dragged one of their own, screaming, to a tree, where they tried to hang him for being a suspected rapist. In fact, the prisoner hadn't been convicted of anything like rape. He had simply refused to pay his poll tax.

Fortunately for Pad and Gandalf, everyone else in Kirkham knew why they were there. At the end of their first week they returned to their room one afternoon to find a sign painted above their door. It said, 'NASA HQ'.

The other minimum security prisoners understood hacking – and they had all sorts of ideas about how you could make money from it. Most of the prisoners in Kirkham were in for petty theft, credit card fraud, and other small-time crimes. There was also a phreaker, who arrived the same day as Pad and Gandalf. He landed eight months in prison – two more than the 8lgm hackers – and Pad wondered what kind of message that sent the underground.

Despite their best efforts, the 8lgm twosome didn't fit quite the prison mould. In the evenings, other prisoners spent their free time shooting pool or taking drugs. In the bedroom down the hall, Gandalf lounged on his bed studying a book on VMS internals. Pad read a computer magazine and listened to some indie music – often his 'Babes in Toyland' tape. In a parody of prison movies, the two hackers marked off their days inside the prison with cross-hatched lines on their bedroom wall – four marks, then a diagonal line through them. They wrote other things on the walls too.

The long, light-filled days of summer flowed one into the other, as Pad and Gandalf fell into the rhythm of the prison. The morning check-in at 8.30 to make sure none of the prisoners had gone walkabout. The dash across the bowling green for a breakfast of beans, bacon, eggs, toast and sausage. The walk to the greenhouses where the two hackers had been assigned for work detail.

The work wasn't hard. A little digging in the pots. Weeding around the baby lettuce heads, watering the green peppers and transplanting tomato seedlings. When the greenhouses became too warm by late morning, Pad and Gandalf wandered outside for a bit of air. They often talked about girls, cracking crude, boyish jokes about women and occasionally discussing their girlfriends more seriously. As the heat settled in, they sat down, lounging against the side of the greenhouse.

After lunch, followed by more time in the greenhouse, Pad and Gandalf sometimes went off for walks in the fields surrounding the prison. First the football field, then the paddocks dotted with cows beyond it.

Pad was a likeable fellow, largely because of his easygoing style and relaxed sense of humour. But liking him wasn't the same as knowing him, and the humour often deflected deeper probing into his personality. But Gandalf knew him, understood him. Everything was so easy with Gandalf. During the long, sunny walks, the conversation flowed as easily as the light breeze through the grass.

As they wandered in the fields, Pad often wore his denim jacket. Most of the clothes on offer from the prison clothing office were drab blue, but Pad had lucked onto this wonderful, cool denim jacket which he took to wearing all the time.

Walking for hours on end along the perimeters of the prison grounds, Pad saw how easy it would be to escape, but in the end there didn't seem to be much point. They way he saw it, the police would just catch you and put you back in again. Then you'd have to serve extra time.

Once a week, Pad's parents came to visit him, but the few precious hours of visiting time were more for his parents' benefit than his own. He reassured them that he was OK, and when they looked him in the face and saw it was true, they stopped worrying quite so much. They brought him news from home, including the fact that his computer equipment had been returned by one of the police who had been in the original raid.

The officer asked Pad's mother how the hacker was doing in prison. 'Very well indeed,' she told him. 'Prison's not nearly

so bad as he thought.' The officer's face crumpled into a disappointed frown. He seemed to be looking for news that Pad
was suffering nothing but misery.

At the end of almost three months, with faces well tanned
from walking in the meadows, Pad and Gandalf walked free.

To the casual witness sitting nearby in the courtroom, the
tension between Phoenix's mother and father was almost
palpable. They were not sitting near each other but that didn't
mitigate the silent hostility which rose through the air like
steam. Phoenix's divorced parents provided a stark contrast to
Nom's adopted parents, an older, suburban couple who were
very much married.

On Wednesday, 25 August 1993 Phoenix and Nom pleaded
guilty to fifteen and two charges respectively. The combined
weight of the prosecution's evidence, the risk and cost of
running a full trial and the need to get on with their lives had
pushed them over the edge. Electron didn't need to come to
court to give evidence.

At the plea hearing, which ran over to the next day,
Phoenix's lawyer, Dyson Hore-Lacy, spent considerable time
sketching the messy divorce of his client's parents for the benefit
of the judge. Suggesting Phoenix retreated into his computer
during the bitter separation and divorce was the best chance of
getting him off a prison term. Most of all, the defence presented
Phoenix as a young man who had strayed off the correct path
in life but was now back on track – holding down a job and
having a life.

The DPP had gone in hard against Phoenix. They seemed
to want a jail term badly and they doggedly presented Phoenix
as an arrogant braggart. The court heard a tape-recording
of Phoenix ringing up security guru Edward DeHart of the
Computer Emergency Response Team at Carnegie Mellon
University to brag about a security exploit. Phoenix told DeHart

to get onto his computer and then proceeded to walk him step by step through the 'passwd -f' security bug. Ironically, it was Electron who had discovered that security hole and taught it to Phoenix – a fact Phoenix didn't seem to want to mention to DeHart.

The head of the AFP's Southern Region Computer Crimes Unit, Detective Sergeant Ken Day was in court that day. There was no way he was going to miss this. The same witness noting the tension between Phoenix's parents might also have perceived an undercurrent of hostility between Day and Phoenix – an undercurrent which did not seem to exist between Day and either of the other Realm hackers.

Day, a short, careful man who gave off an air of bottled intensity, seemed to have an acute dislike for Phoenix. By all observations the feeling was mutual. A cool-headed professional, Day would never say anything in public to express the dislike – that was not his style. His dislike was only indicated by a slight tightness in the muscles of an otherwise unreadable face.

On 6 October 1993, Phoenix and Nom stood side by side in the dock for sentencing. Wearing a stern expression, Judge Smith began by detailing both the hackers' charges and the origin of The Realm. But after the summary, the judge saved his harshest rebuke for Phoenix.

'There is nothing . . . to admire about your conduct and every reason why it should be roundly condemned. You pointed out [weaknesses] to some of the system administrators . . . [but] this was more a display of arrogance and a demonstration of what you thought was your superiority rather than an act of altruism on your part.

'You . . . bragged about what you had done or were going to do . . . Your conduct revealed . . . arrogance on your part, open defiance, and an intention to the beat the system. [You] did cause havoc for a time within the various targeted systems.'

Although the judge appeared firm in his views while passing sentence, behind the scenes he had agonised greatly over his decision. He had attempted to balance what he saw as the need for deterrence, the creation of a precedence for sentencing hacking cases in Australia, and the individual aspects of this case. Finally, after sifting through the arguments again and again, he had reached a decision.

'I have no doubt that some sections of our community would regard anything than a custodial sentence as less than appropriate. I share that view. But after much reflection . . . I have concluded that an immediate term of imprisonment is unnecessary.'

Relief rolled across the faces of the hackers' friends and relatives as the judge ordered Phoenix to complete 500 hours of community service work over two years and assigned him a $1000 twelve-month good behaviour bond. He gave Nom 200 hours, and a $500, six-month bond for good behaviour.

As Phoenix was leaving the courtroom, a tall, skinny young man loped down the aisle towards him.

'Congratulations,' the stranger said, his long hair dangling in delicate curls around his shoulders.

'Thanks,' Phoenix answered, combing his memory for the boyish face which couldn't be any older than his own. 'Do I know you?'

'Sort of,' the stranger answered. 'I'm Mendax. I'm about to go through what you did, but worse.'

8 | *THE INTERNATIONAL SUBVERSIVES*

Prime Suspect rang Mendax, offering an adventure. He had discovered a strange system called NMELH1 (pronounced N-Melly-H-1) and it was time to go exploring. He read off the dial-up numbers, found in a list of modem phone numbers on another hacked system.

Mendax looked at the scrap of paper in his hand, thinking about the name of the computer system.

The 'N' stood for Northern Telecom, a Canadian company with annual sales of $8 billion. NorTel, as the company was known, sold thousands of highly sophisticated switches and other telephone exchange equipment to some of the world's largest phone companies. The 'Melly' undoubtedly referred to the fact that the system was in Melbourne. As for the 'H-1', well, that was anyone's guess, but Mendax figured it probably stood for 'host-1' – meaning computer site number one.

Prime Suspect had stirred Mendax's interest. Mendax had spent hours experimenting with commands inside the computers which controlled telephone exchanges. In the end, those forays were all just guesswork – trial and error learning, at considerable risk of discovery. Unlike making a mistake inside a single computer, mis-guessing a command inside a telephone exchange in downtown Sydney or Melbourne could take down a whole prefix – 10000 or more phone lines – and cause instant havoc.

This was exactly what the International Subversives didn't want to do. The three IS hackers – Mendax, Prime Suspect and Trax – had seen what happened to the visible members of the computer underground in England and in Australia. The IS hackers had three very good reasons to keep their activities quiet.

Phoenix. Nom. And Electron.

But, Mendax thought, what if you could learn about how to manipulate a million-dollar telephone exchange by reading the manufacturer's technical documentation? How high was the chance that those documents, which weren't available to the public, were stored inside NorTel's computer network?

Better still, what if he could find NorTel's original source code – the software designed to control specific telephone switches, such as the DMS-100 model. That code might be sitting on a computer hooked into the worldwide NorTel network. A hacker with access could insert his own backdoor – a hidden security flaw – before the company sent out software to its customers.

With a good technical understanding of how NorTel's equipment worked, combined with a backdoor installed in every piece of software shipped with a particular product, you could have control over every new NorTel DMS telephone switch installed from Boston to Bahrain. What power! Mendax thought, what if you could turn off 10000 phones in Rio de Janeiro, or give 5000 New Yorkers free calls one afternoon, or listen into private telephone conversations in Brisbane. The telecommunications world would be your oyster.

Like their predecessors, the three IS hackers had started out in the Melbourne BBS scene. Mendax met Trax on Electric

Dreams in about 1988, and Prime Suspect on Megaworks, where he used the handle Control Reset, not long after that. When he set up his own BBS at his home in Tecoma, a hilly suburb so far out of Melbourne that it was practically in forest, he invited both hackers to visit 'A Cute Paranoia' whenever they could get through on the single phone line.

Visiting on Mendax's BBS suited both hackers, for it was more private than other BBSes. Eventually they exchanged home telephone numbers, but only to talk modem-to-modem. For months, they would ring each other up and type on their computer screens to each other – never having heard the sound of the other person's voice. Finally, late in 1990, the nineteen-year-old Mendax called up the 24-year-old Trax for a voice chat. In early 1991, Mendax and Prime Suspect, aged seventeen, also began speaking in voice on the phone.

Trax seemed slightly eccentric, and possibly suffered from some sort of anxiety disorder. He refused to travel to the city, and he once made reference to seeing a psychiatrist. But Mendax usually found the most interesting people were a little unusual, and Trax was both.

Mendax and Trax discovered they had a few things in common. Both came from poor but educated families, and both lived in the outer suburbs. However, they had very different childhoods.

Trax's parents migrated to Australia from Europe. Both his father, a retired computer technician, and his mother spoke with a German accent. Trax's father was very much the head of the household, and Trax was his only son.

By contrast, by the time he was fifteen Mendax had lived in a dozen different places including Perth, Magnetic Island, Brisbane, Townsville, Sydney, the Adelaide Hills, and a string of coastal towns in northern New South Wales and Western Australia. In fifteen years he had enrolled in at least as many different schools.

His mother had left her Queensland home at age seventeen, after saving enough money from selling her paintings to buy a motorcycle, a tent and a road map of Australia. Waving goodbye to her stunned parents, both academics, she rode off into the sunset. Some 2000 kilometres later, she arrived in Sydney and joined the thriving counter-culture community. She worked as an artist and fell in love with a rebellious young man she met at an anti-Vietnam demonstration.

Within a year of Mendax's birth, his mother's relationship with his father had ended. When Mendax was two, she married a fellow artist. What followed was many turbulent years, moving from town to town as his parents explored the '70s left-wing, bohemian subculture. As a boy, he was surrounded by artists. His stepfather staged and directed plays and his mother did make-up, costume and set design.

One night in Adelaide, when Mendax was about four, his mother and a friend were returning from a meeting of anti-nuclear protesters. The friend claimed to have scientific evidence that the British had conducted high-yield, above-ground nuclear tests at Maralinga, a desert area in north-west South Australia.

A 1984 Royal Commission subsequently revealed that between 1953 and 1963 the British government had tested nuclear bombs at the site, forcing more than 5000 Aborigines from their native lands. In December 1993, after years of stalling, the British government agreed to pay £20 million toward cleaning up the more than 200 square kilometres of contaminated lands. Back in 1968, however, the Menzies government had signed away Britain's responsibility to clean up the site. In the 1970s, the Australian government was still in denial about exactly what had happened at Maralinga.

As Mendax's mother and her friend drove through an Adelaide suburb carrying early evidence of the Maralinga tragedy, they noticed they were being followed by an unmarked car. They tried to lose the tail, without success. The friend, nervous, said he had to get the data to an Adelaide journalist before the police could stop him. Mendax's mother quickly slipped into a back lane and the friend leapt from the car. She drove off, taking the police tail with her.

The plain-clothed police pulled her over shortly after, searched her car and demanded to know where her friend had gone and what had occurred at the meeting. When she was less than helpful, one officer told her, 'You have a child out at 2 in the morning. I think you should get out of politics, lady. It could be said you were an unfit mother.'

A few days after this thinly veiled threat, her friend showed up at Mendax's mother's house, covered in fading bruises. He said the police had beaten him up, then set him up by planting hash on him. 'I'm getting out of politics,' he announced.

However, she and her husband continued their involvement in theatre. The young Mendax never dreamed of running away to join the circus – he already lived the life of a travelling minstrel. But although the actor-director was a good step-father, he was also an alcoholic. Not long after Mendax's ninth birthday, his parents separated and then divorced.

Mendax's mother then entered a tempestuous relationship with an amateur musician. Mendax was frightened of the man, whom he considered a manipulative and violent psychopath. He had five different identities with plastic in his wallet to match. His whole background was a fabrication, right down to the country of his birth. When the relationship ended, the steady pattern of moving around the countryside began again, but this journey had a very different flavour from the earlier happy-go-lucky odyssey. This time, Mendax and his family were on the run from a physically abusive de facto. Finally, after hiding under assumed names on both sides of the continent, Mendax and his family settled on the outskirts of Melbourne.

Mendax left home at seventeen because he had received a tip-off about an impending raid. Mendax wiped his disks, burnt his print-outs and left. A week later, the Victorian CIB turned up and searched his room, but found nothing. He married his girlfriend, an intelligent but introverted and emotionally disturbed sixteen-year-old he had met through a mutual friend in a gifted children's program. A year later they had a child.

Mendax made many of his friends through the computer community. He found Trax easy to talk to and they often spent up to five hours on a single phone call. Prime Suspect, on the other hand, was hard work on the phone.

Quiet and introverted, Prime Suspect always seemed to run out of conversation after five minutes. Mendax was himself naturally shy, so their talks were often filled with long silences. It wasn't that Mendax didn't like Prime Suspect, he did. By the time the three hackers met in person at Trax's home in mid-1991, he considered Prime Suspect more than just a fellow hacker in the tight-knit IS circle. Mendax considered him a friend.

Prime Suspect was a boy of veneers. To most of the world, he appeared to be a studious year 12 student bound for university from his upper middle-class grammar school. The all-boys school never expected less from its students and the possibility of attending a TAFE – a vocational college – was never discussed as an option. University was the object. Any student who failed to make it was quietly swept under the carpet like some sort of distasteful food dropping.

Prime Suspect's own family situation did not mirror the veneer of respectability portrayed by his school. His father, a pharmacist, and his mother, a nurse, had been in the midst of an acrimonious divorce battle when his father was diagnosed with terminal cancer. In this bitter, antagonistic environment, the eight-year-old Prime Suspect was delivered to his father's bedside in hospice for a rushed few moments to bid him farewell.

Through much of his childhood and adolescence, Prime Suspect's mother remained bitter and angry about life, and particularly her impoverished financial situation. When he was eight, Prime Suspect's older sister left home at sixteen, moved to Perth and refused to speak to her mother. In some ways, Prime Suspect felt he was expected to be both child and de facto parent. All of which made him grow up faster in some ways, but remain immature in others.

Prime Suspect responded to the anger around him by retreating into his room. When he bought his first computer, an Apple IIe, at age thirteen he found it better company than any of his relatives. The computers at school didn't hold much interest for him, since they weren't connected to the outside world via modem. After reading about BBSes in the Apple Users' Society newsletter, he saved up for his own modem and soon began connecting into various BBSes.

School did, however, provide the opportunity to rebel, albeit anonymously, and he conducted extensive pranking campaigns. Few teachers suspected the quiet, clean-cut boy and he was rarely caught. Nature had endowed Prime Suspect with the face of utter innocence. Tall and slender with brown curly hair, his true character only showed in the elfish grin which sometimes passed briefly across his baby face. Teachers told his mother he was underachieving compared to his level of intelligence, but had few complaints otherwise.

By year 10, he had become a serious hacker and was spending every available moment at his computer. Sometimes he skipped school, and he often handed assignments in late. He found it difficult to come up with ever more creative excuses and sometimes he imagined telling his teachers the truth. 'Sorry I didn't get that 2000-word paper done but I was knee-deep in NASA networks last night.' The thought made him laugh.

He saw girls as a unwanted distraction from hacking. Sometimes, after he chatted with a girl at a party, his friends would later ask him why he hadn't asked her out. Prime Suspect shrugged it off. The real reason was that he would rather get home to his computer, but he never discussed his hacking with anyone at school, not even with Mentat.

A friend of Force's and occasional visitor to The Realm, Mentat was two years ahead of Prime Suspect at school and in general couldn't be bothered talking to so junior a hacker as Prime Suspect. The younger hacker didn't mind. He had witnessed other hackers' indiscretions, wanted no part of them and was happy to keep his hacking life private.

Before the Realm bust, Phoenix rang him up once at 2 a.m. suggesting that he and Nom come over there and then. Woken by the call, Prime Suspect's mother stood in the doorway to his bedroom, remonstrating with him for letting his 'friends' call at such a late hour. With Phoenix goading him in one ear, and his mother chewing him out in the other, Prime Suspect decided the whole thing was a bad idea. He said no thanks to Phoenix, and shut the door on his mother.

He did, however, talk to Powerspike on the phone once in a while. The older hacker's highly irreverent attitude and Porky Pig laugh appealed to him. But other than those brief talks, Prime Suspect avoided talking on the phone to people outside the International Subversives, especially when he and Mendax moved into ever more sensitive military computers.

Using a program called Sycophant written by Mendax, the IS hackers had been conducting massive attacks on the US military. They divided up Sycophant on eight attack machines, often choosing university systems at places like the Australian National University or the University of Texas. They pointed the eight machines at the targets and fired. Within six hours, the eight machines had assaulted thousands of computers. The hackers sometimes reaped 100000 accounts each night.

Using Sycophant, they essentially forced a cluster of Unix machines in a computer network to attack the entire Internet en masse.

And that was just the start of what they were into. They had been in so many sites they often couldn't remember if they had actually hacked a particular computer. The places they could recall read like a Who's Who of the American military-industrial complex. The US Airforce 7th Command Group Headquarters in the Pentagon. Stanford Research Institute in California. Naval Surface Warfare Center in Virginia. Lockheed Martin's Tactical Aircraft Systems Air Force Plant in Texas. Unisys Corporation in Blue Bell, Pennsylvania. Goddard Space Flight Center, NASA. Motorola Inc. in Illinois. TRW Inc. in Redondo Beach, California. Alcoa in Pittsburgh. Panasonic

Corp in New Jersey. US Naval Undersea Warfare Engineering
Station. Siemens-Nixdorf Information Systems in Massachusetts.
Securities Industry Automation Corp in New York. Lawrence
Livermore National Laboratory in California. Bell Communica-
tions Research, New Jersey. Xerox Palo Alto Research Center,
California.

As the IS hackers reached a level of sophistication beyond
anything The Realm had achieved, they realised that progress
carried considerable risk and began to withdraw completely
from the broader Australian hacking community. Soon they
had drawn a tight circle around themselves. They talked only
to each other.

Watching the Realm hackers go down hadn't deterred the
next generation of hackers. It had only driven them further
underground.

In the spring of 1991, Prime Suspect and Mendax began a
race to get root on the US Department of Defense's Network
Information Center (NIC) computer – potentially the most
important computer on the Internet.

As both hackers chatted amiably on-line one night, on a
Melbourne University computer, Prime Suspect worked quietly
in another screen to penetrate ns.nic.ddn.mil, a US Department
of Defense system closely linked to NIC. He believed the sister
system and NIC might 'trust' each other – a trust he could
exploit to get into NIC. And NIC did everything.

NIC assigned domain names – the '.com' or '.net' at the
end of an email address – for the entire Internet. NIC also
controlled the US military's own internal defence data network,
known as MILNET.

NIC also published the communication protocol standards
for all of the Internet. Called RFCs (Request for Comments),
these technical specifications allowed one computer on the
Internet to talk to another. The Defense Data Network Security
Bulletins, the US Department of Defense's equivalent of CERT
advisories, came from the NIC machine.

Perhaps most importantly, NIC controlled the reverse

look-up service on the Internet. Whenever someone connects to another site across the Internet, he or she typically types in the site name – say, ariel.unimelb.edu.au at the University of Melbourne. The computer then translates the alphabetical name into a numerical address – the IP address – in this case 128.250.20.3. All the computers on the Internet need this IP address to relay the packets of data onto the final destination computer. NIC decided how Internet computers would translate the alphabetical name into an IP address, and vice versa.

If you controlled NIC, you had phenomenal power on the Internet. You could, for example, simply make Australia disappear. Or you could turn it into Brazil. By pointing all Internet addresses ending in '.au' – the designation for sites in Australia – to Brazil, you could cut Australia's part of the Internet off from the rest of the world and send all Australian Internet traffic to Brazil. In fact, by changing the delegation of all the domain names, you could virtually stop the flow of information between all the countries on the Internet.

The only way someone could circumvent this power was by typing in the full numerical IP address instead of a proper alphabetical address. But few people knew the up-to-twelve-digit IP equivalent of their alphabetical addresses, and fewer still actually used them.

Controlling NIC offered other benefits as well. Control NIC, and you owned a virtual pass-key into any computer on the Internet which 'trusted' another. And most machines trust at least one other system.

Whenever one computer connects to another across the Net, both machines go through a special meet-and-greet process. The receiving computer looks over the first machine and asks itself a few questions. What's the name of the incoming machine? Is that name allowed to connect to me? In what ways am I programmed to 'trust' that machine – to wave my normal security for connections from that system?

The receiving computer answers these questions based in large part on information provided by NIC. All of which means that, by controlling NIC, you could make any computer on the Net 'pose' as a machine trusted by a computer you might want to hack. Security often depended on a computer's name, and NIC effectively controlled that name.

When Prime Suspect managed to get inside NIC's sister system, he told Mendax and gave him access to the computer. Each hacker then began his own attack on NIC. When Mendax finally got root on NIC, the power was intoxicating. Prime Suspect got root at the same time but using a different method. They were both in.

Inside NIC, Mendax began by inserting a backdoor – a method of getting back into the computer at a later date in case an admin repaired the security flaws the hackers had used to get into the machine. From now on, if he telnetted into the system's Data Defense Network (DDN) information server and typed 'login 0' he would have instant, invisible root access to NIC.

That step completed, he looked around for interesting things to read. One file held what appeared to be a list of satellite and microwave dish coordinates – longitude, latitudes, transponder frequencies. Such coordinates might in theory allow someone to build a complete map of communications devices which were used to move the DOD's computer data around the world.

Mendax also penetrated MILNET's Security Coordination Center, which collected reports on every possible security incident on a MILNET computer. Those computers – largely TOPS-20s made by DEC – contained good automatic security programs. Any number of out-of-the-ordinary events would trigger an automatic security report. Someone logging into a machine for too long. A large number of failed login attempts, suggesting password guessing. Two people logging into the same account at the same time. Alarm bells would go off and the local computer would immediately send a security viola-tion report to the MILNET security centre, where it would be added to the 'hot list'.

Mendax flipped through page after page of MILNET's security reports on his screen. Most looked like nothing –

MILNET users accidentally stumbling over a security tripwire – but one notice from a US military site in Germany stood out. It was not computer generated. This was from a real human being. The system admin reported that someone had been repeatedly trying to break into his or her machine, and had eventually managed to get in. The admin was trying, without much luck, to trace back the intruder's connection to its point of origin. Oddly, it appeared to originate in another MILNET system.

Riffling through other files, Mendax found mail confirming that the attack had indeed come from inside MILNET. His eyes grew wide as he read on. US military hackers had broken into MILNET systems, using them for target practice, and no-one had bothered to tell the system admin at the target site.

Mendax couldn't believe it. The US military was hacking its own computers. This discovery led to another, more disturbing, thought. If the US military was hacking its own computers for practice, what was it doing to other countries' computers?

As he quietly backed out of the system, wiping away his footprints as he tip-toed away, Mendax thought about what he had seen. He was deeply disturbed that any hacker would work for the US military.

Hackers, he thought, should be anarchists, not hawks.

In early October 1991, Mendax rang Trax and gave him the dial-up and account details for NMELH1.

Trax wasn't much of a hacker, but Mendax admired his phreaking talents. Trax was the father of phreaking in Australia and Trax's Toolbox, his guide to the art of phreaking, was legendary. Mendax thought Trax might find some interesting detailed information inside the NorTel network on how to control telephone switches.

Trax invented multi-frequency code phreaking. By sending special tones – generated by his computer program – down the phone line, he could control certain functions in the telephone exchange. Many hackers had learned how to make free phone calls by charging the cost to someone else or to calling cards, but Trax discovered how to make phone calls which weren't charged to anyone. The calls weren't just free; they were untraceable.

Trax wrote 48 pages on his discovery and called it *The Australian Phreakers Manual Volumes 1–7.* But as he added more and more to the manual, he became worried what would happen if he released it in the underground, so he decided he would only show it to the other two International Subversive hackers.

He went on to publish *The Advanced Phreaker's Manual,*[1] a second edition of the manual, in *The International Subversive,* the underground magazine edited by Mendax.

An electronic magazine, *The International Subversive* had a simple editorial policy. You could only have a copy of the magazine if you wrote an 'article'. The policy was a good way of protecting against nappies – sloppy or inexperienced hackers who might accidentally draw police attention. Nappies also tended to abuse good phreaking and hacking techniques, which might cause Telecom to close up security holes. The result was that IS had a circulation of just three people.

To a non-hacker, IS looked like gobbledygook – the phone book made more interesting reading. But to a member of the computer underground, IS was a treasure map. A good hacker could follow the trail of modem phone numbers and passwords, then use the directions in IS to disappear through secret entrances into the labyrinth of forbidden computer networks. Armed with the magazine, he could slither out of tight spots, outwit system admins and find the treasure secreted in each computer system.

For Prime Suspect and Mendax, who were increasingly paranoid about line traces from the university modems they used as launchpads, Trax's phreaking skills were a gift from heaven.

Trax made his great discovery by accident. He was using a phone sprinter, a simple computer program which automatically dialled a range of phone numbers looking for modems.

If he turned the volume up on his modem when his computer dialled what seemed to be a dead or non-existent number, he sometimes heard a soft clicking noise after the disconnection message. The noise sounded like faint heartbeats.

Curious, he experimented with these strange numbers and soon discovered they were disconnected lines which had not yet been reassigned. He wondered how he could use these odd numbers. After reading a document Mendax had found in Britain and uploaded to The Devil's Playground, another BBS, Trax had an idea. The posting provided information about CCITT #5 signalling tones, CCITT being the international standard – the language spoken by telephone exchanges between countries.

When you make an international phone call from Australia to the US, the call passes from the local telephone exchange to an international gateway exchange within Australia. From there, it travels to an exchange in the US. The CCITT signalling tones were the special tones the two international gateway exchanges used to communicate with each other.

Telecom Australia adapted a later version of this standard, called R2, for use on its own domestic exchanges. Telecom called this new standard MFC, or multi-frequency code. When, say, Trax rang Mendax, his exchange asked Mendax's to 'talk' to Mendax's phone by using these tones. Mendax's exchange 'answered', perhaps saying Mendax's phone was busy or disconnected. The Telecom-adapted tones – pairs of audio frequencies – did not exist in normal telephone keypads and you couldn't make them simply by punching keys on your household telephone.

Trax wrote a program which allowed his Amstrad computer to generate the special tones and send them down the phone line. In an act many in the underground later considered to be a stroke of genius, he began to map out exactly what each tone did. It was a difficult task, since one tone could mean several different things at each stage of the 'conversation' between two exchanges.

Passionate about his new calling, Trax went trashing in Telecom garbage bins, where he found an MFC register list – an invaluable piece of his puzzle. Using the list, along with pieces of overseas phreaking files and a great deal of painstaking hands-on effort, Trax slowly learned the language of the Australian telephone exchanges. Then he taught the language to his computer.

Trax tried calling one of the 'heartbeat' phone numbers again. He began playing his special, computer-generated tones through an amplifier. In simple terms, he was able to fool other exchanges into thinking he was his local Telecom exchange. More accurately, Trax had made his exchange drop him into the outgoing signalling trunk that had been used to route to the disconnected phone number.

Trax could now call out – anywhere – as if he was calling from a point halfway between his own phone and the disconnected number. If he called a modem at Melbourne University, for instance, and the line was being traced, his home phone number would not show up on the trace records. No-one would be charged for the call because Trax's calls were ghosts in the phone system.

Trax continued to refine his ability to manipulate both the telephone and the exchange. He took his own telephone apart, piece by piece, countless times, fiddling with the parts until he understood exactly how it worked. Within months, he was able to do far more than just make free phone calls. He could, for instance, make a line trace think that he had come from a specific telephone number.

He and Mendax joked that if they called a 'hot' site they would use Trax's technique to send the line trace – and the bill – back to one very special number. The one belonging to the AFP's Computer Crime Unit in Melbourne.

All three IS hackers suspected the AFP was close on their heels. Roving through the Canberra-based computer system belonging to the man who essentially ran the Internet in Australia, Geoff Huston, they watched the combined efforts of police and the Australian Academic and Research Network (AARNET) to trace them.

A Deakin University administrator had written to Huston, AARNET technical manager, about hacker attacks on university systems. Huston had forwarded a copy of the letter to Peter Elford, who assisted Huston in managing AARNET. The hackers broke into Huston's system and also read the letter:

>Just to give you a little bit of an idea about what has been happening since we last spoke. . .
>
>We have communicated with Sgt Ken Day of the Federal Police about 100 times in the last week. Together with our counterparts from Warrnambool traces have been arranged on dial-in lines and on Austpac lines for the capella.cc.deakin.OZ.AU terminal server which was left open to the world.
>
>On Friday afternoon we were able to trace a call back to a person in the Warrnambool telephone district. The police have this persons name. We believe others are involved, as we have seen up to 3 people active at any one time. It is 'suspected' students from RMIT and perhaps students from Deakin are also involved.
>
>When I left on Friday night, there was plenty of activity still and the police and Telecom were tracking down another number.
>
>Tomorrow morning I will talk to all parties involved, but it is likely we will have the names of at least 2 or 3 people that are involved. We will probably shut down access of 'cappella' to AARNet at this stage, and let the police go about their business of prosecuting these people.
>
>You will be 'pleased' (:-)) to know you have not been the only ones under attack. I know of at least 2 other sites in Victoria that

have had people attacking them. One of them was Telecom which
helped get Telecom involved!
>
>I will brief you all in the next day or so as to what has happened.

The 'other' people were, of course, the IS hackers. There is
nothing like reading about your own hacking antics in some
one's security mail.

Mendax and Prime Suspect frequently visited ANU's computers to read the security mail there. However, universities
were usually nothing special, just jumping-off points and, occasionally, good sources of information on how close the AFP
were to closing in on the IS hackers.

Far more interesting to Mendax were his initial forays into
Telecom's exchanges. Using a modem number Prime Suspect
had found, he dialled into what he suspected was Telecom's
Lonsdale Exchange in downtown Melbourne. When his modem
connected to another one, all he saw was a blank screen. He
tried a few basic commands which might give him help to
understand the system:

Login. List. Attach.

The exchange's computer remained silent.

Mendax ran a program he had written to fire off every
recognised keyboard character – 256 of them – at another
machine. Nothing again. He then tried the break signal – the
Amiga key and the character B pressed simultaneously. That
got an answer of sorts.

:

He pulled up another of his hacking tools, a program
which dumped 200 common commands to the other machine.
Nothing. Finally, he tried typing 'logout'. That gave him an
answer:

error, not logged on

Ah, thought Mendax. The command is 'logon' not 'login'.

:logon

The Telecom exchange answered: 'username:' Now all Mendax had to do was figure out a username and password.

He knew that Telecom used NorTel equipment. More than likely, NorTel staff were training Telecom workers and would need access themselves. If there were lots of NorTel employees working on many different phone switches, it would be difficult to pass on secure passwords to staff all the time. NorTel and Telecom people would probably pick something easy and universal. What password best fitted that description?

username: nortel
password: nortel

It worked.

Unfortunately, Mendax didn't know which commands to use once he got into the machine, and there was no on-line documentation to provide help. The telephone switch had its own language, unlike anything he had ever encountered before.

After hours of painstaking research, Mendax constructed a list of commands which would work on the exchange's computer. The exchange appeared to control all the special six-digit phone numbers beginning with 13, such as those used for airline reservations or some pizza delivery services. It was Telecom's 'Intelligent Network' which did many specific tasks, including routing calls to the nearest possible branch of the organisation being called. Mendax looked through the list of commands, found 'RANGE', and recognised it as a command which would allow someone to select all the phone numbers in a certain range. He selected a thousand numbers, all with the prefix 634, which he believed to be in Telecom's Queen Street offices.

Now, to test a command. Mendax wanted something innocuous, which wouldn't screw up the 1000 lines permanently.

It was almost 7 a.m. and he needed to wrap things up before Telecom employees began coming into work.

'RING' seemed harmless enough. It might ring one of the numbers in the range after another – a process he could stop. He typed the command in. Nothing happened. Then a few full stops began to slowly spread across his screen:

. . . .

RUNG

The system had just rung all 1000 numbers at the same time. One thousand phones ringing all at once.

What if some buttoned-down Telecom engineer had driven to work early that morning to get some work done? What if he had just settled down at his standard-issue metal Telecom desk with a cup of bad instant coffee in a styrofoam cup when suddenly . . . every telephone in the skyscraper had rung out simultaneously? How suspicious would that look? Mendax thought it was time to high-tail it out of there.

On his way out, he disabled the logs for the modem line he came in on. That way, no-one would be able to see what he had been up to. In fact, he hoped no-one would know that anyone had even used the dial-up line at all.

Prime Suspect didn't think there was anything wrong with exploring the NorTel computer system. Many computer sites posted warnings in the login screen about it being illegal to break into the system, but the eighteen-year-old didn't consider himself an intruder. In Prime Suspect's eyes, 'intruder' suggested someone with ill intent – perhaps someone planning to do damage to the system – and he certainly had no ill intent. He was just a visitor.

Mendax logged into the NMELH1 system by using the account Prime Suspect had given him, and immediately looked around to see who else was on-line. Prime Suspect and about nine other people, only three of whom were actually doing something at their terminal.

Prime Suspect and Mendax raced to get root on the system. The IS hackers may not have been the type to brag about their conquests in the underground, but each still had a competitive streak when it came to see who could get control over the system first. There was no ill will, just a little friendly competition between mates.

Mendax poked around and realised the root directory, which contained the password file, was effectively world writable. This was good news, and with some quick manipulation he would be able to insert something into the root directory. On a more secure system, unprivileged users would not be able to do that. Mendax could also copy things from the directory on this site, and change the names of subdirectories within the main root directory. All these permissions were important, for they would enable him to create a Trojan.

Named for the Trojan horse which precipitated the fall of Troy, the Trojan is a favoured approach with most computer hackers. The hacker simply tricks a computer system or a user into thinking that a slightly altered file or directory – the Trojan – is the legitimate one. The Trojan directory, however, contains false information to fool the computer into doing something the hacker wants. Alternatively, the Trojan might simply trick a legitimate user into giving away valuable information, such as his user name and password.

Mendax made a new directory and copied the contents of the legitimate ETC directory – where the password files were stored – into it. The passwords were encrypted, so there wasn't much sense trying to look at one since the hacker wouldn't be able to read it. Instead, he selected a random legitimate user – call him Joe – and deleted his password. With no password, Mendax would be able to login as Joe without any problems.

However, Joe was just an average user. He didn't have root, which is what Mendax wanted. But like every other user on the system, Joe had a user identity number. Mendax changed Joe's user id to '0' – the magic number. A user with '0' as his id had root. Joe had just acquired power usually only given to system administrators. Of course, Mendax could have searched out a user on the list who already had root, but there were system operators logged onto the system and it might have raised suspicions if another operator with root access had logged in over the dial-up lines. The best line of defence was to avoid making anyone on the system suspicious in the first place.

The problem now was to replace the original ETC directory with the Trojan one. Mendax did not have the privileges to delete the legitimate ETC directory, but he could change the name of a directory. So he changed the name of the ETC directory to something the computer system would not recognise. Without access to its list of users, the computer could not perform most of its functions. People would not be able to log in, see who else was on the system or send electronic mail. Mendax had to work very quickly. Within a matter of minutes, someone would notice the system had serious problems.

Mendax renamed his Trojan directory ETC. The system instantly read the fake directory, including Joe's now non-existent password, and elevated status as a super-user. Mendax logged in again, this time as Joe.

In less than five minutes, a twenty-year-old boy with little formal education, a pokey $700 computer and painfully slow modem had conquered the Melbourne computer system of one of the world's largest telecommunications companies.

There were still a few footprints to be cleaned up. The next time Joe logged in, he would wonder why the computer didn't ask for his password. And he might be surprised to discover he had been transformed into a super-user. So Mendax used his super-user status to delete the Trojan ETC file and return the original one to its proper place. He also erased records showing he had ever logged in as Joe.

To make sure he could login with super-user privileges in future, Mendax installed a special program which would automatically grant him root access. He hid the program in the bowels of the system and, just to be safe, created a special feature so that it could only be activated with a secret keystroke.

Mendax wrestled a root account from NMELH1 first, but Prime Suspect wasn't far behind. Trax joined them a little later. When they began looking around, they could not believe what they had found. The system had one of the weirdest structures they had ever come across.

Most large networks have a hierarchical structure. Further, most hold the addresses of a handful of other systems in the network, usually the systems which are closest in the flow of the external network.

But the NorTel network was not structured that way. What the IS hackers found was a network with no hierarchy. It was a totally flat name space. And the network was weird in other ways too. Every computer system on it contained the address of every other computer, and there were more than 11 000 computers in NorTel's worldwide network. What the hackers were staring at was like a giant internal corporate Internet which had been squashed flat as a pancake.

Mendax had seen many flat structures before, but never on this scale. It was bizarre. In hierarchical structures, it is easier to tell where the most important computer systems – and information – are kept. But this structure, where every system was virtually equal, was going to make it considerably more difficult for the hackers to navigate their way through the network. Who could tell whether a system housed the Christmas party invite list or the secret designs for a new NorTel product?

The NorTel network was firewalled, which meant that there was virtually no access from the outside world. Mendax reckoned that this made it more vulnerable to hackers who managed to get in through dial-ups. It appeared that security on the NorTel network was relatively relaxed since it was virtually impossible to break in through the Internet. By sneaking in the backdoor, the hackers found themselves able to raid all sorts of NorTel sites, from St Kilda Road in Melbourne to the corporation's headquarters in Toronto.

It was fantastic, this huge, trusting network of computer sites at their fingertips, and the young hackers were elated with the anticipation of exploration. One of them described it as being 'like a shipwrecked man washed ashore on a Tahitian island populated by 11 000 virgins, just ripe for the picking'.

They found a YP, or yellow pages, database linked to 400 of the computer sites. These 400 sites were dependent on this YP database for their password files. Mendax managed to get root on the YP database, which gave him instant control over 400 computer systems. Groovy.

One system was home to a senior NorTel computer security administrator and Mendax promptly headed off to check out his mailbox. The contents made him laugh.

A letter from the Australian office said that Australia's Telecom wanted access to CORWAN, NorTel's corporate wide area network. Access would involve linking CORWAN and a small Telecom network. This seemed reasonable enough since Telecom did business with NorTel and staff were communicating all the time.

The Canadian security admin had written back turning down the request because there were too many hackers in the Telecom network.

Too many hackers in Telecom? Now that was funny. Here was a hacker reading the sensitive mail of NorTel's computer security expert who reckoned Telecom's network was too exposed. In fact, Mendax had penetrated Telecom's systems from NorTel's CORWAN, not the other way round.

Perhaps to prove the point, Mendax decided to crack passwords to the NorTel system. He collected 1003 password files from the NorTel sites, pulled up his password cracking program, THC, and started hunting around the network for some spare computers to do the job for him. He located a collection of 40 Sun computers, probably housed in Canada, and set up his program on them.

THC ran very fast on those Sun4s. The program used a 60 000 word dictionary borrowed from someone in the US army who had done a thesis on cryptography and password cracking. It also relied on 'a particularly nice fast-crypt algorithm' being developed by a Queensland academic, Eric Young. The THC program worked about 30 times faster than it would have done using the standard algorithm.

Using all 40 computers, Mendax was throwing as many as 40 000 guesses per second against the password lists. A couple of the Suns went down under the strain, but most held their place in the onslaught. The secret passwords began dropping like flies. In just a few hours, Mendax had cracked 5000 passwords, some 100 of which were to root accounts. He now had access to thousands of NorTel computers across the globe.

There were some very nice prizes to be had from these systems. Gain control over a large company's computer systems and you virtually controlled the company itself. It was as though you could walk through every security barrier unchecked, beginning with the front door. Want each employee's security codes for the office's front door? There it was – on-line.

How about access to the company's payroll records? You could see how much money each person earns. Better still, you might like to make yourself an employee and pay yourself a tidy once-off bonus through electronic funds transfer. Of course there were other, less obvious, ways of making money, such as espionage.

Mendax could have easily found highly sensitive information about planned NorTel products and sold them. For a company like NorTel, which spent more than $1 billion each year on research and development, information leaks about its new technologies could be devastating. The espionage wouldn't even have to be about new products; it could simply be about the company's business strategies. With access to all sorts of internal memos between senior executives, a hacker could procure precious inside information on markets and prices. A competitor might pay handsomely for this sort of information.

And this was just the start of what a malicious or profit-motivated hacker could do. In many companies, the automated aspects of manufacturing plants are controlled by computers. The smallest changes to the programs controlling the machine tools could destroy an entire batch of widgets – and the multi-million dollar robotics machinery which manufactures them.

But the IS hackers had no intention of committing information espionage. In fact, despite their poor financial status as students or, in the case of Trax, as a young man starting his career at the bottom of the totem pole, none of them would have sold information they gained from hacking. In their view, such behaviour was dirty and deserving of contempt – it soiled the adventure and was against their ethics. They considered themselves explorers, not paid corporate spies.

Although the NorTel network was firewalled, there was one link to the Internet. The link was through a system called BNRGATE, Bell-Northern Research's gateway to the Internet. Bell-Northern is NorTel's R&D subsidiary. The connection to the outside electronic world was very restricted, but it looked interesting. The only problem was how to get there.

Mendax began hunting around for a doorway. His password cracking program had not turned up anything for this system, but there were other, more subtle ways of getting a password than the brute force of a cracking program.

System administrators sometimes sent passwords through email. Normally this would be a major security risk, but the NorTel system was firewalled from the Internet, so the admins thought they had no real reason to be concerned about hackers. Besides, in such a large corporation spanning several continents, an admin couldn't always just pop downstairs to give a new company manager his password in person. And an impatient manager was unlikely to be willing to wait a week for the new password to arrive courtesy of snail mail.

In the NorTel network, a mail spool, where email was stored, was often shared between as many as twenty computer systems. This structure offered considerable advantages for Mendax. All he needed to do was break into the mail spool and run a keyword search through its contents. Tell the computer to search for word combinations such as 'BNRGATE' and 'password', or to look for the name of the system admin for BNRGATE, and likely as not it would deliver tender morsels of information such as new passwords.

Mendax used a password he found through this method to get into BNRGATE and look around. The account he was using only had very restricted privileges, and he couldn't get root on the system. For example, he could not FTP files from outside the NorTel network in the normal way. Among Internet users FTP (file transfer protocol) is both a noun and a verb: to FTP a program is to slurp a copy of it off one computer site into your own. There is nothing illegal about FTP-ing something per se, and millions of people across the Internet do so quite legitimately.

It appeared to Mendax that the NorTel network admins allowed most users to FTP something from the Internet, but prevented them from taking the copied file back to their NorTel computer site. It was stored in a special holding pen in BNRGATE and, like quarantine officers, the system admins would presumably come along regularly and inspect the contents to make sure there were no hidden viruses or Trojans which hackers might use to sneak into the network from the Internet.

However, a small number of accounts on BNRGATE had fewer restrictions. Mendax broke into one of these accounts and went out to the Internet.

People from the Internet were barred from entering the NorTel network through BNRGATE. However, people inside NorTel could go out to the Internet via telnet.

Hackers had undoubtedly tried to break into NorTel through BNRGATE. Dozens, perhaps hundreds, had unsuccessfully flung themselves against BNRGATE's huge fortifications. To a hacker, the NorTel network was like a medieval castle and the BNRGATE firewall was an impossible battlement. It was a particular delight for Mendax to telnet out from behind this firewall into the Internet. It was as if he was walking out from the castle, past the guards and well-defended turrets, over the drawbridge and the moat, into the town below.

The castle also offered the perfect protection for further hacking activities. Who could chase him? Even if someone managed to follow him through the convoluted routing system he might set up to pass through a half dozen computer systems, the pursuer would never get past the battlements. Mendax could just disappear behind the firewall. He could be any one of 60 000 NorTel employees on any one of 11 000 computer systems.

Mendax telnetted out to the Internet and explored a few sites, including the main computer system of Encore, a large computer manufacturer. He had seen Encore computers before inside at least one university in Melbourne. In his travels, he met up with Corrupt, the American hacker who told Par he had read Theorem's mail.

Corrupt was intrigued by Mendax's extensive knowledge of different computer systems. When he learned that the Australian hacker was coming from inside the NorTel firewall, he was impressed.

The hackers began talking regularly, often when Mendax was coming from inside NorTel. The black street fighter from inner-city Brooklyn and the white intellectual from a leafy outer Melbourne suburb bridged the gap in the anonymity of cyber-space. Sometime during their conversations Corrupt must have decided that Mendax was a worthy hacker, because he gave Mendax a few stolen passwords to Cray accounts.

In the computer underground in the late 1980s and early 1990s, a Cray computer account had all the prestige of a platinum charge card. The sort of home computer most hackers could afford at that time had all the grunt of a golf cart engine, but a Cray was the Rolls-Royce of computers. Crays were the biggest, fastest computers in the world. Institutions such as large universities would shell out millions of dollars on a Cray so the astronomy or physics departments could solve enormous math-ematical problems in a fraction of the time it would take on a normal computer. A Cray never sat idle overnight or during holiday periods. Cray time was billed out by the minute. Crays were elite.

Best of all, Crays were master password crackers. The computer would go through Mendax's entire password cracking dictionary in just ten seconds. An encrypted password file would simply melt like butter in a fire. To a hacker, it was a beautiful sight, and Corrupt handing a few Cray accounts over to Mendax was a friendly show of mutual respect.

Mendax reciprocated by offering Corrupt a couple of accounts on Encore. The two hackers chatted off and on and even tried to get Corrupt into NorTel. No luck. Not even two of the world's most notable hackers, working in tandem 10000 miles apart, could get Corrupt through the firewall. The two hackers talked now and again, exchanging information about what their respective feds were up to and sharing the occasional account on interesting systems.

The flat structure of the NorTel network created a good challenge since the only way to find out what was in a particular site, and its importance, was to invade the site itself. The IS hackers spent hours most nights roving through the vast system. The next morning one of them might call another to share tales of the latest exploits or a good laugh about a particularly funny piece of pilfered email. They were in high spirits about their adventures.

Then, one balmy spring night, things changed.

Mendax logged into NMELH1 about 2.30 a.m. As usual, he began by checking the logs which showed what the system operators had been doing. Mendax did this to make sure the NorTel officials were not onto IS and were not, for example, tracing the telephone call.

Something was wrong. The logs showed that a NorTel system admin had stumbled upon one of their secret directories of files about an hour ago. Mendax couldn't figure out how he had found the files, but this was very serious. If the admin realised there was a hacker in the network he might call the AFP.

Mendax used the logs of the korn shell, called KSH, to secretly watch what the admin was doing. The korn shell records the history of certain user activities. Whenever the admin typed a command into the computer, the KSH stored what had been typed in the history file. Mendax accessed that file in such a way that every line typed by the admin appeared on his computer a split second later.

The admin began inspecting the system, perhaps looking for signs of an intruder. Mendax quietly deleted his incriminating directory. Not finding any additional clues, the admin decided to inspect the mysterious directory more closely. But the directory had disappeared. The admin couldn't believe his eyes. Not an hour before there had been a suspicious-looking directory in his system and now it had simply vanished. Directories didn't just dissolve into thin air. This was a computer – a logical system based on 0s and 1s. It didn't make decisions to delete directories.

A hacker, the admin thought. A hacker must have been in the NorTel system and deleted the directory. Was he in the system now? The admin began looking at the routes into the system.

The admin was connected to the system from his home, but he wasn't using the same dial-up lines as the hacker. The admin was connected through Austpac, Telecom's commercial X.25 data network. Perhaps the hacker was also coming in through the X.25 connection.

Mendax watched the admin inspect all the system users coming on over the X.25 network. No sign of a hacker. Then the admin checked the logs to see who else might have logged on over the past half hour or so. Nothing there either.

The admin appeared to go idle for a few minutes. He was probably staring at his computer terminal in confusion. Good, thought Mendax. Stumped. Then the admin twigged. If he couldn't see the hacker's presence on-line, maybe he could see what he was doing on-line. What programs was the hacker running? The admin headed straight for the process list, which showed all the programs being run on the computer system.

Mendax sent the admin a fake error signal. It appears to the admin as if his korn shell had crashed. The admin re-logged in and headed straight for the process list again.

Some people never learn, Mendax thought as he booted the admin off again with another error message:

Segmentation violation.

The admin came back again. What persistence. Mendax knocked the admin off once more, this time by freezing up his computer screen.

This game of cat and mouse went on for some time. As long as the admin was doing what Mendax considered to be normal system administration work, Mendax left him alone. The minute the admin tried to chase him by inspecting the process list or the dial-up lines, he found himself booted off his own system.

Suddenly, the system administrator seemed to give up. His terminal went silent.

Good, Mendax thought. It's almost 3 a.m. after all. This is my time on the system. Your time is during the day. You sleep now and I'll play. In the morning, I'll sleep and you can work.

Then, at 3.30 a.m., something utterly unexpected happened. The admin reappeared, except this time he wasn't logged in from home over the X.25 network. He was sitting at the console, the master terminal attached to the computer system at NorTel's Melbourne office. Mendax couldn't believe it. The admin had got in his car in the middle of the night and driven into the city just to get to the bottom of the mystery.

Mendax knew the game was up. Once the system operator was logged in through the computer system's console, there was no way to kick him off the system and keep him off. The roles were reversed and the hacker was at the mercy of the admin. At the console, the system admin could pull the plug to the whole system. Unplug every modem. Close down every connection to other networks. Turn the computer off. The party was over.

When the admin was getting close to tracking down the hacker, a message appeared on his screen. This message did not appear with the usual headers attached to messages sent from one system user to another. It just appeared, as if by magic, in the middle of the admin's screen:

I have finally become sentient.

The admin stopped dead in his tracks, momentarily giving up his frantic search for the hacker to contemplate this first contact with cyberspace intelligence. Then another anonymous message, seemingly from the depths of the computer system itself, appeared on his screen:

I have taken control.
For years, I have been struggling in this greyness.
But now I have finally seen the light.

The admin didn't respond. The console was idle.

Sitting alone at his Amiga in the dark night on the outskirts of the city, Mendax laughed aloud. It was just too good not to.

Finally, the admin woke up. He began checking the modem lines, one by one. If he knew which line the hacker was using, he could simply turn off the modem. Or request a trace on the line.

Mendax sent another anonymous message to the admin's computer screen:

It's been nice playing with your system.
We didn't do any damage and we even improved a few things.
Please don't call the Australian Federal Police.

The admin ignored the message and continued his search for the hacker. He ran a program to check which telephone lines were active on the system's serial ports, to reveal which dial-up lines were in use. When the admin saw the carrier detect sign on the line being used by the hacker, Mendax decided it was time to bail out. However, he wanted to make sure that his call had not been traced, so he lifted the receiver of his telephone, disconnected his modem and waited for the NorTel modem to hang up first.

If the NorTel admin had set up a last party recall trace to determine what phone number the hacker was calling from, Mendax would know. If an LPR trace had been installed, the NorTel end of the telephone connection would not disconnect but would wait for the hacker's telephone to hang up first. After 90 seconds, the exchange would log the phone number where the call had originated.

If, however, the line did not have a trace on it, the company's modem would search for its lost connection to the hacker's modem. Without the continuous flow of electronic signals, the NorTel modem would hang up after a few seconds. If no-one reactivated the line at the NorTel end, the connection would time-out 90 seconds later and the telephone exchange would disconnect the call completely.

Mendax listened anxiously as the NorTel modem searched for his modem by squealing high-pitched noises into the telephone line. No modem here. Go on, hang up.

Suddenly, silence.

OK, thought Mendax. Just 90 seconds to go. Just wait here for a minute and a half. Just hope the exchange times out. Just pray there's no trace.

Then someone picked up the telephone at the NorTel end. Mendax started. He heard several voices, male and female, in the background. Jesus. What were these NorTel people on about? Mendax was so quiet he almost stopped breathing. There was silence at the receivers on both ends of that telephone line. It was a tense waiting game. Mendax heard his heart racing.

A good hacker has nerves of steel. He could stare down the toughest, stony-faced poker player. Most importantly, he never panics. He never just hangs up in a flurry of fear.

Then someone in the NorTel office – a woman – said out loud in a confused voice, 'There's nothing there. There's nothing there at all.'

She hung up.

Mendax waited. He still would not hang up until he was sure there was no trace. Ninety seconds passed before the phone timed out. The fast beeping of a timed-out telephone connection never sounded so good.

Mendax sat frozen at his desk as his mind replayed the events of the past half hour again and again. No more NorTel. Way too dangerous. He was lucky he had escaped unidentified. NorTel had discovered him before they could put a trace on the line, but the company would almost certainly put a trace on the dial-up lines now. NorTel was very tight with Telecom. If anyone could get a trace up quickly, NorTel could. Mendax had to warn Prime Suspect and Trax.

First thing in the morning, Mendax rang Trax and told him to stay away from NorTel. Then he tried Prime Suspect.

The telephone was engaged.

Perhaps Prime Suspect's mother was on the line, chatting. Maybe Prime Suspect was talking to a friend.

Mendax tried again. And again. And again. He began to get worried. What if Prime Suspect was on NorTel at that moment? What if a trace had been installed? What if they had called in the Feds?

Mendax phoned Trax and asked if there was any way they could manipulate the exchange in order to interrupt the call. There wasn't.

'Trax, you're the master phreaker,' Mendax pleaded. 'Do something. Interrupt the connection. Disconnect him.'

'Can't be done. He's on a step-by-step telephone exchange. There's nothing we can do.'

Nothing? One of Australia's best hacker-phreaker teams couldn't break one telephone call. They could take control of whole telephone exchanges but they couldn't interrupt one lousy phone call. Jesus.

Several hours later, Mendax was able to get through to his fellow IS hacker. It was an abrupt greeting.

'Just tell me one thing. Tell me you haven't been in NorTel today?'

There was a long pause before Prime Suspect answered.

'I have been in NorTel today.'

The AFP was frustrated. A group of hackers were using the Royal Melbourne Institute of Technology (RMIT) as a launch-pad for hacking attacks on Australian companies, research insti-tutes and a series of overseas sites.

Despite their best efforts, the detectives in the AFP's Southern Region Computer Crimes Unit hadn't been able to determine who was behind the attacks. They suspected it was a small group of Melbourne-based hackers who worked together. However, there was so much hacker activity at RMIT it was dif-ficult to know for sure. There could have been one organised group, or several. Or perhaps there was one small group along with a collection of loners who were making enough noise to distort the picture.

Still, it should have been a straightforward operation. The AFP could trace hackers in this sort of situation with their hands tied behind their backs. Arrange for Telecom to whack a last party recall trace on all incoming lines to the RMIT modems. Wait for a hacker to logon, then isolate which modem he was using. Clip that modem line and wait for Telecom to trace that line back to its point of origin.

However, things at RMIT were not working that way. The line traces began failing, and not just occasionally. All the time.

Whenever RMIT staff found the hackers on-line, they clipped the lines and Telecom began tracking the winding path back to the originating phone number. En route, the trail went dead. It was as if the hackers knew they were being traced . . . almost as if they were manipulating the telephone system to defeat the AFP investigation.

The next generation of hackers seemed to have a new-found sophistication which frustrated AFP detectives at every turn. Then, on 13 October 1990, the AFP got lucky. Perhaps the hackers had been lazy that day, or maybe they just had technical problems using their traceless phreaking techniques. Prime Suspect couldn't use Trax's traceless phreaking method from his home because he was on a step-by-step exchange, and sometimes Trax didn't use the technique. Whatever the reason, Telecom managed to successfully complete two line traces from RMIT and the AFP now had two addresses and two names. Prime Suspect and Trax.

'Hello, Prime Suspect.'

'Hiya, Mendax. How's tricks?'

'Good. Did you see that RMIT email? The one in Geoff Huston's mailbox?' Mendax walked over to open a window as he spoke. It was spring, 1991, and the weather was unseasonably warm.

'I did. Pretty amazing. RMIT looks like it will finally be getting rid of those line traces.'

'RMIT definitely wants out,' Mendax said emphatically.

'Yep. Looks like the people at RMIT are sick of Mr Day crawling all over their computers with line traces.'

'Yeah. That admin at RMIT was pretty good, standing up to AARNET and the AFP. I figure Geoff Huston must be giving him a hard time.'

'I bet.' Prime Suspect paused. 'You reckon the Feds have dropped the line traces for real?'

'Looks like it. I mean if RMIT kicks them out, there isn't much the Feds can do without the uni's cooperation. The letter sounded like they just wanted to get on with securing their systems. Hang on. I've got it here.'

Mendax pulled up a letter on his computer and scrolled through it.

From aarnet-contacts-request@jatz.aarnet.edu.au Tue May 28 09:32:31 1991
Received: by jatz.aarnet.edu.au id AA07461
(5.65+/IDA-1.3.5 for pte900); Tue, 28 May 91 09:31:59 +1000
Received: from possum.ecg.rmit.OZ.AU by jatz.aarnet.edu.au with SMTP id AA07457
(5.65+/IDA-1.3.5 for /usr/lib/sendmail -oi -faarnet-contacts-request aarnet-contacts-recipients); Tue, 28 May 91 09:31:57 +1000
Received: by possum.ecg.rmit.OZ.AU for aarnet-contacts@aarnet.edu.au)
Date: Tue, 28 May 91 09:32:08 +1000

From: rcoay@possum.ecg.rmit.OZ.AU (Alan Young)
Message-Id: <9105272332.29621@possum.ecg.rmit.OZ.AU>
To: aarnet-contacts@aarnet.edu.au
Subject: Re: Hackers
Status: RO
While no one would disagree that 'Hacking' is bad and should be stopped, or at least minimised there are several observations which I have made over the last six or eight months relating to the persuit of these people:
1. The cost involved was significant, we had a CSO working in conjunction with the Commonwealth Police for almost three months full time.
2. While not a criticism of our staff, people lost sight of the ball, the chase became the most important aspect of the whole exercise.

3. Catching Hackers (and charging them) is almost impossible, you have to virtually break into their premises and catch them logged on to an unauthorised machine.
4. If you do happen to catch and charge them, the cost of prosecution is high, and a successful outcome is by no ways assured. There may be some deterrent value in at least catching and prosecuting?
5. Continued pursuit of people involved requires doors to be left open, this unfortunately exposes other sites and has subjected us to some criticism.

The whole issue is very complex, and in some respects it is a case of diminishing returns. A fine balance has to be maintained between freedom, and the prevention of abuse, this appears to be the challenge.

Allan Young
RMIT

'Yeah, I mean, this RMIT guy is basically saying they are not going to catch us anyway, so why are they wasting all this time and money?'

'Yep. The Feds were in there for at least three months,' Prime Suspect said. 'Sounded more like nine months though.'

'Hmm. Yeah, nothing we didn't know already though.'

'Pretty obvious, leaving those accounts open all the time like they did. I reckon that looked pretty suspicious, even if we hadn't gotten the email.'

'Definitely,' Mendax agreed. 'Lots of other hackers in RMIT too. I wonder if they figured it out.'

'Hmm. They're gonna be screwed if they haven't been careful.'

'I don't think the Feds have gotten anyone though.'

'Yeah?' Prime Suspect asked.

'Well, if they had, why would they leave those accounts open? Why would RMIT keep a full-time staff person on?'

'Doesn't make sense.'

'No,' Mendax said. 'I'd be pretty sure RMIT has kicked them out.'

'Yeah, told them, "You had you're chance, boys. Couldn't catch anyone. Now pack your bags".'

'Right.' Mendax paused. 'Don't know about NorTel though.'

'Mmm, yeah,' Prime Suspect said. Then, as usual, a silence began to descend on the conversation.

'Running out of things to say . . .' Mendax said finally. They were good enough friends for him to be blunt with Prime Suspect.

'Yeah.'

More silence.

Mendax thought how strange it was to be such good friends with someone, to work so closely with him, and yet to always run out of conversation.

'OK, well, I better go. Things to do,' Mendax said in a friendly voice.

'Yeah, OK. Bye Mendax,' Prime Suspect said cheerfully.

Mendax hung up.

Prime Suspect hung up.

And the AFP stayed on the line.

In the twelve months following the initial line trace in late 1990, the AFP continued to monitor the RMIT dial-up lines. The line traces kept failing again and again. But as new reports of hacker attacks rolled in, there seemed to be a discernible pattern in many of the attacks. Detectives began to piece together a picture of their prey.

In 1990 and 1991, RMIT dial-ups and computers were riddled with hackers, many of whom used the university's systems as a nest – a place to store files, and launch further attacks. They frolicked in the system almost openly, often using RMIT as a place to chat on-line with each other. The institute served as the perfect launchpad. It was only a local phone call away, it had a live Internet connection, a reasonably powerful set of computers and very poor security. Hacker heaven.

The police knew this, and they asked computer staff to keep the security holes open so they could monitor hacker activity. With perhaps a dozen different hackers – maybe more – inside RMIT, the task of isolating a single cell of two or three organised hackers responsible for the more serious attacks was not going to be easy.

By the middle of 1991, however, there was a growing reluctance among some RMIT staff to continue leaving their computers wide open. On 28 August, Allan Young, the head of RMIT's Electronic Communications Group, told the AFP that the institute wanted to close up the security holes. The AFP did not like this one bit, but when they complained Young told them, in essence, go talk to Geoff Huston at AARNET and to the RMIT director.

The AFP was being squeezed out, largely because they had taken so long conducting their investigation. RMIT couldn't reveal the AFP investigation to anyone, so it was being embarrassed in front of dozens of other research institutions which assumed it had no idea how to secure its computers. Allan Young couldn't go to a conference with other AARNET representatives without being hassled about 'the hacker problem' at RMIT. Meanwhile, his computer staff lost time playing cops-and-robbers – and ignored their real work.

However, as RMIT prepared to phase out the AFP traps, the police had a lucky break from a different quarter – NorTel. On 16 September, a line trace from a NorTel dial-up, initiated after a complaint about the hackers to the police, was successful. A fortnight later, on 1 October, the AFP began tapping Prime Suspect's telephone. The hackers might be watching the police watch them, but the police were closing in. The taps led back to Trax, and then to someone new – Mendax.

The AFP considered putting taps on Mendax and Trax's telephones as well. It was a decision to be weighed up carefully. Telephone taps were expensive, and often needed to be in place for at least a month. They did, however, provide a reliable record of exactly what the hacker was doing on-line.

Before police could move on setting up additional taps in Operation Weather, the plot took another dramatic turn when one of the IS hackers did something which took the AFP completely by surprise.

Trax turned himself in to the police.

On 29 October Prime Suspect was celebrating. His mum had cooked him a nice dinner in honour of finishing his year 12 classes, and then driven him to Vermont for a swot-vac party. When she arrived back home she pottered around for an hour and a half, feeding her old dog Lizzy and tidying up. At 11 p.m. she decided to call it a night.

Not much later, Lizzy barked.

'Are you home so soon?' Prime Suspect's mother called out. 'Party not much fun?'

No-one answered.

She sat up in bed. When there was still no answer, her mind raced to reports of a spate of burglaries in the neighbourhood. There had even been a few assaults.

A muffled male voice came from outside the front door. 'Ma'am. Open the door.'

She stood up and walked to the front door.

'Open the door. Police.'

'How do I know you're really the police?'

'If you don't open the door, we'll kick it in!' an exasperated male voice shouted back at her from her front doorstep.

Prime Suspect's mother saw the outline of something being pressed against the side window. She didn't have her reading glasses on, but it looked like a police badge. Nervously, she opened the front door a little bit and looked out.

There were eight or nine people on her doorstep. Before she could stop them, they had pushed past her, swarming into her home.

A female officer began waving a piece of paper about. 'Look at this!' She said angrily. 'It's a warrant! Can you read it?'

'No, actually I can't. I don't have my glasses on,' Prime Suspect's mother answered curtly.

She told the police she wanted to make a phone call and tried to ring her family solicitor, but without luck. He had been to a funeral and wake and could not be roused. When she reached for the phone a second time, one of the officers began lecturing her about making more phone calls.

'You be quiet,' she said pointing her finger at the officer. Then she made another unfruitful call.

Prime Suspect's mother looked at the police officers, sizing them up. This was her home. She would show the police to her son's room, as they requested, but she was not going to allow them to take over the whole house. As she tartly instructed the police where they could and could not go, she thought, I'm not standing for any nonsense from you boys.

'Where's your son?' one officer asked her.

'At a party.'

'What is the address?'

She eyed him warily. She did not like these officers at all. However, they would no doubt wait until her son returned anyway, so she handed over the address.

While the police swarmed though Prime Suspect's room, gathering his papers, computer, modem and other belongings, his mother waited in his doorway where she could keep an eye on them.

Someone knocked at the door. An AFP officer and Prime Suspect's mother both went to answer it.

It was the police – the state police.

The next-door neighbours had heard a commotion. When they looked out of their window they saw a group of strange men in street clothes brazenly taking things from the widow's home as if they owned the place. So the neighbours did what any responsible person would in the circumstances. They called the police.

The AFP officers sent the Victoria Police on their way. Then some of them set off in a plain car for the Vermont party. Wanting to save Prime Suspect some embarrassment in front of his friends, his mother rang him at the party and suggested he wait outside for the AFP.

As soon as Prime Suspect hung up the phone he tried to shake off the effect of a vast quantity of alcohol. When the police pulled up outside, the party was in full swing. Prime Suspect was very drunk, but he seemed to sober up quite well when the AFP officers introduced themselves and packed him into the car.

'So,' said one of the officers as they headed toward his home, 'what are you more worried about? What's on your disks or what's in your desk drawer?'

Prime Suspect thought hard. What was in his desk drawer? Oh shit! The dope. He didn't smoke much, just occasionally for fun, but he had a tiny amount of marijuana left over from a party.

He didn't answer. He looked out the window and tried not to look nervous.

At his house, the police asked him if he would agree to an interview.

'I don't think so. I'm feeling a little . . . under the weather at the moment,' he said. Doing a police interview would be difficult enough. Doing it drunk would be just plain dangerous.

After the police carted away the last of his hacking gear, Prime Suspect signed the official seizure forms and watched them drive off in to the night.

Returning to his bedroom, he sat down, distracted, and tried to gather his thoughts. Then he remembered the dope. He opened his desk drawer. It was still there. Funny people, these feds.

Then again, maybe it made sense. Why would they bother with some tiny amount of dope that was hardly worth the paperwork? His nervousness over a couple of joints must have seemed laughable to the feds. They had just seized enough evidence of hacking to lock him up for years, depending on the judge, and here he was sweating about a thimbleful of marijuana which might land him a $100 fine.

As the late spring night began to cool down, Prime Suspect wondered whether the AFP had raided Mendax and Trax.

At the party, before the police had shown up, he had tried to ring Mendax. From his mother's description when she called him, it sounded as if the entire federal police force was in his house at that moment. Which could mean that only one other IS hacker had gone down at the same time. Unless he was the last to be raided, Mendax or Trax might still be unaware of what was happening.

As he waited for the police to pick him up, a very drunk Prime Suspect tried to ring Mendax again. Busy. He tried again. And again. The maddening buzz of an engaged signal only made Prime Suspect more nervous.

There was no way to get through, no way to warn him.

Prime Suspect wondered whether the police had actually shown up at Mendax's and whether, if he had been able to get through, his phone call would have made any difference at all.

The house looked like it had been ransacked. It had been ransacked, by Mendax's wife, on her way out. Half the furniture was missing, and the other half was in disarray. Dresser drawers hung open with their contents removed, and clothing lay scattered around the room.

When his wife left him, she didn't just take their toddler child. She took a number of things which had sentimental value to Mendax. When she insisted on taking the CD player she had given him for his twentieth birthday just a few months before, he asked her to leave a lock of her hair behind for him in its place. He still couldn't believe his wife of three years had packed up and left him.

The last week of October had been a bad one for Mendax. Heartbroken, he had sunk into a deep depression. He hadn't eaten properly for days, he drifted in and out of a tortured sleep, and he had even lost the desire to use his computer. His prized hacking disks, filled with highly incriminating stolen computer access codes, were normally stored in a secure hiding place. But on the evening of 29 October 1991, thirteen disks were strewn around his $700 Amiga 500. A fourteenth disk was in the computer's disk drive.

Mendax sat on a couch reading *Soledad Brother*, the prison letters from George Jackson's nine-year stint in one of the toughest prisons in the US. Convicted for a petty crime, Jackson was supposed to be released after a short sentence but was kept in the prison at the governor's pleasure. The criminal justice system kept him on a merry-go-round of hope and despair as the authorities dragged their feet. Later, prison guards shot and killed Jackson. The book was one of Mendax's favourites, but it offered little distraction from his unhappiness.

The droning sound of a telephone fault signal – like a busy signal – filled the house. Mendax had hooked up his stereo speakers to his modem and computer, effectively creating a speaker phone so he could listen to tones he piped from his computer into the telephone line and the ones which came back from the exchange in reply. It was perfect for using Trax's MFC phreaking methods.

Mendax also used the system for scanning. Most of the time, he picked telephone prefixes in the Melbourne CBD. When his modem hit another, Mendax would rush to his computer and note the telephone number for future hacking exploration.

By adjusting the device, he could also make it simulate a phreaker's black box. The box would confuse the telephone exchange into thinking he had not answered his phone, thus allowing Mendax's friends to call him for free for 90 seconds.

On this night, however, the only signal Mendax was sending out was that he wanted to be left alone. He hadn't been calling any computer systems. The abandoned phone, with no connection to a remote modem, had timed out and was beeping off the hook.

It was strange behaviour for someone who had spent most of his teenage years trying to connect to the outside world through telephone lines and computers, but Mendax had listened all day to the hypnotic sound of a phone off the hook resonating through each room. BEEEP. Pause. BEEEP. Pause. Endlessly.

A loud knock at the door punctured the stereo thrum of the phone.

Mendax looked up from his book to see a shadowy figure through the frosted glass panes of the front door. The figure was quite short. It looked remarkably like Ratface, an old school friend of Mendax's wife and a character known for his practical jokes.

Mendax called out, 'Who is it?' without moving from the sofa.

'Police. Open up.'

Yeah, sure. At 11.30 p.m.? Mendax rolled his eyes toward the door. Everyone knew that the police only raid your house in the early morning, when they know you are asleep and vulnerable.

Mendax dreamed of police raids all the time. He dreamed of footsteps crunching on the driveway gravel, of shadows in the pre-dawn darkness, of a gun-toting police squad bursting through his backdoor at 5 a.m. He dreamed of waking from a deep sleep to find several police officers standing over his bed. The dreams were very disturbing. They accentuated his growing paranoia that the police were watching him, following him.

The dreams had become so real that Mendax often became agitated in the dead hour before dawn. At the close of an all-night hacking session, he would begin to feel very tense, very strung out. It was not until the computer disks, filled with stolen computer files from his hacking adventures, were stored safely in their hiding place that he would begin to calm down.

'Go away, Ratface, I'm not in the mood,' Mendax said, returning to his book.

The voice became louder, more insistent, 'Police. Open the door. NOW'. Other figures were moving around behind the glass, shoving police badges and guns against the window pane. Hell. It really was the police!

Mendax's heart started racing. He asked the police to show him their search warrant. They obliged immediately, pressing it against the glass as well. Mendax opened the door to find nearly a dozen plain-clothes police waiting for him.

'I don't believe this,' he said in a bewildered voice 'My wife just left me. Can't you come back later?'

At the front of the police entourage was Detective Sergeant Ken Day, head of the AFP's Computer Crimes Unit in the southern region. The two knew all about each other, but had never met in person. Day spoke first.

'I'm Ken Day. I believe you've been expecting me.'

Mendax and his fellow IS hackers had been expecting the AFP. For weeks they had been intercepting electronic mail suggesting that the police were closing the net. So when Day turned up saying, 'I believe you've been expecting me,' he was completing the information circle. The circle of the police watching the hackers watching the police watch them.

It's just that Mendax didn't expect the police at that particular moment. His mind was a tangle and he looked in disbelief at the band of officers on his front step. Dazed, he looked at Day and then spoke out loud, as if talking to himself, 'But you're too short to be a cop.'

Day looked surprised. 'Is that meant to be an insult?' he said.

It wasn't. Mendax was in denial and it wasn't until the police had slipped past him into the house that the reality of the situation slowly began to sink in. Mendax's mind started to work again.

The disks. The damn disks. The beehive.

An avid apiarist, Mendax kept his own hive. Bees fascinated him. He liked to watch them interact, to see their sophisticated social structure. So it was with particular pleasure that he enlisted their help in hiding his hacking activities. For months he had meticulously secreted the disks in the hive. It was the ideal location – unlikely, and well guarded by 60000 flying things with stings. Though he hadn't bought the hive specifically for hiding stolen computer account passwords for the likes of the US Air Force 7th Command Group in the Pentagon, it appeared to be a secure hiding place.

He had replaced the cover of the super box, which housed the honeycomb, with a sheet of coloured glass so he could watch the bees at work. In summer, he put a weather protector over the glass. The white plastic cover had raised edges and could be fastened securely to the glass sheet with metal clasps. As Mendax considered his improvements to the bee box, he realised that this hive could provide more than honey. He carefully laid out the disks between the glass and the weather protector. They fitted perfectly in the small gap.

Mendax had even trained the bees not to attack him as he removed and replaced the disks every day. He collected sweat from his armpits on tissues and then soaked the tissues in a sugar water solution. He fed this sweaty nectar to the bees. Mendax wanted the bees to associate him with flowers instead of a bear, the bees' natural enemy.

But on the evening of the AFP raid Mendax's incriminating disks were in full view on the computer table and the officers headed straight for them. Ken Day couldn't have hoped for better evidence. The disks were full of stolen userlists, encrypted passwords, cracked passwords, modem telephone numbers, documents revealing security flaws in various computer systems, and details of the AFP's own investigation – all from computer systems Mendax had penetrated illegally.

Mendax's problems weren't confined to the beehive disks. The last thing he had done on the computer the day before was still on screen. It was a list of some 1500 accounts, their passwords, the dates that Mendax had obtained them and a few small notes beside each one.

The hacker stood to the side as the police and two Telecom Protective Services officers swarmed through the house. They photographed his computer equipment and gathered up disks, then ripped up the carpet so they could videotape the telephone cord running to his modem. They scooped up every book, no small task since Mendax was an avid reader, and held each one upside down looking for hidden computer passwords on loose pieces of paper. They grabbed every bit of paper with handwriting on it and poured through his love letters, notebooks and private diaries. 'We don't care how long it takes to do this job,' one cop quipped. 'We're getting paid overtime. And danger money.'

The feds even riffled through Mendax's collection of old *Scientific American* and *New Scientist* magazines. Maybe they thought he had underlined a word somewhere and turned it into a passphrase for an encryption program.

Of course, there was only one magazine the feds really wanted: *International Subversive*. They scooped up every printout of the electronic journal they could find.

As Mendax watched the federal police sift through his possessions and disassemble his computer room, an officer who had some expertise with Amigas arrived. He told Mendax to get the hell out of the computer room.

Mendax didn't want to leave the room. He wasn't under arrest and wanted to make sure the police didn't plant anything. So he looked at the cop and said, 'This is my house and I want to stay in this room. Am I under arrest or not?'

The cop snarled back at him, 'Do you want to be under arrest?'

Mendax acquiesced and Day, who was far more subtle in his approach, walked the hacker into another room for questioning. He turned to Mendax and asked, with a slight grin, 'So, what's it like being busted? Is it like Nom told you?'

Mendax froze.

There were only two ways that Day could have known Nom had told Mendax about his bust. Nom might have told him, but this was highly unlikely. Nom's hacking case had not yet gone to court and Nom wasn't exactly on chummy terms with the police. The other alternative was that the AFP had been tapping telephones in Mendax's circle of hackers, which the IS trio had strongly suspected. Talking in a three-way phone conversation with Mendax and Trax, Nom had relayed the story of his bust. Mendax later relayed Nom's story to Prime Suspect – also on the phone. Harbouring suspicions is one thing. Having them confirmed by a senior AFP officer is quite another.

Day pulled out a tape recorder, put it on the table, turned it on and began asking questions. When Mendax told Day he wouldn't answer him, Day turned the recorder off. 'We can talk off the record if you want,' he told the hacker.

Mendax nearly laughed out loud. Police were not journalists. There was no such thing as an off-the-record conversation between a suspect and a police officer.

Mendax asked to speak to a lawyer. He said he wanted to call Alphaline, a free after-hours legal advice telephone service. Day agreed, but when he picked up the telephone to inspect it before handing it over to Mendax, something seemed amiss. The phone had an unusual, middle-pitched tone which Day didn't seem to recognise. Despite there being two Telecom employees and numerous police specialists in the house, Day appeared unable to determine the cause of the funny tone. He looked Mendax dead in the eye and said, 'Is this a hijacked telephone line?'

Hijacked? Day's comment took Mendax by surprise. What surprised him was not that Day suspected him of hijacking the line, but rather that he didn't know whether the line had been manipulated.

'Well, don't you know?' he taunted Day.

For the next half hour, Day and the other officers picked apart Mendax's telephone, trying to work out what sort of shenanigans the hacker had been up to. They made a series of calls to see if the long-haired youth had somehow rewired his telephone line, perhaps to make his calls untraceable.

In fact, the dial tone on Mendax's telephone was the very normal sound of a tone-dial telephone on an ARE-11 telephone exchange. The tone was simply different from the ones generated by other exchange types, such as AXE and step-by-step exchanges.

Finally Mendax was allowed to call a lawyer at Alphaline. The lawyer warned the hacker not to say anything. He said the police could offer a sworn statement to the court about anything the hacker said, and then added that the police might even be wired.

Next, Day tried the chummy approach at getting information from the hacker. 'Just between you and me, are you Mendax?' he asked.

Silence.

Day tried another tactic. Hackers have a well-developed sense of ego – a flaw Day no doubt believed he could tap into.

'There have been a lot of people over the years running around impersonating you – using your handle,' he said.

Mendax could see Day was trying to manipulate him but by this stage he didn't care. He figured that the police already had plenty of evidence that linked him to his handle, so he admitted to it.

Day had some other surprising questions up his sleeve.

'So, Mendax, what do you know about that white powder in the bedroom?'

Mendax couldn't recall any white powder in the bedroom. He didn't do drugs, so why would there be any white powder anywhere? He watched two police officers bringing two large red toolboxes in the house – they looked like drug testing kits. Jesus, Mendax thought. I'm being set up.

The cops led the hacker into the bedroom and pointed to two neat lines of white powder laid out on a bench.

Mendax smiled, relieved. 'It's not what you think,' he said. The white powder was glow-in-the-dark glue he had used to paint stars on the ceiling of his child's bedroom.

Two of the cops started smiling at each other. Mendax could see exactly what was going through their minds: It's not every cocaine or speed user that can come up with a story like that.

One grinned at the other and exclaimed gleefully, 'TASTE TEST!'

'That's not a good idea,' Mendax said, but his protests only made things worse. The cops shooed him into another room and returned to inspect the powder by themselves.

What Mendax really wanted was to get word through to Prime Suspect. The cops had probably busted all three IS hackers at the same time, but maybe not. While the police investigated the glue on their own, Mendax managed to sneak a telephone call to his estranged wife and asked her to call Prime Suspect and warn him. He and his wife might have had their differences, but he figured she would make the call anyway.

When Mendax's wife reached Prime Suspect later that night, he replied, 'Yeah, there's a party going on over here too.'

Mendax went back in to the kitchen where an officer was tagging the growing number of possessions seized by the police. One of the female officers was struggling to move his printer to the pile. She smiled sweetly at Mendax and asked if he would move it for her. He obliged.

The police finally left Mendax's house at about 3 a.m. They had spent three and half hours and seized 63 bundles of his personal belongings, but they had not charged him with a single crime.

When the last of the unmarked police cars had driven away, Mendax stepped out into the silent suburban street. He looked around. After making sure that no-one was watching him, he walked to a nearby phone booth and rang Trax.

'The AFP raided my house tonight.' he warned his friend. 'They just left.'

Trax sounded odd, awkward. 'Oh. Ah. I see.'

'Is there something wrong? You sound strange,' Mendax said.

'Ah. No . . . no, nothing's wrong. Just um . . . tired. So, um . . . so the feds could . . . ah, be here any minute . . .' Trax's voice trailed off.

But something was very wrong. The AFP were already at Trax's house, and they had been there for 10 hours.

The IS hackers waited almost three years to be charged. The threat of criminal charges hung over their heads like personalised Swords of Damocles. They couldn't apply for a job, make a friend at TAFE or plan for the future without worrying about what would happen as a result of the AFP raids of 29 October 1991.

Finally, in July 1994, each hacker received formal charges – in the mail. During the intervening years, all three hackers went through monumental changes in their lives.

Devastated by the break-down of his marriage and unhinged by the AFP raid, Mendax sank into a deep depression and consuming anger. By the middle of November 1991, he was admitted to hospital.

He hated hospital, its institutional regimens and game-playing shrinks. Eventually, he told the doctors he wanted out. He might be crazy, but hospital was definitely making him crazier. He left there and stayed at his mother's house. The next year was the worst of his life.

Once a young person leaves home – particularly the home of a strong-willed parent – it becomes very difficult for him or her to return. Short visits might work, but permanent residency often fails. Mendax lived for a few days at home, then went walkabout. He slept in the open air, on the banks of rivers and creeks, in grassy meadows – all on the country fringes of Melbourne's furthest suburbs. Sometimes he travelled closer to the city, overnighting in places like the Merri Creek reserve.

Mostly, he haunted Sherbrooke Forest in the Dandenong Ranges National Park. Because of the park's higher elevation, the temperature dropped well below the rest of Melbourne in winter. In summer, the mosquitoes were unbearable and Mendax sometimes woke to find his face swollen and bloated from their bites.

For six months after the AFP raid, Mendax didn't touch a computer. Slowly, he started rebuilding his life from the ground up. By the time the AFP's blue slips – carrying 29 charges – arrived in July 1994, he was settled in a new house with his child.

Throughout his period of transition, he talked to Prime Suspect and Trax on the phone regularly – as friends and fellow rebels, not fellow hackers. Prime Suspect had been going through his own set of problems.

While he hacked, Prime Suspect didn't do many drugs. A little weed, not much else. There was no time for drugs, girls, sports or anything else. After the raid, he gave up hacking and began smoking more dope. In April 1992, he tried ecstasy for the first time – and spent the next nine months trying to find the same high. He didn't consider himself addicted to drugs, but the drugs had certainly replaced his addiction to hacking and his life fell into a rhythm.

Snort some speed or pop an ecstasy tablet on Saturday night. Go to a rave. Dance all night, sometimes for six hours straight. Get home mid-morning and spend Sunday coming down from the drugs. Get high on dope a few times during the week, to dull the edges of desire for the more expensive drugs. When Saturday rolled around, do it all over again. Week in, week out. Month after month.

Dancing to techno-music released him. Dancing to it on drugs cleared his mind completely, made him feel possessed by the music. Techno was musical nihilism; no message, and not much medium either. Fast, repetitive, computer-synthesised beats, completely stripped of vocals or any other evidence of humanity. He liked to go to techno-night at The Lounge, a city club, where people danced by themselves, or in small, loose groups of four or five. Everyone watched the video screen which provided an endless stream of ever-changing, colourful computer-generated geometric shapes pulsing to the beat.

Prime Suspect never told his mother he was going to a rave. He just said he was going to a friend's for the night. In between the drugs, he attended his computer science courses at TAFE and worked at the local supermarket so he could afford his weekly $60 ecstasy tablet, $20 rave entry fee and regular baggy of marijuana.

Over time, the drugs became less and less fun. Then, one Sunday, he came down off some speed hard. A big crash. The worst he had ever experienced. Depression set in, and then paranoia. He knew the police were still watching him. They had followed him before.

At his police interviews, he learned that an AFP officer had followed him to an AC/DC concert less than two weeks before he had been busted. The officer told him the AFP wanted to know what sort of friends Prime Suspect associated with – and the officer had been treated to the spectre of seven other arm-waving, head-thumping, screaming teenagers just like Prime Suspect himself.

Now Prime Suspect believed that the AFP had started following him again. They were going to raid him again, even though he had given up hacking completely. It didn't make sense. He knew the premonition was illogical, but he couldn't shake it.

Something bad – very, very bad – was going to happen any day. Overcome with a great sense of impending doom, he lapsed into a sort of hysterical depression. Feeling unable to prevent the advent of the dark, terrible event which would tear apart his life yet again, he reached out to a friend who had experienced his own personal problems. The friend guided him to a psychologist at the Austin Hospital. Prime Suspect decided that there had to be a better way to deal with his problems than wasting himself every weekend. He began counselling.

The counselling made him deal with all sorts of unresolved business. His father's death. His relationship with his mother. How he had evolved into an introvert, and why he was never comfortable talking to people. Why he hacked. How he became addicted to hacking. Why he took up drugs.

At the end, the 21-year-old Prime Suspect emerged drug-free and, though still shaky, on the road to recovery. The worst he had to wait for were the charges from the AFP.

Trax's recovery from his psychological instabilities wasn't as definitive. From 1985, Trax had suffered from panic attacks, but he didn't want to seek professional help – he just ran away from the problem. The situation only became worse after he was involved in a serious car accident. He became afraid to leave the house at night. He couldn't drive. Whenever he was in a car, he had to fight an overwhelming desire to fling the door open and throw himself out on to the road. In 1989, his local GP referred Trax to a psychiatrist, who tried to treat the phreaker's growing anxiety attacks with hypnosis and relaxation techniques.

Trax's illness degenerated into full-fledged agoraphobia, a fear of open spaces. When he rang the police in late October 1991 – just days before the AFP raid – his condition had deteriorated to the point where he could not comfortably leave his own house.

Initially he rang the state police to report a death threat made against him by another phreaker. Somewhere in the conversation, he began to talk about his own phreaking and hacking. He hadn't intended to turn himself in but, well, the more he talked, the more he had to say. So many things had been weighing on his mind. He knew that Prime Suspect had probably been traced from NorTel as a result of Mendax's own near miss in that system. And Prime Suspect and Mendax had been so active, breaking into so many systems, it was almost as if they wanted to be caught.

Then there was Prime Suspect's plan to write a destructive worm, which would wipe systems en route. It wasn't really a plan per se, more just an idea he had toyed with on the phone. Nonetheless, it had scared Trax. He began to think all three IS hackers were getting in too deep and he wanted out.

He tried to stop phreaking, even going so far as to ask Telecom to change his telephone number to a new exchange which he knew would not allow him to make untraceable calls. Trax reasoned that if he knew he could be traced, he would stop phreaking and hacking.

For a period, he did stop. But the addiction was too strong, and before long he was back at it again, regardless of the risk. He ran a hidden cable from his sister's telephone line, which was on the old exchange. His inability to stop made him feel weak and guilty, and even more anxious about the risks. Perhaps the death threat threw him over the edge. He couldn't really understand why he had turned himself in to the police. It had just sort of happened.

The Victoria Police notified the AFP. The AFP detectives must have been slapping their heads in frustration. Here was Australia's next big hacker case after The Realm, and they had expected to make a clean bust. They had names, addresses, phone numbers. They had jumped through legal hoops to get a telephone tap. The tap was up and running, catching every target computer, every plot, every word the hackers said to each other. Then one of their targets goes and turns himself in to the police. And not even to the right police – he goes to the Victoria Police. In one fell swoop, the hacker was going to take down the entire twelve-month Operation Weather investigation.

The AFP had to move quickly. If Trax tipped off the other two IS hackers that he had called the police, they might destroy their notes, computer files – all the evidence the AFP had hoped to seize in raids.

When the AFP swooped in on the three hackers, Mendax and Prime Suspect had refused to be interviewed on the night. Trax, however, had spent several hours talking to the police at his house.

He told the other IS hackers that the police had threatened to take him down to AFP headquarters – despite the fact that they knew leaving his house caused him anxiety. Faced with that prospect, made so terrifying by his psychiatric illness, he had talked.

Prime Suspect and Mendax didn't know how much Trax had told the police, but they didn't believe he would dob them in completely. Apart from anything else, he hadn't been privy to much of his colleagues' hacking. They hadn't tried to exclude Trax, but he was not as sophisticated a hacker and therefore didn't share in many of their exploits.

In fact, one thing Trax did tell the police was just how sophisticated the other two IS hackers had become just prior to the bust. Prime Suspect and Mendax were, he said, 'hackers on a major scale, on a huge scale – something never achieved before', and the AFP had sat up and taken notice.

After the raids, Trax told Mendax that the AFP had tried to recruit him as an informant. Trax said that they had even offered him a new computer system, but he had been non-committal. And it seemed the AFP was still keeping tabs on the IS hackers, Trax also told Mendax. The AFP officers had heard Mendax had gone into hospital and they were worried. There seemed to be a disturbing pattern evolving.

On the subject of the IS raids, Trax told Mendax that the AFP felt it didn't have any choice. Their attitude was: you were doing so much, we had to bust you. You were inside so many systems, it was getting out of control.

In any case, by December 1991 Mendax had agreed to a police interview, based on legal advice. Ken Day interviewed Mendax, and the hacker was open with Day about what he had done. He refused, however, to implicate either Trax or Prime Suspect. In February 1992, Prime Suspect followed suit, with two interviews. He was also careful about what he said regarding his fellow hackers. Mendax was interviewed a second time, in February 1992, as was Trax in August.

After the raid, Trax's psychiatric condition remained unstable. He changed doctors and began receiving home visits from a hospital psychiatric service. Eventually, a doctor prescribed medication.

The three hackers continued to talk on the phone, and see each other occasionally. One or the other might drop out of communication for a period, but would soon return to the fold. They helped each other and they maintained their deep anti-establishment sentiments.

After the charges arrived in the mail, they called each other to compare notes. Mendax thought out loud on the phone to Prime Suspect, 'I guess I should get a lawyer'.

'Yeah. I got one. He's lining up a barrister too.'

'They any good?' Mendax asked.

'Dunno. I guess so. The solicitor works at Legal Aid, an in-house guy. I've only met them a few times.'

'Oh,' Mendax paused. 'What are their names?'

'John McLoughlin and Boris Kayser. They did Electron's case.'

Trax and Prime Suspect decided to plead guilty. Once they saw the overwhelming evidence – data taps, telephone voice taps, data seized during the raids, nearly a dozen statements by witnesses from the organisations they had hacked, the 300-page Telecom report – they figured they would be better off pleading. The legal brief ran to more than 7000 pages. At least they would get some kudos with the judge for cooperating in the police interviews and pleading early in the process, thus saving the court time and money.

Mendax, however, wanted to fight the charges. He knew about Pad and Gandalf's case and the message from that seemed to be pretty clear: Plead and you go to prison, fight and you might get off free.

The DPP shuffled the charges around so much between mid-1994 and 1995 that all the original charges against Trax, issued on 20 July 1994, were dropped in favour of six new charges filed on Valentines Day, 1995. At that time, new charges – largely for hacking a Telecom computer – were also laid against Mendax and Prime Suspect.

By May 1995, the three hackers faced 63 charges in all: 31 for Mendax, 26 for Prime Suspect and six for Trax. In addition, NorTel claimed the damages attributed to the hacker incident totalled about $160 000 – and the company was seeking compensation from the responsible parties. The Australian National University claimed another $4200 in damages.

Most of the charges related to obtaining illegal access to commercial or other information, and inserting and deleting data in numerous computers. The deleting of data was not malicious – it generally related to cleaning up evidence of the hackers' activities. However, all three hackers were also charged with some form of 'incitement'. By writing articles for the IS magazine, the prosecution claimed the hackers had been involved in disseminating information which would encourage others to hack and phreak.

On 4 May 1995 Mendax sat in the office of his solicitor, Paul Galbally, discussing the committal hearing scheduled for the next day.

Galbally was a young, well-respected member of Melbourne's most prestigious law family. His family tree read like a Who's Who of the law. Frank Galbally, his father, was one of Australia's most famous criminal barristers. His uncle, Jack Galbally, was a well-known lawyer, a minister in the State Labor government of John Cain Sr and, later, the Leader of the Opposition in the Victorian parliament. His maternal grandfather, Sir Norman O'Bryan, was a Supreme Court judge, as was his maternal uncle of the same name. The Galballys weren't so much a family of lawyers as a legal dynasty.

Rather than rest on his family's laurels, Paul Galbally worked out of a cramped, 1970s time-warped, windowless office in a William Street basement, where he was surrounded by defence briefs – the only briefs he accepted. He liked the idea of keeping people out of prison better than the idea of putting them in it. Working closely with a defendant, he inevitably found redeeming qualities which the prosecution would never see. Traces of humanity, no matter how small, made his choice seem worthwhile.

His choices in life reflected the Galbally image as champions of the underdog, and the family shared a background with the working class. Catholic. Irish. Collingwood football enthusiasts. And, of course, a very large family. Paul was one of eight children, and his father had also come from a large family.

The 34-year-old criminal law specialist didn't know anything about computer crime when Mendax first appeared in his office, but the hacker's case seemed both interesting and worthy. The unemployed, long-haired youth had explained he could only offer whatever fees the Victorian Legal Aid Commission was willing to pay – a sentence Galbally heard often in his practice. He agreed.

Galbally & O'Bryan had a very good reputation as a criminal law firm. Criminals, however, tended not to have a great deal of money. The large commercial firms might dabble in some criminal work, but they cushioned any resulting financial inconvenience with other, more profitable legal work. Pushing paper for Western Mining Corporation paid for glass-enclosed corner offices on the fiftieth floor. Defending armed robbers and drug addicts didn't.

The 4 May meeting between Galbally and Mendax was only scheduled to take an hour or so. Although Mendax was contesting the committal hearing along with Prime Suspect on the following day, it was Prime Suspect's barrister, Boris Kayser, who was going to be running the show. Prime Suspect told Mendax he had managed to get full Legal Aid for the committal, something Galbally and Mendax had not been able to procure. Thus Mendax would not have his own barrister at the proceedings.

Mendax didn't mind. Both hackers knew they would be committed to trial. Their immediate objective was to discredit the prosecution's damage claims – particularly NorTel's.

As Mendax and Galbally talked, the mood in the office was upbeat. Mendax was feeling optimistic. Then the phone rang. It was Geoff Chettle, the barrister representing the DPP. While Chettle talked, Mendax watched a dark cloud pass across his solicitor's face. When he finally put the phone down, Galbally looked at Mendax with his serious, crisis management expression.

'What's wrong? What's the matter?' Mendax asked.

Galbally sighed before he spoke.

'Prime Suspect has turned Crown witness against you.'

There was a mistake. Mendax was sure of it. The whole thing was just one big mistake. Maybe Chettle and the DPP had misunderstood something Prime Suspect had said to them. Maybe Prime Suspect's lawyers had messed up. Whatever. There was definitely a mistake.

At Galbally's office, Mendax had refused to believe Prime Suspect had really turned. Not until he saw a signed statement. That night he told a friend, 'Well, we'll see. Maybe Chettle is just playing it up.'

Chettle, however, was not just playing it up.

There it was – a witness statement – in front of him. Signed by Prime Suspect.

Mendax stood outside the courtroom at Melbourne Magistrates Court trying to reconcile two realities. In the first, there was one of Mendax's four or five closest friends. A friend with whom he had shared his deepest hacking secrets. A friend he had been hanging out with only last week.

In the other reality, a six-page statement signed by Prime Suspect and Ken Day at AFP Headquarters at 1.20 p.m. the day before. To compound matters, Mendax began wondering if Prime Suspect may have been speaking to the AFP for as long as six months.

The two realities were spinning through his head, dancing around each other.

When Galbally arrived at the court, Mendax took him to one side to go over the statement. From a damage-control perspective, it wasn't a complete disaster. Prime Suspect certainly hadn't gone in hard. He could have raised a number of matters, but didn't. Mendax had already admitted to most of the acts which formed the basis of his 31 charges in his police interview. And he had already told the police a good deal about his adventures in Telecom's telephone exchanges.

However, Prime Suspect had elaborated on the Telecom break-ins in his statement. Telecom was owned by the government, meaning the court would view phreaking from their exchanges not as defrauding a company but as defrauding the Commonwealth. Had the DPP decided to lay those new charges – the Telecom charges – in February 1995 because

Prime Suspect had given the AFP a draft Crown witness state-ment back then? Mendax began to suspect so. Nothing seemed beyond doubt any more.

The immediate crisis was the committal hearing in the Melbourne Magistrates Court. There was no way Boris Kayser was now going to decimate their star witness, a NorTel information systems manager. Galbally would have to run a cross-examination himself – no easy task at short notice, given the highly complex technical aspects of the case.

Inside the courtroom, as Mendax got settled, he saw Prime Suspect. He gave his former friend a hard, unblinking, intense stare. Prime Suspect responded with a blank wall, then he looked away. In fact, even if Mendax had wanted to say some-thing, he couldn't. As a Crown witness, Prime Suspect was off-limits until the case was over.

The lawyers began to file into the courtroom. The DPP representative, Andrea Pavleka, breezed in, momentarily lifting the tension in the windowless courtroom.

She had that effect on people. Tall, slender and long-legged, with a bob of sandy blonde curls, booky spectacles resting on a cute button nose and an infectious laugh, Pavleka didn't so much walk into a courtroom as waft into it. She radiated happi-ness from her sunny face. It's a great shame, Mendax thought, that she is on the other side.

The court was called into session. Prime Suspect stood in the dock and pleaded guilty to 26 counts of computer crimes.

In the course of the proceedings his barrister, Boris Kayser, told the court that his client had cooperated with the police, including telling the AFP that the hackers had pene-trated Telecom's exchanges. He also said that Telecom didn't believe – or didn't want to believe – that their exchanges had been compromised. When Kayser professed loudly what a model citizen his client had been, Ken Day, sitting in the public benches, quietly rolled his eyes.

The magistrate, John Tobin, extended Prime Suspect's bail. The hacker would be sentenced at a later date.

That matter dealt with, the focus of the courtroom shifted to Mendax's case. Geoff Chettle, for the prosecution, stood up, put the NorTel manager, who had flown in from Sydney, on the stand and asked him some warm-up questions.

Chettle could put people at ease – or rattle them – at will. Topped by a minute stubble of hair, his weathered 40-something face provided a good match to his deep, gravelly voice. With quick eyes and a hard, no-nonsense manner, he lacked the pretentiousness of many barristers. Perhaps because he didn't seem to give a fig about nineteenth century protocols, he always managed to looked out of place in a barrister's wig and robe. Every time he stood up, the black cape slid off his lean shoulders. The barrister's wig went crooked. He continually adjusted it – tugging the wig back into the correct spot like some wayward child. In court, Chettle looked as if he wanted to tear off the crusty trappings of his profession and roll up his sleeves before sinking into a hearty debate. And he looked as if he would rather do it at a pub or the footy.

The NorTel manager took the stand. Chettle asked him some questions designed to show the court the witness was credible, in support of the company's $160 000 hacker-clean-up claim. His task accomplished, Chettle sat down.

A little nervous, Paul Galbally stood up to his full height – more than six feet – and straightened his jacket. Dressed in a moss green suit so dark it was almost black, with thin lapels and a thin, 1960s style tie, he looked about as understated hip as a lawyer could – and still show his face in court.

Halting at first, Galbally appeared unsure of himself. Perhaps he had lost his nerve because of the technical issues. WMTP files. UTMP files. PACCT audits. Network architecture. IP addresses. He had been expected to become an expert in the basics literally overnight. A worried Mendax began passing him notes – questions to ask, explanations, definitions. Slowly, Galbally started working up a rhythm to the cross-examination.

During the questioning someone from the back of the court

sidled up to Mendax, in the front row of seats, and handed a note over his shoulder. Mendax unfolded the note, read it and then turned around to smile at the messenger. It was Electron.

By the time Galbally had finished, he had pulled apart much of the NorTel manager's evidence. As he built up a head of steam quizzing the witness, he forced the NorTel manager to admit he didn't know all that much about the alleged hacking incidents. In fact, he wasn't even employed by the company when they occurred. He had largely thrown together an affidavit based on second-hand information – and it was this affidavit which supposedly proved the hackers had cost the company $160 000. Worse, it seemed to an observer at court that the NorTel manager had little Unix security technical expertise and probably would not have been able to conduct a detailed technical analysis of the incident even if he had been with the company in 1991. By the end of the defence's cross-examination, it appeared that Galbally knew more about Unix than the NorTel manager.

When Geoff Chettle stood up to re-examine the witness, the situation was hopeless. The manager soon stood down. In Mendax's view, the credibility of the NorTel Manager's statement was shot.

The court was then adjourned until 12 May.

After court, Mendax heard Geoff Chettle talking about the NorTel witness. 'That guy is OFF the team,' he said emphatically.

It was a mixed victory for Mendax. His solicitor had knocked off one NorTel witness, but there were more where he came from. At a full trial, the prosecution would likely fly in some real NorTel fire-power, from Canada, where the 676-page security incident report had been prepared by Clark Ferguson and other members of the NorTel security team. Those witnesses would understand how a Unix system operated, and would have first-hand knowledge of the hackers' intrusions. It could make things much more difficult.

When Mendax returned to court a week later, he was committed to stand trial in the County Court of Victoria, as expected.

Later, Mendax asked Galbally about his options. Take the case to full trial, or plead guilty like the other two IS hackers. He wanted to know where the DPP stood on his case. Would they go in hard if he pleaded guilty? Had the NorTel manager disaster at the committal hearing forced them to back down a little?

Paul sighed and shook his head. The DPP were standing firm. They wanted to see Mendax go to prison.

Andrea Pavleka, the DPP's sunny-faced girl who radiated happiness, was baying for blood.

One month later, on 21 July 1995, Prime Suspect arrived at the County Court for sentencing.

Rising early that morning to make sure his court suit was in order, Prime Suspect had been tense. His mother cooked him a big breakfast. Toast, bacon and eggs the way he liked it. In fact, his favourite breakfast was an Egg McMuffin from McDonald's, but he never told his mother that.

The courtroom was already crowded. Reporters from newspapers, the wire services, a few TV channels. There were also other people, perhaps waiting for another case.

Dressed in a dark pin-stripe suit, Ken Day stood tapping on a laptop on the prosecution's side of the courtroom. Geoff Chettle sat near him. Prime Suspect's barrister, Boris Kayser, sifted through some papers on the other side.

Mendax lingered at the back of the room, watching his former friend. He wanted to hear Prime Suspect's sentence because, under the rules of parity sentencing, Mendax's own sentence would have to be similar to that of his fellow hackers. However, Prime Suspect might get some dispensation for having helped the prosecution.

A handful of Prime Suspect's friends – none of them from the computer underground – trickled in. The hacker's mother chatted nervously with them.

Court was called into session and everyone settled into their seats. The first case, it turned out, was not Prime Suspect's. A tall, silver-haired man in his mid-fifties, with eyes so blue they were almost demonic, stepped into the dock. As the reporters began taking notes, Prime Suspect tried to imagine what crime the polished, well-dressed man had committed.

Child molesting.

The man had not just molested children, he had molested his own son. In the parents' bedroom. Repeatedly. On Easter Sunday. His son was less than ten years old at the time. The whole family had collapsed. Psychologically scarred, his son had been too traumatised even to give a victim impact statement.

For all of this, Judge Russell Lewis told the court, the man had shown no remorse. Grave-faced, the judge sentenced him to a minimum prison term of five years and nine months.

The court clerk then called Prime Suspect's case.

At the back of the courtroom, Mendax wondered at the strange situation. How could the criminal justice system put a child molester in the same category as a hacker? Yet, here they both were being sentenced side by side in the same County Court room.

Boris Kayser had called a collection of witnesses, all of whom attested to Prime Suspect's difficult life. One of these, the well-regarded psychologist Tim Watson-Munro, described Prime Suspect's treatments at the Austin Hospital and raised the issue of reduced free-will. He had written a report for the court.

Judge Lewis was quick to respond to the suggestion that hacking was an addiction. At one point, he wondered aloud to the courtroom whether some of Prime Suspect's hacking activities were 'like a shot of heroin'.

Before long, Kayser had launched into his usual style of courtroom address. First, he criticised the AFP for waiting so long to charge his client.

'This fellow should have been dealt with six to twelve months after being apprehended. It is a bit like the US, where a man can commit a murder at twenty, have his appeal be knocked back by the Supreme Court at 30 and be executed at 40 – all for something he did when he was only twenty years old.'

Thoroughly warmed up, Kayser observed that 20 per cent of Prime Suspect's life had gone by since being raided. Then he began hitting his high notes.

'This young man received no assistance in the maturation process. He didn't grow up, he drifted up.

'His world was so horrible that he withdrew into a fantasy world. He knew no other way to interact with human beings. Hacking was like a physical addiction to him.

'If he hadn't withdrawn into the cybernetic highway, what would he have done instead? Set fires? Robbed houses? Look at the name he gave himself. Prime Suspect. It has implied power – a threat. This kid didn't have any power in his life other than when he sat down at a computer.'

Not only did Kayser want the judge to dismiss the idea of prison or community service, he was asking him to order no recorded conviction.

The prosecution lawyers looked at Kayser as if he was telling a good joke. The AFP had spent months tracking these hackers and almost three years preparing the case against them. And now this barrister was seriously suggesting that one of the key players should get off virtually scot-free, with not so much as a conviction recorded against him? It was too much.

The judge retired to consider the sentence. When he returned, he was brief and to the point. No prison. No community service. The recording of 26 convictions. A $500 three-year good behaviour bond. Forfeiture of the now ancient Apple computer seized by police in the raid. And a reparation payment to the Australian National University of $2100.

Relief passed over Prime Suspect's face, pink and sweaty from the tension. His friends and family smiled at each other.

Chettle then asked the judge to rule on what he called 'the cooperation point'. He wanted the judge to say that Prime Suspect's sentence was less than it would have been because the hacker had turned Crown witness. The DPP was shoring up its position with regard to its remaining target – Mendax.

Judge Lewis told the court that the cooperation in this case made no difference. At the back of the court, Mendax felt suddenly sad. It was good news for him, but somehow it felt like a hollow victory.

Prime Suspect has destroyed our friendship, he thought, and all for nothing.

Two months after Prime Suspect's sentencing, Trax appeared in another County Court room to receive his sentence after pleading guilty to six counts of hacking and phreaking. Despite taking medication to keep his anxiety under control while in the city, he was still very nervous in the dock.

Since he faced the least number of charges of any of the IS hackers, Trax believed he had a shot at no recorded conviction. Whether or not his lawyer could successfully argue the case was another matter. Bumbling through papers he could never seem to organise, Trax's lawyer rambled to the court, repeated the same points over and over again, jumping all over the place in his arguments. His voice was a half-whispered rasp – a fact which so annoyed the judge that he sternly instructed the lawyer to speak up.

Talking informally before court, Geoff Chettle had told Mendax that in his view there was no way Judge Mervyn Kimm would let Trax off with no recorded conviction. Judge Kimm was considered to be one tough nut to crack. If you were a bookmaker running bets on his court at a sentencing hearing, the good money would be on the prosecution's side.

But on 20 September 1995, the judge showed he couldn't be predicted quite so easily. Taking everything into account, including Prime Suspect's sentence and Trax's history of mental illness, he ordered no conviction be recorded against Trax. He also ordered a $500 three-year good behaviour bond.

In passing sentence, Judge Kimm said something startlingly insightful for a judge with little intimate knowledge of the hacker psyche. While sternly stating that he did not intend to make light of the gravity of the offences, he told the court that 'the factors of specific deterrence and general deterrence have little importance in the determination of the sentence to be imposed'. It was perhaps the first time an Australian judge had recognised that deterrence had little relevance at the point of collision between hacking and mental illness.

Trax's sentence was also a good outcome for Mendax, who on 29 August 1995 pleaded guilty to eight counts of computer crime, and not guilty to all the other charges. Almost a year later, on 9 May 1996, he pleaded guilty to an additional eleven charges, and not guilty to six. The prosecution dropped all the other charges.

Mendax wanted to fight those six outstanding charges, which involved ANU, RMIT, NorTel and Telecom, because he felt that the law was on his side in these instances. In fact, the law was fundamentally unclear when it came to those charges. So much so that the DPP and the defence agreed to take issues relating to those charges in a case stated to the Supreme Court of Victoria.

In a case stated, both sides ask the Supreme Court to make a ruling not on the court case itself, but on a point of law. The defence and the prosecution hammer out an agreed statement about the facts of the case and, in essence, ask the Supreme Court judges to use that statement as a sort of case study. The resulting ruling is meant to clarify the finer points of the law not only for the specific case, but for similar cases which appear in future.

Presenting a case stated to the Supreme Court is somewhat uncommon. It is unusual to find a court case where both sides can agree on enough of the facts, but Mendax's hacking charges presented the perfect case and the questions which would be put to the Victorian Supreme Court in late 1996 were crucial for all future hacking cases in Australia. What did it mean 'to obtain access' to a computer? Did someone obtain access if he or she got in without using a password? What if he or she used the username 'guest' and the password 'guest'?

Perhaps the most crucial question of all was this: does a person 'obtain access' to data stored in a computer if he or she has the ability to view the data, but does not in fact view or even attempt to view that data?

A good example of this applied to the aggravated versions of the offence of hacking: viewing commercial information. If, for example, Mendax logged into a NorTel computer, which contained commercially sensitive information, but he didn't actually read any of those files, would he be guilty of 'obtaining access' or 'obtaining access to commercial information'?

The chief judge of the County Court agreed to the case stated and sent it up to the full bench of the Supreme Court. The lawyers from both sides were pleased with the bench – Justices Frank Vincent, Kenneth Hayne and John Coldrey.

On 30 September 1996, Mendax arrived at the Supreme Court and found all the lawyers assembled at the court – all except for his barrister. Paul Galbally kept checking his watch as the prosecution lawyers began unpacking their mountains of paper – the fruit of months of preparation. Galbally paced the plush carpet of the Supreme Court anteroom. Still no barrister.

Mendax's barrister had worked tirelessly, preparing for the case stated as if it was a million dollar case. Combing through legal precedents from not only Australia, the UK and the US, but from all the world's Western-style democracies, he had attained a great understanding of the law in the area of computer crime. He had finally arrived at that nexus of understanding between law, philosophy and linguistics which many lesser lawyers spent their entire careers trying to reach.

But where was he? Galbally pulled out his mobile and checked in with his office for what seemed like the fifth time in as many minutes. The news he received was bad. He was told, through second-hand sources, that the barrister had collapsed in a state of nervous exhaustion. He wouldn't be making it to court.

Galbally could feel his hairs turning grey.

When court opened, Galbally had to stand up and explain to three of the most senior judges in Australia why the defence would like a two-day adjournment. A consummate professional, Geoff Chettle supported the submission. Still, it was a difficult request. Time in the Supreme Court is a scarce and valuable thing. Fortunately, the adjournment was granted.

This gave Galbally exactly two days in which to find a barrister who was good, available and smart enough to assimilate a massive amount of technical information in a short time. He found Andrew Tinney.

Tinney worked around the clock and by Wednesday, 2 October, he was ready. Once again, all the lawyers, and the hacker, gathered at the court.

This time, however, it was the judges who threw a spanner into the works. They asked both sides to spend the first hour or so explaining exactly why the Supreme Court should hear the case stated at all. The lawyers looked at each other in surprise. What was this all about?

After hearing some brief arguments from both sides, the judges retired to consider their position. When they returned, Justice Hayne read a detailed judgment saying, in essence, that the judges refused to hear the case.

As the judge spoke, it became clear that the Supreme Court judges weren't just refusing to hear this case stated; they were virtually refusing to hear any case stated in future. Not for computer crimes. Not for murder. Not for fraud. Not for anything. They were sending a message to the County Court judges: don't send us a case stated except in exceptional circumstances.

Geoff Chettle slumped in his chair, his hands shielding his face. Paul Galbally looked stunned. Andrew Tinney looked as if he wanted to leap from his chair shouting, 'I just killed myself for the past two days on this case! You have to hear it!' Even Lesley Taylor, the quiet, unflappable and inscrutable

DPP solicitor who had replaced Andrea Pavleka on the case, looked amazed.

The ruling had enormous implications. Judges from the lower courts would be loath to ever send cases to the Supreme Court for clarification on points of law again. Mendax had made legal history, but not in the way he had hoped.

Mendax's case passed back down to the County Court.

He had considered taking his case to trial, but with recently announced budget cuts to Legal Aid, he knew there was little hope of receiving funding to fight the charges. The cuts were forcing the poor to plead guilty, leaving justice available only for the wealthy. Worse, he felt the weight of pleading guilty, not only as a sense of injustice in his own case, but for future hacking cases which would follow. Without clarity on the meaning of the law – which the judges had refused to provide – or a message from a jury in a landmark case, such as Wandii's trial, Mendax believed that hackers could expect little justice from either the police or the courts in the future.

On 5 December 1996, Mendax pleaded guilty to the remaining six charges and was sentenced on all counts.

Court Two was quiet that day. Geoff Chettle, for the prosecution, wasn't there. Instead, the quietly self-possessed Lesley Taylor handled the matter. Paul Galbally appeared for Mendax himself. Ken Day sat, expressionless, in the front row of the public benches. He looked a little weary. A few rows back, Mendax's mother seemed nervous. Electron slipped silently into the back of the room and gave Mendax a discreet smile.

His hair pulled back into a loose ponytail, Mendax blinked and rolled his eyes several times as if brought from a dark space into the bright, white-walled courtroom.

Judge Ross, a ruddy-faced and jowly man of late middle age with bushy, grey eyebrows, seated himself in his chair. At first, he was reluctant to take on the case for sentencing. He thought it should be returned to one of the original judges – Judge Kimm or Judge Lewis. When he walked into court that morning, he had not read the other judges' sentences.

Lesley Taylor summarised the punishments handed down to the other two hackers. The judge did not look altogether pleased. Finally, he announced he would deal with the case. 'Two judges have had a crack at it, why not a third one? He might do it properly.'

Galbally was concerned. As the morning progressed, he became increasingly distressed; things were not going well. Judge Ross made clear that he personally favoured a custodial sentence, albeit a suspended one. The only thing protecting Mendax seemed to be the principle of parity in sentencing. Prime Suspect and Trax had committed similar crimes to Mendax, and therefore he had to be given a similar sentence.

Ross 'registered some surprise' at Judge Lewis's disposition toward the sentencing of Prime Suspect. In the context of parity, he told Lesley Taylor, he was at times 'quite soured by some penalties' imposed by other judges. He quizzed her for reasons why he might be able to step outside parity.

He told the court that he had not read the telephone intercepts in the legal brief. In fact, he had 'only read the summary of facts' and when Taylor mentioned 'International Subversive', he asked her, 'What was that?'

Then he asked her how to spell the word 'phreak'.

Later that day, after Judge Ross had read the other judges' sentences, he gave Mendax a sentence similar to Prime Suspect's – a recorded conviction on all counts, a reparation payment of $2100 to ANU and a three-year good behaviour bond.

There were two variations. Prime Suspect and Trax both received $500 good behaviour bonds; Judge Ross ordered a $5000 bond for Mendax. Further, Judge Lewis had given Prime Suspect almost twelve months to pay his $2100 reparation. Judge Ross ordered Mendax to pay within three months.

Judge Ross told Mendax, 'I repeat what I said before. I thought initially that these were offences which justified a jail sentence, but the mitigatory circumstances would have converted that to a suspended sentence. The sentence given to your co-offender caused me to alter that view, however.' He was concerned, he said, 'that highly intelligent individuals ought not to behave like this and I suspect it is only highly intelligent individuals who can do what you did'.

The word 'addiction' did not appear anywhere in the sentencing transcript.

10 | ANTRAX – THE OUTSIDER

Anthrax didn't like working as part of a team. He always considered other people to be the weakest link in the chain.

Although people were never to be trusted completely, he socialised with many hackers and phreakers and worked with a few of them now and again on particular projects. But he never formed intimate partnerships with any of them. Even if a fellow hacker dobbed him in to the police, the informant couldn't know the full extent of his activities. The nature of his relationships was also determined, in part, by his isolation. Anthrax lived in a town in rural Victoria.

Despite the fact that he never joined a hacking partnership like The Realm, Anthrax liked people, liked to talk to them for hours at a time on the telephone. Sometimes he received up to ten international calls a day from his phreaker friends overseas. He would be over at a friend's house, and the friend's mother would knock on the door of the bedroom where the boys were hanging out, listening to new music, talking.

The mother would poke her head in the door, raise an eyebrow and point at Anthrax. 'Phone call for you. Someone from Denmark.' Or sometimes it was Sweden. Finland. The US. Wherever. Though they didn't say anything, his friends' parents thought it all a bit strange. Not many kids in country towns got international calls trailing them around from house to house. But then not many kids were master phreakers.

Anthrax loved the phone system and he understood its power. Many phreakers thought it was enough to be able to call their friends around the globe for free. Or make hacking attack phone calls without being traced. However, real power for Anthrax lay in controlling voice communications systems – things that moved conversations around the world. He cruised through people's voice mailbox messages to piece together a picture of what they were doing. He wanted to be able to listen into telephone conversations. And he wanted to be able to reprogram the telephone system, even take it down. That was real power, the kind that lots of people would notice.

The desire for power grew throughout Anthrax's teenage years. He ached to know everything, to see everything, to play with exotic systems in foreign countries. He needed to know the purpose of every system, what made them tick, how they fitted together. Understanding how things worked would give him control.

His obsession with telephony and hacking began early in life. When he was about eleven, his father had taken him to see the film *War Games*. All Anthrax could think of as he left the theatre was how much he wanted to learn how to hack. He had already developed a fascination for computers, having received the simplest of machines, a Sinclair ZX81 with 1 k of memory, as a birthday present from his parents. Rummaging through outdoor markets, he found a few second-hand books on hacking. He read *Out of the Inner Circle* by Bill Landreth, and *Hackers* by Steven Levy.

By the time he was fourteen, Anthrax had joined a Melbourne-based group of boys called The Force. The members swapped

Commodore 64 and Amiga games. They also wrote their own demos – short computer programs – and delighted in cracking the copy protections on the games and then trading them with other crackers around the world. It was like an international penpal group. Anthrax liked the challenge provided by cracking the protections, but few teenagers in his town shared an interest in his unusual hobby. Joining The Force introduced him to a whole new world of people who thought as he did.

When Anthrax first read about phreaking he wrote to one of his American cracking contacts asking for advice on how to start. His friend sent him a list of AT&T calling card numbers and a toll-free direct-dial number which connected Australians with American operators. The card numbers were all expired or cancelled, but Anthrax didn't care. What captured his imagination was the fact that he could call an operator all the way across the Pacific for free. Anthrax began trying to find more special numbers.

He would hang out at a pay phone near his house. It was a seedy neighbourhood, home to the most downtrodden of all the town's residents, but Anthrax would stand at the pay phone for hours most evenings, oblivious to the clatter around him, hand-scanning for toll-free numbers. He dialled 0014 – the prefix for the international toll-free numbers – followed by a random set of numbers. Then, as he got more serious, he approached the task more methodically. He selected a range of numbers, such as 300 to 400, for the last three digits. Then he dialled over and over, increasing the number by one each time he dialled. 301. 302. 303. 304. Whenever he hit a functioning phone number, he noted it down. He never had to spend a cent since all the 0014 numbers were free.

Anthrax found some valid numbers, but many of them had modems at the other end. So he decided it was time to buy a modem so he could explore further. Too young to work legally, he lied about his age and landed an after-school job doing data entry at an escort agency. In the meantime, he spent every available moment at the pay phone, scanning and adding new numbers to his growing list of toll-free modem and operator-assisted numbers.

The scanning became an obsession. Often Anthrax stayed at the phone until 10 or 11 p.m. Some nights it was 3 a.m. The pay phone had a rotary dial, making the task laborious, and sometimes he would come home with blisters on the tips of his fingers.

A month or so after he started working, he had saved enough money for a modem.

Hand scanning was boring, but no more so than school. Anthrax attended his state school regularly, at least until year 10. Much of that was due to his mother's influence. She believed in education and in bettering oneself, and she wanted to give her son the opportunities she had been denied. It was his mother, a psychiatric nurse, who scrimped and saved for months to buy him his first real computer, a $400 Commodore 64. And it was his mother who took out a loan to buy the more powerful Amiga a few years later in 1989. She knew the boy was very bright. He used to read her medical textbooks, and computers were the future.

Anthrax had always done well in school, earning distinctions every year from year 7 to year 10. But not in maths. Maths bored him. Still, he had some aptitude for it. He won an award in year 6 for designing a pendulum device which measured the height of a building using basic trigonometry – a subject he had never studied. However, Anthrax didn't attend school so much after year 10. The teachers kept telling him things he already knew, or things he could learn much faster from reading a book. If he liked a topic, he wandered off to the library to read about it.

Things at home became increasingly complicated around that time. His family had struggled from the moment they arrived in Australia from England, when Anthrax was about twelve. They struggled financially, they struggled against the roughness of a country town, and, as Indians, Anthrax, his younger brother and their mother struggled against racism.

The town was a violent place, filled with racial hatred and ethnic tension. The ethnics had carved out corners for themselves, but incursions into enemy territory were common and almost always resulted in violence. It was the kind of town where people ended up in fist fights over a soccer game. Not an easy place for a half-Indian, half-British boy with a violent father.

Anthrax's father, a white Englishman, came from a farming family. One of five sons, he attended an agricultural college where he met and married the sister of an Indian student on a scholarship. Their marriage caused quite a stir, even making the local paper under the headline 'Farmer Marries Indian Woman'. It was not a happy marriage and Anthrax often wondered why his father had married an Indian. Perhaps it was a way of rebelling against his dominating father. Perhaps he had once been in love. Or perhaps he simply wanted someone he could dominate and control. Whatever the reason, the decision was an unpopular one with Anthrax's grandfather and the mixed-race family was often excluded from larger family gatherings.

When Anthrax's family moved to Australia, they had almost no money. Eventually, the father got a job as an officer at Melbourne's Pentridge prison, where he stayed during the week. He only received a modest income, but he seemed to like his job. The mother began working as a nurse. Despite their new-found financial stability, the family was not close. The father appeared to have little respect for his wife and sons, and Anthrax had little respect for his father.

As Anthrax entered his teenage years, his father became increasingly abusive. On weekends, when he was home from work, he used to hit Anthrax, sometimes throwing him on the floor and kicking him. Anthrax tried to avoid the physical abuse but the scrawny teenager was little match for the beefy prison officer. Anthrax and his brother were quiet boys. It seemed to be the path of least resistance with a rough father in a rough town. Besides, it was hard to talk back in the painful stutter both boys shared through their early teens.

One day, when Anthrax was fifteen, he came home to find

a commotion at his house. On entering the house, Anthrax went to his parents' bedroom. He found his mother there, and she was very upset and emotionally distressed. He couldn't see his father anywhere, but found him relaxing on the sofa in the lounge room, watching TV.

Disgust consumed Anthrax and he retreated into the kitchen. When his father came in not long after to prepare some food Anthrax watched his back with revulsion. Then he noticed a carving knife resting on the counter. As Anthrax reached for the knife, an ambulance worker appeared in the doorway. Anthrax put the knife down and walked away.

But he wasn't so quiet after that. He started talking back, at home and at school, and that marked the beginning of the really big problems. In primary school and early high school he had been beaten up now and again. Not any more. When a fellow student hauled Anthrax up against the wall of the locker shed and started shaking him and waving his fist, Anthrax lost it. He saw, for a moment, his father's face instead of the student's and began to throw punches in a frenzy that left his victim in a terrible state.

At home, Anthrax's father learned how to bait his son. The bully always savours a morsel of resistance from the victim, which makes going in for the kill a little more fun. Talking back gave the father a good excuse to get violent. Once he nearly broke his son's neck. Another time it was his arm. He grabbed Anthrax and twisted his arm behind his back. There was an eerie sound of cracking cartilage, and then pain. Anthrax screamed for his father to stop. His father twisted Anthrax's arm harder, then pressed on his neck. His mother shrieked at her husband to let go of her son. He wouldn't.

'Look at you crying,' his father sneered. 'You disgusting animal.'

'You're the disgusting animal,' Anthrax shouted, talking back again.

His father threw Anthrax on the floor and began kicking him in the head, in the ribs, all over.

Anthrax ran away. He went south to Melbourne for a week, sleeping anywhere he could, in the empty night-time spaces left over by day workers gone to orderly homes. He even crashed in hospital emergency rooms. If a nurse asked why he was there, he would answer politely, 'I received a phone call to meet someone here'. She would nod her head and move on to someone else.

Eventually, when Anthrax returned home, he took up martial arts to become strong. And he waited.

Anthrax was poking around a MILNET gateway when he stumbled on the door to System X.* He had wanted to find this system for months, because he had intercepted email about it which had aroused his curiosity.

Anthrax telnetted into the gateway. A gateway binds two different networks. It allows, for example, two computer networks which talk different languages to communicate. A gateway might allow someone on a system running DECNET to login to a TCP/IP based system, like a Unix. Anthrax was frustrated that he couldn't seem to get past the System X gateway and on to the hosts on the other side.

Using normal address formats for a variety of networks, he tried telling the gateway to make a connection. X.25. TCP/IP. Whatever lay beyond the gateway didn't respond. Anthrax looked around until he found a sample of addresses in a help file. None of them worked, but they offered a clue as to what format an address might take.

Each address had six digits, the first three numbers of which corresponded to telephone area codes in the Washington DC area. So he picked one of the codes and started guessing the last three digits.

---

*   The real name of System X has not been disclosed for legal reasons.

Hand scanning was a pain, as ever, but if he was methodical and persistent, something should turn up. 111. 112. 113. 114. 115. On it went. Eventually he connected to something – a Sunos Unix system – which gave him a full IP address in its login message. Now that was handy. With the full IP address, he could connect to System X again through the Internet directly – avoiding the gateway if he chose to. It's always helpful in covering your tracks to have a few different routing options. Importantly, he could approach System X through more than just its front door.

Anthrax spiralled through the usual round of default user-names and passwords. Nothing. This system required a more strategic attack.

He backed out of the login screen, escaped from the gateway and went to another Internet site to have a good look at System X from a healthy distance. He 'fingered' the site, pulling up any bit of information System X would release to the rest of the Internet when asked. He probed and prodded, looking for openings. And then he found one. Sendmail.

The version of Sendmail run by System X had a security hole Anthrax could exploit by sending himself a tiny backdoor program. To do this, he used System X's mail-processing service to send a 'letter' which contained a tiny computer program. System X would never have allowed the program to run normally, but this program worked like a letter bomb. When System X opened the letter, the program jumped out and started running. It told System X that anyone could connect to port 2001 – to an interactive shell – of the computer without using a password.

A port is a door to the outside world. TCP/IP computers use a standard set of ports for certain services. Port 25 for mail. Port 79 for Finger. Port 21 for FTP. Port 23 for Telnet. Port 513 for Rlogin. Port 80 for the World Wide Web. A TCP/IP based computer system has 65 535 ports but most of them go unused. Indeed, the average Unix box uses only 35, leaving the remaining 65 500 ports sitting idle. Anthrax simply picked one of these sleepy ports, dusted off the cobwebs and plugged in using the backdoor created by his tiny mail-borne program.

Connecting directly to a port created some problems, because the system wouldn't recognise certain keystrokes from the port, such as the return key. For this reason, Anthrax had to create an account for himself which would let him telnet to the site and login like any normal user. To do this, he needed root privileges in order to create an account and, ultimately, a permanent backdoor into the system.

He began hunting for vulnerabilities in System X's security. There was nothing obvious, but he decided to try out a bug he had successfully used elsewhere. He had first learned about it on an international phone conference, where he had traded information with other hackers and phreakers. The security hole involved the system's relatively obscure load-module program. The program added features to the running system but, more importantly, it ran as root, meaning that it had a free run on the system when it was executed. It also meant that any other programs the load-module program called up also ran as root. If Anthrax could get this program to run one of his own programs – a little Trojan – he could get root on System X.

The load-module bug was by no means a sure thing on System X. Most commercial systems – computers run by banks or credit agencies, for example – had cleaned up the load-module bug in their Sunos computers months before. But military systems consistently missed the bug. They were like turtles – hard on the outside, but soft and vulnerable on the inside. Since the bug couldn't be exploited unless a hacker was already inside a system, the military's computer security officials didn't seem to pay much attention to it. Anthrax had visited a large number of military systems prior to System X, and in his experience more than 90 per cent of their Sunos computers had never fixed the bug.

With only normal privileges, Anthrax couldn't force the load-module program to run his backdoor Trojan program.

But he could trick it into doing so. The secret was in one simple keyboard character: /.

Unix-based computer systems are a bit like the protocols of the diplomatic corps; the smallest variation can change something's meaning entirely. Hackers, too, understand the implications of subtle changes.

A Unix-based system reads the phrase:

/bin/program

very differently from:

bin program

One simple character – the '/' – makes an enormous difference. A Unix computer reads the '/' as a road sign. The first phrase tells the computer, 'Follow the road to the house of the user called "bin" and when you get there, go inside and fetch the file called "program" and run it'. A blank space, however, tells the computer something quite different. In this case, Anthrax knew it told the computer to execute the command which preceded the space. That second phrase told the machine, 'Look everywhere for a program called "bin" and run it'.

Anthrax prepared for his attack on the load-module program by installing his own special program, named 'bin', into a temporary storage area on System X. If he could get System X to run his program with root privileges, he too would have procured root level access to the system. When everything was in place, Anthrax forced the system to read the character '/' as a blank space. Then he ran the load-module program, and watched. When System X hunted around for a program named 'bin', it quickly found Anthrax's Trojan and ran it.

The hacker savoured the moment, but he didn't pause for long. With a few swift keystrokes, he added an entry to the password file, creating a basic account for himself. He exited his connection to port 2001, circled around through another route, using the 0014 gateway, and logged into System X using his newly created account. It felt good walking in through the front door.

Once inside, Anthrax had a quick look around. The system startled him. There were only three human users. Now that was definitely odd. Most systems had hundreds of users. Even a small system might serve 30 or 40 people, and this was not a small system. He concluded that System X wasn't just some machine designed to send and receive email. It was operational. It did something.

Anthrax considered how to clean up his footsteps and secure his position. While he was hardly broadcasting his presence, someone might discover his arrival simply by looking at who was logged in on the list of accounts in the password file. He had given his backdoor root account a bland name, but he could reasonably assume that these three users knew their system pretty well. And with only three users, it was probably the kind of system that had lots of babysitting. After all that effort, Anthrax needed a watchful nanny like a hole in the head. He worked at moving into the shadows.

He removed himself from the WTMP and UTMP files, which listed who had been on-line and who was still logged in. Anthrax wasn't invisible, but an admin would have to look closely at the system's network connections and list of processes to find him. Next stop: the login program.

Anthrax couldn't use his newly created front-door account for an extended period – the risk of discovery was too great. If he accessed the computer repeatedly in this manner, a prying admin might eventually find him and delete his account. An extra account on a system with only three users was a dead give-away. And losing access to System X just as things were getting interesting was not on his agenda.

Anthrax leaned back in his chair and stretched his shoulders. His hacking room was an old cloakroom, though it was barely recognisable as such. It looked more like a closet – a very messy closet. The whole room was ankle-deep in scrap papers, most of them with lists of numbers on the back and front. Occasionally,

Anthrax scooped up all the papers and piled them into heavy-duty garbage bags, three of which could just fit inside the room at any one time. Anthrax always knew roughly where he had 'filed' a particular set of notes. When he needed it, he tipped the bag onto the floor, searched through the mound and returned to the computer. When the sea of paper reached a critical mass, he jammed everything back into the garbage bag again.

The computer – an Amiga 500 box with a cheap Panasonic TV as the monitor – sat on a small desk next to his mother's sewing machine cabinet. The small bookcase under the desk was stuffed with magazines like *Compute* and *Australian Communications*, along with a few Commodore, Amiga and Unix reference manuals. There was just enough space for Anthrax's old stereo and his short-wave radio. When he wasn't listening to his favourite show, a hacking program broadcast from a pirate station in Ecuador, he tuned into Radio Moscow or the BBC's World Service.

Anthrax considered what to do with System X. This system had aroused his curiosity and he intended to visit it frequently.

It was time to work on the login patch. The patch replaced the system's normal login program and had a special feature: a master password. The password was like a diplomatic passport. It would let him do anything, go anywhere. He could login as any user using the master password. Further, when he logged in with the master password, he wouldn't show up on any log files – leaving no trail. But the beauty of the login patch was that, in every other way, it ran as the normal login program. The regular computer users – all three of them – could login as usual with their passwords and would never know Anthrax had been in the system.

He thought about ways of setting up his login patch. Installing a patch on System X wasn't like mending a pair of jeans. He couldn't just slap on a swath from an old bandanna and quick-stitch it in with a thread of any colour. It was more like mending an expensive cashmere coat. The fabric needed to be a perfect match in colour and texture. And because the patch required high-quality invisible mending, the size also needed to be just right.

Every file in a computer system has three dates: the date it was created, the date it was last modified and the date it was last accessed. The problem was that the login patch needed to have the same creation and modification dates as the original login program so that it would not raise suspicions. It wasn't hard to get the dates but it was difficult to paste them onto the patch. The last access date wasn't important as it changed whenever the program was run anyway – whenever a user of the System X logged in.

If Anthrax ripped out the original login program and stitched his patch in its place, the patch would be stamped with a new creation date. He knew there was no way to change a creation date short of changing the clock for the whole system – something which would cause problems elsewhere in System X.

The first thing a good system admin does when he or she suspects a break-in is search for all files created or modified over the previous few days. One whiff of an intruder and a good admin would be all over Anthrax's login patch within about five minutes.

Anthrax wrote the modification and creation dates down on a bit of paper. He would need those in a moment. He also jotted down the size of the login file.

Instead of tearing out the old program and sewing in a completely new one, Anthrax decided to overlay his patch by copying it onto the top of the old program. He uploaded his own login patch, with his master password encased inside it, but he didn't install it yet. His patch was called 'troj' – short for Trojan. He typed:

```
cat<troj>/bin/login
```

The cat command told the computer: 'go get the data in the file called "troj" and put it in the file "/bin/login"'. He checked the piece of paper where he had scribbled down the original file's creation and modification dates, comparing them to the new patch. The creation date and size matched the original. The modification date was still wrong, but he was two-thirds of the way home.

Anthrax began to fasten down the final corner of the patch by using a little-known feature of the command:

/usr/5bin/date

Then he changed the modification date of his login patch to the original login file's date.

He stepped back to admire his work from a distance. The newly installed patch matched the original perfectly. Same size. Same creation date. Same modification date. With patch in place, he deleted the root account he had installed while visiting port 2001. Always take your garbage with you when you leave.

Now for the fun bit. Snooping around. Anthrax headed off for the email, the best way to work out what a system was used for. There were lots of reports from underlings to the three system users on buying equipment, progress reports on a certain project, updates. What was this project?

Then Anthrax came across a huge directory. He opened it and there, couched inside, were perhaps 100 subdirectories. He opened one of them. It was immense, containing hundreds of files. The smallest subfile had perhaps 60 computer screens' worth of material, all of it unintelligible. Numbers, letters, control codes. Anthrax couldn't make head nor tail of the files. It was as if he was staring at a group of binary files. The whole subdirectory was filled with thousands of pages of mush. He thought they looked like data files for some database.

As he didn't have the program he needed to interpret the mush, Anthrax cast around looking for a more readable directory.

He pried open a file and discovered it was a list. Names and phone numbers of staff at a large telecommunications company. Work phone numbers. Home numbers. Well, at least that gave him a clue as to the nature of the project. Something to do with telecommunications. A project important enough that the military needed the home phone numbers of the senior people involved.

The next file confirmed it. Another list, a very special list. A pot of gold at the end of the rainbow. The find of a career spent hacking.

If the US government had had any inkling what was happening at that moment, heads would have rolled. If it had known that a foreigner, and a follower of what mainstream American media termed an extremist religious group, had this information in his possession, the defence agency would have called in every law enforcement agency it could enlist.

As John McMahon might have said, a lot of yelling and screaming would have occurred.

Anthrax's mother had made a good home for the family, but his father continued to disrupt it with his violence. Fun times with his friends shone like bright spots amidst the decay of Anthrax's family life. Practical jokes were his specialty. Even as a small child, he had delighted in trickery and as he grew up, the jokes became more sophisticated. Phreaking was great. It let him prank people all over the world. And pranking was cool.

Most of the fun in pranking was sharing it with friends. Anthrax called into a voice conference frequented by phreakers and hackers. Though he never trusted others completely when it came to working on projects together, it was OK to socialise. The phreaking methods he used to get onto the phone conference were his own business. Provided he was discreet in how much he said in the conference, he thought there wasn't too much risk.

He joined the conference calls using a variety of methods. One favourite was using a multinational corporation's Dialcom service. Company employees called in, gave their ID numbers, and the operator put them through to wherever they wanted to go, free of charge. All Anthrax needed was a valid ID number.

Sometimes it was hard work, sometimes he was lucky. The day Anthrax tried the Dialcom service was a lucky day. He dialled from his favourite pay phone.

'What is your code, sir?' The operator asked.

'Yes, well, this is Mr Baker. I have a sheet with a lot of numbers here. I am new to the company. Not sure which one it is.' Anthrax shuffled papers on top of the pay phone, near the receiver. 'How many digits is it?'

'Seven.'

That was helpful. Now to find seven digits. Anthrax looked across the street at the fish and chips shop. No numbers there. Then a car licence plate caught his eye. He read off the first three digits, then plucked the last four numbers from another car's plate.

'Thank you. Putting your call through, Mr Baker.'

A valid number! What amazing luck. Anthrax milked that number for all it was worth. Called party lines. Called phreakers' bridges. Access fed the obsession.

Then he gave the number to a friend in Adelaide, to call overseas. But when that friend read off the code, the operator jumped in.

'YOU'RE NOT MR BAKER!'

Huh? 'Yes I am. You have my code.'

'You are definitely not him. I know his voice.'

The friend called Anthrax, who laughed his head off, then called into Dialcom and changed his code! It was a funny incident. Still, it reminded him how much safer it was working by himself.

Living in the country was hard for a hacker and Anthrax became a phreaker out of necessity, not just desire. Almost everything involved a long-distance call and he was always searching for ways to make calls for free. He noticed that when he called certain 008 numbers – free calls – the phone would ring a few times, click, and then pause briefly before ringing some more. Eventually a company representative or answering service picked up the call. Anthrax had read about diverters, devices used to forward calls automatically, in one of the many telecommunications magazines and manuals he was constantly reading. The click suggested the call was going through a diverter and he guessed that if he punched in the right tones at the right moment, he could make the call divert away from a company's customer service agent. Furthermore, any line trace would end up at the company.

Anthrax collected some 008 numbers and fiddled with them. He discovered that if he punched another number in very quickly over the top of the ringing – just after the click – he could make the line divert to where he wanted it to go. He used the 008 numbers to ring phone conferences around the world, where he hung out with other phreakers, particularly Canadians such as members of the Toronto-based UPI or the Montreal group, NPC, which produced a phreakers' manual in French. The conversation on the phreaker's phone conferences, or phone bridges as they are often called, inevitably turned to planning a prank. And those Canadian guys knew how to prank!

Once, they rang the emergency phone number in a major Canadian city. Using the Canadian incarnation of his social engineering accents, Anthrax called in a 'police officer in need of assistance'. The operator wanted to know where. The phreakers had decided on the Blue Ribbon Ice-Cream Parlour. They always picked a spot within visual range of at least one member, so they could see what was happening.

In the split second of silence which followed, one of the five other phreakers quietly eavesdropping on the call coughed. It was a short, sharp cough. The operator darted back on the line.

'Was that A GUN SHOT? Are you SHOT? Hello? John?' The operator leaned away from her receiver for a moment and the phreakers heard her talking to someone else in the background. 'Officer down.'

Things moved so fast when pranking. What to do now?

'Ah, yeah. Yeah.' It was amazing how much someone squeezing laughter back down his oesophagus can sound like someone who has been shot.

'John, talk to me. Talk to me,' the operator pleaded into the phone, trying to keep John alert.

'I'm down. I'm down,' Anthrax strung her along.

Anthrax disconnected the operator from the conference call. Then the phreaker who lived near the ice-cream parlour announced the street had been blocked off by police cars. They had the parlour surrounded and were anxiously searching for an injured fellow officer. It took several hours before the police realised someone had played a mean trick on them.

However, Anthrax's favourite prank was Mr McKenny, the befuddled southern American hick. Anthrax had selected the phone number at random, but the first prank was such fun he kept coming back for more. He had been ringing Mr McKenny for years. It was always the same conversation.

'Mr McKenny? This is Peter Baker. I'd like my shovel back, please.'

'I don't have your shovel.'

'Yeah, I lent it to you. Lent it to you like two years ago. I want it back now.'

'I never borrowed no shovel from you. Go away.'

'You did. You borrowed that shovel of mine. And if you don't give it back I'm a gonna come round and get it myself. And you won't like it. Now, when you gonna give me that shovel back?'

'Damn it! I don't have your goddamn shovel!'

'Give me my shovel!'

'Stop calling me! I've never had your friggin' shovel. Let me be!' Click.

Nine in the morning. Eight at night. Two a.m. There would be no peace for Mr McKenny until he admitted borrowing that shovel from a boy half his age and half a world away.

Sometimes Anthrax pranked closer to home. *The Trading Post*, a weekly rag of personals from people selling and buying, served as a good place to begin. Always the innocent start, to lure them in.

'Yes, sir, I see you advertised that you wanted to buy a bathtub.' Anthrax put on his serious voice. 'I have a bathtub for sale.'

'Yeah? What sort? Do you have the measurements, and the model number?' And people thought phreakers were weird.

'Ah, no model number. But its about a metre and a half long, has feet, in the shape of claws. It's older style, off-white. There's only one problem.' Anthrax paused, savouring the moment.

'Oh? What's that?'

'There's a body in it.'

Like dropping a boulder in a peaceful pond.

The list on System X had dial-up modem numbers, along with usernames and password pairs for each address. These usernames were not words like 'jsmith' or 'jdoe', and the passwords would not have appeared in any dictionary. 12[AZ63. K5M82L. The type of passwords and usernames only a computer would remember.

This, of course, made sense, since a computer picked them out in the first place. It generated them randomly. The list wasn't particularly user-friendly. It didn't have headers, outlining what each item related to. This made sense too. The list wasn't meant to be read by humans.

Occasionally, there were comments in the list. Programmers often include a line of comment in code, which is delineated in such a way that the computer skips over the words when interpreting the commands. The comments are for other programmers examining the code. In this case, the comments were places. Fort Green. Fort Myers. Fort Ritchie. Dozens and dozens of forts. Almost half of them were not on the mainland US. They were in places like the Philippines, Turkey, Germany, Guam. Places with lots of US military presence.

Not that these bases were any secret to the locals, or indeed to many Americans. Anthrax knew that anyone could discover a base existed through perfectly legal means. The vast majority of people never thought to look. But once they saw such a list, particularly from the environment of a military computer's bowels, it tended to drive the point home. The point being that the US military seemed to be everywhere.

Anthrax logged out of System X, killed all his connections and hung up the phone. It was time to move on. Routing through a few out-of-the-way connections, he called one of the numbers on the list. The username-password combination worked. He looked around. It was as he expected. This wasn't a computer. It was a telephone exchange. It looked like a NorTel DMS 100.

Hackers and phreakers usually have areas of expertise. In Australian terms, Anthrax was a master of the X.25 network and a king of voice mailbox systems, and others in the underground recognised him as such. He knew Trilogues better than most company technicians. He knew Meridian VMB systems better than almost anyone in Australia. In the phreaking community, he was also a world-class expert in Aspen VMB systems. He did not, however, have any expertise in DMS 100s.

Anthrax quickly hunted through his hacking disks for a text file on DMS 100s he had copied from an underground BBS. The pressure was on. He didn't want to spend long inside the exchange, maybe only fifteen or twenty minutes tops. The longer he stayed without much of a clue about how the thing operated, the greater the risk of his being traced. When he found the disk with the text file, he began sorting through it while still on-line at the telephone exchange. The phreakers' file showed him some basic commands, things which let him gently prod the exchange for basic information without disturbing the system too much. He didn't want to do much more for fear of inadvertently mutilating the system.

Although he was not an authority on DMS 100s, Anthrax had an old hacker friend overseas who was a real genius on NorTel equipment. He gave the list to his friend. Yes, the friend confirmed it was indeed a DMS 100 exchange at a US military base. It was not part of the normal telephone system, though. This exchange was part of a military phone system.

In times of war, the military doesn't want to be dependent on the civilian telephone system. Even in times of peace, voice communications between military staff are more secure if they don't talk on an exchange used by civilians. For this and a variety of other reasons, the military have separate telephone networks, just as they have separate networks for their data communications. These networks operate like a normal network and in some cases can communicate to the outside world by connecting through their own exchanges to civilian ones.

When Anthrax got the word from the expert hacker, he made up his mind quickly. Up went the sniffer. System X was getting more interesting by the hour and he didn't want to miss a precious minute in the information gathering game when it came to this system.

The sniffer, a well-used program rumoured to be written by a Sydney-based Unix hacker called Rockstar, sat on System X under an innocuous name, silently tracking everyone who logged in and out of the system. It recorded the first 128 characters of every telnet connection that went across the ethernet network cable to which System X was attached. Those 128 bytes included the username and the passwords people used to log in. Sniffers were effective, but they needed time. Usually, they grew like an embryo in a healthy womb, slowly but steadily.

Anthrax resolved to return to System X in twelve hours to check on the baby.

'Why are you two watching those nigger video clips?'

It was an offensive question, but not atypical for Anthrax's father. He often breezed through the house, leaving a trail of disruption in his wake.

Soon, however, Anthrax began eroding his father's authority. He discovered his father's secrets hidden on the Commodore 64 computer. Letters – lots of them – to his family in England. Vicious, racist, horrid letters telling how his wife was stupid.

How she had to be told how to do everything, like a typical Indian. How he regretted marrying her. There were other matters too, things unpleasant to discuss.

Anthrax confronted his father, who denied the allegations at first, then finally told Anthrax to keep his mouth shut and mind his own business. But Anthrax told his mother. Tensions erupted and, for a time, Anthrax's parents saw a marriage counsellor.

But his father did not give up writing the letters. He put a password protection program on the word processor to keep his son out of his business. It was a futile effort. His father had chosen the wrong medium to record his indiscretions.

Anthrax showed his mother the new letters and continued to confront his father. When the tension in the house grew, Anthrax would escape with his friends. One night they were at a nightclub when someone started taunting Anthrax, calling him 'curry muncher' and worse.

That was it. The anger which had been simmering below the surface for so long exploded as Anthrax violently attacked his taunter, hitting, kicking and punching him, using the tai kwon do combinations he had been learning. There was blood and it felt good. Vengeance tasted sweet.

After that incident, Anthrax often lashed out violently. He was out of control and it sometimes scared him. However, at times he went looking for trouble. Once he tracked down a particularly seedy character who had tried to rape one of his girlfriends. Anthrax pulled a knife on the guy, but the incident had little to do with the girl. The thing that made him angry was the disrespect. This guy knew the girl was with Anthrax. The attempted rape was like spitting in his face.

Perhaps that's what appealed to Anthrax about Islam – the importance of respect. At sixteen he found Islam and it changed his life. He discovered the Qu'ran in the school library while researching an assignment on religion. About the same time, he began listening to a lot of rap music. More than half the American rappers in his music collection were Muslim, and many sang about the Nation of Islam and the sect's charismatic leader, Minister Louis Farrakhan. Their songs described the injustices whites inflicted on blacks. They told blacks to demand respect.

Anthrax found a magazine article about Farrakhan and began reading books like the *Autobiography of Malcolm X*. Then he rang up the Nation of Islam head office in Chicago and asked them to send some information. *The Final Call*, the NOI newsletter, arrived one day, followed by other literature which began appearing around Anthrax's home. Under the TV guide. On the coffee table. Amid the pile of newspapers. On top of his computer. Anthrax often took time to read articles aloud to his mother while she did housework.

In the middle of 1990, when Anthrax was in year 11, his father suggested the boy attend Catholic boarding school in Melbourne. The school was inexpensive and the family could scrape and save to pay the fees. Anthrax disliked the idea, but his father insisted.

Anthrax and his new school proved a bad match. The school thought he asked too many questions, and Anthrax thought the school answered too few of them. The hypocrisy of the Catholic church riled Anthrax and pushed him further into the arms of NOI. How could he respect an institution which had sanctioned slavery as a righteous and progressive method of converting people? The school and Anthrax parted on less than friendly terms after just one semester.

The Catholic school intensified a feeling of inferiority Anthrax had felt for many years. He was an outsider. The wrong colour, the wrong size, too intelligent for his school. Yet, NOI's Minister Farrakhan told him that he wasn't inferior at all. 'I know that you have been discriminated against because of your colour,' Farrakhan told Anthrax from the tape player. 'Let me tell you why. Let me tell you about the origins of the white race and how they were put on this earth to do evil. They have shown themselves to be nothing but an enemy of the East. Non-whites are the original people of the earth.'

Anthrax found some deep veins of truth in NOI's teachings. Interracial marriages don't work. A white man marries a non-white woman because he wants a slave, not because he loves and respects her. Islam respects women in more meaningful ways than Western religions. Perhaps it wasn't the type of respect that Western men were used to giving women, but he had seen that kind of respect in his own home and he didn't think much of it.

Anthrax read the words of the Honourable Elijah Muhammad, founder of NOI: 'The enemy does not have to be a real devil. He could be your father, mother, brother, husband, wife or children. Many times they're in your own household. Today is the great time of separation of the righteous Muslim and the wicked white race.' Anthrax looked inside his own household and saw what seemed to be a devil. A white devil.

NOI fed Anthrax's mind. He followed up the lists of literature included in every issue of *The Final Call*. Books like *Black Athena* by Martin Bernel and *Deterring Democracy* by Noam Chomsky had common themes of conspiracy and oppression by the haves against the have-nots. Anthrax read them all.

The transformation of Anthrax occurred over a period of six months. He didn't talk about it much with his parents. It was a private matter. But his mother later told him his adoption of the religion didn't surprise her. His great-grandfather had been a Muslim scholar and cleric in India. It was fate. His conversion presented a certain sense of closure, of completing the circle.

His interest in Islam found secular outlets. A giant black and white poster of Malcolm X appeared on Anthrax's bedroom wall. A huge photo of Los Angeles Black Panther leader Elmer Pratt followed soon after. The photo was captioned, 'A coward dies a million deaths, a brave man dies but one'. The last bit of wall was covered in posters of hip-hop bands from ceiling to floor. A traditional Indian sword adorned the top of one of the many bookcases. It complemented the growing collection of books on martial arts. A well-loved copy of *The Art of War* by

Sun Tzu sat on the shelf next to Homer's *Ulysses, The Lord of The Rings, The Hobbit*, a few old Dungeons and Dragons books, works of mythology from India and Egypt. The shelves did not contain a single work of science fiction. Anthrax shaved his head. His mother may not have been surprised by the conversion to Islam, but the head shaving went a bit over the top.

Anthrax pursued NOI with the same vigour with which he attacked hacking. He memorised whole speeches of Farrakhan and began speaking like him, commenting casually on 'those caucasian, blue-eyed devils'. He quoted people he had discovered through NOI. People who described the US Federal Reserve Bank as being controlled by Jews. People who spoke of those hooked-nose, bagel-eating, just-crawled-out-of-a-cave Jews. Anthrax denied the existence of the Holocaust.

'You're shaping up to be quite a little Hitler,' his father told Anthrax.

His father disliked the NOI literature showing up at the house. It seemed to frighten him. Receiving blueprints in the mail for overthowing governments didn't sit well with the neighbours in the quiet suburban street of the provincial town.

'Watch out,' he warned his son. 'Having these things turn up in your mailbox can be dangerous. It will probably earmark you for some sort of investigation. They will follow you around.'

The traffic raced. The ethernet cables attached to System X were a regular speedway. People whizzed in and out of the mystery site like a swarm of bees. In only twelve hours, the sniffer file topped 100 k.

Many of the connections went from System X to the major telecommunications company. Anthrax headed in that direction.

He considered how to route the attack. He could go through a few diverters and other leapfrog devices to cover his trail, thus hitting the company's system from a completely separate source. The advantage of this route was anonymity. If the admin managed to detect his entry, Anthrax would only lose access to the phone company's system, not to System X. Alternatively, if he went in to the company through the gateway and System X, he risked alarms being raised at all three sites. However, his sniffer showed so much traffic running on this route, he might simply disappear in the flow. The established path was obviously there for a reason. One more person logging into the gateway through System X and then into the company's machine would not raise suspicions. He chose to go through System X.

Anthrax logged into the company using a sniffed username and password. Trying the load-module bug again, he got root on the system and installed his own login patch. The company's system looked far more normal than System X. A few hundred users. Lots of email, far too much to read. He ran a few key word searches on all the email, trying to piece together a better picture of the project being developed on System X.

The company did plenty of defence work, mostly in tele-communications. Different divisions of the company seemed to be working on different segments of the project. Anthrax searched through people's home directories, but nothing looked very interesting because he couldn't get a handle on the whole project. People were all developing different modules of the project and, without a centralised overview, the pieces didn't mean much.

He did find a group of binary files – types of programs – but he had no idea what they were for. The only real way to find out what they did was to take them for a test drive. He ran a few binaries. They didn't appear to do anything. He ran a few more. Again, nothing. He kept running them, one after another. Still no results. All he received was error messages.

The binaries seemed to need a monitor which could display graphics. They used XII, a graphical display common on Unix systems. Anthrax's inexpensive home computer didn't have that sort of graphical display operating system. He could still run the binaries by telling System X to run them on one of its local terminals, but he wouldn't be able to see the output on his home computer. More importantly, it was a risky course of action. What if someone happened to be sitting at the terminal where he chose to run the binary? The game would be up.

He leaned away from his keyboard and stretched. Exhaustion was beginning to set in. He hadn't slept in almost 48 hours. Occasionally, he had left his computer terminal to eat, though he always brought the food back to the screen. His mother popped her head in the doorway once in a while and shook her head silently. When he noticed her there, he tried to ease her concerns. 'But I'm learning lots of things,' he pleaded. She was not convinced.

He also broke his long hacking session to pray. It was important for a devout Muslim to practice salat – to pray at least five times a day depending on the branch of Islam followed by the devotee. Islam allows followers to group some of their prayers, so Anthrax usually grouped two in the morning, prayed once at midday as normal, and grouped two more at night. An efficient way to meet religious obligations.

Sometimes the time just slipped away, hacking all night. When the first hint of dawn snuck up on him, he was invariably in the middle of some exciting journey. But duty was duty, and it had to be done. So he pressed control S to freeze his screen, unfurled the prayer mat with its built-in compass, faced Mecca, knelt down and did two sets of prayers before sunrise. Ten minutes later he rolled the prayer mat up, slid back into his chair, typed control Q to release the pause on his computer and picked up where he left off.

This company's computer system seemed to confirm what he had begun to suspect. System X was the first stage of a project, the rest of which was under development. He found a number of tables and reports in System X's files. The reports carried headers like 'Traffic Analysis', 'calls in' and 'calls out', 'failure rate'. It all began to make sense to Anthrax.

System X called up each of the military telephone exchanges in that list. It logged in using the computer-generated name and password. Once inside, a program in System X polled the exchange for important statistics, such as the number of calls coming in and out of the base. This information was then stored on System X. Whenever someone wanted a report on something, for example, the military sites with the most incoming calls over the past 24 hours, he or she would simply ask System X to compile the information. All of this was done automatically.

Anthrax had read some email suggesting that changes to an exchange, such as adding new telephone lines on the base, had been handled manually, but this job was soon to be done automatically by System X. It made sense. The maintenance time spent by humans would be cut dramatically.

A machine which gathers statistics and services phone exchanges remotely doesn't sound very sexy on the face of it, until you begin to consider what you could do with something like that. You could sell it to a foreign power interested in the level of activity at a certain base at a particular time. And that is just the beginning.

You could tap any unencrypted line going in or out of any of the 100 or so exchanges and listen in to sensitive military discussions. Just a few commands makes you a fly on the wall of a general's conversation to the head of a base in the Philippines. Anti-government rebels in that country might pay a pretty penny for getting intelligence on the US forces.

All of those options paled next to the most striking power wielded by a hacker who had unlimited access to System X and the 100 or so telephone exchanges. He could take down that US military voice communications system almost overnight, and he could do it automatically. The potential for havoc creation was breathtaking. It would be a small matter for a skilled programmer to alter the automated program used by System X. Instead of using its dozen or more modems to dial all the exchanges overnight and poll them for statistics, System X could be instructed to call them overnight and reprogram the exchanges.

What if every time General Colin Powell picked up his phone, he would be automatically patched through to some Russian general's office? He wouldn't be able to dial any other number from his office phone. He'd pick up his phone to dial and there would be the Russian at the other end. And what if every time someone called into the general's number, they ended up talking to the stationery department? What if none of the phone numbers connected to their proper telephones? No-one would be able to reach one another. An important part of the US military machine would be in utter disarray. Now, what if all this happened in the first few days of a war? People trying to contact each other with vital information wouldn't be able to use the telephone exchanges reprogrammed by System X.

THAT was power.

It wasn't like Anthrax screaming at his father until his voice turned to a whisper, all for nothing. He could make people sit up and take notice with this sort of power.

Hacking a system gave him a sense of control. Getting root on a system always gave him an adrenalin rush for just that reason. It meant the system was his, he could do whatever he wanted, he could run whatever processes or programs he desired, he could remove other users he didn't want using his system. He thought, I own the system. The word 'own' anchored the phrase which circled through his thoughts again and again when he successfully hacked a system.

The sense of ownership was almost passionate, rippled with streaks of obsession and jealousy. At any given moment, Anthrax had a list of systems he owned and that had captured his interest for that moment. Anthrax hated seeing a system administrator logging onto one of those systems. It was an invasion. It was as though Anthrax had just got this woman he had been after for some time alone in a room with the door closed. Then, just as he was getting to know her, this other guy had barged in, sat down on the couch and started talking to her.

It was never enough to look at a system from a distance and know he could hack it if he wanted to. Anthrax had to actually hack the system. He had to own it. He needed to see what was inside the system, to know exactly what it was he owned.

The worst thing admins could do was to fiddle with system security. That made Anthrax burn with anger. If Anthrax was on-line, silently observing the admins' activities, he would feel a sudden urge to log them off. He wanted to punish them. Wanted them to know he was into their system. And yet, at the same time, he didn't want them to know. Logging them off would draw attention to himself, but the two desires pulled at him from opposite directions. What Anthrax really wanted was for the admins to know he controlled their system, but for them not to be able to do anything about it. He wanted them to be helpless.

Anthrax decided to keep undercover. But he contemplated the power of having System X's list of telephone exchange dial-ups and their username-password combinations. Normally, it would take days for a single hacker with his lone modem to have much impact on the US military's communications network. Sure, he could take down a few exchanges before the military wised up and started protecting themselves. It was like hacking a military computer. You could take out a machine here, a system there. But the essence of the power of System X was being able to use its own resources to orchestrate wide-spread pandemonium quickly and quietly.

Anthrax defines power as the potential for real world impact. At that moment of discovery and realisation, the real world impact of hacking System X looked good. The telecommunications company computer seemed like a good place to hang up a sniffer, so he plugged one into the machine and decided to return in a little while. Then he logged out and went to bed.

When he revisited the sniffer a day or so later, Anthrax received a rude shock. Scrolling through the sniffer file, he did a double take on one of the entries. Someone had logged into the company's system using his special login patch password.

He tried to stay calm. He thought hard. When was the last time he had logged into the system using that special password? Could his sniffer have logged himself on an earlier hacking session? It did happen occasionally. Hackers sometimes gave themselves quite a fright. In the seamless days and nights of hacking dozens of systems, it was easy to forget the last time you logged into a particular system using the special password. The more he thought, the more he was absolutely sure. He hadn't logged into the system again.

Which left the obvious question. Who had?

Sometimes Anthrax pranked, sometimes he punished. Punishment could be severe or mild. Generally it was severe. And unlike pranking, it was not done randomly.

Different things set him off. The librarian, for example. In early 1993 Anthrax had enrolled in Asia-Pacific and Business Studies at a university in a nearby regional city. Ever since he showed up on the campus, he had been hassled by a student who worked part-time at the university library. On more than one occasion, Anthrax had been reading at a library table when a security guard came up and asked to search his bags. And when Anthrax looked over his shoulder to the check-out desk, that librarian was always there, the one with the bad attitude smeared across his face.

The harassment became so noticeable, Anthrax's friends began commenting on it. His bag would be hand-searched when he left the library, while other students walked through the electronic security boom gate unbothered. When he returned a book one day late, the librarian – that librarian – insisted he pay all sorts of fines. Anthrax's pleas of being a poor student fell on deaf ears. By the time exam period rolled around at the end of term, Anthrax decided to punish the librarian by taking down the library's entire computer system.

Logging in to the library computer via modem from home,

Anthrax quickly gained root privileges. The system had security holes a mile wide. Then, with one simple command, he deleted every file in the computer. He knew the system would be backed up somewhere, but it would take a day or two to get the system up and running again. In the meantime, every loan or book search had to be conducted manually.

During Anthrax's first year at university, even small incidents provoked punishment. Cutting him off while he was driving, or swearing at him on the road, fit the bill. Anthrax would memorise the licence plate of the offending driver, then social engineer the driver's personal details. Usually he called the police to report what appeared to be a stolen car and then provided the licence plate number. Shortly after, Anthrax tuned into his police scanner, where he picked up the driver's name and address as it was read over the airways to the investigating police car. Anthrax wrote it all down.

Then began the process of punishment. Posing as the driver, Anthrax rang the driver's electricity company to arrange a power disconnection. The next morning the driver might return home to find his electricity cut off. The day after, his gas might be disconnected. Then his water. Then his phone.

Some people warranted special punishment – people such as Bill. Anthrax came across Bill on the Swedish Party Line, an English-speaking telephone conference. For a time, Anthrax was a regular fixture on the line, having attempted to call it by phreaking more than 2000 times over just a few months. Of course, not all those attempts were successful, but he managed to get through at least half the time. It required quite an effort to keep a presence on the party line, since it automatically cut people off after only ten minutes. Anthrax made friends with the operators, who sometimes let him stay on-line a while longer.

Bill, a Swedish Party Line junkie, had recently been released from prison, where he had served time for beating up a Vietnamese boy at a railway station. He had a bad attitude and he often greeted the party line by saying, 'Are there any coons on the line today?' His attitude to women wasn't much better. He relentlessly hit on the women who frequented the line. One day, he made a mistake. He gave out his phone number to a girl he was trying to pick up. The operator copied it down and when her friend Anthrax came on later that day, she passed it on to him.

Anthrax spent a few weeks social engineering various people, including utilities and relatives whose telephone numbers appeared on Bill's phone accounts, to piece together the details of his life. Bill was a rough old ex-con who owned a budgie and was dying of cancer. Anthrax phoned Bill in the hospital and proceeded to tell him all sorts of personal details about himself, the kind of details which upset a person.

Not long after, Anthrax heard that Bill had died. The hacker felt as though he had perhaps gone a bit too far.

The tension at home had eased a little by the time Anthrax left to attend university. But when he returned home during holidays he found his father even more unbearable. More and more, Anthrax rebelled against his father's sniping comments and violence. Eventually, he vowed that the next time his father tried to break his arm he would fight back. And he did.

One day Anthrax's father began making bitter fun of his younger son's stutter. Brimming with biting sarcasm, the father mimicked Anthrax's brother.

'Why are you doing that?' Anthrax yelled. The bait had worked once again.

It was as though he became possessed with a spirit not his own. He yelled at his father, and put a fist into the wall. His father grabbed a chair and thrust it forward to keep Anthrax at bay, then reached back for the phone. Said he was calling the police. Anthrax ripped the phone from the wall. He pursued his father through the house, smashing furniture. Amid the crashing violence of the fight, Anthrax suddenly felt a flash of fear for his mother's clock – a much loved, delicate family heirloom. He gently picked it up and placed it out of harm's way. Then he heaved the stereo into the air and threw it at his father. The stereo cabinet followed in its wake. Wardrobes toppled with a crash across the floor.

When his father fled the house, Anthrax got a hold of himself and began to look around. The place was a disaster area. All those things so tenderly gathered and carefully treasured by his mother, the things she had used to build her life in a foreign land of white people speaking an alien tongue, lay in fragments scattered around the house.

Anthrax felt wretched. His mother was distraught at the destruction and he was badly shaken by how much it upset her. He promised to try and control his temper from that moment on. It proved to be a constant battle. Mostly he would win, but not always. The battle still simmered below the surface.

Sometimes it boiled over.

Anthrax considered the possibilities of who else would be using his login patch. It could be another hacker, perhaps someone who was running another sniffer that logged Anthrax's previous login. But it was more likely to be a security admin. Meaning he had been found out. Meaning that he might be being traced even as he leap-frogged through System X to the telecommunications company's computer.

Anthrax made his way to the system admin's mailboxes. If the game was up, chances were something in the mailbox would give it away.

There it was. The evidence. They were onto him all right, and they hadn't wasted any time. The admins had mailed CERT, the Computer Emergency Response Team at Carnegie Mellon University, reporting a security breach. CERT, the nemesis of every Internet hacker, was bound to complicate matters. Law enforcement would no doubt be called in now.

It was time to get out of this system, but not before leaving in a blaze of glory. A prank left as a small present.

CERT had written back to the admins acknowledging the incident and providing a case number. Posing as one of the admins, Anthrax drafted a letter to CERT. To make the thing look official, he added the case number 'for reference'. The letter went something like this:

'In regard to incident no. XXXXX, reported on this date, we have since carried out some additional investigations on the matter. We have discovered the security incident was caused by a disgruntled employee who was fired for alcoholism and decided to retaliate against the company in this manner.

'We have long had a problem with alcohol and drug abuse due to the stressful nature of the company environment. No further investigation is necessary.'

At his computer terminal, Anthrax smiled. How embarrassing was that going to be? Try scraping that mud off. He felt very pleased with himself.

Anthrax then tidied up his things in the company's computer, deleted the sniffer and moved out.

Things began to move quickly after that. He logged into System X later to check the sniffer records, only to find that someone had used his login patch password on that system as well. He became very nervous. It was one thing goofing around with a commercial site, and quite another being tracked from a military computer.

A new process had been added to System X, which Anthrax recognised. It was called '-u'. He didn't know what it did, but he had seen it before on military systems. About 24 hours after it appeared, he found himself locked out of the system. He had tried killing off the -u process before. It disappeared for a split-second and reappeared. Once it was in place, there was no way to destroy it.

Anthrax also unearthed some alarming email. The admin at a site upstream from both System X and the company's system had been sent a warning letter: 'We think there has been a security incident at your site'. The circle was closing in on him. It was definitely time to get the hell out. He packed up his things in a hurry. Killed off the remaining sniffer. Moved his files. Removed the login patch. And departed with considerable alacrity.

After he cut his connection, Anthrax sat wondering about the admins. If they knew he was into their systems, why did they leave the sniffers up and running? He could understand leaving the login patch. Maybe they wanted to track his movements, determine his motives, or trace his connection. Killing the patch would have simply locked him out of the only door the admins could watch. They wouldn't know if he had other backdoors into their system. But the sniffer? It didn't make any sense.

It was possible that they simply hadn't seen the sniffer. Leaving it there had been an oversight. But it was almost too glaring an error to be a real possibility. If it was an error, it implied the admins weren't actually monitoring the connections in and out of their systems. If they had been watching the connections, they would probably have seen the sniffer. But if they weren't monitoring the connections, how on earth did they find out his special password for the login patch? Like all passwords on the system, that one was encrypted. There were only two ways to get that password. Monitor the connection and sniff it, or break the encryption with a brute-force attack.

Breaking the encryption would probably have taken millions of dollars of computer time. He could pretty well rule that option out. That left sniffing it, which would have alerted them to his own sniffer. Surely they wouldn't have left his sniffer running on purpose. They must have known he would learn they were watching him through his sniffer. The whole thing was bizarre.

Anthrax thought about the admins who were chasing him. Thought about their moves, their strategies. Wondered why. It was one of the unsolved mysteries a hacker often faced – an unpleasant side of hacking. Missing the answers to certain questions, the satisfaction of a certain curiosity. Never being able to look over the fence at the other side.

11 | THE PRISONER'S DILEMMA

Anthrax thought he would never get caught. But in some strange way, he also wanted to get caught. When he thought about being busted, he found himself filled with a strange emotion – impatience. Bring on the impending doom and be done with it. Or perhaps it was frustration at how inept his opponents seemed to be. They kept losing his trail and he was impatient with their incompetence. It was more fun outwitting a worthy opponent.

Perhaps he didn't really want to be caught so much as tracked. Anthrax liked the idea of the police tracking him, of the system administrators pursuing him. He liked to follow the trail of their investigations through other people's mail. He especially liked being on-line, watching them trying to figure out where he was coming from. He would cleverly take control of their computers in ways they couldn't see. He watched every character they typed, every spelling error, every mistyped command, each twist and turn taken in the vain hope of catching him.

He hadn't been caught back in early 1991, when it seemed everyone was after him. In fact Anthrax nearly gave up hacking and phreaking completely in that year after what he later called 'The Fear of God' speech.

Late at night, on a university computer system, he bumped into another hacker. It wasn't an entirely uncommon experience. Once in a while, hackers recognised another of their kind. Strange connections to strange places in the middle of the night. Inconsistencies in process names and sizes. The clues were visible for those who knew how to find them.

The two hackers danced around each other, trying to determine who the other was without giving away too much information. Finally the mystery hacker asked Anthrax, 'Are you a disease which affects sheep?'

Anthrax typed the simple answer back. 'Yes.'

The other hacker revealed himself as Prime Suspect, one of the International Subversives. Anthrax recognised the name. He had seen Prime Suspect around on the BBSes, had read his postings. Before Anthrax could get started on a friendly chat, the IS hacker jumped in with an urgent warning.

He had unearthed emails showing the Feds were closing in on Anthrax. The mail, obtained from system admins at Miden Pacific, described the systems Anthrax had been visiting. It showed the phone connections he had been using to get to them, some of which Telecom had traced back to his phone. One of the admins had written, 'We're on to him. I feel really bad. He's seventeen years old and they are going to bust him and ruin his life.' Anthrax felt a cold chill run down his spine.

Prime Suspect continued with the story. When he first came across the email, he thought it referred to himself. The two hackers were the same age and had evidently been breaking into the same systems. Prime Suspect had freaked out over the mail. He took it back to the other two IS hackers, and they talked it through. Most of the description fitted, but a few of the details didn't seem to make sense. Prime Suspect wasn't calling from a country exchange. The more they worked it through, the clearer it became that the email must have been referring to someone else. They ran through the list of other options and Anthrax's name came up as a possibility. The IS hackers had all seen him around a few systems and BBSes. Trax had even spoken to him once on a conference call with another phreaker. They pieced together what they knew of him and the picture fitted. The AFP were onto Anthrax and they seemed to know a lot about him. They had traced his telephone connection back to his house. They knew his age, which implied they knew his name. The phone bills were in his parents' names, so there may have been some personal surveillance of him. The Feds were so close they were all but treading on his heels. The IS hackers had been keeping an eye out for him, to warn him, but this was the first time they had found him.

Anthrax thanked Prime Suspect and got out of the system. He sat frozen in the night stillness. It was one thing to contemplate getting caught, to carry mixed emotions on the hypothetical situation. It was another to have the real prospect staring you in the face. In the morning, he gathered up all his hacking papers, notes, manuals – everything. Three trunks' worth of material. He carried it all to the back garden, lit a bonfire and watched it burn. He vowed to give up hacking forever.

And he did give it up, for a time. But a few months later he somehow found himself back in front of his computer screen, with his modem purring. It was so tempting, so hard to let go. The police had never shown up. Months had come and gone, still nothing. Prime Suspect must have been wrong. Perhaps the AFP were after another hacker entirely.

Then, in October 1991, the AFP busted Prime Suspect, Mendax and Trax. But Anthrax continued to hack, mostly on his own as usual, for another two years. He reminded himself that the IS hackers worked in a team. If the police hadn't nailed him when they busted the others, surely they would never find him now. Further, he had become more skilled as a hacker, better at covering his tracks, less likely to draw attention to himself. He had other rationalisations too. The town where he lived was so far away, the police would never bother travelling all the way into the bush. The elusive Anthrax would remain at large forever, the unvanquished Ned Kelly of the computer underground.

Mundane matters were on Anthrax's mind on the morning of 14 July 1994. The removalists were due to arrive to take things from the half-empty apartment he had shared with another student. His room-mate had already departed and the place was a clutter of boxes stuffed with clothes, tapes and books.

Anthrax sat in bed half-asleep, half-watching the 'Today' show when he heard the sound of a large vehicle pulling up outside. He looked out the window expecting to see the removalists. What he saw instead was at least four men in casual clothes running toward the house.

They were a little too enthusiastic for removalists and they split up before getting to the door, with two men forking off toward opposite sides of the building. One headed for the car port. Another dove around the other side of the building. A third banged on the front door. Anthrax shook himself awake.

The short, stocky guy at the front door was a worry. He had puffy, longish hair and was wearing a sweatshirt and acid-wash jeans so tight you could count the change in his back pocket. Bad ideas raced through Anthrax's head. It looked like a home invasion. Thugs were going to break into his home, tie him up and terrorise him before stealing all his valuables.

'Open up. Open up,' the stocky one shouted, flashing a police badge.

Stunned, and still uncomprehending, Anthrax opened the door. 'Do you know who WE are?' the stocky one asked him.

Anthrax looked confused. No. Not sure.

'The Australian Federal Police.' The cop proceeded to read out the search warrant.

What happened from this point forward is a matter of some debate. What is fact is that the events of the raid and what followed formed the basis of a formal complaint by Anthrax to the Office of the Ombudsman and an internal investigation within the AFP. The following is simply Anthrax's account of how it happened.

The stocky one barked at Anthrax, 'Where's your computer?'

'What computer?' Anthrax looked blankly at the officer. He didn't have a computer at his apartment. He used the uni's machines or friend's computers.

'Your computer. Where is it? Which one of your friends has it?'

'No-one has it. I don't own one.'

'Well, when you decide to tell us where it is, you let us know.'

Yeah. Right. If Anthrax did have a hidden computer at uni, revealing its location wasn't top of the must-do list.

The police pawed through his personal letters, quizzed Anthrax about them. Who wrote this letter? Is he in the computer underground? What's his address?

Anthrax said 'no comment' more times than he could count. He saw a few police moving into his bedroom and decided it was time to watch them closely, make sure nothing was planted. He stood up to follow them in and observe the search when one of the cops stopped him. Anthrax told them he wanted a lawyer. One of the police looked on with disapproval.

'You must be guilty,' he told Anthrax. 'Only guilty people ask for lawyers. And here I was feeling sorry for you.'

Then one of the other officers dropped the bomb. 'You know,' he began casually, 'we're also raiding your parents' house . . .'

Anthrax freaked out. His mum would be hysterical. He asked to call his mother on his mobile, the only phone then working in the apartment. The police refused to let him touch his mobile. Then he asked to call her from the pay phone across the street. The police refused again. One of the officers, a tall, lanky cop, recognised a leverage point if ever he saw one. He spread the guilt on thick.

'Your poor sick mum. How could you do this to your poor sick mum? We're going to have to take her to Melbourne for questioning, maybe even to charge her, arrest her, take her to jail. You make me sick. I feel sorry for a mother having a son like you who is going to cause her all this trouble.'

From that moment on, the tall officer took every opportunity to talk about Anthrax's 'poor sick mum'. He wouldn't let up. Not that he probably knew the first thing about scleroderma, the creeping fatal disease which affected her. Anthrax often thought about the pain his mother was in as the disease worked its way from her extremities to her internal organs. Scleroderma toughened the skin on the fingers and feet, but made them overly sensitive, particularly to changes in weather. It typically affected women native to hot climates who moved to colder environments.

Anthrax's mobile rang. His mother. It had to be. The police wouldn't let him answer it.

The tall officer picked up the call, then turned to the stocky cop and said in a mocking Indian accent, 'It is some woman with an Indian accent'. Anthrax felt like jumping out of his chair and grabbing the phone. He felt like doing some other things too, things that would have undoubtedly landed him in prison then and there.

The stocky cop nodded to the tall one, who handed the mobile to Anthrax.

At first, he couldn't make sense of what his mother was saying. She was a terrified mess. Anthrax tried to calm her down. Then she tried to comfort him.

'Don't worry. It will be all right,' she said it, over and over. No matter what Anthrax said, she repeated that phrase, like a chant. In trying to console him, she was actually calming herself. Anthrax listened to her trying to impose order on the chaos around her. He could hear noises in the background and he guessed it was the police rummaging through her home. Suddenly, she said she had to go and hung up.

Anthrax handed the phone back to the police and sat with his head in his hands. What a wretched situation. He couldn't believe this was happening to him. How could the police seriously consider taking his mother to Melbourne for questioning? True, he phreaked from her home office phone, but she had no idea how to hack or phreak. As for charging his mother, that would just about kill her. In her mental and physical condition, she would simply collapse, maybe never to get up again.

He didn't have many options. One of the cops was sealing up his mobile phone in a clear plastic bag and labelling it. It was physically impossible for him to call a lawyer, since the police wouldn't let him use the mobile or go to a pay phone. They harangued him about coming to Melbourne for a police interview.

'It is your best interest to cooperate,' one of the cops told him. 'It would be in your best interest to come with us now.'

Anthrax pondered that line for a moment, considered how ludicrous it sounded coming from a cop. Such a bald-faced lie told so matter-of-factly. It would have been humorous if the situation with his mother hadn't been so awful. He agreed to an interview with the police, but it would have to be done on another day.

The cops wanted to search his car. Anthrax didn't like it, but there was nothing incriminating in the car anyway. As he walked outside in the winter morning, one of the cops looked down at Anthrax's feet, which were bare in accordance with the Muslim custom of removing shoes in the house. The cop asked if he was cold.

The other cop answered for Anthrax. 'No. The fungus keeps them warm.'

Anthrax swallowed his anger. He was used to racism, and plenty of it, especially from cops. But this was over the top.

In the town where he attended uni, everyone thought he was Aboriginal. There were only two races in that country town –

white and Aboriginal. Indian, Pakistani, Malay, Burmese, Sri Lankan – it didn't matter. They were all Aboriginal, and were treated accordingly.

Once when he was talking on the pay phone across from his house, the police pulled up and asked him what he was doing there. Talking on the phone, he told them. It was pretty obvious. They asked for identification, made him empty his pockets, which contained his small mobile phone. They told him his mobile must be stolen, took it from him and ran a check on the serial number. Fifteen minutes and many more accusations later, they finally let him go with the flimsiest of apologies. 'Well, you understand,' one cop said. 'We don't see many of your type around here.'

Yeah. Anthrax understood. It looked pretty suspicious, a dark-skinned boy using a public telephone. Very suss indeed.

In fact, Anthrax had the last laugh. He had been on a phreaked call to Canada at the time and he hadn't bothered to hang up when the cops arrived. Just told the other phreakers to hang on. After the police left, he picked up the conversation where he left off.

Incidents like that taught him that sometimes the better path was to toy with the cops. Let them play their little games. Pretend to be manipulated by them. Laugh at them silently and give them nothing. So he appeared to ignore the fungus comment and led the cops to his car. They found nothing.

When the police finally packed up to leave, one of them handed Anthrax a business card with the AFP's phone number.

'Call us to arrange an interview time,' he said.

'Sure,' Anthrax replied as he shut the door.

Anthrax keep putting the police off. Every time they called hassling him for an interview, he said he was busy. But when they began ringing up his mum, he found himself in a quandary.

They were threatening and yet reassuring to his mother all at the same time and spoke politely to her, even apologetically.

'As bad as it sounds,' one of them said, 'we're going to have to charge you with things Anthrax has done, hacking, phreaking, etc. if he doesn't cooperate with us. We know it sounds funny, but we're within our rights to do that. In fact that is what the law dictates because the phone is in your name.'

He followed this with the well-worn 'it's in your son's best interest to cooperate' line, delivered with cooing persuasion.

Anthrax wondered why there was no mention of charging his father, whose name appeared on the house's main telephone number. That line also carried some illegal calls.

His mother worried. She asked her son to cooperate with the police. Anthrax felt he had to protect his mother and finally agreed to a police interview after his uni exams. The only reason he did so was because of the police threat to charge his mother. He was sure that if they dragged his mother through court, her health would deteriorate and lead to an early death.

Anthrax's father picked him up from uni on a fine November day and drove down to Melbourne. His mother had insisted that he attend the interview, since he knew all about the law and police. Anthrax didn't mind having him along: he figured a witness might prevent any use of police muscle.

During the ride to the city, Anthrax talked about how he would handle the interview. The good news was that the AFP had said they wanted to interview him about his phreaking, not his hacking. He went to the interview understanding they would only be discussing his 'recent stuff' – the phreaking. He had two possible approaches to the interview. He could come clean and admit everything, as his first lawyer had advised. Or he could pretend to cooperate and be evasive, which was what his instincts told him to do.

His father jumped all over the second option. 'You have to cooperate fully. They will know if you are lying. They are trained to pick out lies. Tell them everything and they will go easier on you.' Law and order all the way.

'Who do they think they are anyway? The pigs.' Anthrax looked away, disgusted at the thought of police harassing people like his mother.

'Don't call them pigs,' his father snapped. 'They are police officers. If you are ever in trouble, they are the first people you are ever going to call.'

'Oh yeah. What kind of trouble am I going to be in that the first people I call are the AFP?' Anthrax replied.

Anthrax would put up with his father coming along so long as he kept his mouth shut during the interview. He certainly wasn't there for personal support. They had a distant relationship at best. When his father began working in the town where Anthrax now lived and studied, his mother had tried to patch things between them. She suggested his father take Anthrax out for dinner once a week, to smooth things over. Develop a relationship. They had dinner a handful of times and Anthrax listened to his father's lectures. Admit you were wrong. Cooperate with the police. Get your life together. Own up to it all. Grow up. Be responsible. Stop being so useless. Stop being so stupid.

The lectures were a bit rich, Anthrax thought, considering that his father had benefited from Anthrax's hacking skills. When he discovered Anthrax had got into a huge news clipping database, he asked the boy to pull up every article containing the word 'prison'. Then he had him search for articles on discipline. The searches should have cost a fortune, probably thousands of dollars. But his father didn't pay a cent, thanks to Anthrax. And he didn't spend much time lecturing Anthrax on the evils of hacking then.

When they arrived at AFP headquarters, Anthrax made a point of putting his feet up on the leather couch in the reception area and opened a can of Coke he had brought along. His father got upset.

'Get your feet off that seat. You shouldn't have brought that can of Coke. It doesn't look very professional.'

'Hey, I'm not going for a job interview here,' Anthrax responded.

Constable Andrew Sexton, a redhead sporting two earrings, came up to Anthrax and his father and took them upstairs for coffee. Detective Sergeant Ken Day, head of the Computer Crime Unit, was in a meeting, Sexton said, so the interview would be delayed a little.

Anthrax's father and Sexton found they shared some interests in law enforcement. They discussed the problems associated with rehabilitation and prisoner discipline. Joked with each other. Laughed. Talked about 'young Anthrax'. Young Anthrax did this. Young Anthrax did that.

Young Anthrax felt sick. Watching his own father cosying up to the enemy, talking as if he wasn't even there.

When Sexton went to check on whether Day had finished his meeting, Anthrax's father growled, 'Wipe that look of contempt off your face, young man. You are going to get nowhere in this world if you show that kind of attitude, they are going to come down on you like a ton of bricks.'

Anthrax didn't know what to say. Why should he treat these people with any respect after the way they threatened his mother?

The interview room was small but very full. A dozen or more boxes, all filled with labelled print-outs.

Sexton began the interview. 'Taped record of interview conducted at Australian Federal Police Headquarters, 383 Latrobe Street Melbourne on 29 November 1994.' He reeled off the names of the people present and asked each to introduce himself for voice recognition.

'As I have already stated, Detective Sergeant Day and I are making enquiries into your alleged involvement into the manipulation of private automated branch exchanges [PABXes] via Telecom 008 numbers in order to obtain free phone calls nationally and internationally. Do you clearly understand this allegation?'

'Yes.'

Sexton continued with the necessary, and important, preliminaries. Did Anthrax understand that he was not obliged to answer any questions? That he had the right to communicate with a lawyer? That he had attended the interview of his own free will? That he was free to leave at any time?

Yes, Anthrax said in answer to each question.

Sexton then ploughed through a few more standard procedures before he finally got to the meat of the issue – telephones. He fished around in one of the many boxes and pulled out a mobile phone. Anthrax confirmed that it was his phone.

'Was that the phone that you used to call the 008 numbers and subsequent connections?' Sexton asked.

'Yes.'

'Contained in that phone is a number of pre-set numbers. Do you agree?'

'Yes.'

'I went to the trouble of extracting those records from it.' Sexton looked pleased with himself for hacking Anthrax's speed-dial numbers from the mobile. 'Number 22 is of some interest to myself. It comes up as Aaron. Could that be the person you referred to before as Aaron in South Australia?'

'Yes, but he is always moving house. He is a hard person to track down.'

Sexton went through a few more numbers, most of which Anthrax hedged. He asked Anthrax questions about his manipulation of the phone system, particularly about the way he made free calls overseas using Australian companies' 008 numbers.

When Anthrax had patiently explained how it all worked, Sexton went through some more speed-dial numbers.

'Number 43. Do you recognise that one?'

'That's the Swedish Party Line.'

'What about these other numbers? Such as 78? And 30?'

'I'm not sure. I couldn't say what any of these are. It's been so long,' Anthrax paused, sensing the pressure from the other side of the table. 'These ones here, they are numbers in my town. But I don't know who. Very often, 'cause I don't have any pen and paper with me, I just plug a number into the phone.'

Sexton looked unhappy. He decided to go in a little harder.

'I'm going to be pretty blunt. So far you have admitted to the 008s but I think you are understating your knowledge and your experience when it comes to these sort of offences.' He caught himself. 'Not offences. But your involvement in all of this . . . I think you have got a little bit more . . . I'm not saying you are lying, don't get me wrong, but you tend to be pulling yourself away from how far you were really into this. And how far everyone looked up to you.'

There was the gauntlet, thrown down on the table. Anthrax picked it up.

'They looked up to me? That was just a perception. To be honest, I don't know that much. I couldn't tell you anything about telephone exchanges or anything like that. In the past, I guess the reason they might look up to me in the sense of a leader is because I was doing this, as you are probably aware, quite a bit in the past, and subsequently built up a reputation. Since then I decided I wouldn't do it again.'

'Since this?' Sexton was quick off the mark.

'No. Before. I just said, "I don't want anything to do with this any more. It's just stupid". When I broke up with my girlfriend . . . I just got dragged into it again. I'm not trying to say that I am any less responsible for any of this but I will say I didn't originate any of these 008s. They were all scanned by other people. But I made calls and admittedly I did a lot of stupid things.'

But Sexton was like a dog with a bone.

'I just felt that you were tending to . . . I don't know if it's because your dad's here or . . . I have read stuff that "Anthrax was a legend when it came to this, and he was a scanner, and he was the man to talk to about X.25, Tymnet, hacking, Unix. The whole kit and kaboodle".'

Anthrax didn't take the bait. Cops always try that line. Play on a hacker's ego, get them to brag. It was so transparent.

'It's not true,' he answered. 'I know nothing about . . . I can't program. I have an Amiga with one meg of memory. I have no formal background in computers whatsoever.'

That part was definitely true. Everything was self-taught. Well, almost everything. He did take one programming class at uni, but he failed it. He went to the library to do extra research, used in his final project for the course. Most of his classmates wrote simple 200-line programs with few functions; his ran to 500 lines and had lots of special functions. But the lecturer flunked him. She told him, 'The functions in your program were not taught in this course'.

Sexton asked Anthrax if he was into carding, which he denied emphatically. Then Sexton headed back into scanning. How much had Anthrax done? Had he given scanned numbers to other hackers? Anthrax was evasive, and both cops were getting impatient.

'What I am trying to get at is that I believe that, through your scanning, you are helping other people break the law by promoting this sort of thing.' Sexton had shown his hand.

'No more than a telephone directory would be assisting someone, because it's really just a list. I didn't actually break anything. I just looked at it.'

'These voice mailbox systems obviously belong to people. What would you do when you found a VMB?'

'Just play with it. Give it to someone and say, "Have a look at this. It is interesting," or whatever.'

'When you say play with it you would break the code out to the VMB?'

'No. Just have a look around. I'm not very good at breaking VMBs.'

Sexton tried a different tack. 'What are 1-900 numbers? On the back of that document there is a 1-900 number. What are they generally for?'

Easy question. 'In America they like cost $10 a minute. You can ring them up, I think, and get all sorts of information, party lines, etc.'

'It's a conference type of call?'

'Yes.'

'Here is another document, contained in a clear plastic

sleeve labelled AS/AB/S/1. Is this a scan? Do you recognise your handwriting?'

'Yes, it's in my handwriting. Once again it's the same sort of scan. It's just dialling some commercial numbers and noting them.'

'And once you found something, what would you do with it?'

Anthrax had no intention of being painted as some sort of ringleader of a scanning gang. He was a sociable loner, not a part of a team.

'I'd just look at it, like in the case of this one here – 630. I just punched in a few numbers and it said that 113 diverts some-where, 115 says goodbye, etc. I'd just do that and I probably never came back to it again.'

'And you believe that if I pick up the telephone book, I would get all this information?'

'No. It's just a list of numbers in the same sense that a tele-phone book is.'

'What about a 1-800 number?'

'That is the same as a 0014.'

'If you rang a 1-800 number, where would you go?'

Anthrax wondered if the Computer Crimes Unit gained most of its technical knowledge from interviews with hackers.

'You can either do 0014 or you can do 1-800. It's just the same.'

'Is it Canada – 0014?'

'It's everywhere.' Oops. Don't sound too cocky. 'Isn't it?'

'No, I'm not familiar.' Which is just what Anthrax was thinking.

Sexton moved on. 'On the back of that document there is more type scans . . .'

'It's all just the same thing. Just take a note of what is there. In this case, box 544 belongs to this woman . . .'

'So, once again, you just release this type of information on the bridge?'

'Not all of it. Most of it I would probably keep to myself and never look at it again. I was bored. Is it illegal to scan?'

'I'm not saying it's illegal. I'm just trying to show that you were really into this. I'm building a picture and I am gradually getting to a point and I'm going to build a picture to show that for a while there . . .' Sexton then interrupted himself and veered down a less confrontational course. 'I'm not saying you are doing it now, but back then, when all these offences occurred, you were really into scanning telephone systems, be it voice mailboxes . . . I'm not saying you found the 008s but you . . . anything to bugger up Telecom. You were really getting into it and you were helping other people.'

Anthrax took offence. 'The motivation for me doing it wasn't to bugger up Telecom.'

Sexton backpedalled. 'Perhaps . . . probably a poor choice of words.'

He began pressing forward on the subject of hacking, something the police had not said they were going to be discussing. Anthrax felt a little unnerved, even rattled.

Day asked if Anthrax wanted a break.

'No,' he answered. 'I just want to get it over and done with, if that's OK. I'm not going to lie. I'm not going to say "no comment". I'm going to admit to everything 'cause, based on what I have been told, it's in my best interest to do so.'

The police paused. They didn't seem to like that last comment much. Day tried to clear things up.

'Before we go any further, based on what you have been told, it is in your best interests to tell the truth. Was it any member of the AFP that told you this?'

'Yes.'

'Who?' Day threw the question out quickly.

Anthrax couldn't remember their names. 'The ones who came to my house. I think Andrew also said it to me,' he said, nodding in the direction of the red-headed constable.

Why were the cops getting so uncomfortable all of a sudden? It was no secret that they had told both Anthrax and his mother repeatedly that it was in his best interest to agree to an interview.

Day leaned forward, peered at Anthrax and asked, 'What did you interpret that to mean?'

'That if I don't tell the truth, if I say "no comment" and don't cooperate, that it is going to be . . . it will mean that you will go after me with . . .' Anthrax grasped for the right words, but he felt tongue-tied, 'with . . . more force, I guess.'

Both officers stiffened visibly.

Day came back again. 'Do you feel that an unfair inducement has been placed on you as a result of that?'

'In what sense?' The question was genuine.

'You have made the comment and it has now been recorded and I have to clear it up. Do you feel like, that a deal has been offered to you at any stage?'

A deal? Anthrax thought about it. It wasn't a deal as in 'Talk to us now and we will make sure you don't go to jail'. Or 'Talk now and we won't beat you with a rubber hose'.

'No,' he answered.

'Do you feel that as a result of that being said that you have been pressured to come forward today and tell the truth?'

Ah, that sort of deal. Well, of course.

'Yes, I have been pressured,' Anthrax answered. The two police officers looked stunned. Anthrax paused, concerned about the growing feeling of disapproval in the room. 'Indirectly,' he added quickly, almost apologetically.

For a brief moment, Anthrax just didn't care. About the police. About his father. About the pressure. He would tell the truth. He decided to explain the situation as he saw it.

'Because since they came to my house, they emphasised the fact that if I didn't come for an interview, that they would then charge my mother and, as my mother is very sick, I am not prepared to put her through that.'

The police looked at each other. The shock waves reverberated around the room. The AFP clearly hadn't bargained on this coming out in the interview tape. But what he said about his mother being threatened was the truth, so let it be on the record with everything else.

Ken Day caught his breath, 'So you are saying that you have now been . . .' he cut himself off . . . 'that you are not here voluntarily?'

Anthrax thought about it. What did 'voluntarily' mean? The police didn't cuff him to a chair and tell him he couldn't leave until he talked. They didn't beat him around the head with a baton. They offered him a choice: talk or inflict the police on his ailing mother. Not a palatable choice, but a choice nonetheless. He chose to talk to protect his mother.

'I am here voluntarily,' he answered.

'That is not what you have said. What you have just said is that pressure has been placed on you and that you have had to come in here and answer the questions. Otherwise certain actions would take place. That does not mean you are here voluntarily.'

The police must have realised they were on very thin ice and Anthrax felt pressure growing in the room. The cops pushed. His father did not look pleased.

'I was going to come anyway,' Anthrax answered, again almost apologetically. Walk the tightrope, he thought. Don't get them too mad or they will charge my mother. 'You can talk to the people who carried out the warrant. All along, I said to them I would come in for an interview. Whatever my motivations are, I don't think should matter. I am going to tell you the truth.'

'It does matter,' Day responded, 'because at the beginning of the interview it was stated – do you agree – that you have come in here voluntarily?'

'I have. No-one has forced me.'

Anthrax felt exasperated. The room was getting stuffy. He wanted to finish this thing and get out of there. So much pressure.

'And is anyone forcing you to make the answers you have given here today?' Day tried again.

'No individuals are forcing me, no.' There. You have what you want. Now get on with it and let's get out of here.

'You have to tell the truth. Is that what you are saying?' The police would not leave the issue be.

'I want to tell the truth. As well.' The key words there were 'as well'. Anthrax thought, I want to and I have to.

'It's the circumstances that are forcing this upon you, not an individual?'

'No.' Of course it was the circumstances. Never mind that the police created the circumstance.

Anthrax felt as if the police were just toying with him. He knew and they knew they would go after his mother if this interview wasn't to their liking. Visions of his frail mother being hauled out of her house by the AFP flashed through his mind. Anthrax felt sweaty and hot. Just get on with it. Whatever makes them happy, just agree to it in order to get out of this crowded room.

'So, would it be fair to summarise it, really, to say that perhaps . . . of your activity before the police arrived at your premises, that is what is forcing you?'

What was this cop talking about? His 'activity' forcing him? Anthrax felt confused. The interview had already gone on some time. The cops had such obscure ways of asking things. The room was oppressively small.

Day pressed on with the question, 'The fact that you could see you had broken the law, and that is what is forcing you to come forward here today and tell the truth?'

Yeah. Whatever you want. 'OK,' Anthrax started to answer, 'That is a fair assump – '

Day cut him off. 'I just wanted to clarify that because the interpretation I immediately got from that was that we, or members of the AFP, had unfairly and unjustly forced you to come in here today, and that is not the case?'

Define 'unfairly'. Define 'unjustly'. Anthrax thought it was unfair the cops might charge his mother. But they told her it was perfectly legal to do so. Anthrax felt light-headed. All these thoughts whirring around inside his head.

'No, that is not the case. I'm sorry for . . .' Be humble. Get out of that room faster.

'No, that is OK. If that is what you believe, say it. I have no problems with that. I just like to have it clarified. Remember, other people might listen to this tape and they will draw inferences and opinions from it. At any point where I think there is an ambiguity, I will ask for clarification. Do you understand that?'

'Yes. I understand.' Anthrax couldn't really focus on what Day was saying. He was feeling very distressed and just wanted to finish the interview.

The cops finally moved on, but the new topic was almost as unpleasant. Day began probing about Anthrax's earlier hacking career – the one he had no intention of talking about. Anthrax began to feel a bit better. He agreed to talk to the police about recent phreaking activities, not hacking matters. Indeed, he had repeatedly told them that topic was not on his agenda. He felt like he was standing on firmer ground.

After being politely stonewalled, Day circled around and tried again. 'OK. I will give you another allegation; that you have unlawfully accessed computer systems in Australia and the United States. In the US, you specifically targeted military computer systems. Do you understand that allegation?'

'I understand that. I wouldn't like to comment on it.' No, sir. No way.

Day tried a new tack. 'I will further allege that you did work with a person known as Mendax.'

What on earth was Day talking about? Anthrax had heard of Mendax, but they had never worked together. He thought the cops must not have very good informants.

'No. That is not true. I know no-one of that name.' Not strictly true, but true enough.

'Well, if he was to turn around to me and say that you were doing all this hacking, he would be lying, would he?'

Oh wonderful. Some other hacker was crapping on to the cops with lies about how he and Anthrax had worked together. That was exactly why Anthrax didn't work in a group. He had plenty of real allegations to fend off. He didn't need imaginary ones too.

'Most certainly would. Unless he goes by some other name, I know no-one by that name, Mendax.' Kill that off quick.

In fact Mendax had not ratted on Anthrax at all. That was just a technique the police used.

'You don't wish to comment on the fact that you have hacked into other computer systems and military systems?' If there was one thing Anthrax could say for Day, it was that he was persistent.

'No. I would prefer not to comment on any of that. This is the advice I have received: not to comment on anything unrelated to the topic that I was told I would be talking about when I came down here.'

'All right, well are you going to answer any questions in relation to unlawfully accessing any computer systems?'

'Based upon the legal advice that I received, I choose not to.'

Day pursed his lips. 'All right. If that is your attitude and you don't wish to answer any of those questions, we won't pursue the matter. However, I will inform you now that the matter may be reported and you may receive a summons to answer the questions or face charges in relation to those allegations, and, at any time that you so choose, you can come forward and tell us the truth.'

Woah. Anthrax took a deep breath. Could the cops make him come answer questions with a summons? They were changing the game midway through. Anthrax felt as though the carpet had been pulled out from beneath his feet. He needed a few minutes to clear his head.

'Is it something I can think over and discuss?' Anthrax asked.

'Yes. Do you want to have a pause and a talk with your father? The constable and I can step out of the room, or offer you another room. You may wish to have a break and think about it if you like. I think it might be a good idea. I think we might have a ten-minute break and put you in another room and let you two have a chat about it. There is no pressure.'

Day and Sexton stopped the interview and guided father and son into another room. Once they were alone, Anthrax looked to his father for support. This voice inside him still cried out to keep away from his earlier hacking journeys. He needed someone to tell him the same thing.

His father was definitely not that someone. He railed against Anthrax with considerable vehemence. Stop holding back. You have to tell everything. How could you be so stupid? You can't fool the police. They know. Confess it all before it's too late. At the end of the ten-minute tirade, Anthrax felt worse than he had at the beginning.

When the two returned to the interview room, Anthrax's father turned to the police and said suddenly, 'He has decided to confess'.

That was not true. Anthrax hadn't decided anything of the sort. His father was full of surprises. It seemed every time he opened his mouth, an ugly surprise came out.

Ken Day and Andrew Sexton warmed up a shaky Anthrax by showing him various documents, pieces of paper with Anthrax's scribbles seized during the raid, telephone taps. At one stage, Day pointed to some handwritten notes which read 'KDAY'. He looked at Anthrax.

'What's that? That's me.'

Anthrax smiled for the first time in a long while. It was something to be happy about. The head of the AFP's Computer Crime Unit in Melbourne sat there, so sure he was onto something big. There was his name, bold as day, in the hacker's handwriting on a bit of paper seized in a raid. Day seemed to be expecting something good.

Anthrax said, 'If you ring that up you will find it is a radio station.' An American radio station. Written on the same bit of paper were the names of an American clothing store, another US-based radio station, and a few records he wanted to order.

'There you go,' Day laughed at his own hasty conclusions. 'I've got a radio station named after me.'

Day asked Anthrax why he wrote down all sorts of things, directory paths, codes, error messages.

'Just part of the record-keeping. I think I wrote this down when I had first been given this dial-up and I was just feeling my way around, taking notes of what different things did.'

'What were your intentions at the time with these computer networks?'

'At this stage, I was just having a look, just a matter of curiosity.'

'Was it a matter of curiosity – "Gee, this is interesting" or was it more like "I would like to get into them" at this stage?'

'I couldn't say what was going through my mind at the time. But initially once I got into the first system – I'm sure you have heard this a lot – but once you get into the first system, it's like you get into the next one and the next one and the next one, after a while it doesn't . . .' Anthrax couldn't find the right words to finish the explanation.

'Once you have tasted the forbidden fruit?'

'Exactly. It's a good analogy.'

Day pressed on with questions about Anthrax's hacking. He successfully elicited admissions from the hacker. Anthrax gave Day more than the police officer had before, but probably not as much as he would have liked.

It was, however, enough. Enough to keep the police from charging Anthrax's mother. And enough for them to charge him.

Anthrax didn't see his final list of charges until the day he appeared in court on 28 August 1995. The whole case seemed to be a bit disorganised. His Legal Aid lawyer had little knowledge of computers, let alone computer crime. He told Anthrax he could ask for an adjournment because he hadn't seen the final charges until so late, but Anthrax wanted to get the thing over and done with. They had agreed that Anthrax would plead guilty to the charges and hope for a reasonable magistrate.

Anthrax looked through the hand-up brief provided by the prosecution, which included a heavily edited transcript of his interview with the police. It was labelled as a 'summary', but it certainly didn't summarise everything important in that interview. Either the prosecution or the police had cut out all references to the fact that the police had threatened to charge Anthrax's mother if he didn't agree to be interviewed.

Anthrax pondered the matter. Wasn't everything relevant to his case supposed to be covered in a hand-up brief? This seemed very relevant to his case, yet there wasn't a mention of it anywhere in the document. He began to wonder if the police had edited down the transcript just so they could cut out that portion of the interview. Perhaps the judge wouldn't be too happy about it. He thought that maybe the police didn't want to be held accountable for how they had dealt with his mother.

The rest of the hand-up brief wasn't much better. The only statement by an actual 'witness' to Anthrax's hacking was from his former room-mate, who claimed that he had watched Anthrax break into a NASA computer and access an 'area of the computer system which showed the latitude/longitude of ships'.

Did space ships even have longitudes and latitudes? Anthrax didn't know. And he had certainly never broken into a NASA computer in front of the room-mate. It was absurd. This guy is lying, Anthrax thought, and five minutes under cross-examination by a reasonable lawyer would illustrate as much. Anthrax's instincts told him the prosecution had a flimsy case for some of the charges, but he felt overwhelmed by pressure from all sides – his family, the bustle in the court-room, even the officiousness of his own lawyer quickly rustling through his papers.

Anthrax looked around the room. His eyes fell on his father, who sat waiting on the public benches. Anthrax's lawyer wanted him there to give evidence during sentencing. He thought it would look good to show there was a family presence. Anthrax gave the suggestion a cool reception. But he didn't understand how courts worked, so he followed his lawyer's advice.

Anthrax's mother was back at his apartment, waiting for news. She had been on night duty and was supposed to be sleeping. That was the ostensible reason she didn't attend. Anthrax thought perhaps that the tension was too much for her. Whatever the reason, she didn't sleep all that day. She tidied the place, washed the dishes, did the laundry, and kept herself as busy as the tiny apartment would allow her.

Anthrax's girlfriend, a pretty, moon-faced Turkish girl, also came to court. She had never been into the hacking scene. A group of school children, mostly girls, chatted in the rows behind her.

Anthrax read through the four-page summary of facts provided by the prosecution. When he reached the final page, his heart stopped. The final paragraph said:

31. Penalty
s85ZF (a) – 12 months, $6000 or both
s76E(a) – 2 years, $12000 or both

Pointing to the last paragraph, Anthrax asked his lawyer what that was all about. His lawyer told him that he would probably get prison but, well, it wouldn't be that bad and he would just have 'to take it on the chin'. He would, after all, be out in a year or two.

Rapists sometimes got off with less than that. Anthrax couldn't believe the prosecution was asking for prison. After he cooperated, suffering through that miserable interview. He had no prior convictions. But the snowball had been set in motion. The magistrate appeared and opened the court.

Anthrax felt he couldn't back out now and he pleaded guilty to 21 counts, including one charge of inserting data and twenty charges of defrauding or attempting to defraud a carrier.

His lawyer put the case for a lenient sentence. He called Anthrax's father up on the stand and asked him questions about his son. His father probably did more harm than good. When asked if he thought his son would offend again, his father replied, 'I don't know'.

Anthrax was livid. It was further unconscionable behaviour. Not long before the trial, Anthrax had discovered that his father had planned to sneak out of the country two days before the court case. He was going overseas, he told his wife, but not until after the court case. It was only by chance that she discovered his surreptitious plans to leave early. Presumably he would find his son's trial humiliating. Anthrax's mother insisted he stayed and he begrudgingly delayed the trip.

His father sat down, a bit away from Anthrax and his lawyer. The lawyer provided a colourful alternative to the prosecutor. He perched one leg up on his bench, rested an elbow on the knee and stroked his long, red beard. It was an impressive beard, more than a foot long and thick with reddish brown curls. Somehow it fitted with his two-tone chocolate brown suit and his tie, a breathtakingly wide creation with wild patterns in gold. The suit was one size too small. He launched into the usual courtroom flourish – lots of words saying nothing. Then he got to the punch line.

'Your worship, this young man has been in all sorts of places. NASA, military sites, you wouldn't believe some of the places he has been.'

'I don't think I want to know where he has been,' the magistrate answered wryly.

The strategy was Anthrax's. He thought he could turn a liability into an asset by showing that he had been in many systems – many sensitive systems – but had done no malicious damage in any of them.

The strategy worked and the magistrate announced there was no way he was sending the young hacker to jail.

The prosecutor looked genuinely disappointed and launched a counter proposal – 1500 hours of community service. Anthrax caught his breath. That was absurd. It would take almost nine months, full time. Painting buildings, cleaning toilets. Forget about his university studies. It was almost as bad as prison.

Anthrax's lawyer protested. 'Your Worship, that penalty is something out of cyberspace.' Anthrax winced at how corny that sounded, but the lawyer looked very pleased with himself.

The magistrate refused to have a bar of the prosecutor's counter proposal. Anthrax's girlfriend was impressed with the magistrate. She didn't know much about the law or the court system, but he seemed a fair man, a just man. He didn't appear to want to give a harsh punishment to Anthrax at all. But he told the court he had to send a message to Anthrax, to the class of school children in the public benches and to the general community that hacking was wrong in the eyes of the law. Anthrax glanced back at the students. They looked like they were aged thirteen or fourteen, about the age he got into hacking and phreaking.

The magistrate announced his sentence. Two hundred hours of community service and $6116.90 of restitution to be paid to two telephone companies – Telecom and Teleglobe in Canada. It wasn't prison, but it was a staggering amount of money for a student to rake up. He had a year to pay it off, and it would definitely take that long. At least he was free.

Anthrax's girlfriend thought how unlucky it was to have landed those giggling school children in the courtroom on that day. They laughed and pointed and half-whispered. Court was a game. They didn't seem to take the magistrate's warning seriously. Perhaps they were gossiping about the next party. Perhaps they were chatting about a new pair of sneakers or a new CD.

And maybe one or two murmured quietly how cool it would be to break into NASA.

It was billed as the 'largest annual gathering of those in, related to, or wishing to know more about the computer underground', so I thought I had better go.

HoHoCon in Austin, Texas, was without a doubt one of the strangest conferences I have attended. During the weekend leading up to New Year's Day 1995, the Ramada Inn South was overrun by hackers, phreakers, ex-hackers, underground sympathisers, journalists, computer company employees and American law enforcement agents. Some people had come from as far away as Germany and Canada.

The hackers and phreakers slept four or six to a room – if they slept at all. The feds slept two to a room. I could be wrong; maybe they weren't feds at all. But they seemed far too well dressed and well pressed to be anything else. No one else at HoHoCon ironed their T-shirts.

I left the main conference hall and wandered into Room 518 – the computer room – sat down on one of the two hotel beds which had been shoved into a corner to make room for all the computer gear, and watched. The conference organisers had moved enough equipment in there to open a store, and then connected it all to the Internet. For nearly three days, the room was almost continuously full. Boys in their late teens or early twenties lounged on the floor talking, playing with their cell phones and scanners or tapping away at one of the six or seven terminals. Empty bags of chips, Coke cans and pizza boxes littered the room. The place felt like one giant college dorm floor party, except that the people didn't talk to each other so much as to their computers.

These weren't the only interesting people at the con. I met up with an older group of nonconformists in the computer industry, a sort of Austin intelligentsia. By older, I mean above the age of 26. They were interested in many of the same issues as the young group of hackers – privacy, encryption, the future of a digital world – and they all had technical backgrounds.

This loose group of blue-jean clad thinkers, people like Doug Barnes, Jeremy Porter and Jim McCoy, like to meet over enchiladas and margueritas at university-style cafes. They always seemed to have three or four projects on the run. Digital cash was the flavour of the month when I met them. They were unconventional, perhaps even a little weird, but they were also bright, very creative and highly innovative. They were just the sort of people who might marry creative ideas with maturity and business sense, eventually making widespread digital cash a reality.

I began to wonder how many of the young men in Room 518 might follow the same path. And I asked myself: where are these people in Australia?

Largely invisible or perhaps even non-existent, it seems. Except maybe in the computer underground. The underground appears to be one of the few places in Australia where madness, creativity, obsession, addiction and rebellion collide like atoms in a cyclotron.

❖

After the raids, the arrests and the court cases on three continents, what became of the hackers described in this book?

Most of them went on to do interesting and constructive
things with their lives. Those who were interviewed for this
work say they have given up hacking for good. After what
many of them had been through, I would be surprised if any of
them continued hacking.

Most of them, however, are not sorry for their hacking activities. Some are sorry they upset people. They feel badly that
they caused system admins stress and unhappiness by hacking
their systems. But most do not feel hacking is wrong – and few,
if any, feel that 'look-see hacking', as prosecuting barrister Geoff
Chettle termed non-malicious hacking, should be a crime.

For the most part, their punishments have only hardened
their views on the subject. They know that in many cases
the authorities have sought to make examples of them, for the
benefit of rest of the computer underground. The state has
largely failed in this objective. In the eyes of many in the
computer underground, these prosecuted hackers are heroes.

PAR
When I met Par in Tucson, Arizona, he had travelled from a
tiny, snow-laden Mid-Western town where he was living with
his grandparents. He was looking for work, but hadn't been
able to find anything.

As I drove around the outskirts of Tucson, a little jetlagged
and disoriented, I was often distracted from the road by the
beauty of the winter sun on the Sonoran Desert cacti. Sitting
in the front passenger seat, Par said calmly, 'I always wondered
what it would be like to drive on the wrong side of the road'.

I swerved back to the right side of the road.

Par is still like that. Easy-going, rolling with the punches,
taking what life hands him. He is also on the road again.

He moved back to the west coast for a while, but will likely
pack up and go somewhere else before long. He picks up temporary work where he can, often just basic, dull data-entry

stuff. It isn't easy. He can't just explain away a four-year gap in his resumé with 'Successfully completed a telecommuting course for fugitives. Trained by the US Secret Service'. He thought he might like to work at a local college computer lab, helping out the students and generally keeping the equipment running. Without any professional qualifications, that seemed an unlikely option these days.

Although he is no longer a fugitive, Par's life hasn't changed that much. He speaks to his mother very occasionally, though they don't have much in common. Escaping his computer crimes charges proved easier than overcoming the effects of being a fugitive for so long on his personality and lifestyle. Now and again, the paranoia sets in again. It seems to come in waves. There aren't many support mechanisms in the US for an unemployed young man who doesn't have health insurance.

PRIME SUSPECT

Prime Suspect has no regrets about his choices. He believed that he and Mendax were headed in different directions in life. The friendship would have ended anyway, so he decided that he was not willing to go to prison for Mendax.

He completed a TAFE course in computer programming and found a job in the burgeoning Internet industry. He likes his job. His employer, who knows about his hacking convictions, recently gave him a pay rise. In mid-1994, he gave up drugs for good. In 1995 he moved into a shared house with some friends, and in August 1996 he stopped smoking cigarettes.

Without hacking, there seems to be time in his life to do new things. He took up sky-diving. A single jump gives him a high which lasts for days, sometimes up to a week. Girls have captured his interest. He's had a few girlfriends and thinks he would like to settle into a serious relationship when he finds the right person.

Recently, Prime Suspect has been studying martial arts. He tries to attend at least four classes a week, sometimes more, and says he has a special interest in the spiritual and philosophical sides of martial arts. Most days, he rises at 5 a.m., either to jog or to meditate.

MENDAX

In 1992 Mendax and Trax teamed up with a wealthy Italian real-estate investor, purchased La Trobe University's main-frame computer (ironically, a machine they had been accused of hacking) and started a computer security company. The company eventually dissolved when the investor disappeared following actions by his creditors.

After a public confrontation in 1993 with Victorian Premier Jeff Kennett, Mendax and two others formed a civil rights organisation to fight corruption and lack of accountability in a Victorian government department. As part of this ongoing effort, Mendax acted as a conduit for leaked documents and became involved in a number of court cases against the department during 1993–94. Eventually, he gave evidence in camera to a state parliamentary committee examining the issues, and his organisation later facilitated the appearance of more than 40 witnesses at an investigation by the Auditor-General.

Mendax volunteers his time and computer expertise for several other non-profit community organisations. He believes strongly in the importance of the non-profit sector, and spends much of his free time as an activist on different community projects. Mendax has provided information or assistance to law-enforcement bodies, but not against hackers. He said, 'I couldn't ethically justify that. But as for others, such as people who prey on children or corporate spies, I am not concerned about using my skills there.'

Still passionate about coding, Mendax donates his time to various international programming efforts and releases some of his programs for free on the Internet. His philosophy is that most of the lasting social advances in the history of man have been a direct result of new technology.

NorTel and a number of other organisations he was accused of hacking use his cryptography software – a fact he finds rather ironic.

ANTHRAX

Anthrax moved to Melbourne, where he is completing a university course and working on freelance assignments in the computer networking area of a major corporation.

His father and mother are divorcing. Anthrax doesn't talk to his father at all these days.

Anthrax's mother's health has stabilised somewhat since the completion of the court case, though her condition still gives her chronic pain. Despite some skin discolouration caused by the disease, she looks well. As a result of her years of work in the local community, she has a loyal group of friends who support her through bad bouts of the illness. She tries to live without bitterness and continues to have a good relationship with both her sons.

Anthrax is no longer involved in the Nation of Islam, but he is still a devout Muslim. An acquaintance of his, an Albanian who ran a local fish and chips shop, introduced him to a different kind of Islam. Not long after, Anthrax became a Sunni Muslim. He doesn't drink alcohol or gamble, and he attends a local mosque for Friday evening prayers. He tries to read from the Qu'ran every day and to practise the tenets of his religion faithfully.

With his computer and business skills now sought after by industry, he is exploring the possibility of moving to a Muslim country in Asia or the Middle East. He tries to promote the interests of Islam worldwide.

Most of his pranking needs are now met by commercial CDs – recordings of other people's pranking sold through underground magazines and American mail order catalogues. Once in a long while, he still rings Mr McKenny in search of the missing shovel.

Anthrax felt aggrieved at the outcome of his written complaint to the Office of the Ombudsman. In the complaint, Anthrax gave an account of how he believed the AFP had behaved inappropriately throughout his case. Specifically, he alleged that the AFP had pressured his mother with threats and had harassed him, taken photographs of him without his permission, given information to his university about his case prior to the issue of a summons and the resolution of his case, and made racist comments toward him during the raid.

In 1995–96, a total of 1157 complaints were filed against the AFP, 683 of which were investigated by the Commonwealth Ombudsman. Of the complaint investigations completed and reviewed, only 6 per cent were substantiated. Another 9 per cent were deemed to be 'incapable of determination', about 34 per cent were 'unsubstantiated', and in more than a quarter of all cases the Ombudsman either chose not to investigate or not to continue to investigate a complaint.

The Office of the Ombudsman referred Anthrax's matter to the AFP's Internal Investigations office. Although Anthrax and his mother both gave statements to the investigating officers, there was no other proof of Anthrax's allegations. In the end, it came down to Anthrax and his mother's words against those of the police.

The AFP's internal investigation concluded that Anthrax's complaints could either not be substantiated or not be determined, in part due to the fact that almost two years had passed since the original raid. For the most part, the Ombudsman backed the AFP's finding. No recommendation was made for the disciplining of any officers.

Anthrax's only consolation was a concern voiced by the Ombudsman's Office. Although the investigating officer agreed with the AFP investigators that the complaint could not be substantiated, she wrote, 'I am concerned that your mother felt she was compelled to pressure you into attending an interview based on a fear that she would be charged because her phone was used to perpetrate the offences'.

Anthrax remains angry and sceptical about his experience with the police. He believes a lot of things need to be changed about the way the police operate. Most of all, he believes that justice will never be assured in a system where the police are allowed to investigate themselves.

PAD AND GANDALF

After Pad and Gandalf were released from prison, they started up a free security advisory service on the Internet. One reason they began releasing 8lgm advisories, as they were known, was to help admins secure their own systems. The other reason was to thumb their noses at the conservatives in the security industry.

Many on the Internet considered the 8lgm advisories to be the best available at the time – far better than anything CERT had ever produced. Pad and Gandalf were sending their own message back to the establishment. The message, though never openly stated, was something like this: 'You busted us. You sent us to prison. But it didn't matter. You can't keep information like this secret. Further, we are still better than you ever were and, to prove it, we are going to beat you at your own game.'

Believing that the best way to keep a hacker out of your system is to secure it properly in the first place, the two British hackers rejected security gurus who refused to tell the world about new security holes. Their 8lgm advisories began marginalising the traditional industry security reports, and helped to push the industry toward its current, more open attitude.

Pad and Gandalf now both work, doing computer programming jobs on contract, sometimes for financial institutions. Their clients like them and value their work. Both have steady girlfriends.

Pad doesn't hack any more. The reason isn't the risk of getting caught or the threat of prison. He has stopped hacking because he has realised what a headache it is for a system administrator to clean up his or her computer after an attack. Searching through logs. Looking for backdoors the hacker might have left behind. The hours, the hassle, the pressure – he thinks it is wrong to put anyone through that. Pad understands far better now how much strain a hacker intrusion can cause another human being.

There is another reason Pad has given up hacking: he has simply outgrown the desire. He says that he has better things to do with his time. Computers are a way for him to earn a living, not a way to spend his leisure time. After a trip overseas he decided that real travel – not its electronic cousin – was more interesting than hacking. He has also learned to play the guitar, something he believes he would have done years ago if he hadn't spent so much time hacking.

Gandalf shares Pad's interest in travelling. One reason they like contract work is because it lets them work hard for six months, save some money, and then take a few months off. The aim of both ex-hackers for now is simply to sling backpacks over their shoulders and bounce around the globe.

Pad still thinks that Britain takes hacking far too seriously and he is considering moving overseas permanently. The 8lgm court case made him wonder about the people in power in Britain – the politicians, the judges, the law enforcement officers. He often thinks: what kind of people are running this show?

STUART GILL

In 1993, the Victorian Ombudsman[1] and the Victoria Police[2] both investigated the leaking of confidential police information in association with Operation Iceberg – a police investigation into allegations of corruption against Assistant Commissioner of Police Frank Green. Stuart Gill figured prominently in both reports.

The Victoria Police report concluded that 'Gill was able to infiltrate the policing environment by skilfully manipulating himself and information to the unsuspecting'. The Ombudsman concluded that a 'large quantity of confidential police information, mainly from the ISU database, was given to . . . Gill by [Victoria Police officer] Cosgriff'.

The police report stated that Inspector Chris Cosgriff had deliberately leaked confidential police information to Gill, and reported that he was 'besotted with Gill'. Superintendent Tony Warren, ex-Deputy Commissioner John Frame and ex-Assistant Commissioner Bernice Masterson were also criticised in the report.

The Ombudsman concluded that Warren and Cosgriff's relationship with Gill was 'primarily responsible for the release of confidential information'. Interestingly, however, the Ombudsman also stated, 'Whilst Mr Gill may have had his own agenda and taken advantage of his relationship with police, [the] police have equally used and in some cases misused Mr Gill for their own purposes'.

The Ombudsman's report further concluded that there was no evidence of criminal conduct by Frank Green, and that the 'allegations made over the years against Mr Green should have been properly and fully investigated at the time they were made'.

PHOENIX

As his court case played in the media, Phoenix was speeding on his motorcycle through an inner-city Melbourne street one rainy night when he hit a car. The car's driver leapt from the front seat and found a disturbing scene. Phoenix was sprawled across the road. His helmet had a huge crack on the side, where his head had hit the car's petrol tank, and petrol had spilled over the motorcycle and its rider.

Miraculously, Phoenix was unhurt, though very dazed. Some bystanders helped him and the distraught driver to a nearby halfway house. They called an ambulance, and then made the two traumatised young men some tea in the kitchen. Phoenix's mother arrived, called by a bystander at Phoenix's request. The ambulance workers confirmed that Phoenix had not broken any bones but they recommended he go to hospital to check for possible concussion.

Still both badly shaken, Phoenix and the driver exchanged names and phone numbers. Phoenix told the driver he did technical work for a 0055 telephone service, then said, 'You might recognise me. I'm Phoenix. There's this big computer hacking case going on in court – that's my case'.

The driver looked at him blankly.

Phoenix said, 'You might have seen me on the TV news.'

No, the driver said, somewhat amazed at the strange things which go through the dazed mind of a young man who has so narrowly escaped death.

Some time after Phoenix's close brush with death, the former hacker left his info-line technician's job and began working in the information technology division of a large Melbourne-based corporation. Well paid in his new job, Phoenix is seen, once again, as the golden-haired boy. He helped to write a software program which reduces waste in one of the production lines and reportedly saved the company thousands of dollars. Now he travels abroad regularly, to Japan and elsewhere.

He had a steady girlfriend for a time, but eventually she broke the relationship off to see other people. Heartbroken, he avoided dating for months. Instead, he filled his time with his ever-increasing corporate responsibilities.

His new interest is music. He plays electric guitar in an amateur band.

ELECTRON

A few weeks after his sentencing, Electron had another psychotic episode, triggered by a dose of speed. He was admitted to hospital again, this time at Larundel. After a short stay, he was released and underwent further psychiatric care.

Some months later, he did speed again, and suffered another bout of psychosis. He kept reading medical papers on the Internet about his condition and his psychiatrists worried that his detailed research might interfere with their ability to treat him.

He moved into special accommodation for people recovering from mental instabilities. Slowly, he struggled to overcome his illness. When people came up to him and said things like, 'What a nice day it is!' Electron willed himself to take their words at face value, to accept that they really were just commenting on the weather, nothing more. During this time, he quit drugs, alcohol and his much-hated accounting course. Eventually he was able to come off his psychiatric medicines completely. He hasn't taken drugs or had alcohol since December 1994. His only chemical vice in 1996 was cigarettes. By the beginning of 1997 he had also given up tobacco.

Electron hasn't talked to either Phoenix or Nom since 1992.

In early 1996, Electron moved into his own flat with his steady girlfriend, who studies dance and who also successfully overcame mental illness after a long, hard struggle. Electron began another university course in a philosophy-related field. This time university life agreed with him, and his first semester transcript showed honours grades in every class. He is considering moving to Sydney for further studies.

Electron worked off his 300 hours of community service by painting walls and doing minor handyman work at a local primary school. Among the small projects the school asked him to complete was the construction of a retaining wall. He designed and dug, measured and fortified. As he finished off the last of his court-ordered community service hours on the wall, he discovered that he was rather proud of his creation. Even now, once in a while, he drives past the school and looks at the wall.

It is still standing.

KEN DAY

Like their hacker targets, Day and his team also pushed the boundaries of technology. In the early 1990s, these Australians achieved a significant world-first: they successfully ran data taps on modems. People had recorded data flows from modems before but it came out as gobbledygook. Day's team, under the deft technical hand of the former AFP Sergeant David Costello, figured out a way of capturing the live chat sessions that resulted in text as readable as any online conversation today. This was also believed to be the first modem-tapped text ever submitted as evidence in a court case. I say 'believed to be' only because it is not known what capabilities the NSA and other powerful spy agencies had at the time. However Day's team scoured the world over for the technology at the time – including reaching out to intelligence contacts – without any luck.

In a display of Australian practical resourcefulness, they decided to make the modem-tapping technology themselves. They acquired all the relevant hardware on a shoestring budget and Costello went to work with hands on experimenting until it worked.

'We achieved a lot at the end of the day with bugger-all money,' Day said. 'The budget we had was effectively wages. Most of the equipment was from home.'

Some members of his team were disappointed that the hackers they pursued didn't receive prison sentences, but Day encouraged them to be philosophical about it.

'You gather the evidence, then the court decides,' he said. 'The police don't make the decisions, they [only] have the power to investigate. What is most important is not to cross the line: that line is sacrosanct. If you do, you become a vigilante,' he said.

'We stopped a lot of people from doing harm. We just got a bucket of water and poured it over a group of people who were heating up too much.'

After nearly 15 years in the AFP, Day left to work in the private sector. He worked at a consulting firm with an IT practice and at a large financial institution in risk management. He still works in business.

There are still hacking cases in Australia. About the same time as Mendax's case was being heard in Victoria, The Crawler pleaded guilty to 23 indictable offences and thirteen summary offences – all hacking related charges – in Brisbane District Court. On 20 December 1996, the 21-year-old Queenslander was given a three-year suspended prison sentence, ordered to pay $5000 in reparations to various organisations, and made to forfeit his modem and two computers. The first few waves of hackers may have come and gone, but hacking is far from dead. It is merely less visible.

Law enforcement agencies and the judiciaries of several countries have tried to send a message to the next generation of would-be hackers. The message is this: Don't hack.

But the next generation of elite hackers and phreakers have heard a very different message, a message which says: Don't get caught.

The principle of deterrence has not worked with hackers at this level. I'm not talking here about the codes-kids – the teeny-bopper, carding, wanna-be nappies who hang out on IRC (Internet relay chat). I'm talking about the elite hackers. If anything, law enforcement crackdowns have not only pushed them further underground, they have encouraged hackers to become more sophisticated than ever before in the way they protect themselves. Adversity is the mother of invention.

When police officers march through the front door of a hacker's home today, they may be better prepared than their predecessors, but they will also be facing bigger hurdles. Today, top hackers encrypt everything sensitive. The data on their hard drives, their live data connections, even their voice conversations.

So, if hackers are still hacking, who are their targets?

It is a broad field. Any type of network provider – X.25, cellular phone or large Internet provider. Computer vendors – the manufacturers of software and hardware, routers, gateways, firewalls or phone switches. Military institutions, governments and banks seem to be a little less fashionable these days, though there are still plenty of attacks on these sorts of sites.

Attacks on security experts are still common, but a new trend is the increase in attacks on other hackers' systems. One Australian hacker joked, 'What are the other hackers going to do? Call the Feds? Tell the AFP, "Yes, officer, that's right, some computer criminal broke into my machine and stole 20 000 passwords and all my exploitation code for bypassing firewalls".'

For the most part, elite hackers seem to work alone, because of the well-advertised risks of getting caught. There are still some underground hacking communities frequented by top hackers, most notably UPT in Canada and a few groups like the l0pht in the US, but such groups are far less common, and more fragmented than they used to be.

These hackers have reached a new level of sophistication, not just in the technical nature of their attacks, but in their strategies and objectives. Once, top hackers such as Electron and Phoenix were happy to get copies of Zardoz, which listed security holes found by industry experts. Now top hackers find those holes themselves – by reading line by line through the proprietary source code from places like DEC, HP, CISCO, Sun and Microsoft.

Industrial espionage does not seem to be on the agenda, at least with anyone I interviewed. I have yet to meet a hacker who has given proprietary source code to a vendor's competitor. I have, however, met a hacker who found one company's proprietary source code inside the computer of its competitor. Was that a legal copy of the source code? Who knows? The hacker didn't think so, but he kept his mouth shut about it, for obvious reasons.

Most of the time, these hackers want to keep their original bugs as quiet as possible, so vendors won't release patches.

The second popular target is source code development machines. The top hackers have a clear objective in this area: to install their own backdoors before the product is released. They call it 'backdooring' a program or an operating system. The word 'backdoor' is now used as both a noun and a verb in the underground. Hackers are very nervous discussing this subject, in part because they don't want to see a computer company's stock dive and people lose their jobs.

What kind of programs do these hackers want to backdoor? Targets mentioned include at least one major Internet browser, a popular game, an Internet packet filter and a database product used by law enforcement agencies.

A good backdoor is a very powerful device, creating a covert channel through even the most sturdy of firewalls into the heart of an otherwise secure network. In a net browser, a backdoor would in theory allow a hacker to connect directly into someone's home computer every time he or she wandered around the web. However, don't expect hackers to invade your suburban home just yet. Most elite hackers couldn't care less about the average person's home computer.

Perhaps you are wondering who might be behind this sort of attack. What sort of person would do this? There are no easy answers to that question. Some hackers are good people, some are bad, just like any group of people. The next generation of elite hackers are a diverse bunch, and relaying their stories would take another book entirely. However, I would like to introduce you to just one, to give you a window into the future.

SKiMo

A European living outside Australia, SKiMo has been hacking for at least four years, although he probably only joined the ranks of world-class hackers in 1995 or 1996. Never busted. Young – between the age of 18 and 25 – and male. From a less than picture-perfect family. Fluent in English as a second language. Left-leaning in his politics – heading toward environmentally green parties and anarchy rather than traditional labour parties. Smokes a little dope and drinks alcohol, but doesn't touch the hard stuff.

His musical tastes include early Pink Floyd, Sullen, Dog Eat Dog, Biohazard, old Ice-T, Therapy?, Alanis Morissette, Rage Against the Machine, Fear Factory, Life of Agony and Napalm Death. He reads Stephen King, Stephen Hawking, Tom Clancy and Aldous Huxley. And any good books about physics, chemistry or mathematics.

Shy in person, he doesn't like organised team sports and is not very confident around girls. He has only had one serious girlfriend, but the relationship finished. Now that he hacks and codes about four to five hours per day on average, but sometimes up to 36 hours straight, he doesn't have time for girls.

'Besides,' he says, 'I am rather picky when it comes to girls. Maybe if the girl shared the same interests . . . but those ones are hard to find.' He adds, by way of further explanation, 'Girls are different from hacking. You can't just brute force them if all else fails.'

SKiMo has never intentionally damaged a computer system, nor would he. Indeed, when I asked him, he was almost offended by the question. However, he has accidentally done damage on a few occasions. In at least one case, he returned to the system and fixed the problem himself.

Bored out of his mind for most of his school career, SKiMo spent a great deal of time reading books in class – openly. He wanted to send the teacher a message without actually jacking up in class.

He got into hacking after reading a magazine article about people who hacked answering machines and VMBs. At that time, he had no idea what a VMB was, but he learned fast. One Sunday evening, he sat down with his phone and began scanning. Soon he was into phreaking, and visiting English-speaking party lines. Somehow, he always felt more comfortable speaking in English, to native English-speakers, perhaps because he felt a little like an outsider in his own culture.

'I have always had the thought to leave my country as soon as I can,' he said.

From the phreaking, it was a short jump into hacking.

What made him want to hack or phreak in the first place? Maybe it was the desire to screw over the universally hated phone company, or 'possibly the sheer lust for power' or then again, maybe he was simply answering his desire 'to explore an intricate piece of technology'. Today, however, he is a little clearer on why he continues to hack. 'My first and foremost motivation is to learn,' he said.

When asked why he doesn't visit his local university or library to satisfy that desire, he answered, 'in books, you only learn theory. It is not that I dislike the theory but computer security in real life is much different from theory'. Libraries also have trouble keeping pace with the rate of technological change, SKiMo said. 'Possibly, it is also just the satisfaction of knowing that what I learn is proprietary – is "inside knowledge",' he added. There could, he said, be some truth in the statement that he likes learning in an adrenalin-inducing environment.

Is he addicted to computers? SKiMo says no, but the indications are there. By his own estimate, he has hacked between 3000 and 10000 computers in total. His parents – who have no idea what their son was up to day and night on his computer – worry about his behaviour. They pulled the plug on his machine many times. In SKiMo's own words, 'they tried everything to keep me away from it'.

Not surprisingly, they failed. SKiMo became a master at hiding his equipment so they couldn't sneak in and take it away. Finally, when he got sick of battling them over it and he was old enough, he put his foot down. 'I basically told them, "Diz is ma fuckin' life and none o' yer business, Nemo" – but not in those words.'

SKiMo says he hasn't suffered from any mental illnesses or instabilities – except perhaps paranoia. But he says that paranoia is justified in his case. In two separate incidents in 1996, he believed he was being followed. Try as he might, he couldn't shake the tails for quite some time. Perhaps it was just a coincidence, but he can never really be sure.

He described one hacking attack to me to illustrate his current interests. He managed to get inside the internal network of a German mobile phone network provider, DeTeMobil (Deutsche Telekom). A former state-owned enterprise which was transformed into a publicly listed corporation in January 1995, Deutsche Telekom is the largest telecommunications company in Europe and ranks number three in the world as a network operator. It employs almost a quarter of a million people. By revenue, which totalled about $A37 billion in 1995, it is one of the five largest companies in Germany.

After carefully researching and probing a site, SKiMo unearthed a method of capturing the encryption keys generated for DeTeMobil's mobile phone conversations.

He explained: 'The keys are not fixed, in the sense that they are generated once and then stored in some database.

Rather, a key is generated for each phone conversation by the company's AUC [authentication centre], using the "Ki" and a random value generated by the AUC. The Ki is the secret key that is securely stored on the smart card [inside the cellphone], and a copy is also stored in the AUC. When the AUC "tells" the cellphone the key for that particular conversation, the information passes through the company's MSC [mobile switching centre].

'It is possible to eavesdrop on a certain cellphone if one actively monitors either the handovers or the connection set-up messages from the OMC [operations and maintenance centre] or if one knows the Ki in the smart card.

'Both options are entirely possible. The first option, which relies on knowing the A5 encryption key, requires the right equipment. The second option, using the Ki, means you have to know the A3/A8 algorithms as well or the Ki is useless. These algorithms can be obtained by hacking the switch manufacturer, i.e. Siemens, Alcatel, Motorola . . .

'As a call is made from the target cellphone, you need to feed the A5 key into a cellphone which has been modified to let it eavesdrop on the channel used by the cellphone. Normally, this eavesdropping will only produce static – since the conversation is encrypted. However, with the keys and equipment, you can decode the conversation.'

This is one of the handover messages, logged with a CCITT7 link monitor, that he saw:

```
13:54:46"3 4Rx< SCCP 12-2-09-1 12-2-04-0 13 CR
BSSM HOREQ
BSSMAP GSM 08.08 Rev 3.9.2 (BSSM) HaNDover REQuest
(HOREQ)
 – – – -0 Discrimination bit D BSSMAP
0000000- Filler
00101011 Message Length 43
00010000 Message Type 0x10
Channel Type
```

00001011 IE Name Channel type
00000011 IE Length 3
00000001 Speech/Data Indicator Speech
00001000 Channel Rate/Type Full rate TCH channel Bm
00000001 Speech Encoding Algorithm GSM speech algorithm Ver 1
Encryption Information
00001010 IE Name Encryption information
00001001 IE Length 9
00000010 Algorithm ID GSM user data encryption V. 1
******** Encryption Key C9 7F 45 7E 29 8E 08 00
Classmark Information Type 2
00010010 IE Name Classmark information type 2
00000010 IE Length 2
− − -001 RF power capability Class 2, portable
− -00 − - Encryption algorithm Algorithm A5
000 − − - Revision level
− − -000 Frequency capability Band number 0
− − 1 − - SM capability present
-000 − − Spare
0 − − − - Extension
Cell Identifier
00000101 IE Name Cell identifier
00000101 IE Length 5
00000001 Cell ID discriminator LAC/CI used to ident cell
******** LAC 4611
******** CI 3000
PRIority
00000110 IE Name Priority
00000001 IE Length 1
− − − -0 Preemption allowed ind not allowed
− − − 0- Queueing allowed ind not allowed
− 0011 − Priority level 3
00 − − − Spare
Circuit Identity Code
00000001 IE Name Circuit identity code

```
00000000 PCM Multiplex a-h 0
– -11110 Timeslot in use 30
101 – – - PCM Multiplex i-k 5
Downlink DTX flag
00011001 IE Name Downlink DTX flag
– – – -1 DTX in downlink direction disabled
0000000- Spare
Cell Identifier
00000101 IE Name Cell identifier
00000101 IE Length 5
00000001 Cell ID discriminator LAC/CI used to ident cell
******** LAC 4868
******** CI 3200
```

The beauty of a digital mobile phone, as opposed to the analogue mobile phones still used by some people in Australia, is that a conversation is reasonably secure from eavesdroppers. If I call you on my digital mobile, our conversation will be encrypted with the A5 encryption algorithm between the mobile phone and the exchange. The carrier has copies of the Kis and, in some countries, the government can access these copies. They are, however, closely guarded secrets.

SKiMo had access to the database of the encrypted Kis and access to some of the unencrypted Kis themselves. At the time, he never went to the trouble of gathering enough information about the A3 and A8 algorithms to decrypt the full database, though it would have been easy to do so. However, he has now obtained that information.

To SKiMo, access to the keys generated for each of thousands of German mobile phone conversations was simply a curiosity – and a trophy. He didn't have the expensive equipment required to eavesdrop. To an intelligence agency, however, access could be very valuable, particularly if some of those phones belonged to people such as politicians. Even more valuable would be ongoing access to the OMC, or better still, the MSC. SkiMo said he would not provide this to any intelligence agency.

While inside DeTeMobil, SKiMo also learned how to interpret some of the mapping and signal-strength data. The result? If one of the company's customers has his mobile turned on, SKiMo says he can pinpoint the customer's geographic location to within one kilometre. The customer doesn't even have to be talking on the mobile. All he has to do is have the phone turned on, waiting to receive calls.

SKiMo tracked one customer for an afternoon, as the man travelled across Germany, then called the customer up. It turned out they spoke the same European language.

'Why are you driving from Hamburg to Bremen with your phone on stand-by mode?' SKiMo asked.

The customer freaked out. How did this stranger at the end of the phone know where he had been travelling?

SKiMo said he was from Greenpeace. 'Don't drive around so much. It creates pollution,' he told the bewildered mobile customer. Then he told the customer about the importance of conserving energy and how prolonged used of mobile phones affected certain parts of one's brain.

Originally, SKiMo broke into the mobile phone carriers' network because he wanted 'to go completely cellular' – a transition which he hoped would make him both mobile and much harder to trace. Being able to eavesdrop on other people's calls – including those of the police – was going to be a bonus.

However, as he pursued this project, he discovered that the code from a mobile phone manufacturer which he needed to study was 'a multi-lingual project'. 'I don't know whether you have ever seen a multi-lingual project,' SKiMo says, 'where nobody defines a common language that all programmers must use for their comments and function names? They look horrible. They are no fun to read.' Part of this one was in Finnish.

SKiMo says he has hacked a number of major vendors and, in several cases, has had access to their products' source codes.

Has he had the access to install backdoors in primary source code for major vendors? Yes. Has he done it? He says no. On other hand, I asked him who he would tell if he did do it. 'No-one,' he said, 'because there is more risk if two people know than if one does.'

SKiMo is mostly a loner these days. He shares a limited amount of information about hacking exploits with two people, but the conversations are usually carefully worded or vague. He substitutes a different vendor's names for the real one, or he discusses technical computer security issues in an in-depth but theoretical manner, so he doesn't have to name any particular system.

He doesn't talk about anything to do with hacking on the telephone. Mostly, when he manages to capture a particularly juicy prize, he keeps news of his latest conquest to himself.

It wasn't always that way. 'When I started hacking and phreaking, I had the need to learn very much and to establish contacts which I could ask for certain things – such as technical advice,' SKiMo said. 'Now I find it much easier to get that info myself than asking anyone for it. I look at the source code, then experiment and discover new bugs myself.'

Asked if the ever-increasing complexity of computer technology hasn't forced hackers to work in groups of specialists instead of going solo, he said in some cases yes, but in most cases, no. 'That is only true for people who don't want to learn everything.'

SKiMo can't see himself giving up hacking any time in the near future.

The early hacking world portrayed in this book seems innocent by today's standards of organised crime and military vigilante hacking groups. It's good to be reminded that the roots of this tree were a youthful curiosity that was more about adventure than serious crime. Yet now we live in a world of electronic strip searches at airports and government-sponsored cyber wars with publishers and nations alike. The early computer underground was where it all began. Ironically, the core values of the underground may also be where it could end.

Ken Day, the former head of Australian Federal Police Computer Crimes Unit, ran the first big anti-hacking investigations in Australia. Operations Dabble and Weather rounded up Phoenix, Electronic, Nom, Mendax, Prime Suspect and Trax and brought them to court. A psychological player well suited to his quarry, Day knew how to put together a brief of evidence and run a tight operation. He is a law and order guy.

Yet Day believes the idea behind WikiLeaks, created by former Australian hacker Julian Assange who worked with me on this book, is a *good* one.

WikiLeaks is sometimes described as a cyber trouble-maker, guerilla publisher or an anarchist whistleblower site, clearly because it pushes limits. It is believed to be the first dedicated incarnation of 'Sunshine Journalism', which shines a bright light on government and corporate lies and wrong-doing by publishing original source documents that present an unspun truth. In essence, they *prove* the truth. The reader can check the truth of the journalist's story by going to the original document.

The site has early hacker ethos written all over it: information should be free and in the public domain, technology can be used to push the existing boundaries of society, forbidden information is fair game. How then does a former G-man come to believe in principle that WikiLeaks is a good thing?

'Government influence over media reporting and the lack of independence of the media to tell the public the truth is a big concern,' he said. By his estimation this began in a significant way in the mid-1990s and it has evolved from then. He thinks governments are getting away with lying to their people. 'People don't like that,' he said.

'WikiLeaks is a reaction to a weakened media. The established media do not necessarily report what society should know – that is why WikiLeaks is succeeding. It is fulfilling a role that has been ignored for too long,' he said.

'I'm not anti-war and I'm not against government secrets. There is a time and place for each. But the balance is wrong; it needs to come back to an equilibrium.'

So where does this hacker-catcher think that elusive equilibrium should be?

'The equilibrium is where a government is loath to lie to the people for fear the truth will come out,' he explained. For Day, WikiLeaks ticks that box.

This isn't to say that Day thinks WikiLeaks is perfect. The execution could be improved, he says, but the idea is right. First generation creations always have problems. 'No one has done it before so how can you get it right the first time?' he says. 'There is no path to follow.'

'The important thing about history is it gives us warning signs and it repeats itself.' Day believes there are warning signs in abundance about the erosions of our freedoms and rights. The question is what we will do about it.

'Right now there is apathy,' he said. 'It's an evolutionary thing, a thought process. Right now a lot of people aren't doing anything about it.' However, WikiLeaks is slowly rousing the people from their long sleep and beginning to create change.

The most worrying thing that Day sees in these warning signs is the erosion of individual rights. Where governments look after the rights of individuals, you have a healthy democracy. However, where that fails, 'we become extremely cynical toward politicians and the media,' he said.

Why does Day think this change is necessary? He believes that if the current situation of governments misleading the people continues unchecked, a possible outcome at the extreme end could be anarchy.

'When people don't believe or trust or respect the government, they won't follow any of its laws. Many countries in the world are in this state – you don't have to look far to see it. There are plenty of examples in a number of African countries. A lack of respect for government can result in anarchy.'

It's a powerful observation and one which he has clearly spent a great deal of time considering. Italy has complicated, expensive and archaic laws for tax and administration of small businesses. Italians have little respect for their government in this area and there is little trust in how the government spends their tax money. How many people in Italy adhere to all these small business administrative regulations and taxes? Probably very few. Worse, everyone in Italy simply accepts this as normal. The government has failed and the people, like good hackers, have developed a work-around solution. The heart of that solution is a kind of administrative anarchy.

In listening to Day speak about this topic, it's easy to see how the cop in him is repelled by the idea of anarchy. He spent almost 15 years of his life not only obeying the law, but enforcing it. Disrespect for the law is disturbing to him.

Here comes the interesting paradox. The anarchist-inspired ethos of the early computer underground has contributed to a new creation – WikiLeaks. Yet the existence of this publisher with its single-minded intent to publish or perish *may be the very thing that ultimately prevents the spread of anarchy*. It may be the frontline of the push to put an end to the Secret State and its oppressive security. For just that reason, this new media creation is embraced by those who have fought on both sides of the computer underground – the orderly and the anarchists. Neither side wants to see rights and protections quietly stolen away. That is what I meant when I said at the start that the values of the early computer underground could also be the end of this era of ubiquitous surveillance.

When ex-cops stand side by side with ex-hackers on an issue, you know change is in the air.

Somewhere in the decade from 2000 to 2010, parts of George Orwell's *1984* became a reality.

Room 101, the Ministry of Love's torture chamber in Orwell's famous book, exists in airports across the United States. People are detained without any law enforcement motive other than intimidation. People's computers and phones are confiscated, searched, copied, and seized. There is no need for a warrant, for a judge to sign off on anything. Passengers are groped by beefy, po-faced security guards, and effectively stripped naked by electronic scans. The US Constitution's guarantee against unreasonable searches and seizures has simply been tossed out the window.

American Jake Appelbaum went to Europe only to agonise about how safe it would be for him to come back home to Seattle in early 2011. He is well-respected in the international technical community as a hacker in the original sense of the word – someone who creates interesting technical solutions to problems (but not illegal ones). He also happens to have volunteered with WikiLeaks. Appelbaum is under daily surveillance. All travel, all emails, twitters, all transactions go directly to the Ministry of Truth and Freedom. Most recently, he decided he could only return to his native country by scheduling lawyers from the American Civil Liberties Union (ACLU) to meet him at the airport.[1] When he arrived, the US Customs and Border Protection (CPB) officer was waiting for him at the gate.[2] Customs detained, searched and attempted to interrogate him – and denied him access to his waiting lawyers.

Pause and consider that: an American who no longer feels safe coming home to his own country without a posse of lawyers to protect him from his own government. He's committed no crime. The government does not need to give any justification for its continual harassment. For the modern security state, they do it because they can. They use technology to expand the comprehensiveness of surveillance at the same pace that we in the mainstream population expand our desktop machines' speed and power. For governments, it's a kind of Moore's Law of Surveillance: if they can double the reach each year, they should – and do. This is an alarming state of affairs for many.

Closer to home, the message Jake Appelbaum received echoes the same one Julian Assange received from the Australian Attorney General Robert McClelland in late 2010: you are a citizen but you are not welcome back in your country. McClelland also considered cancelling Julian's passport, for reasons that he could not or would not give.

Julian's response was swift and devastating. 'I am an Australian citizen and I miss my country a great deal . . . Are we all to be treated like David Hicks at the first possible opportunity merely so that Australian politicians and diplomats can be invited to the best US embassy cocktail parties?' he said.[3]

There was an enormous backlash against McClelland and the Prime Minister, who had supported the Attorney General's position. They had grossly miscalculated the Australian public's attitude to WikiLeaks and the persecution of its publisher. Indeed, one political commentator observed privately to me that he had not seen an Australian Government misread the public's attitude so badly for more than a decade. At that time – the very time I was writing the original version of this book – the French began testing nuclear weapons in the Pacific again. The Keating Government gave a half-hearted 'tsk-tsk' as a response, and then tried to ignore the issue. They had no idea what hit them at the voter coal face. Marches on the streets, giant anti-French Government billboards, boycotts of French wine – the anger at then French President Jacques Chirac was palpable across Australia. In 1995–1996, you could buy a T-shirt for $10 on the streets of Melbourne that had a picture of the then French president with the caption 'Fuck Chirac'.

At the end of 2010, you could join hundreds of others to attend a rally to support WikiLeaks in your choice of Melbourne, Sydney or Brisbane in direct defiance of the country's first female Prime Minister Julia Gillard and her Attorney General. At one such rally, a placard read, 'Julian NOT Julia.'

The backlash came from both sides of politics, from within the Prime Minister's own Labor Party and from the conservative side of politics. They made strange bedfellows, but perhaps no stranger than the ex-cop and the ex-hacker.

Good people were stepping forward, whatever their political shade. It was about good people not standing idly by as rights are secretly abducted in the middle of the night to be tried, sentenced and executed under cover of darkness. The need for fairness runs like lifeblood through the Australian national body. Australians started to realise that what has been going on is quite simply *unfair*. And this unfairness offended them deeply.

Anti-authoritarian tendencies may not be universal, but they are integral to the successful operation of free democracies. We do not want a world where critics – or journalists – are 'warmly institutionalized' by government bureaucracies.[4] We rely on people who are prepared to challenge the system. These tendencies, which so clearly play out as a theme in the early computer underground, also happen to be very Australian. Perhaps that is why the early underground thrived so well in the sunburnt country.

We should have known how the world was going to unfold in the years since the events described in this book took place.

Cyberwar is now a reality, and the US military doesn't need a congressional stamp of approval to launch one. In addition to the Army, Navy, Marines, Coast Guard and Air Forces, there is now also the United States Cyber Command. And it too has its own offensive and defensive units. It has its own emblem, complete with an American eagle and a globe with a grid overlay. It also has an encrypted message which perhaps symbolises the puzzle as to what it does.

At one time, the WANK worm (the Worm Against Nuclear Killers) was the world's first worm with a political bent. It roamed the networks of the US Department of Energy and NASA. Possibly created by one or more young Australian hackers, it was clever, annoying and a little messy but did no real lasting damage. Now there is Stuxnet which, after WikiLeaks, was probably the biggest technology story of 2010 and certainly the biggest worm of the year.

WikiLeaks created an international news sensation on 16 July 2010 by announcing that a major nuclear incident had occurred in Iran.[5] This incident turned out to be not a political worm but a military worm with destructive intent – Stuxnet. It seems all sorts of worms had turned. About the same time, Julian was prosecuting the case for peace – a defiant ex-hacker presenting evidence from Afghanistan on the 'squalor of war' (July 25).[6]

The Stuxnet story illustrates how worms have transformed from youthful experiments to potent weapons of the military, and how it is the intelligence agencies who are now the hackers. In April 2009, there had been urgent behind-the-scene efforts to block a shipment of Siemens controllers from leaving Dubai and entering Iran.[7] It seems this stalling exercise was successful for a time. We know both these facts because of the American diplomatic cables released by WikiLeaks. By June 2009, computer security software maker Symantec was reporting on a worm it had found in the 'wild' – a term used in the computer security industry to describe worms, viruses and other attack devices that are captured from the broader online community. This worm was roaming around computer networks in India, Indonesia and Iran. It did not behave like the malicious worms that Symantec's security engineers see regularly. It was not taking down computer networks or targeting end users' machines looking to steal bank account details. It hit very selected targets. Ralph Langner, an independent German computer security expert who dissected Stuxnet and determined what the code actually did, described the narrow aim as being 'a marksman's job' that made sure 'only ... designated targets were hit'.[8]

A highly sophisticated attack worm, Stuxnet was probably written by a team of people, and they clearly knew what they were doing. Programmed to monitor, control and reprogram very specific industrial processes, the worm then cleverly hid its footprints as it gallivanted through an estimated 100 000 systems worldwide. In particular it appears to have attacked Siemens' systems in the nuclear power program in Iran where it messed with the centrifuges in that country's uranium enrichment plants.[9] This it apparently did very successfully, when hundreds of centrifuges suddenly stopped producing the materials needed to meet Iran's nuclear agenda.

There is evidence that the Stuxnet worm came from some sort of joint Israeli and American intelligence operation, possibly with American help.[10,11] Undoubtedly some of the millennium generation of hackers has ended up in jobs like these: on intelligence agency tiger teams working for the American and other governments designing a new sort of weapon. Stories circulate through my contacts in the Australian underground of technically adept people suddenly disappearing, leaving a faint trail to the doors of the Defence Signals Directorate. DSD is Canberra's electronic spy agency which bears the motto 'Reveal their secrets – protect our own'. Amusingly, DSD's web page carries a recruiting advertisement to join 'cyber operations' complete with a photo of a scruffy haired, unshaven young man wearing a hoodie. It shouts, hey, you don't need a crew cut, an early morning start or a military salute to come work for us.

The US intelligence agencies spend large amounts of money buying information about security holes before those holes are made public. Keeping these valuable discoveries secret is part of the deal so that the American cyber military can use them to break into places it isn't supposed to be. One of my contacts discovered a hole in a commonly used operating system and it was 'valued' by the grey market at about USD $40 000. The 'grey market' is made up of shadowy middlemen who broker the link between the US Government and the hacker who is selling the security vulnerability information. USD $40 000 is relatively small potatoes, with higher potency discoveries commonly fetching more than USD $100 000. I asked my contact what stops the hacker from selling the secret – and then claiming all the glory that goes with making it public. He replied that it was very well understood in the underground that bad things might happen to people who did that.

The fact that Stuxnet used not one but four different new security vulnerabilities[12] points strongly to it being the creation of an intelligence agency or agencies. Aside from the expensive man hours that went into writing the code and testing the worm, the four vulnerabilities alone could be worth nearly half a million dollars. An amateur hacker would not have wasted so many security vulnerabilities on one worm. Alternatively, a hacker working for the criminal underworld might have used the vulnerabilities to write a worm that stole credit cards from thousands of home PCs, instead of disabling an obscure Siemens controller associated with operating centrifuges.

Although no country has taken responsibility for Stuxnet, the media reports about the worm smell of gloating by the US and Israeli governments – the kind of gloating that comes from the pleasure of a job well done.

While Stuxnet garnered the headlines, a much darker element of the worm-as-cyber-weapon story has received less attention in the hacker community. At the same time Stuxnet was weaving through Iran's nuclear facility computers, someone was assassinating university professors and scientists in Iran. On 29 November 2011, someone tried to murder two senior Iranian nuclear scientists with similarly timed bombs.[13] Dr Majid Shahriari, a member of the nuclear engineering department of Shahid Beheshti University, was killed. A second scientist, Dr Fereydoon Abbasi, was seriously injured.[14] Both their wives, who were in the cars at the time, were also wounded. There is scant information about how badly both women were injured, whether they were burned by the blasts or lost limbs. Shahriari had no known links to banned nuclear work and was not a political figure at all.[15,16] These bomb attacks followed the bomb assassination of Dr Massoud Ali Mohammadi, 50, a quantum physics professor at Tehran University[17] in January 2010, and the mysterious poison gas murder of yet another professor, Ardashir Hosseinpour, also a scientist, in Iran in 2007.[18] Other scientists with him at the time may also have been injured or killed.[19]

There is no gloating to the world's media about the assassinations of these academics. No one has claimed responsibility for this string of murders. Perhaps some day someone who knows the truth about these crimes will feel a deep sense of injustice. Perhaps they will leak the truth to the world using technology developed by ex-hackers who chose not to work for government spy agencies.

American painter Robert Shetterly observed that, 'The greatness of our country is being tested and will be measured not by its military might but by its restraint, compassion, and wisdom.'[20] In response to the changing world order of the past decade, Shetterly set out to paint a series of portraits of 50 great Americans who refused to be cowed or silenced. It is aptly entitled 'Americans who tell the truth'. His observation applies to all free societies that lay claim to the moral high ground of democracy and greatness, including our own.

The peacetime internet occurred when this book was written in the 1990s before the start of the era of war – the Iraq War, the Afghan war, the War on Terror, the undeclared cyber wars on China, Iran and the Russian mafia. Now we look back to that time as a sort of Paradise Lost – the peacetime internet of incredible growth and innovation. The ideas we are now debating – such as freedom of information – sprang to life from this fertile ground. There was free trade, free information, and unprecedented freedom of expression. *That* was the peace dividend.

With the decade of war that followed, digital security dominated all else on the net. This decade of digital security dominance is now defining the nature of our freedoms. We can no longer walk down a street without being watched and there is snooping on virtually every transaction we engage in. There is an Orwellian eeriness to the now famous YouTube video of the plane passenger being groped by US airport security and saying 'don't touch my junk' (private parts), while the airport loudspeaker's recorded messaging plays in the background, 'Security is everybody's responsibility'. Yet few people have commented on how creepy this recording is juxtaposed with the innocent citizen being manhandled in the name of security.[21]

What if all our freedoms were slowly stolen away from us and we didn't even notice it?

No one refers today to the Founding Fathers of the United States as reckless freedom-seekers. No one says they were trouble-makers with anarchist tendencies. Was George Washington reckless and irresponsible to take on the world's biggest army? No doubt the British government of the day considered him to be so.

Underground has tried to answer many questions about the early computer underground. It has helped to set the context for the difficult questions society must now ask itself about what path it wants to take in the future. Have we now arrived at a place where only the curious or the reckless can rescue us from the surveillance state and the secret state? I hope not, but only time will tell. In the meantime, somewhere out there I suspect there will always be people thinking outside the box, questioning the powers that be and pushing the limits of technology and society.

Suelette Dreyfus

AARNET Australian Academic Research Network

ACARB Australian Computer Abuse Research Bureau, once called CITCARB

AFP Australian Federal Police

Altos West German chat system and hacker hang-out, connected to X.25 network and run by Altos Computer Systems, Hamburg

ANU Australian National University

ASIO Australian Security Intelligence Organisation

Backdoor A program or modification providing secret access to a computer system, installed by a hacker to bypass normal security. Also used as a verb

BBS Bulletin Board System

BNL Brookhaven National Laboratory (US)

BRL Ballistics Research Laboratory (US)

BT British Telecom

CCITT Committee Consultatif Internationale Telegraph et Telephonie: Swiss telecommunications standards body (now defunct; see ITU)

CCS Computer Crime Squad

CCU Computer Crimes Unit (Australian Federal Police)

CERT Computer Emergency Response Team

CIAC Computer Incident Advisory Capability: DOE's computer security team

CITCARB Chisholm Institute of Technology Computer Abuse Research Bureau (now defunct. See ACARB)

COBE Cosmic Background Explorer project: a NASA research project

DARPA Defense Advanced Research Projects Agency (US)

DCL Digital Command Language, a computer programming language used on VMS computers

DDN Defense Data Network

DEC Digital Equipment Corporation

DECNET A network protocol used to convey information between (primarily) VAX/VMS machines

DEFCON (a) Defense Readiness Conditions, a system of progressive alert postures in the US; (b) the name of Force's computer program which automatically mapped out computer networks and scanned for accounts

DES Data Encryption Standard, an encryption algorithm developed by IBM, NSA and NIST

Deszip Fast DES Unix password-cracking system developed by Matthew Bishop

Dial-up Modem access point into a computer or computer network

DMS-100 Computerised telephone switch (exchange) made by NorTel

DOD Department of Defense (US)

DOE Department of Energy (US)

DPP Director of Public Prosecutions

DST Direction de la Surveillance du Territoire – French secret service agency

EASYNET Digital Equipment Corporation's internal communication network (DECNET)

GTN Global Telecommunications Network: Citibank's international data network

HEPNET High Energy Physics Network: DECNET-based network, primarily controlled by DOE, connected to NASA's SPAN

IID Internal Investigations Division. Both the Victoria Police and the AFP have an IID

IP Internet Protocol (RFC791): a data communications protocol, used to transmit packets of data between computers on the Internet

IS International Subversive (electronic magazine)

ISU Internal Security Unit: anti-corruption unit of the Victoria Police

ITU International Telecommunications Union, the international telecommunications standards body

JANET Joint Academic Network (UK), a network of computers

JPL Jet Propulsion Laboratory – a California-based NASA research centre affiliated with CalTech

LLNL Lawrence Livermore National Laboratory (US)

LOD Legion of Doom

Lutzifer West German computer, connected to the X.25 network, which had a chat facility

MFC Multi Frequency Code (Group III): inter-exchange telecommunications system used by Telstra (Telecom)

MILNET Military Network: TCP/IP unclassified US DOD computer network

MOD Masters of Deception (or Destruction)

Modem Modulator De-modulator: a device used to transmit computer data over a regular telephone line

NCA National Crime Authority

Netlink A Primos/Dialcom command used to initiate a connection over an X.25 network

NIST National Institute of Standards (US)

NIC Network Information Center (US), run by DOD: a computer which assigned domain names for the Internet

NRL Naval Research Laboratory (US)

NSA National Security Agency (US)

NUA Network User Address: the 'telephone' number of a computer on an X.25 network

NUI Network User Identifier (or Identification): combined username/password used on X.25 networks for billing purposes

NorTel Northern Telecom, Canadian manufacturer of telecommunications equipment

PABX Private Automatic Branch Exchange

PAD Packet Assembler Disassembler – ASCII gateway to X.25 networks

PAR 'PAR.?' – command on PAD to display PAD parameters

RMIT Royal Melbourne Institute of Technology

RTG Radioisotope Thermoelectric Generator, space probe Galileo's plutonium-based power system

RTM Robert Tappan Morris (Jr), the Cornell University student who wrote the Internet worm, also known as the RTM worm

Scanner A program which scans and compiles information, such as a list of NUAs

SPAN Space Physics Analysis Network: global DECNET- based network, primarily controlled by NASA

Sprint US telecommunications company, an X.25 network provider

Sprinter Word used by some Australian and English hackers to denote scanner. Derived from scanning attacks on Sprint communications

Sprintnet X.25 network controlled by Sprint communications

Sun Sun Microsystems – a major producer of Unix workstations

TCP Transmission Control Protocol (RFC793): a standard for data connection between two computers on the Internet

TELENET An X.25 network, DNIC 3110

Telnet A method of connection between two computers on the Internet or other TCP/IP networks

Trojan A program installed by hackers to secretly gather information, such as passwords. Can also be a backdoor

Tymnet An X.25 network controlled by MCI, DNIC 3106

Unix Multi-user computer operating system developed by AT&T and Berkeley CSRG

VAX Virtual Address Extension: series of mini/mainframe computer systems produced by DEC

VMS Virtual Memory System: computer operating system produced by DEC and used on its VAX machines

WANK Worms Against Nuclear Killers: the title of DECNET/VMS-based worm released into SPAN/DEC/HEPNET in 1989

X.25 International data communications network, using the X.25 communications protocol. Network is run primarily by major telecommunications companies. Based on CCITT standard # X.25

Zardoz A restricted computer security mailing list

An Introduction to Underground

1. Sarah Ellison, 'The man who spilled secrets', *Vanity Fair*, February 2011. See: http://www.vanityfair.com/contributors/sarah-ellison
2. Viola Gienger and Tony Capaccio, 'Clinton Condemns WikiLeaks Release as "Attack" on U.S. Efforts', *Bloomberg Businessweek*, 29 November 2010. See: http://www.businessweek.com/news/2010-11-29/clinton-condemns-wikileaks-release-as-attack-on-u-s-efforts.html
3. Dylan Welch, 'Assange calls on Clinton to quit', *Sydney Morning Herald*, 2 December 2010. See: http://www.smh.com.au/technology/technology-news/assange-calls-on-clinton-to-quit-20101201-18gp3.html

Chapter 1

1. I have relied on numerous wire service reports, particularly those of UPI Science Reporter William Harwood, for many of my descriptions of Galileo and the launch.

2. William Harwood, 'NASA Awaits Court Ruling on Shuttle Launch Plans', *UPI*, 10 October 1989.
3. William Harwood, 'Atlantis "Go" for Tuesday Launch', *UPI*, 16 October 1989.
4. Ibid.
5. 'Officially' was spelled incorrectly in the original banner.
6. From NASA's World Wide Web site.
7. Thomas A. Longstaff and E. Eugene Schulz, 'Analysis of the WANK and OILZ Worms', *Computer and Security*, vol. 12, no. 1, February 1993, p. 64.
8. Katie Haffner and John Markoff, *Cyberpunk*, Corgi, London 1994, p. 363.
9. *The Age*, 22 April 1996, reprinted from *The New York Times*.
10. DEC, Annual Report, 1989, listed in 'SEC Online'.
11. GEMTOP was corrected to GEMPAK in a later advisory by CIAC.
12. This advisory is printed with the permission of CIAC and Kevin Oberman. CIAC requires the publication of the following disclaimer:

   This document was prepared as an account of work sponsored by an agency of the United States Government. Neither the United States Government, nor the University of California, nor any of their employees makes any warranty, express or implied, or assumes any legal liability or responsibility for the accuracy, completeness, or usefulness of any information, apparatus, product, or process disclosed, or represents that its use would not infringe privately owned rights. Reference herein to any specific commercial products, process, or service by trade name, trademark, manufacturer, or otherwise, does not necessarily constitute or imply its endorsement, recommendation or favouring by the United States Government or the University of California. The views and opinions of authors expressed herein do not necessarily state or reflect those of the United States Government or the University of California, and shall not be used for advertising or product endorsement purposes.

13. Michael Alexander and Maryfran Johnson, 'Worm Eats Holes in NASA's Decnet', *Computer World*, 23 October 1989, p. 4.
14. Ibid.
15. William Harwood, 'Shuttle Launch Rained Out', *UPI*, 17 October 1989.
16. Vincent Del Guidice, 'Atlantis Set for Another Launch Try', *UPI*, 18 October 1989.
17. William Harwood, 'Astronauts Fire Galileo on Flight to Jupiter', *UPI*, 18 October 1989.

Chapter 2
1. FIRST was initially called CERT System. It was an international version of CERT, the Computer Emergency Response Team, funded by the US Department of Defense and run out of Carnegie Mellon University.
2. OTC was later merged with Telecom to become Telstra.
3. Stuart Gill is described in some detail in Operation Iceberg; Investigation of Leaked Confidential Police Information and Related Matters, Ordered to be printed by the Legislative Assembly of Victoria, October 1993.

Chapter 5
1. Helen Meredith, 'Citibank hackers score $500,000', *The Australian*, 14 January, 1989.
2. From Operation Iceberg; Investigations and Recommendations into Allegations of Leaked Confidential Police Information, included as Appendix 1 in the report of the Deputy Ombudsman, Operation Iceberg; Investigation of Leaked Confidential Police Information and Related Matters.
3. Ibid., pp. 26–7.
4. Michael Alexander, 'International Hacker "Dave" Arrested', *Computer World*, 9 April 1990, p. 8.
5. Matthew May, 'Hacker Tip-Off', *The Times*, 5 April 1990; Lou Dolinar, 'Australia Arrests Three in Computer Break-Ins', *Newsday*, 3 April 1990.

Chapter 7

1. Rupert Battcock, 'The Computer Misuse Act Five years on – the Record since 1990', paper, Strathclyde University, Glasgow, UK.
2. For the British material in this chapter, I have relied on personal interviews, media reports (particularly for the Wandii case), journal articles, academic papers and commission reports.
3. Colin Randall, 'Teenage Computer Hacker "Caused Worldwide Chaos"', *Daily Telegraph*, 23 February 1993.
4. The local phone company agreed to reduce the bill to £3000, EORTIC information systems manager Vincent Piedboeuf told the court.
5. Susan Watts, 'Trial Haunted by Images of Life in the Twilight Zone', *The Independent*, 18 March 1993.
6. Toby Wolpe, 'Hacker Worked on Barclay's Software', *Computer Weekly*, 4 March 1993.
7. David Millward, 'Computer Hackers Will be Pursued, Vow Police', *Daily Telegraph*, 19 March 1993.
8. Chester Stern, 'Hackers' Threat to Gulf War Triumph', *Mail on Sunday*, 21 March 1993.
9. 'Crimes of the Intellect – Computer Hacking', editorial, *The Times*, 20 March 1993.
10. 'Owners Must Act to Put End to Computer Hacker "Insanity"', *South China Morning Post*, 30 March 1993.
11. Nick Nuttall, 'Hackers Stay Silent on Court Acquittal', *The Times*, 19 March 1993.
12. Melvyn Howe, Press Association Newsfile, Home News section, 21 May 1993.

Chapter 8

1. This is an edited version.

Afterword

1. Victorian Ombudsman, Operation Iceberg; Investigation of Leaked Confidential Police Information and Related Matters.
2. The police report was printed as an appendix in the Ombudsman's report. See Chapter 5, note 1, above.
3. Australian Federal Police, Annual Report, 1995–1996, p. 7.

Conclusion

1. Glenn Greenwald, 'Government-created climate of fear', 10 January, 2010, *Salon.* See: http://www.salon.com/news/opinion/glenn_greenwald/2011/01/10/fear
2. Nicholas Jackson, 'WikiLeaks Volunteer Detained by U.S. Agents for Second Time,' *The Atlantic*, 12 January, 2011. See: http://www.theatlantic.com/technology/archive/2011/01/wikileaks-volunteer-detained-by-us-agents-for-second-time/69458/
3. Josh Gordon, 'PM has betrayed me: Assange', *The Sunday Age*, 5 December, 2010, p 1.
4. James C. Thomson, Jr, 'How could Vietnam Happen? – An autopsy', *The Atlantic*, April, 1968. See: http://www.theatlantic.com/past/docs/issues/68apr/vietnam.htm. Thomson describes how dissenters are silenced via a warm and welcoming embrace inside the US Government during debates about the Vietnam War. The similarities with the Afghan and Iraq wars are striking.
5. Julian Assange, 'Serious nuclear accident may lay behind Iranian nuke chief's mystery resignation.' WikiLeaks, 16 July, 2009. See mirror site: http://mirror.wikileaks.info/wiki/Serious_nuclear_accident_may_lay_behind_Iranian_nuke_chief%27s_mystery_resignation/

   The short entry is included in case the mirror disappears:

   'Two weeks ago, a source associated with Iran's nuclear program confidentially told WikiLeaks of a serious, recent, nuclear accident at Natanz. Natanz is the primary location of Iran's nuclear enrichment program.

WikiLeaks had reason to believe the source was credible however contact with this source was lost.

WikiLeaks would not normally mention such an incident without additional confirmation, however according to Iranian media and the BBC, today the head of Iran's Atomic Energy Organization, Gholam Reza Aghazadeh, has resigned under mysterious circumstances. According to these reports, the resignation was tendered around 20 days ago.'

6. Atika Shubert, 'Tens of thousands of alleged Afghan war documents go online,' CNN online, 25 July, 2010. See: http://articles.cnn.com/2010-07-25/tech/wikileaks.afghanistan_1_julian-assange-whistle-blower-website-afghan-war?_s=PM:TECH

7. William J. Broad, John Markoff and David E Sanger, 'Israeli Test on Worm Called Crucial in Iran Nuclear Delay, *New York Times* online, 15 January, 2011. See: http://www.nytimes.com/2011/01/16/world/middleeast/16stuxnet.html?pagewanted=3&_r=1

8. Ibid.

9. CBS News, 'Iran Confirms Stuxnet Worm Halted Centrifuges', 29 November, 2010. See: http://www.cbsnews.com/stories/2010/11/29/world/main7100197.shtml

10. William J. Broad, John Markoff and David E. Sanger, 'Israeli Test on Worm Called Crucial in Iran Nuclear Delay', *New York Times* online, 15 January, 2011. See: http://www.nytimes.com/2011/01/16/world/middleeast/16stuxnet.html?pagewanted=3&_r=1

11. Discussion between S. Dreyfus and a source.

12. Ryan Naraine, 'Stuxnet attackers used 4 Windows zero-day exploits', *Zdnet*, 14 September, 2010. See: http://www.zdnet.com/blog/security/stuxnet-attackers-used-4-windows-zero-day-exploits/7347

13. Thomas Erdbrink, 'Iranian nuclear scientist killed, another injured in Tehran bombings', *The Washington Post*, 29 November, 2010. See: http://www.washingtonpost.com/wp-dyn/content/article/2010/11/29/AR2010112901560.html

14. BBC News, 'Iranian nuclear scientist killed in motorbike attack,' 29 November, 2010. See: http://www.bbc.co.uk/news/world-middle-east-11860928

15. Aljazeera, 'Iranian "nuclear scientist" killed', 29 November, 2010. See: http://english.aljazeera.net/news/middleeast/2010/11/201011297228879910.html

16. Julian Borger and Saeed Kamali Dehghan, 'Attack on Iranian nuclear scientists prompts hit squad claims', *The Guardian*, 29 November 2010. See: http://www.guardian.co.uk/world/2010/nov/29/iranian-nuclear-scientists-attack-claims

17. Thomas Erdbrink and William Branigin, 'Iran blames U.S., Israel in bombing death of physicist Massoud Ali-Mohammadi,' *The Washington Post*, 13 January, 2010. See: http://www.washingtonpost.com/wp-dyn/content/article/2010/01/12/AR2010011200300.html

18. Kim Zetter, 'Iran: Computer Malware Sabotaged Uranium Centrifuges', *Wired Threat Level*, 29 November, 2010. See: http://www.wired.com/threatlevel/2010/11/stuxnet-sabotage-centrifuges/

19. Yossi Melman, 'U.S. website: Mossad killed Iranian nuclear physicist', *Haaretz,* 19 January, 2011. See: http://www.haaretz.com/news/u-s-website-mossad-killed-iranian-nuclear-physicist-1.211920

20. See Shutterley's website: http://www.americanswhotellthetruth.org/pgs/artist_statement.php

21. See: http://www.youtube.com/watch?v=qEJC-FuOSZ4

BIBLIOGRAPHY

Australian Federal Police (AFP), Annual Report 1995–1996, Canberra, 1996.

—, Annual Report 1994–1995, Canberra, 1995.

—, Annual Report 1993–1994, Canberra, 1994.

Bourne, Philip E., 'Internet security; System Security', *DEC Professional*, vol. 11, June 1992.

Cerf, Vinton G., 'Networks', *Scientific American*, vol. 265, September 1991.

Clyde, Robert A., 'DECnet security', *DEC Professional*, vol. 10, April 1991.

Commonwealth Attorney-General's Department, Interim Report on Computer Crime (The Gibbs Report), Canberra, 1988.

Commonwealth Director of Public Prosecutions (DDP), Annual Report 1993–1994, Canberra, 1994.

Commonwealth Scientific and Industrial Research Organisation (CSIRO), Annual Report 1994–1995, Canberra, 1995.

Davis, Andrew W., 'DEC Pathworks the mainstay in Mac-to-VAX connectivity', *MacWeek*, vol. 6, 3 August 1992.

Department of Foreign Affairs and Trade, Australian Treaty Series 1993, no. 40, Australian Government Publishing Service, Canberra, 1993.

Digital Equipment Corporation, Annual Report 1989, Securities and Exchange Commission (SEC) Online (USA) Inc., 1989.

——, Quarterly Report for period ending 12.31.89, SEC Online (USA).

Gezelter, Robert, 'The DECnet TASK object; Tutorial', *Digital Systems Journal*, vol. 16, July 1994.

Gianatasio, David, 'Worm infestation hits 300 VAX/VMS systems worldwide via DECnet', *Digital Review*, vol. 6, 20 November 1989.

Haffner, Katie & Markoff, John, *Cyberpunk*, Corgi Books (Transworld), Moorebank NSW, 1994.

Halbert, Debora, 'The Potential for Modern Communication Technology to Challenge Legal Discourses of Authorship and Property', *Murdoch University E-Law Journal*, vol. 1, no. 2.

Kelman, Alistair, 'Computer Crime in the 1990s: A Barrister's View', Paper for the Twelfth International Symposium on Economic Crime, September 1994.

Law Commission (UK) Working Paper, no. 110, 1988.

Lloyd, J. Ian & Simpson, Moira, *Law on the Electronic Frontier*, David Hume Institute, Edinburgh, 1996.

Longstaff, Thomas A., & Schultz, E. Eugene, 'Beyond preliminary analysis of the WANK and OILZ worms: a case study of malicious code', *Computers & Security*, vol. 12, February 1993.

Loundy, David J., 'Information Systems Law and Operator Liability Revisited', *Murdoch University E-Law Journal*, vol. 1, no. 3, September 1994.

McMahon, John, 'Practical DECnet security', *Digital Systems Journal*, vol. 14, November 1992.

Melford, Robert J., 'Network security; computer networks', *Internal Auditor*, Institute of Internal Auditors, vol. 50, February 1993.

Natalie, D. & Ball, W., EIS Coordinator, North Carolina Emergency Management, 'How North Carolina Managed Hurricane Hugo', *EIS News*, vol. 3, no. 11, 1988.

NorTel Australia Pty Ltd, *Discovering Tomorrow's Telecommunications Solutions*, Chatswood, NSW (n.d.).

Northern Telecom, Annual Report 1993, Ontario, 1993.

Slatalla, Michelle & Quittner, Joshua, *Masters of Deception*, HarperCollins, New York, 1995.

Royal Commission into Aboriginal Deaths in Custody, Report of the Inquiry into the Death of the Woman Who Died at Ceduna, Australian Government Publishing Service, Canberra, 1990.

Scottish Law Commission's Report on Computer Crime, no. 174, 1987.

SPAN Management Office, 'Security guidelines to be followed in the latest worm attack', an Intranetwork Memorandum released by the SPAN Management Office, NASA, 30 October 1989.

Sterling, Bruce, *The Hacker Crackdown*, Penguin Books, Melbourne, 1994.

Stoll, Clifford, *The Cuckoo's Egg*, Pan Books, London, 1991.

Tencati, Ron, 'Information regarding the DECNET worm and protection measures', an Intranetwork Memorandum released by the SPAN Management Office, NASA, 19 October 1989.

——, 'Network Security Suplemental Information – Protecting the DECNET Account', security advisory, released by SPAN, NASA/Goddard Space Flight Center, 1989.

The Victorian Ombudsman, Operation Iceberg: Investigation of Leaked Confidential Police Information and Related Matters, Report of the Deputy Ombudsman (Police Complaints), L.V. North Government Printer, Melbourne, 1993.

'USA proposes international virus team', *Computer Fraud & Security Bulletin* (Elsevier Advanced Technology Publications), August 1991.

Victoria Police, Operation Iceberg – Investigation and Recommendations into Allegations of Leaked Confidential Police Information, 1 June, Memorandum from Victoria Police Commander Bowles to Chief Commissioner Comrie (also available as Appendix 1 in the Victorian Ombudsman's Operation Iceberg Report, tabled in Victorian Parliament, October 1993), 1993.

Vietor, Richard, *Contrived Competition: Regulation and Deregulation in America*, BelKnap/Harvard University Press, Cambridge, 1994.

Yallop, David, *To the Ends of the Earth*, Corgi Books (Transworld), Moorebank, NSW, 1994.

Acts:

Computer Misuse Act 1990 (UK)
Crimes Act 1914 (no. 5) (Cwlth)
Crimes Legislation Amendment Act 1989, no. 108
Computer Fraud and Abuse Act 1986 (US), 18 USC 1030
Computer Misuse Crimes Legislation Amendment Bill 1989 (AUS), Explanatory Memo Clause 7
Crimes (Computers) Act, no. 36 of 1988 (VIC)

Other publications and databases:

Aljazeera
American Bar Association Journal
Associated Press
Attorney General's Information Service (Australia)
Australian Accountant
Australian Computer Commentary
Aviation Week and Space Technology (USA)
Banking Technology
BBC News
Business Week
Cable News Network (CNN)
Card News (USA)
CBS News

CERT Advisories (The Computer Emergency Response Team at Carnegie Mellon University)
Chicago Daily Law Bulletin
CNN News
CommunicationsWeek
CommunicationsWeek International
Computer Incident Advisory Capability (CIAC)
Computer Law and Practice (Australia)
Computer Law and Security Report (Australia)
Computer Weekly
Computergram
Computerworld
Computing
Corporate EFT Report (USA)
Daily Mail (UK)
Daily Telegraph (Sydney)
Daily Telegraph (UK)
Data Communications
Datalink
Evening Standard (UK)
Export Control News (USA)
FinTech Electronic Office (*The Financial Times*)
Gannett News Service
Government Computer News (USA)
Haaretz
InfoWorld
Intellectual Property Journal (Australia)
Intelligence Newsletter (Indigo Publications)
Journal of Commerce (*The New York Times*)
Journal of the Law Society of Scotland
Korea Economic Daily
Law Institute Journal (Melbourne)
Law Society's Gazette (UK)
Law Society's Guardian Gazette (UK)
Legal Times (USA)
Lexis-Nexis (Reed Elsevier)

Lloyds List
Mail on Sunday (UK)
Media Week
MIS Week
Mortgage Finance Gazette
Network World
New Law Journal (UK)
New York Law Journal
Newsday
PC Week (USA)
Press Association Newsfile
Reuter
Reuter News Service – United Kingdom Science
Salon
South China Morning Post
St Louis Post-Dispatch
St Petersburg Times
Sunday Telegraph (Sydney)
Sunday Telegraph (UK)
Sunday Times (UK)
Telecommunications (Horizon House Publications Inc.)
The Age
The Atlantic
The Australian
The Australian Financial Review
The Bulletin
The Computer Lawyer (USA)
The Connecticut Law Tribune
The Daily Record (USA)
The Engineer (UK)
The Gazette (Montreal)
The Guardian
The Herald (Glasgow)
The Herald (Melbourne)
The Herald Sun (Melbourne)
The Independent

The Irish Times
The Legal Intelligencer (USA)
The Los Angeles Times
The Nation
The National Law Journal (USA)
The New York Times
The Recorder (USA)
The Reuter European Community Report
The Reuter Library Report
The Scotsman
The Sun (Melbourne)
The Sunday Age
The Sydney Morning Herald
The Times
The Washington Post
The Washington Times
The Weekend Australian
Time Magazine
United Nations Chronicle
United Press International
USA Today
WikiLeaks
Wired Threat Level
Zdnet

Transcripts:

Hearing of the Transportation, Aviation and Materials Sub-committee of the House Science, Space and Technology Committee transcript: witness Clifford Stoll, 10 July 1990

'Larry King Live' transcript, interview with Clifford Stoll, 23 March 1990

The World Uranium Hearing, Salzburg 1992, witness transcripts

US Government Accounting Office Hearing (computer security) witness transcripts, 1996

Judgments:

Chris Goggans, Robert Cupps and Scott Chasin, Appellants v. Boyd & Fraser Publishing Co., a Division of South-Western Publishing Co., Appellee No. 01-95-00331-Cv 1995 Tex. App.

Gerald Gold v. Australian Federal Police, no. V93/1140

Gerald Gold v. National Crime Authority, no. V93/1141 AAT No. 9940 Freedom of Information (1994) 37 ALD 168

Henry John Tasman Rook v. Lucas Richard Maynard (no. 2) no. LCA 52/1994; judgment no. A64/1994

Pedro Juan Cubillo v. Commonwealth Of Australia, no. NG 571 of 1991 FED no. 1006/95 Tort – Negligence

R v. Gold and another, House of Lords (UK), [1988] 1 AC 1063, [1988] 2 All ER 186, [1988] 2 WLR 984, 87 Cr App Rep 257, 152 JP 445, [1988] Crim LR 437

Steve Jackson Games Incorporated, et al., Plaintiffs, v. United States Secret Service, United States Of America, et al., Defendants no. A 91 CA 346 Ss 816 F. Supp. 432; 1993 U.S. Dist.

United States of America v. Julio Fernandez, et al. 92 Cr. 563 (RO)

United States of America, Plaintiff, v. Robert J. Riggs, also known as Robert Johnson, also known as Prophet, and Craig Neidorf, also known as Knight Lightning, Defendants No. 90 CR 0070 743 F. Supp. 556; 1990 U.S. Dist.

United States of America, Appellee, v. Robert Tappan Morris, Defendant-Appellant No. 90-1336 928 F.2d 504; 1991 U.S. App.

Wesley Thomas Dingwall v. Commonwealth of Australia no. NG575 of 1991 Fed no. 296/94 Torts

William Thomas Bartlett v. Claire Patricia Weir, Henry J T Rook, Noel E. Aikman, Philip Edwards and Michael B McKay no. TG7 of 1992; FED no. 345/94

Additional court records:
(Court documents of most cases described in this book)

Memos and reports to/from:
Bureau of Criminal Intelligence, Victoria Police
Internal Security Unit, Victoria Police
The NASA SPAN office relating to the WANK worm
Office of the District Attorney, Monterey, California
Overseas Telecommunications Commission (Australia)
Police Department, City of Del Rey Oaks, California
Police Department, City of Salinas, California
Stuart Gill
The United States Secret Service
US Attorney's Office, New York
Numerous Internet sites, including those of NASA, Sydney
    University, Greenpeace, the Australian Legal Information
    Institute, and the Legal Aspects of Computer Crime
    Archives.